Enthusiastic Ideas

Also by Gary Henry

More Enthusiastic Ideas
Diligently Seeking God
Reaching Forward

Enthusiastic Ideas

*A Good Word for Every Day
of the Year*

Gary Henry

WordPoints
Frankfort, Kentucky
WordPoints.com

WordPoints Daybook Series - Volume 1
Enthusiastic Ideas
A Good Word for Each Day of the Year

First Edition. Copyright © 2012 by Gary Henry
Printed in the United States of America

ISBN 978-0-9713710-2-6 – Print Edition

WordPoints
238 West Main Street, Suite 200
Frankfort, KY 40601

502-682-2603

Web: *wordpoints.com*
E-mail: *garyhenry@wordpoints.com*

For

Phil Henry

my brother and most faithful friend

CONTENTS

JANUARY

FEBRUARY

MARCH

APRIL

MAY

JUNE

JULY

AUGUST

SEPTEMBER

OCTOBER

NOVEMBER

DECEMBER

PREFACE

IN 1995, THE MOST TRAUMATIC EVENT IN MY LIFE TO THAT POINT OCCURRED. My wife and the mother of our two sons felt that she could no longer remain within our marriage, and so she left that relationship to find another life.

In the ensuing months, as I struggled to adapt to the painful realities of single-parenthood, I tried to learn everything I could that might help me win back my wife's love. Those efforts were not successful, unfortunately, but one of the things I did back then has resulted in this book — *Enthusiastic Ideas: A Good Word for Each Day of the Year.*

I began to keep a notebook. Not a journal exactly, just a notebook in which I would write down truths and principles I needed to be reminded of. I remember writing to myself that if I ever expected my wife to come back, I would need to offer her the gift of certain unconditional things: love, security, listening, acceptance, and several others.

At first, my list of "gift words" was fairly short, but it didn't take me long to think of a number of other qualities that I should be prepared to give, if I got the chance. And as the list grew, it began to be clear that these were not just things a husband should want to give his wife — they were gifts that all of us should want to give to those we love.

After that, the list started evolving into a more general list of "positive words." No longer looking for just "gift words," I included other words that might be looked at in a positive way. At the height of this word-collecting period, I could hardly read a book or an article without checking to see if it contained any words I hadn't thought of. I don't recall ever actually going through the dictionary, but it's hard to imagine that many good words eluded my search. I was pretty thorough, if not methodical. By the time things settled down, I had over eight hundred nouns, each of which I thought was suggestive of *something worth including in a human being's character and conduct.*

I posted my list of words on a website I was maintaining back then, and I still chuckle when I remember some of the comments I received from readers: "Henry, what's with this crazy list of words? What can anybody do with just a list of . . . *words?*"

Well, I happen to believe that words are very special things. I love them, I respect them, and I believe that getting "thinky" about the words we use is a very healthy exercise.

So I've written a book that gives you a single positive word to think about every twenty-four hours: *a good word every day.* Like my other books, this one is a daybook. There is a short, one-page reading for each day of the year, and what I'd like you to do is read the book at the rate of one page per day. Sure, you can browse ahead or go back and review. That's fine. Just promise me you'll really *meditate* on no more than one page each day. If you'll try this habit, you might like it.

With a few of the words, you may wonder what's so positive about them. I've written, for example, about things like *abstinence, admonition,* and *apologies.* Words like these don't belong in the "positive mental attitude" lexicon, do they? Maybe not, but let's give them a fair chance. Like people, some words wear their positive qualities on the surface, while others aren't seen to be good without a deeper look. As J. R. R. Tolkien liked to say, "All that is gold does not glitter."

And, yes, since I collected over eight hundred words, I have enough for more than one year. A second volume of these readings is not only possible; it has already been written. Next year, *More Enthusiastic Ideas* will be coming to a bookstore near you, unless God has other plans.

Over the years, I have profited as much as anyone from writers and speakers in the "positive mental attitude" genre. We do need to think more positively, and doing so is a great help. But the only positive thinking that matters is the kind that results in our doing what is *right.* And if better self-esteem is what we want, then we need to start living not only with strength but also with *honor.* I hope you'll agree.

Finally, may I caution you never to use the expression "mere words." Words are never "mere." They are strong and beautiful. Use them carefully, for language is both a powerful gift and a serious stewardship. Say nothing you will not be pleased to meet on Judgment Day.

G.P.H.

Enthusiastic Ideas

The written word preserves what otherwise might
be lost among the impressions that inundate our lives.
Thoughts, insights, and perceptions constantly threaten
to leave us before we have the opportunity to grasp their
meaning ... Reflection slows matters down. It analyzes
what was previously unexamined, and opens doors to
different interpretations of what was there all along.
Writing, by encouraging reflection, intensifies life.

— *Helena Hjalmarsson*

BEGINNINGS

The tragedy of life is not that it ends so soon,
but that we wait so long to begin it.

W. M. LEWIS

WITH THE DAWNING OF EVERY NEW DAY WE'RE GIVEN THE OPPORTUNITY TO MAKE NEW BEGINNINGS. And though we often take it for granted, the clean slate that is offered to us each morning is one of the best things about our sojourn in this world. Why is it that we so rarely seize this advantage? Why are there so many days in which nothing is improved and nothing new is begun?

Perhaps we don't want to be like the dabblers, those unhappy folks who never follow through and are constantly starting over. But the thing that's dishonorable about the dabbler is not that he makes new beginnings; it's just that he fails to do his best and finish his work. Starting over is necessary for him because he frequently gives up and quits trying. But if yesterday's work was the best we could do, then there is nothing dishonorable about seeing today as a fresh start. And if yesterday we failed to do our best, then a new beginning is even more important. We should see today as a chance, after all this time, *to start being what we've always intended to be.*

It may seem ironic, but there is a sense in which those who make the most progress in life are those who go back to the beginning every day and start over. We do need to be persistent, but *improvement* is the main thing we need to be persistent about. Those who finish life well are those who make a habit of beginning anew every day.

But we shouldn't make new beginnings just for our own sakes — we should view them as gifts to our loved ones. Indeed, there are few gifts that bestow any more honor on those around us than to give ourselves to them each day as persons of renewed commitment, eager to explore new territory and build new habitations for the heart. There is in every one of us a better person than our acquaintances have known us to be in the past. Today — *this very day* — we can begin to be that better person. We can make a fresh start that will do our families and our friends much good.

Are you in earnest? Seize this very minute!
What you can do, or dream you can, begin it. Boldness has genius,
power, and magic in it. Only engage, and then the mind grows heated.
Begin, and then the work will be completed.

JOHANN WOLFGANG VON GOETHE

EXCELLENCE

> No one ever attains very eminent success by simply doing what
> is required of him; it is the amount and excellence of what is over and above
> the required that determines the greatness of ultimate distinction.
>
> CHARLES KENDALL ADAMS

WE SHOW GRATITUDE FOR THE GIFT OF LIFE WHEN WE STRIVE FOR THE HIGHEST AND BEST THAT IS WITHIN US. Against the powerful pull of mediocrity, we must exert our best effort. "Good enough" is simply not good enough. In the giving of ourselves, we need to give nothing less than our personal best.

The concept of "excelling" is a noble one. It's unfortunate that we so often think of it in competitive terms, as if the thing that we're to surpass is someone else's performance. But in the highest sense, excellence has to do not with comparisons to other people but our relationship to an objective standard. Just as there is such a thing as beauty, there is such a thing as excellence, and we ought to value it greatly.

Even when we do think of excellence in comparative terms, the thing that we ought to compare ourselves to is our own past effort, not that of some other person. What matters most in life is not how many other people we surpass, but how often we excel what we have previously done. The best lives in the world are lived by those who're always looking to improve themselves, not for competitive advantage but for the inherent value of greater and greater excellence.

Since life is a growth process, we need to see the pursuit of excellence as a continual effort, an ongoing work. There will surely be days when the quality of our efforts is disappointing, perhaps grievously or tragically so. But those who truly wish to excel will not be defeated by individual disappointments. As long as life lasts, there is at least some of our story that remains to be written, and we should determine that the next part will be better than any we've written yet.

A commitment to excellence is possible for every one of us, no matter how insignificant we may think we are. Pursuit of the best is not just for the high and the mighty; it's for every living soul. Indeed, we are never more noble than when we confer our best effort on the simple daily duties that are the stuff of ordinary life.

> Great works do not always lie in our way, but every moment
> we may do little ones excellently, that is, with great love.
>
> FRANCIS DE SALES

PRINCIPLES

> There are *principles* that govern human effectiveness — natural laws
> in the human dimension that are just as real, just as unchanging and
> unarguably "there" as laws such as gravity are in the physical dimension.
>
> STEPHEN R. COVEY

A S WE GROW IN WISDOM, WE COME TO SEE THE VALUE OF LIVING A PRINCIPLED LIFE. Indeed, the worth of the contribution that we make as we live in the world depends upon the faithfulness with which we adhere to true principles. Positive contributions are not made by those governed by moods and trends, but rather by those guided by integrity to proven principles.

Principles are the precepts of honor and effectiveness in human conduct. Analogous to the laws by which the physical cosmos is ordered, principles are the laws by which the moral universe is ordered. They have been known by the wise in all cultures throughout time, and their truth and value have been borne out in the experience of every person since the human race began. "Honesty" is a principle. "Kindness" is another. "Courage" is yet another. The list of principles is long, but it is not mysterious or hard to come by. Each of us carries it within our conscience. Somewhere deep down, we know what is right, and we know what will be effective in the long run.

Principles are permanent. The laws of right and effective conduct do not change. They are inherent in the nature of reality. Civilizations may rise and fall, but there will never come an age when things like "thankfulness" and "unselfishness" have lost their value. The laws of moral conduct are no more apt to be altered than the laws of physics.

Principles are dependable. Because they are unchangeable, principles can be counted on. They are stable, trustworthy guidelines for our conduct. "If one can be certain that his principles are right, he need not worry about the consequences" (Robert Elliott Speer). Without knowing the future, we can act with integrity to principles and have confidence that our actions will lead us in exactly the right direction.

Such dependability is extremely important in our uncertain world. We desperately need more security than is provided by the fads and fashions of pop culture. It's a dangerous world that we live in — too dangerous to trust anything less than permanent principles.

> If the roots are deep, have no fear that the wind will uproot the tree.
>
> CHINESE PROVERB

AWAKENING

A single event can awaken within us a stranger
totally unknown to us. To live is to be born slowly.

ANTOINE DE SAINT-EXUPÉRY

L IFE IS ALWAYS FILLED WITH THE PROMISE OF AWAKENINGS.
In the case of some of us, we have slumbered through life to such
an extent that we're desperately in need of being awakened. Others
have lived their lives more fully and may seem already to have been
awakened. In either case, however, we need to be stirred. Within each
of us lie deep reservoirs of untapped potential. We've hardly more
than begun to be the persons we're capable of being, and on even the
most ordinary day something extraordinary may happen that will
wake us up and show us a wider realm of possibility. There is always
the "danger" that this will happen to us.

Sometimes our awakening is the result of a great event. Births,
marriages, and deaths come to mind, of course, but great awakenings
are often produced by events much more unusual and unexpected
than these. In fact, one of the most pleasurable aspects of life is the
anticipation that around the very next corner may be a surprising situation that will stir us with such hope that we will never be the same.

At other times, we are awakened by a great person. Before our
lives are over most of us will cross paths with one or two individuals whose influence upon us is so profound that they can be said to
have opened our eyes to the lives we were meant to live. When we
look back, we can see that our encounter with these people resulted in
nothing less than a transformation of our character.

Awakenings are almost always to our benefit, at least eventually,
but it's a fact that they often come to us in circumstances surrounded
by sorrow. The boldest and brightest new days that we'll ever see will
often follow dark nights of destructive storm. But storms, perhaps
more than anything else, force upon us new perspectives. And having
passed through sorrow, we find ourselves awakened, opened up, and
more completely alive. The sorrow passes, but the awakening remains.

These things are beautiful beyond belief:
The pleasant weakness that comes after pain,
The radiant greenness that comes after rain,
The deepened faith that follows after grief,
And the awakening to love again.

ANONYMOUS

ASPIRATION

It seems to me we can never give up longing and wishing
while we are thoroughly alive. There are certain things we feel
to be beautiful and good, and we must hunger after them.

GEORGE ELIOT

ONE OF OUR MOST MARVELOUS ENDOWMENTS IS THE ABIL-
ITY TO ASPIRE TO GREATER THINGS THAN THOSE WE'VE
KNOWN IN THE PAST. Unlike other creatures that are bound to what
"is," we are able to contemplate what "can be." We are capable of envisioning values and ideals that reach higher and higher.

Being careful about our aspirations is important for the simple
reason that they determine the quality of our lives and the worthiness of our achievements. Whether thoughtfully considered or not,
our ideals are the things we move toward. James Allen said it well:
"Whatever your present environment may be, you will fall, remain,
or rise with your thoughts, your vision, your ideal. You will become as
small as your controlling desire, or as great as your dominant vision."

It makes good sense to purify and elevate our aspirations daily.
We need to exercise the freedom we've been given and dream of ends
that are more honorable than those we've pursued in the past. In regard to our vision of the future, we need to implement the concept of
"continuous improvement." As the days go by, we should be improving not only what we do but also what we're *trying* to do.

Unfortunately, we are surrounded by forces that would rob us
of our aspirations. We must resist these forces with all our might.
When cynicism and discouragement threaten to drag our dreams into
the gutter, we must defend our dreams. It takes a tenacious character to hold on to ideals that are mocked by our enemies, and when
our dreams are unappreciated by our friends, it takes an even greater
determination to stay the course. But if we ever let go of the things we
long for, it should only be to exchange them for higher longings.

So we need to appreciate the importance of our aspirations. We
need to improve them. We need to hold on to them. But above all, we
need to *desire* them. The highest things that we hope for ought to be
pursued with a heart that is desperately hungry. We're not really living
if we don't let ourselves long for certain things with all our hearts.

To love the beautiful, to desire the good, to do the best.

MOSES MENDELSSOHN

TENDERHEARTEDNESS

The prudence of the best heads is often defeated
by the tenderness of the best hearts.
HENRY FIELDING

AMONG THE VIRTUES VALUED IN OUR AGE, TENDERHEARTED-
NESS IS ONE OF THE MOST UNDERVALUED. In the minds of
many, toughness is the key to success in the real world, and tenderness
is seen as more of a weakness than a strength. The truth is, however,
tenderness can solve a much wider range of problems than its opposite. In the history of our world, the people who have exerted the
greatest real power — power to build, rather than destroy — have
always been people with tender hearts.

The word "tenderheartedness" can mean two different things,
both of which are valuable. In modern usage, tenderheartedness often
means *compassion*. It denotes that one is easily moved by another's
distress. In this sense, the person with a tender heart is one who can
be touched by someone else's suffering and is willing to respond with
mercy. Surely, this is a prime virtue to include in our character.

But tenderheartedness can mean something else: it can mean
that a person has a tender *conscience*. Unlike the individual who has
allowed his conscience to become hard and insensitive, the tender-
hearted person has a conscience that still works. When it is pointed
out that he has erred, he is "touched" by that fact. His heart is still
tender enough to feel genuine, healthy remorse for his failings. And
like other kinds of tenderness, this tenderness of conscience is a potent force, a strength with impressive capabilities. It allows the person
who possesses it to do something that the tough are rarely able to do:
take steps of honest growth and personal improvement.

There are few gifts that we can give to others that are more beneficial than tenderheartedness. Whether it is tenderness of compassion
or tenderness of conscience, this is a quality that can do powerful, life-
changing good. It can move mountains — mountains at which the
"strong" can only curse. And one of the most remarkable things about
it is that, while life lasts, it is never out of our reach. Even the hardest
heart can become more tender if it's willing to make that choice.

When death, the great reconciler, has come, it is
never our tenderness that we regret, but our severity.
GEORGE ELIOT

WHOLEHEARTEDNESS

Purity of heart is to will one thing.

SØREN KIERKEGAARD

THESE DAYS, WE'RE PULLED IN SO MANY DIFFERENT DIREC-TIONS, A TOTAL COMMITMENT TO ANYTHING SEEMS IMPOS-SIBLE. Conflicting values and multiple priorities have become so common that our minds are in danger of going numb. Somehow we must rediscover the meaning and value of "wholeheartedness."

The popular concept of wholeheartedness is that of energy and enthusiasm. When we say that someone did something wholeheartedly we usually mean that it was done exuberantly. But while wholeheartedness includes the idea of energy, there is more to it than that. In its highest sense, the word means *singleness of purpose*. The "whole" heart is the "single" heart; it's the heart that is supremely fixed on one thing and not torn or divided among competing loyalties. The wholehearted person has considered the options, made a decisive commitment to one of them, and is now willing to sacrifice all else to *the passionate pursuit of one great objective.* Few and fortunate are those among us who have learned the power of this kind of commitment. Those who do what they do with all of their hearts live life at a level the rest of us can only imagine.

But life is complicated, isn't it? As G. K. Chesterton noted, "The perplexity of life arises from there being too many interesting things in it for us to be interested properly in any of them." Although each of us should have some "one thing" that is our ultimate passion, we don't have the luxury of thinking about that thing every waking moment. Meals have to be provided, clothes have to be washed, and the roof has to be repaired. Still, we can be more wholehearted in our living. We can give our full attention to each thing in its turn, doing as the Zen maxim advises, "When walking, walk. When eating, eat." Being fully "present" in each moment is a discipline that can save our sanity.

W. H. Auden said, "Choice of attention, to pay attention to this and ignore that, is to the inner life what choice of action is to the outer." Full, healthy human character is impossible unless we exercise the ability to choose our thoughts. And wholeheartedness means that having chosen, we give ourselves completely to the choice we've made.

One man, two loves. No good ever comes of that.

EURIPIDES

CONSCIENTIOUSNESS

Trust that man in nothing
who has not a conscience in everything.

LAURENCE STERNE

F EW OF LIFE'S PLEASURES RIVAL THE DEEP SATISFACTION THAT COMES FROM BEING CONSCIENTIOUS. The knowledge that (a) we've done what is *right,* and (b) we've given our *best effort* to what is right has to rank somewhere near the top of life's most lasting contentments. The old adage contains a truth we need to reconnect with: "The softest pillow is a good conscience."

Conscientiousness deserves a better reputation than it has. It tends to be confused with perfectionism, and the conscientious are often accused of having too many scruples and not enough spontaneity. But submitting our work to the standards of conscience is not a sign of psychological sickness. It's a sign that we care enough about the world to make the best contribution to it that we can.

Those who are conscientious are governed by conscience in everything they do. Even when "it doesn't matter" and even when "no one else will know," they are careful to do what they believe is right. The conscientious steer by true-north principles. They are more concerned with enduring values than with shortcuts and quick fixes.

Those who are conscientious are diligent in what they do. They value quality — quality in character and quality in workmanship. They are thorough, and yes, even scrupulous. Moved by conscience, they take wholesome pride in jobs that are well done, and most of them have gotten used to being called persnickety and old-fashioned.

The bottom line is this: if we wish to have the confidence of others, we must be conscientious. People may say that perfectionism is a hang-up, but when it comes time to put their trust in somebody, they still look for someone who does things the way they ought to be done. When we're sitting back in 24-B, we want the pilot to be the most conscientious person on the plane. So how confident are those who're riding on *your* conduct today? Can they count on your conscience?

Is your conscience clear, with nothing to fear
As you punch the clock each night;
When you leave the job, do your pulses throb
With the thought of a task done right?

FRANK A. COLLINS

January 9
STRAIGHTFORWARDNESS

> Nothing more completely baffles one who is full of tricks and duplicity
> than straightforward and simple integrity in another.
>
> GOTTHOLD EPHRAIM LESSING

HOW REFRESHING IT IS TO DEAL WITH THOSE WHO ARE STRAIGHTFORWARD! In a world where we often have to wonder if we're being told the whole truth, it's like a breath of fresh air when we encounter those faithful folks who actually are what they want others to believe they are. At least this experience is refreshing if we ourselves are honest. If we're not, those who refuse to leave the path of truth are probably sources of great frustration to us.

Straightforwardness can best be understood by looking at its opposite: deviousness. "Devious" comes from a Latin word which meant "away from the road." The devious person is willing to go "out of the way" to get what he wants, following a secret, crooked path if necessary. Skilled at winning people's confidence (at least superficially), the devious operator shows only as much of himself as is "expedient."

By contrast, the straightforward person stays on the high road of openness and honesty. He has no hidden agenda and no desire to manipulate the course of events. There is a simple strength about this person: the strength of truth. There is also a certain peace and relaxation. Not having told the truth selectively (with some parts told to some people and other parts told to others), he has no need to keep track of which version of himself he has presented to which person. He is the "real deal," known by all to be dependably open.

There are few things more valuable than a reputation for straight dealing, and such a reputation ought to be one of our highest priorities. Yet it can't be gained by devious means! We can't depend on the clever use of personality to conjure up the image of character. Smoke and mirrors will not suffice, nor can we always "spin" the truth to our advantage. We must simply be what we wish to appear to be. That's straightforwardness, and that's what people want from us.

> The most agreeable of all companions is a simple, frank person,
> without any high pretensions to an oppressive greatness — one who
> loves life and understands the use of it; obliging alike at all hours; above all,
> of a golden temper, and steadfast as an anchor. For such a one we gladly
> exchange the greatest genius, the most brilliant wit,
> the profoundest thinker.
>
> CHARLES CALEB COLTON

CHARACTER

Unless the vessel is clean,
what you pour into it turns sour.
LATIN PROVERB

CONCERNING CHARACTER, IT'S IMPORTANT TO UNDERSTAND THAT GOOD CHARACTER COMES FROM OUR DECISIONS, NOT FROM OUR CIRCUMSTANCES. Those who spend their lives waiting for their ship to come in, thinking that their true character can't be developed until they get their big break, are turning one of life's great priorities upside-down. Choices concerning our character should come first, not last. If and when we do get the circumstances we're hoping for, if our character isn't what it ought to be those circumstances will turn out to be seriously disappointing. *"Unless the vessel is clean, what you pour into it turns sour."*

But if it's important to think rightly about our character with regard to the future, it's also important to do so with regard to the past. There is a Jewish proverb which says, "A man is what he is — not what he used to be." This is a double-edged truth. On the sobering side, we need to admit that good character in the past is no substitute for good character in the present. What we are is what we are, not what we used to be. Having been a good person at some point in the past doesn't give us a lifetime exemption from any further effort.

The other side of this truth, however, is encouraging. If our character has been bad in the past, that fact does not doom us to having the same character forever. We're not inherently bad; we just need to change for the better. If we do, then our character is what it is, not what it used to be. *Character comes from our decisions, not from our circumstances.* And freedom of the will means that better decisions are ours for the making every single day that we live in the world.

Compared to the things we typically spend our time working on, the building of solid character needs to get more of our attention. What we *are* (our character) is a good deal more important than what we *have* (our possessions). It's even more important than what we *do* (our accomplishments). When the final tally is made, what we will want more than anything is to have had hearts that were true and just.

What lies behind us and what lies before us
are tiny matters compared to what lies within us.
RALPH WALDO EMERSON

RENEWAL

Inside myself is a place where I live all alone,
and that's where you renew your springs that never dry up.
PEARL S. BUCK

NONE OF US HAS ENOUGH INNER STRENGTH TO LAST A LIFE-
TIME. We simply can't make it. If we are to keep going, we must
be "renewed" fairly often. And this process must take place deep inside
of us — in that place where, as Pearl S. Buck said, we "live all alone."
Physical renewal is important, as is emotional renewal, but even more
important is a thing that may be called character renewal. *The choices*
we've made in the past concerning our principles, our values, and our con-
duct will "dry up" if they're not refreshed, improved, and strengthened.

There is little excuse, really, for not tending to our renewal. We
are surrounded by resources to prompt us and help us. The world of
nature is the most obvious one, of course. Even the casual observation
of the land, the sea, and the heavens tends to have a refreshing effect
on us. Indeed, natural things are so powerful that if we had regular
contact with them our renewal would almost take care of itself. But
there are many other things that should have a similar effect: friends,
books, music, and laughter are just a few. If we interact with these
things with any thoughtfulness, we will find ourselves being rejuve-
nated. Our outlook will be refurbished and our energy replenished.

The people who have the greatest impact for good in our world
are those who see themselves as being "new." Like anyone else, they
reach the point of exhaustion from time to time, but unlike others,
they make a point of regularly starting over. They know how to turn
to a fresh page and begin writing something new. And as the years go
by, they feel themselves getting "newer" rather than "older."

If we're not doing what these people do, we need to be reminded
that the only alternative to renewal is decay. For living, personal
beings, there is no middle ground. Either we're developing or we're
deteriorating. And those around us, especially our loved ones, would
dearly love to see us developing! They would be delighted to know
that our inner light is growing stronger and brighter as time goes by.

We die on the day when our lives cease to be illumined
by the steady radiance, renewed daily, of a wonder,
the source of which is beyond all reason.
DAG HAMMARSKJÖLD

January 12
PERSPECTIVE

The last thing one knows is what to put first.
BLAISE PASCAL

PUTTING FIRST THINGS FIRST REQUIRES NOT ONLY DISCIPLINE; IT REQUIRES WISDOM. We can't give priority to the things of first importance if we don't know what they are, and it's wisdom that provides this information. And where does wisdom come from? Usually, it comes from what we call "perspective," the ability to see things from a wider angle and to take in more of the total reality that we're dealing with. There may be times when our wisdom is blocked by a bold-faced lie or an outright untruth, but more often the problem is that we don't see *enough* of the truth. We need to gain a fuller perspective.

It may seem strange, but some of the situations that we see the least adequately are those that we're closest to. It takes better vision than most of us are blessed with to see what's immediately in front of us. We need to back up and look at our circumstances from a more objective distance. Doing this is often the single best thing we can do to improve the quality of our decision-making.

I once knew a man who had served in the Air Force in Colorado Springs, Colorado. He said that there was a certain road in the area that had always intrigued him. It looked as if it might go to some interesting place, but he never knew where it went until one day when he was in the nearby mountains, looking down on the area. From this higher and more complete vantage point, he could see that the road he'd always wondered about actually went to the city dump!

And that's the way it often is with us in our assessment of what's important from day to day. Some courses of action which look intriguing from our present viewpoint may be seen, from a wider angle, to go nowhere but to the "dump." So Norman Cousins was right when he said, "What was most significant about the lunar voyage was not that men set foot on the moon but that they set eye on the earth." Our perspective won't ever be infinite or perfect, and neither will our wisdom, but when we back up as far as we can and see as much as possible, it's amazing what truths suddenly become apparent.

Climb up on some hill at sunrise.
Everybody needs perspective once in a while,
and you'll find it there.
ROBB SAGENDORPH

January 13
RESPONSIBILITY

Duty done is the soul's fireside.

ROBERT BROWNING

YOU'D BE HARD PUT TO NAME A BETTER FEELING THAN THE FEELING OF KNOWING YOU'VE DONE WHAT WAS RIGHT. The simple knowledge that we've acted with integrity, doing to the best of our ability the thing that most needed to be done, is not only one of life's greatest pleasures, it's also one that's widely available. This is a "fireside" that anyone can enjoy at the end of any day.

It's never entirely accurate to say that we had no choice but to do a wrong thing. Responsibility literally means "response-ability," the ability to respond. As free moral agents, we're able to choose our response, no matter what the circumstances may be that confront us and call for a decision. We're never responsible for doing that which is impossible for us; we're only held accountable for doing what we can — and nothing that's truly within our duty is ever out of our reach. "I ought, therefore I can" is how Immanuel Kant put it.

Most of us want to be treated as responsible people. But the key to responsible treatment is *being* responsible. A reputation for responsibility has to be gotten the old-fashioned way: it has to be earned. And having been earned, it has to be maintained carefully. When we violate the principles of responsibility and accountability, it takes a long time to repair the damage that we've done to our name.

We lift a great burden from the shoulders of others when we accept the idea of our own responsibility. When those we deal with every day know that we can be counted on to do what's right and to be accountable for our own actions, they can rest easy in their relationship with us. It's a magnificent gift when we can say to others and mean it, "I will hold up my end of our duties. You can count on me."

"Responsibility" is often looked at as a negative word nowadays, along with "obligation," "duty," and similar words. But doing our duty need not be a dreary business. If we choose, we can listen *appreciatively* to the voice of conscience. It's mostly a matter of how we see life itself: *is it something to be refused or something to be received?*

> I slept and dreamed that life was joy,
> I awoke and saw that life was duty,
> I acted, and behold duty was joy.

RABINDRANATH TAGORE

January 14

EXHILARATION

Suddenly I feel myself transformed and changed; it is joy
unspeakable. My mind is exhilarated; I lose the memory of past
trials; my intelligence is clarified; my desires are satisfied. I grasp
something inwardly as with the embracement of love.

HUGH OF ST. VICTOR

NOW AND THEN WE EXPERIENCE AN EXCITEMENT SO IN-
TENSE THAT WE CALL IT "EXHILARATION." It may not happen
often (and it might not be good if it did), but occasionally we are so
alive and engaged in the moment that the event remains stamped in
our memory forever. These are the "mountaintop" experiences in our
lives, those times when our senses and our sensibilities seem to have
been electrified. It's good that we're able to experience such moments.
The ability to be exhilarated is a thing to be thankful for.

Unfortunately, we tend to fall "asleep" as we get older, and in that
state we fail to be exhilarated by things that should touch us deeply.
We let our minds and hearts be dulled by the duties of daily living.
We lose our openness to the wonder of the world. And consequently,
we forget what it's like to tingle with childlike amazement.

This does not have to happen, however, and we do ourselves a
favor when we make sure that it doesn't. But not only that, we do
others a favor as well. We all know how enjoyable it is to live and
work around the individual whose senses are alive and whose mind is
awake; we can be that individual ourselves if we determine to do so.

Of course, there are some moments so exciting that they would
stir anyone up, even the most jaded. Dangerous moments, for example, are thrilling. (Winston Churchill commented one time that
"nothing in life is so exhilarating as to be shot at without result.") Life
doesn't deliver such extraordinary exhilaration very often, and there is
more to life than the mere seeking of thrills. But when these rare moments come along, they do have the healthy effect of waking us up.

It's a mistake, however, to think that exhilaration can only be
experienced on the mountaintop. In truth, much of what is commonplace can be intensely pleasurable — and the good life will elude us if
we can't taste the tang and the tartness of what is right before us.

Crossing a bare common, in snow puddles, at twilight, under a
clouded sky, without having in my thoughts any occurrence of special
good fortune, I have enjoyed a perfect exhilaration.

RALPH WALDO EMERSON

DISCIPLINE

He that would be superior to external influences
must first become superior to his own passions.

SAMUEL JOHNSON

LIFE PRESENTS US WITH NO GREATER CHALLENGE THAN
WHEN IT ASKS US TO DISCIPLINE OURSELVES. There aren't
many good things that can be accomplished without self-mastery,
but this kind of discipline is as difficult as it is important. To learn to
discipline ourselves effectively, we must usually pass through a painful
apprenticeship. Most of us will fail frequently before we master the
ability to channel our abilities in consistently good directions.

Too often, we spend our training energies learning nothing more
than how to do what we want to do. Having learned that, we then
insist on the right to do what we want. But as Aristotle pointed out,
"What it lies in our power to do, it lies in our power not to do." The
highest form of discipline is the ability to refrain from doing what we
might do in order to achieve goals consistent with what we *ought* to
do. Just because a thing can be done, that doesn't mean it should be
done. Discipline knows the difference. It's able to subordinate impulse
to principle. It knows what to put in . . . and also what to leave out!

Things like self-esteem and self-respect are high priorities with
most people. In view of that, it's ironic that self-discipline is not valued any more than it is. Folks who've been down the road far enough
in life to know what works and what doesn't all report that it's impossible to like ourselves if we don't discipline ourselves. Abraham Joshua
Heschel, for example, said, "Self-respect is the fruit of discipline; the
sense of dignity grows with the ability to say no to oneself."

So the ability to govern ourselves is critical. But as we said at the
beginning, it's very difficult. It's not a skill learned overnight, but one
that comes from growth and training. We need to get in the game and
start learning discipline, but we also need to be patient with ourselves.

The main thing is to decide who we are and what we want. This
sounds simple, but there aren't many people in the world who've really
done it. We can have anything we want, but not everything we want.
Some choices have to be made; some things have to be given up. Let's
not let our lives be marred by things we're too weak to let go of.

Discipline is remembering what you want.

DAVID CAMPBELL

HUMANENESS

> A jeweled pivot on which our lives must turn is the deep
> realization that every person we meet in the course of a day
> is a dignified, essential human soul and that we are being
> guilty of gross inhumanity when we snub or abuse him.
>
> JOSHUA LOTH LIEBMAN

ALL OF US ARE "HUMAN," BUT HOW MANY OF US HAVE LEARNED TO BE "HUMANE"? We should not only conduct ourselves with the honor that should attend our own human lives, but also treat others with the dignity and compassion they deserve, they being creatures with the same nature as we. It is no small feat to deal with those around us, consistently and genuinely, as *human* beings — beings who are not simply mineral, vegetable, or animal . . . but *personal.*

True, there is a sense in which we speak of treating animals humanely. When we use the word in this way, we refer simply to the kind, merciful, and compassionate treatment of animals. This kind of humaneness is by no means unimportant. In fact, how a person treats animals is one measure of that person's character. The Book of Proverbs contains this statement: "A righteous man regards the life of his animal, but the tender mercies of the wicked are cruel."

Yet in its highest sense, humaneness refers to the treatment of other human beings in a "human" way. It means that we never lose sight of their value as persons. And in the end, the willingness to do this usually comes from our having experienced enough failure and sorrow that we're able to empathize and treat them humanely, despite their misjudgments and mistakes. "Through the portals of sorrow we can enter into the suffering of others. Our human compassion is kindled. Our sympathies are awakened" (Sidney Greenberg).

With the means of travel and communication that are available to us now, the world has become a smaller place. Not many days go by that we're not reminded of the larger world that we're a part of. These reminders should make us more humane. "There is no feeling in a human heart that exists in that heart alone — which is not, in some form or degree, in every heart" (George MacDonald). *Whoever we are, you and I have much in common. I should treat you accordingly.*

> There is but one law for all, namely, that law which governs all law,
> the law of our Creator, the law of humanity, justice, equity
> — the law of nature, and of nations.
>
> EDMUND BURKE

ADMIRATION

To love is to admire with the heart;
to admire is to love with the mind.

THÉOPHILE GAUTIER

TO BE ABLE TO ADMIRE — AND TO ADMIRE THINGS THAT ARE TRULY ADMIRABLE — IS A CHARACTER TRAIT WORTH CUL-TIVATING. And mind you, being "able to admire" is a trait that has to be cultivated. If there are few things that we admire, or if the things we admire are not really very worthy, it's probably because we've not worked on keeping our hearts open and we've not educated our hearts to appreciate the better things that life has to offer.

Sometimes we're like the stupid tourist who came out of the Louvre in Paris bragging that he didn't see "what was so great about all that stuff." To him, the doorman simply replied, "Don't you wish you *could* see what was so great about it, sir?" By our failure to admire certain things, we make much more of a comment on ourselves than on the things about which we express our low opinion.

Have you ever given much thought to what the forces are that mold and shape your life the most? Are you, for example, shaped mainly by the love you have for the things you like, or is your life more the result of a reaction against things you don't like? In all honesty, which has been the principal force in molding your character: your admirations or your hostilities? These are probing questions, ones that probably make most of us shift a little uncomfortably in our seats. This uneasiness is evidence of a feeling deep inside us that we ought to give our admirations more priority than we do. These worthy things ought to be given a chance to move us more powerfully.

The fact is, we inhabit a universe chock full of good things to admire. If we want to be powered by a great love for good things, there is no shortage of such things around us. And many of these things come in the form of *people*. So find some things to love and some people to admire. A few years from now, you'll be very glad you did.

To be glad of life because it gives you the chance to love and to work and to play and to look up at the stars — to be satisfied with your possessions but not contented with yourself until you have made the best of them — to despise nothing in the world except falsehood and meanness, and to fear nothing except cowardice — to be governed by your admirations rather than by your disgusts . . . these are little guideposts on the footpath to peace.

HENRY VAN DYKE

SERVANTHOOD

They who give have all things;
they who withhold have nothing.

HINDU PROVERB

MUCH MORE THAN OCCASIONAL ACTS OF SERVICE, WHAT WE NEED IS A SPIRIT OF SERVANTHOOD. Although acts of service are good in and of themselves (and we don't have the spirit of servanthood if we don't actually serve), we would be helped if we worked more on having the *heart* of a servant. In a positive sense, we need to see ourselves as servants, thinking more often of what we can give than of what we can get. We need to have the attitude and the mindset of one who is in the world to serve and not to be served.

To "serve" means to "help." It means to do something that somebody else needs to have done. The servant is first and foremost a giver, an individual whose primary role is to provide and to please.

Learning to have this outlook as our primary way of thinking is a challenge. It's a challenge because from childhood we've been acquiring the habit of self-centeredness. We started out in life thinking that the world existed to serve our needs, and many of us have never grown much beyond that pattern of thought. To learn another way of thinking requires going against the grain of a lifelong disposition.

It's easy, however, to tell whether we've learned the spirit of servanthood. The test is simply this: how do you react when someone *treats* you like a servant? If when treated like a servant you react indignantly, you probably don't see yourself as one, whatever words you may have spoken about the "nobility" of serving others. True servants don't object when others see them as being what they really are!

Albert Schweitzer, who knew the meaning of servanthood if anyone ever did, once told a graduation audience, "I don't know what your destiny will be, but one thing I know: the only ones among you who will be really happy are those who will have sought and found how to serve." Schweitzer was right, of course. And yet we need to be careful. The kind of serving that will make us "really happy" is not rendered for that reason. In our finer moments, we don't serve for the emotional payoff we get. We serve because that's what life is about.

Be ashamed to die unless you have
won some victory for humanity.

HORACE MANN

January 19
SPONTANEITY

Some desire is necessary to keep life in motion,
and he whose real wants are supplied must admit those of fancy.
SAMUEL JOHNSON

O F ALL THE FUELS THAT CAN FIRE US UP, ONE OF THE MOST
WONDERFUL IS SPONTANEITY. Of necessity, we spend the
greater part of our time "taking care of business." Things like food,
clothing, and shelter have to be provided, along with an increasing number of other basic needs. But life can't be about these things
entirely, and the desire (often a very strong one) to break out of our
routines and do something unplanned and unpredictable is not a bad
desire. It must be managed with wisdom, admittedly, but there's no
denying that spontaneity can be a potent force for good in our lives.

It's an unfortunate person who is so busy being "productive"
that he can't be diverted from that once in a while. In the words of
George Santayana, "To condemn spontaneous and delightful occupa-
tions because they are useless for self-preservation shows an uncritical
prizing of life irrespective of its content." And not only that, the truly
productive people are almost always those who know how to blend a
little humor and impulse into their recipe for living.

The benefit and the pleasure of spontaneity are two reasons to
keep up with our regular work. If we procrastinate our regular duties,
we may find that we stay in emergency mode most of the time, doing
things at the last minute that absolutely can't be put off any longer.
In that mode, it's almost impossible to indulge the desire to do things
spontaneously. But those who've kept up with their normal work have
the luxury of being able to lay it aside when a spur-of-the-moment
impulse strikes them. It's a nice reward for having been diligent.

We need to appreciate the spontaneous people who enter our
lives. These free spirits can be exasperating at times, to be sure, but
the truth of the matter is, we're fortunate to have their influence upon
us. It's a privilege to be "inconvenienced" by the person who drops by
in the middle of the morning to say, "Let's go get a cup of coffee."

As we said, spontaneity must be managed with wisdom. But true
wisdom can laugh. It can giggle. It can appreciate a change of plans.
And — believe it or not — wisdom sometimes has no plan at all!

It is a bad plan that admits of no modification.
PUBLILIUS SYRUS

REALISM

> The very greatest mystery is in unsheathed reality itself.
>
> EUDORA WELTY

TRUTH, WE ARE OFTEN TOLD, IS STRANGER THAN FICTION. I would agree, as long as we use the word "strange" to mean "wonderful," i.e. "producing a sense of wonder." Compared to what we sometimes wish to be real or prefer to be real, what is real is almost always more full of wonder. As a writer of some of the twentieth century's greatest fiction, Eudora Welty knew what she was talking about: "The very greatest mystery is in unsheathed reality itself."

A commitment to reality is a good thing. We'd be better off if we made such a commitment more seriously. But doing that isn't always easy. For one thing, it takes *humility*. Reality is a thing that we must bow before with a certain amount of reverence. In addition, a commitment to reality also takes *courage*. "Realists do not fear the results of their study" (Feodor Dostoevsky). Once we sign on to follow the truth, there's no telling where it might lead us before we're done.

But there is one other thing that should be said about realists. Contrary to the popular stereotype, realists are usually people of action. There is a certain type of individual who, under the guise of "realism," is always saying, "It won't work." He never has a better plan, but he knows that the one that has been proposed is going to fail. But that's not realism — it's laziness. As Sydney J. Harris said, "An idealist believes the short run doesn't count. A cynic believes the long run doesn't matter. A realist believes that what is done or left undone in the short run determines the long run." The genuine realist is always willing, with both humility and courage, to *act*. He's willing to do the best thing that he knows to do at the present moment.

What we all want in life is to have people who'll deal with us realistically. We want to be accepted for what we are, even with our blemishes and blunders. But if we want that, shouldn't we deal with others in the same way? Real people, like real life, don't always conform to our wishes. If they did, they wouldn't be as "wonderful."

> Nothing which is at all times and in every way agreeable to us can have objective reality. It is of the very nature of the real that it should have sharp corners and rough edges, that it should be resistant, should be itself. Dream-furniture is the only kind on which you never stub your toes or bang your knee.
>
> C. S. LEWIS

January 21

FEEDBACK

Because of its value, some people have called feedback
"the breakfast of champions." But it isn't the breakfast; it's the
lunch. Vision is the breakfast. Self-correction is the dinner.

STEPHEN R. COVEY

FEEDBACK IS THE THING THAT LETS US KNOW HOW WE'RE
DOING. The word has some other scientific and technical definitions, but in the realm of human relationships, feedback is simply the
information that comes to us from outside our own minds and tells
us what the results of our actions have been. If an employee receives
a performance appraisal from his supervisor, that's feedback. If a student gets an exam back with a grade on it, that's feedback. If a friend
tells you that she was offended by something you said, that's feedback.

Without feedback, it's almost impossible to know whether our
actions have achieved the result that we were hoping for. We may
have our own ideas and impressions about what we've done, but those
impressions can be seriously out of touch with the real facts. Even the
most objective people among us need the benefit of external feedback,
information from outside ourselves that can help us see if there are
any adjustments we need to make in what we're doing.

If we know what's good for us, we will appreciate, rather than
resent, those who give us feedback. There is even a sense in which
we ought to make good use of the feedback we get from enemies. If
a comment is made that contains some truth we need to hear, we'd
be foolish to disregard the truth just because of where it came from.
Indeed, our enemies will sometimes come closer to telling us the truth
than will our friends, who don't want to jeopardize the relationship.

Too often, our lives languish for lack of feedback. We hide from
it, preferring the comfort and security of our own self-image. And
consequently, we stay stuck. We don't make the progress that could be
made if we opened ourselves up to outside information about where
we really are right now. Too embarrassed to be told, "You're still a
beginner," we doom ourselves to the permanent status of beginner.

Building character and competency is a process, and one of the highest-
leverage things we can do in this process is to regularly seek 360-degree
feedback. It takes humility to ask for and receive it. You may have to take
oxygen to get through it. But understanding it and acting wisely with
regard to it can powerfully impact your time and quality of life.

STEPHEN R. COVEY

January 22
IMAGINATION

> The necessity of loyalty between friends, the responsibility
> that the strong owe the infirm, the illusion of ill-gotten gain, the rewards
> of hard work, honesty, and trust — these are enduring truths glimpsed
> and judged first through the imagination, first through art.
>
> MICHAEL DORRIS

IMAGINATION WAS GIVEN TO US NOT ONLY FOR OUR ENTERTAINMENT; IT WAS ALSO GIVEN FOR OUR INSTRUCTION. It's a silly person indeed who, disliking fiction, says that he only enjoys books that are "true." Not only can imaginative works convey truth, they can often do so much more powerfully than an argument or an exposition. It is no accident that the most influential teachers the world has ever known have engaged our imaginations with stories.

None of us has grasped any more than a minute fraction of the totality of what is real. If we were good enough with words to describe in detail every single thing we know to be true, the books we might write would still contain only an infinitesimal part of what there is to know. Deep down, we know this. We know that there is so much more. In our heart of hearts, we feel the tug of great things that lie just outside the boundaries of our present knowledge. We sense their existence, but we can't quite capture them with our words.

Imagination, I believe, is the tool that's been given to us by which we can reach beyond what we know is true and touch things we only have an inkling are true. Joseph Roux said it this way: "That which we know is but little; that which we have a presentiment of is immense; it is in this direction that the poet outruns the learned man."

We need to take better care of our imaginations than we sometimes do. For one thing, we need to be more careful what we *feed* them. Much that we might imagine is not worth imagining, and we ought to steer clear of all that is sordid or selfish. But beyond that, we need to *nurture* our imaginations. If we allow them the exercise they need, they'll grow and become strong. In time, they'll take their place among our best friends. And, as we've said, they'll not only entertain us; they'll teach us. As folks who're both thoughtful and imaginative, we'll learn a lot more than we could with either tool alone.

> You ride astride the imaginary
> in order to hunt down the real.
>
> BREYTEN BREYTENBACH

January 23

CAMARADERIE

It must be obvious to those who take the time to look at human life
that its greatest values lie not in getting things, but in doing them, in doing
them together, in all working toward a common aim, in the experience of
comradeship, of warmhearted one hundred percent human life.

W. T. GRANT

WE OFTEN UNDERESTIMATE THE GOODNESS THAT IS GEN-
ERATED WHEN PEOPLE WORK TOGETHER ON SOMETHING
THAT THEY'RE ALL PASSIONATELY COMMITTED TO. Call it "synergy" or whatever you like, there is something very special that takes
place when two or more people make a mutual assault on a challenge
that would be too much for any of them individually. When the
undertaking is dangerous or physically threatening, the spirit of "camaraderie" is especially deep and meaningful, but we don't have to be
soldiers sharing a foxhole under enemy fire to experience the benefit
of this phenomenon. There are many other ways we can be comrades.

The main ingredient necessary for the spirit of camaraderie is a
common vision or purpose. To be bound together beneficially, a group
must have a goal that is not only held in common but is also felt to be
very important by the group. When two or more people are committed to a goal that is greater than any differences that might separate
them, powerful things are likely to take place. When a group has a goal
greater than its differences, you'd be wise to stand back. It's coming
through, and if you're an obstruction, you're likely to be mowed down.

The wonderful thing about life is that there is no shortage of
good goals that can weld us together. And not only that, we can be
members of more than one group, committed to more than one goal.

These days, most of us live and work in locales where there are
many other people. We find ourselves being with other human beings
whether we want to be or not. But the really good things in life won't
come to us unless we move beyond physical closeness to actual camaraderie. It takes a conscious choice on our part to connect healthily
to those who jostle up against us from day to day. Good, mutually
beneficial relationships are there for the making, and we ought not to
be content to occupy physically adjoining spaces. With at least a few
of these people, we need to become comrades.

A crowd is not company.
OLD SAYING

CRAFTSMANSHIP

Criticism comes easier than craftsmanship.

ZEUXIS

IF WE HAVE TO ADMIT THAT WE SPEND MORE TIME CRITIQU-ING THE WORK OF OTHERS THAN WE DO IMPROVING OUR OWN CRAFTSMANSHIP, THAT'S NOT A GOOD THING. Most of the worthwhile things that human beings are called upon to do require some skill and ability. It's a fact that other people often fail to do their work as skillfully and ably as might be expected, but even so, pointing out that fact is rarely the most productive thing we could be doing with our time. Sharpening our own skills is usually the better choice.

If the word "pride" can ever be used in a good sense, it's probably in the phrase "pride of workmanship." Pride of workmanship is the pleasure that the craftsman has when he finishes a piece of work and knows that it's the very best that he can do. It's one of life's best feelings, actually. And it's sad that so few of us experience it very often.

The quality of our craftsmanship could certainly be improved in the many specific things we do — our work, our hobbies, our community involvement, and so forth — but there is an even more important sense in which we are practicing a craft. A human life as a whole is a thing that has to be made or created. In an overall sense, we are each "building" something that will eventually be finished. Whether the finished product will be one that we can feel good about depends, to a large extent, on how active we are in improving our craftsmanship.

As we give ourselves to our family and friends and coworkers, it's a gratifying thing to know that we're giving them the very best handiwork that we're capable of producing. Surely, some of our peers are people who mean so much to us that we wouldn't ever want to give them anything but our best. But in truth, there is no one we'll ever meet who doesn't deserve the best that we can offer them.

And so let's aspire to being people who know how to craft a human life that's worthy of appreciation. It's a daunting challenge, without a doubt, and it will consume vast reserves of both patience and diligence. But crafting an honorable life is not impossible.

If a great thing can be done at all, it can be done easily.
But it is that kind of ease with which a tree blossoms
after long years of gathering strength.

JOHN RUSKIN

WINSOMENESS

> A person or action which can be described by the [Greek] word *kalos*
> is not only *good;* he or it is also *beautiful.* It therefore has in it the idea of
> goodness which is winsome and attractive. Very often
> the best translation of it is "lovely."
>
> WILLIAM BARCLAY

WINSOMENESS IS ONE KIND OF GOODNESS: IT'S THE KIND OF GOODNESS THAT IS "ATTRACTIVE." When someone is charming or delightful, we're attracted to them. We're pulled toward them. The pull is not a physical force like gravitation or magnetism, yet it sometimes feels that compelling. (Antonyms like "repulsive" or "repellent" share the same metaphor, of course, only in reverse. People with these qualities push us away from them.) "Winsomeness," then, is *attractive* goodness, goodness that pulls with the power of likability.

In ancient times, the Greeks had a special word for this kind of goodness: *kalos.* In contrast to *agathos,* the normal word for "good," *kalos* meant that which was fine or admirable or praiseworthy. If something was *kalos,* it was not only right and correct from a technical viewpoint, but it was also delightful. And these are two very different kinds of goodness, aren't they? We all know people who are scrupulously correct, but their rightness doesn't have much warmth or beauty to it. We know others who are no less concerned to do the right thing, but their goodness is also lovely and inviting. They are winsome!

It's interesting that our English word "winsome" comes from the Old English *wynn,* which simply meant "joy." When we say that a friend has a "winning" smile, we don't just mean that their facial expressions can win us over but that their goodness gives us great joy.

Are you working on your winsomeness? I hope so. And I hope you'll see it as something more than just a personality trait. In reality, it's a character trait. Real winsomeness has a much higher goal than "how to win friends and influence people." It's not a technique to use but a gift to give. It's the imparting of daily grace to those around us.

> A sweet attractive kind of grace,
> A full assurance given by looks,
> Continual comfort in a face,
> The lineaments of Gospel books;
> I trow that countenance cannot lie
> Where thoughts are legible in the eye.
>
> MATTHEW ROYDON

URGENCY

> We cannot put off living until we are ready. The most salient
> characteristic of life is its coerciveness; it is always urgent, "here and now"
> without any possible postponement. Life is fired at us point blank.
>
> JOSÉ ORTEGA Y GASSET

IN VERY MANY CASES, WHATEVER IS WORTH DOING IS NOT ONLY WORTH DOING WELL; IT'S WORTH DOING RIGHT NOW. When we know that there is some good thing to be done and that it would be best to tend to it immediately, procrastination is a dangerous, opportunity-wasting thing. In matters of conscience, at least, we would be better off if we were people whose inward character had more urgency. As Gasset pointed out, "Life is fired at us point blank," and it's usually a mistake to duck or run away.

Much has been written about the bad habit of letting our lives be tyrannized by relatively trivial things that demand our attention, while more important matters go undone. To whatever extent we can distinguish between "urgent" and "important," we do need to resist the tyranny of things that are urgent but not important. I don't deny that. But when I recommend urgency as a positive character trait, I'm saying that we ought to grant a greater urgency to the things that are important. Our view of what's urgent needs to be adjusted.

Almost everybody has had the experience of being given a gift by somebody who couldn't wait for us to open it. When we said, "Thanks, I look forward to finding out what it is," they said, "Go ahead! Open it! Open it!" Do we mind that kind of urgency? Are we put off by it? Certainly not. And the point is that we ought to be giving our very selves to our loved ones with that kind of eagerness.

Whether or not we show a healthy measure of urgency in our hearts probably depends on how we see life in general. The most delightfully urgent people I know happen to be people whose basic response to life is "Yes!" Whatever difficulties they may have to endure, their overarching attitude toward their place in the world is one of gratitude. I'm no more naive about the brokenness of our world than you are, but I submit to you that there is still much grace to be found . . . and to be *acted* upon. The right response is a hearty "Yes!"

> The day is short, the labor long, the workers are idle,
> the reward is great, and the Master is urgent.
>
> MISHNAH

GLADNESS

> Life is short and we never have enough time
> for gladdening the hearts of those who travel the way
> with us. Oh, be swift to love! Make haste to be kind.
>
> HENRI-FRÉDÉRIC AMIEL

IF THERE IS ANYTHING THAT IS BOTH IMPORTANT AND URGENT, "GLADDENING THE HEARTS OF THOSE WHO TRAVEL THE WAY WITH US" WOULD CERTAINLY QUALIFY. Given the amount of gloom that hangs around most people's lives, we never have a greater privilege than when we have the opportunity to impart a little gladness.

In discussing the synonyms *glad, happy, cheerful, lighthearted, joyful,* and *joyous,* the *American Heritage Dictionary* makes this comment on *glad:* "Glad often has reference to the strong feeling that results from gratification of a wish or from satisfaction with immediate circumstances." We make others glad when the things we do for them fulfill a significant longing or desire that they have, especially the longing to be treated with love, respect, and kindness.

Being glad ourselves and giving gladness to others don't require much in the way of raw materials. For gladness to occur, it isn't necessary for some great event to transpire or for some magnificent gesture to be made. Small things can provide great gladness, often better than large ones, and there aren't many days when we don't have numerous chances to give and to enjoy commonplace gladness.

Perhaps one of the deepest sources of gladness should be the knowledge of our own personal identities. Simply put, we ought to be glad to be who we are. Despite our disadvantages, each of us enjoys a set of circumstances that we can rightfully be thankful for. Our individually unique families, our distinct physical and mental characteristics, our geographical places to live and work — all of these things, and many more, are "pastures" that we should be reluctant to trade for any of the "greener" ones that belong to someone else.

Not everything in life gives gladness, of course. But the things that don't are very often those that deepen our gratitude when the darkness finally disappears. What we want are hearts that can feel the whole range of things that *need* to be felt, each in its rightful time.

> In heaven above,
> And earth below, they best can serve true gladness
> Who meet most feelingly the calls of sadness.
>
> WILLIAM WORDSWORTH

LAUGHTER

Keep me away from the wisdom which does not cry,
the philosophy which does not laugh, and the greatness
which does not bow before children.

KAHLIL GIBRAN

WE NEED TO ACCEPT THE FACT THAT THERE ARE SOME THINGS IN LIFE TO WHICH LAUGHTER IS THE RIGHT RESPONSE. Sometimes we act as if we thought laughter were nothing more than a concession to weakness, and that whenever we've indulged in a bit of laughter we need to return to a serious state of mind as quickly as possible. But that's simply not true. We may occasionally laugh when laughter is not appropriate, but the fact remains: there are some things that laughter is the right response to. Not to laugh at things that *should* produce laughter is as unhealthy as it is foolish.

When we encounter something that should cause laughter to bubble up spontaneously inside of us and that doesn't happen, what is the cause? There might be many reasons, some of which would be perfectly understandable, but very often the culprit is simply our pride. We take ourselves too seriously. Our notion of "dignity" or "maturity" is such that it won't let us laugh. But that's unfortunate. As Kahlil Gibran observed, "the philosophy which does not laugh" is not a good philosophy to build our lives upon. It's one to be avoided.

It's a curious fact that sometimes we may be feeling quite mirthful on the inside but no one could tell it by looking at our faces. I suggest that it's a healthy exercise to work on letting physical laughter break out from inside us more often. It's good to feel joyful, but it's even better to *express* that feeling with good, physical laughter!

But what about our relationships with others? Wouldn't it be a good thing if laughter were allowed to enliven our relationships more often? If it would, then here's a good gift that we can give to those whom we love. In our relationships with them, we can do our part to create an environment where it's as safe to laugh as it is to cry. Good relationships can't be made from laughter alone; they also require some sorrow. But on the other hand, if others aren't sure what our response would be if they ever laughed out loud, that's not good either.

Where is home? Home is where the heart can laugh
without shyness. Home is where the heart's tears
can dry at their own pace.

VERNON G. BAKER

ANCHORAGE

Few delights can equal the mere presence
of one whom we trust utterly.
GEORGE MACDONALD

AN "ANCHOR" IS A HEAVY OBJECT ATTACHED TO A VESSEL BY
A CABLE AND CAST OVERBOARD TO KEEP THE VESSEL FROM
MOVING, AND "ANCHORAGE" IS THE CONDITION OF BEING AT
ANCHOR IN A SAFE PLACE. If it's important for ships to find anchorage when they need it, it's even more important, in a figurative sense,
for people to find places where they can be anchored. And the kind of
anchorage we need more often than any other kind is the safety and
security of a relationship in which there is *trust*. When the weather is
stormy, we need someone whose trust will keep us from "moving."

It's a rare person who hasn't been seriously betrayed somewhere
along the way. And that being true, the tendency is for us to retreat
from trust. Having been hurt, we're tempted never to cast anchor in
anyone else's harbor ever again. But that's a temptation we must resist
by all means. We never do ourselves any greater damage than when
we turn away from trust. There is no avoiding our need for anchorage.

Rather than fretting about the scarcity of trustworthy people in
the world, we'd probably do better to work on our own trustworthiness. It's as true with trust as it is with many other things: it is more
blessed to give than to receive. A reputation for trust is not a weak
reputation to have, but rather one of great strength. There's no greater
honor we can aspire to than the honor of being known as persons
who're both trustworthy ourselves and also eager to trust others. We
ought to want others to think of "anchorage" when they think of us.

Anchorage is, in fact, a gift that can be given. It's a thing we can
deliberately choose to extend to those around us. And we ought not
only to give it freely, but appreciate those who've given it freely to us.
If it's been a while since you've thanked someone who has extended
significant trust to you, today would be a fine day to do that.

When people trust us, we are changed forever. Having had someone who gave us anchorage during a storm that could've destroyed us,
we are never the same afterward. It's a gift that keeps on giving.

The comfort of having a friend may be taken away,
but not that of having had one.
SENECA

STEPS

A glimpse is not a vision. But to a man on a
mountain road by night, a glimpse of the next three feet
of road may matter more than a vision of the horizon.

C. S. LEWIS

TO BE WILLING SIMPLY TO TAKE STEPS MAY SEEM LIKE A
SMALL THING, BUT IT'S ACTUALLY A VERY COURAGEOUS
THING AND ALSO ONE THAT'S VERY WISE. Often we don't know
what lies on the distant reaches of our path ahead, but if, as C. S.
Lewis suggested, we have "a glimpse of the next three feet of road,"
then we have the information we need to take the only step that can
actually be taken: *the one immediately in front of us.* The determination
to *take* this step is what makes progress possible in the real world.

Greatness of human character lies not so much in the skill to do
hard things as in the discipline to do easy things in hard moments.
If we miss out on the good life, it won't be for lack of intelligence or
inborn ability; it'll come down to failure in the matter of step-taking.

Looking back at our past, each of us can see that we are where
we are today as a result of the steps that we have or haven't taken
previously, not many of which seemed very significant at the time.
The taking of small steps has a cumulative effect. One thing leads to
another, and the first thing we know, an entire human life has been
brought into being. It's important, therefore, to take our steps decisively, rather than to live by denial and default.

It would probably be difficult to overestimate the value of our
example when we consistently take the steps we know we should take.
Whatever we do, others are watching, whether we know it at the time
or not. We confer a benefit on those around us when we give ourselves to them as *persons who have the courage to take steps.*

We're all trying to move forward in life, aren't we? As we try to
do that, it's not uncommon to encounter obstacles. But the hindrance
represented by these obstacles is often out of all proportion to the
size of the obstacles themselves. Not infrequently, the greatness of the
difficulty lies in our unwillingness to take some simple step that we're
quite capable of taking. And that's a difficulty we can do away with.

Many of our fears are tissue-paper thin, and a single
courageous step would carry us clear through them.

BRENDAN FRANCIS

REDEMPTION

Evil can never be undone, but only purged and redeemed.
DOROTHY L. SAYERS

THE ANONYMOUS LATIN-SPEAKING PROVERBIST WHO ORIGI-NALLY SAID *ERRARE HUMANUM EST* ("TO ERR IS HUMAN") PACKED A GOOD DEAL OF SAD MEANING INTO A FEW WORDS. We do err, don't we? All of us do. And when we've done so, our hearts are later broken when we see our failures honestly. When our failure is one of great or tragic proportions, our sense of sorrow can be deadly.

In its most literal sense, the word "redeem" means "to buy back." More generally, its meaning is "to set free or rescue." When we speak of redemption, what we have in mind is really the coupling of two basic ideas: *deliverance* and *restoration*. To have failed and then to experience redemption is to be given one's life back. It is to be "bought back" from the sentence of death by someone else's grace.

It is a deeply held belief of mine that we live in a world where there is such a thing as redemption. If I didn't believe that, I'm not sure that I would judge human life to be worth continuing.

The gift of redemption, of course, is never unconditional. Indeed, one of the main objects of our existence ought to be discovering what the terms of our redemption are. And not only discovering them, the joyful *embracing* of them ought to be the mainspring of our happiness, even if it is through great suffering that we are to be redeemed.

If you've ever known serious defeat and then been pulled back from your deadly, downward spiral by someone else's grace, you know what it's like to have life breathed back into your lungs redemptively. Shouldn't we all be wanting to be the agents of such grace for others?

One of my favorite scenes in all of Peter Jackson's magnificent screenplay of J. R. R. Tolkien's *Lord of the Rings* is the one where Lady Arwen, cradling an apparently dying Frodo in her arms, prays that he might be spared: "What grace is given me, let it pass to him."

Whatever grace has been given to us (and it is much), can we not be willing, if not eager, for that grace to be passed to those around us? Would we not die, if by our death someone else could live? And if you think others don't deserve the grace by which they could be redeemed, let yourself be reminded of this: neither do you and neither do I.

No creature that deserved redemption would need to be redeemed.
C. S. LEWIS

CONVICTION

> The enemies a person makes by taking a stand
> will have more respect for him than the friends
> he makes by being on the fence.
>
> ANONYMOUS

CONVICTION IS "THE STATE OF BEING CONVINCED." If we're convicted (i.e., convinced) that a certain belief is accurate and that that belief is very important, then we hold it in our hearts deeply and steadfastly. A conviction is more than a whim, a guess, or an opinion. It's an element in a person's deep-down belief system, a part of that person's very principles. And people of strong conviction would rather die than compromise the principles that they are convicted of.

It should be obvious that we could do with a lot more conviction in the world. Too often, we find that people don't really believe anything strongly enough that their ideas would qualify as convictions. And not only that, what convictions we do have are often those we've simply picked up from the news and entertainment media. So most of us would profit from periodically going back and reexamining our basic principles. Do we really believe what we say we believe? Are we willing to make these things a matter of conviction or not?

Conviction doesn't guarantee the truthfulness of a belief, of course. Even if we'd die for what we believe, that doesn't mean we're not mistaken. "Martyrdom has always been a proof of the intensity, never of the correctness of a belief" (Arthur Schnitzler).

All else being equal, however, it is better to be people of conviction than not to be. The only alternative is to spend our lives sitting on the fence on every question — never sure, never taking a stand, and never having the respect of any thoughtful person.

Perhaps we'd do better if we quit paying so much attention to how our convictions are "paying off" at the present moment. Having convictions requires certain qualities of character, and one of them is *trust*. Another is *patience*. Another is *longsuffering*. Just because a principle seems to be headed for defeat right now, that doesn't mean it's not worth standing up for. It's natural that we want to be on the "winning" side, but conviction is content if it is just on the side of *wisdom*.

> Hope is not the conviction that something
> will turn out well but the certainty that something
> makes sense, regardless of how it turns out.
>
> VÁCLAV HAVEL

STATURE

Be free, all worthy spirits,
And stretch yourselves, for greatness and for height.
GEORGE CHAPMAN

IN THE LITERAL SENSE, A PERSON'S STATURE IS THAT PERSON'S PHYSICAL HEIGHT. The word comes from the Latin *stare* ("to stand"), and so stature is how tall a person stands. But we often speak of someone's "standing" in a metaphorical sense. If, for example, a doctor enjoys a high "standing" in the medical community, that would mean that he's highly regarded for integrity, professionalism, technical expertise, and so forth. So aspiring to significant "stature" is more than a matter of wanting to be seven feet tall physically. It's wanting to have a *character* that has some greatness to it, rather than one that is petty and small. And surely that is something we should aspire to.

The average human being is capable of a greater character than most people realize. When it comes to personal growth, most of us settle for far less than we should. We need to reach for more than we do. In the words of Chapman's encouragement: "Be free, all worthy spirits / And stretch yourselves, for greatness and for height."

But why should we do this? Certainly not for reasons that stem from selfish ambition. No, we need to grow toward our greatest stature because that's what life asks of us. It's a privilege to be the persons that we are, and it's a privilege to live in the world that we inhabit. We have a poor concept of stewardship indeed if we're so complacent and indifferent that we don't care whether we realize our potential or not. If nothing else, a failure to grow is a failure to be grateful.

But make no mistake: achieving "stature" or "standing" does require growth! There are no quick fixes, no miraculous three-day plans that will get the job done. Learning to stand tall is a process that not only takes time; it takes a prodigious amount of work.

People of stature are often applauded by their peers. But if we're serious about standing as tall as we can, we need to be careful in the matter of applause. Applause is usually given to those who've done things outwardly that are impressive. But real stature is an inward quality — it's a matter of character. All the "standing" in the world doesn't mean a thing if we don't have the character to go with it.

Stature comes not from height but with depth.
BENJAMIN LICHTENBERG

TRUST

The best proof of love is trust.

JOYCE BROTHERS

IN A SENSE, TRUST IS THE MOST GENEROUS GIFT THAT ONE PERSON CAN GIVE TO ANOTHER. All of us know that we fall short of being completely trustworthy; even if we're generally faithful to our commitments, there have been at least a few times when we've let others down. And so, when someone extends trust to us, we know that they're accepting some risk. In order to benefit us, they're allowing themselves to be made vulnerable. And that's a very generous thing to do. Not only is trust the "best proof of love," as Joyce Brothers puts it, it's also the costliest gift that love can bestow.

Trust is never more beautiful than when it's given as a conscious choice. There are some individuals who are so naturally easy to trust that we find ourselves comfortably drawn in the direction of trusting them. At some point in our relationship, we simply wake up and realize that we've come to trust them. But there are others who, for whatever reason, are not so easy to trust, and when we make the conscious choice to trust them anyway, that's a very beautiful gesture indeed.

We may as well admit it: it takes strength of character to give the gift of trust. In very many cases, the question of whether we will trust another person is not so much a question of their character as it is a question of our own. If you look at your list of relationships and you see that there aren't many people you trust, you may think you've just had the bad luck to be surrounded by an unusual number of traitors. The more likely explanation, however, is that you just haven't developed the internal character to engage in the act of trust.

It's true that we pay a price for trusting other people, but the price of weakness and lack of trust is even higher. To be mistrustful is to be miserable. "You may be deceived if you trust too much, but you will live in torment if you do not trust enough" (Frank Crane).

And not only does mistrust make us miserable, it also erodes our own integrity. Doubters and cynics (those who make a big deal about how few people there are in the world who can be trusted) are very rarely people you'd want to go into business with. So how about you and me? Do we trust others? If not, they probably can't trust us either!

He who mistrusts most should be trusted least.

THEOGNIS

TRUSTWORTHINESS

Put more trust in nobility of character than in an oath.

SOLON

ULTIMATELY, THE ONLY THING THAT WILL MAKE PEOPLE FEEL SAFE IN THEIR INTERACTION WITH US IS THE TRUST-WORTHINESS OF OUR CHARACTER. There are times when our commitments will have to be backed up with oaths, vows, contracts, and collateral, but the bottom line is that if our inward character can't be trusted, these external things aren't enough to make people rest easy in their dealings with us. They'll know that if our commitment to them ever becomes inconvenient, we'll manage to find something in the fine print that will let us set aside our obligation to them.

But speaking of contracts and so forth, people who are truly trustworthy don't mind signing such guarantees. Honorable people don't object to having their word bound by social and legal safeguards, and you should be leery of the fellow who acts offended when you ask him to back up his word with a contract. Indeed, even with promises we make to ourselves, it's often wise to strengthen private promises by placing them on record in some kind of public way. It's not bad to have friends who can come and say, "But you said you would . . . "

But the question of commitments that we make to ourselves raises an important point. One of the things we need most in life is confidence in our own integrity and reliability. We need to be able to trust ourselves, knowing deep inside that we will do whatever we commit ourselves to do. If our past record is such that we ourselves don't have any confidence that we'll follow through, it's not realistic to expect that others will find us trustworthy. So the best thing we can do to be seen as trustworthy by our peers is to practice the daily discipline of making and keeping commitments to ourselves.

Whatever discipline it takes to build trustworthiness, that's a discipline we need to adopt. There are few gifts we can give to others that will be any more appreciated. And trustworthiness is not just a gift; it's an obligation. We owe it to others to do as we say we'll do.

I would be true, for there are those who trust me;
I would be pure, for there are those who care;
I would be strong, for there is much to suffer;
I would be brave, for there is much to dare.

HOWARD A. WHEELER

PRIVACY

The human animal needs a freedom seldom mentioned,
freedom from intrusion. He needs a little privacy quite as much
as he wants understanding or vitamins or exercise or praise.
PHYLLIS MCGINLEY

THE PERSON WHO'S NEVER ALONE IS A PERSON WHO'LL FIND IT HARD TO GROW IN CHARACTER. We certainly do need contact with other human beings, and we even need what might be called *companionship* (more about that tomorrow), but it's a fact that we also need *privacy*. We need times of solitude to reflect, to meditate, and to grow. We need some quiet, private spaces in our lives. And if it's true that we need such spaces, it's also true that it's hard to find them. More and more, our lives are lived in such a way that solitude — at least *significant* solitude — is a rare commodity.

Robert Lindner wrote, "It is in solitude that the works of hand, heart, and mind are always conceived, and in solitude that individuality must be affirmed." By now, the record of the human race is clear: positive contributions to the world are not made except by those who've spent time alone, growing strong in the seasons of life.

Privacy is not the end goal of life, however, and nothing that we've said here is meant to take away from the importance of interaction with others. But as Emerson said, "Isolation must precede true society." If we intend our connections with others to be beneficial, we must first learn the benefit of solitude. Little good will come from our circle of relationships if we haven't grounded ourselves in the virtue of valid principles — and that is almost always done in private.

There are no friends we should appreciate any more than those who're secure enough in their relationship with us that they'll honor our need for privacy. And more than that, those friends are especially valuable who, when we've taken them into our privacy and confided to them some part of our solitude, can be trusted to keep our private matters private. A friend who'll guard the gate to the innermost chambers of our heart is a friend indeed. But the crucial question is not whether we *have* friends like that; it's whether we can *be* friends like that. Those who need us, need us to keep safe their secrets.

Count him not among your friends
who will retail your privacies to the world.
PUBLILIUS SYRUS

COMPANIONSHIP

True happiness is of a retired nature, and an enemy to pomp and noise;
it arises, in the first place, from the enjoyment of one's self; and, in the
next, from the friendship of a few select companions.

JOSEPH ADDISON

OUR HAPPINESS NEEDS A LITTLE PRIVACY, BUT IT ALSO NEEDS
"THE FRIENDSHIP OF A FEW SELECT COMPANIONS," AS
ADDISON SAYS. The qualities of character that we nurture in private
are not meant for our benefit alone; they're meant to be used and
enjoyed within the context of relationships with others. Whatever we
are within the privacy of our own hearts, that person should touch
and influence other human beings in widening circles of contact. And
those who occupy the innermost of these circles are our "companions."

The word "companion" is actually a colorful word. We get it from
the Latin *companio*, which was a compound of two words: *com* ("together") + *panis* ("bread"). A companion, then, is someone with whom
we "break bread," that is, a close associate or comrade. Looking at it
from a slightly different angle, our companions are those who "accompany" us on the road that we have to travel. They're our "company."

Companionableness. What are the qualities of a good companion?
Well, as we suggested in yesterday's reading, one of them is a respect
for our privacy. Good companions enjoy our company, but they also
honor our solitude. But there are other traits as well, and almost all
of them are virtues of character: sympathy, understanding, sense of
humor, kindness, enjoyment of life, curiosity, and many more.

Companionship. Companionable qualities may be delightful, but
they're not much good unless they're used. And so what we need more
of in the world is not merely companionableness; we need more actual
companionship. We need — all of us do — to engage *actively* in the
conduct of companionship. It takes work and it's not always conve-
nient, but the value of it is worth more than diamonds and rubies.

Whoever you are, there'll be those around you who need you to
"accompany" them in some way. They need your companionship. And,
in truth, you need theirs too! It's a fact: human beings are social creatures, and we need a few good folks with whom we can "break bread."

Good company and good discourse
are the very sinews of virtue.

IZAAK WALTON

February 7
BEAUTY

God has given us the Morning Star already: you can go and enjoy
the gift on many fine mornings if you get up early enough. What more,
you may ask, do we want? Ah, but we want so much more — something
the books on aesthetics take little notice of. But the poets
and the mythologies know all about it.

C. S. LEWIS

SOMEWHERE WITHIN EACH OF US, THERE IS A DESIRE FOR
BEAUTY. In fact, this is one of our deepest desires, whether we
recognize it as such or not. And it's not just that we want to see or
hear or touch particular things that are beautiful within our world:
"We want something else which can hardly be put into words — we
want to be united with the beauty we see, to pass into it, to receive it
into ourselves, to bathe in it, to become part of it" (C. S. Lewis).

Isn't this why we're drawn so powerfully toward *personal* beauty?
However much we may be moved by the beauty of things like sunrises
and songs and stories, the beauty of certain *persons* acts on us even
more magnetically. And it's not just their physical beauty that pulls us
toward them; it's almost always a combination of inward and outward
traits that blend together and make us want to know them — and
to be known by them — at the deepest possible level. The beauty of
these individuals is merely a marker, a pointer. It points us toward
something that we have a built-in need for. We may not be able to
define it or describe it, but we know for a fact that we've met people
who stir within us a desperate longing for something we've never
experienced in its fullness or perfection. Let's call this thing Beauty.

But as we all know, beauty is not the only thing in the world;
there is also much ugliness. And so we have a choice to make: will we
give in to the ugliness that taints our lives or will we resist it? I'd like
to encourage you to resist it. When faced with a choice, *choose beauty*.
Learn to appreciate it, and educate your taste for it. Make it one of
your core values, and exhibit it in your character. Love it, and share its
sharp, piercing wonder with others who love it as you do.

Spend all you have for loveliness,
Buy it and never count the cost;
For one white singing hour of peace
Count many a year of strife well lost,
And for a breath of ecstasy
Give all you have been, or could be.

SARA TEASDALE

TRANQUILITY

Calm's not life's crown, though calm is well.

MATTHEW ARNOLD

IF OUR INWARD CHARACTER IS ONE THAT CAN BE CALLED "TRANQUIL," THEN WE HAVE SOMETHING TO ENJOY. Our individual characters are the result of our choices, of course, and we may not have made choices that have led us in the direction of tranquility. If we haven't, perhaps we ought to consider doing so. A calm, peaceful state of mind is not the highest goal that should claim our attention, but rightly considered, it's an honorable thing, worthy of our pursuit.

We say that it's not the highest goal in life simply because there are many things that would be worth sacrificing our tranquility for. For example, suppose a house is burning down and there are young children inside who need to be rescued. No one in his right mind would say, "Well, I'd like to get involved, but I prefer not to disturb my peace of mind." No, we would gladly sacrifice the feeling of tranquility in that moment in order to achieve a higher goal. So peace of mind is like any other kind of peace: what we want is peace, but not peace at any price. Feelings are fine, but life involves a number of considerations more important than how we feel at the present moment.

Come to think of it, one of the things that's more important than the enjoyment of tranquility is being an agent who influences *others* to enjoy that quality. We live in times that are agitated, and most of those whom we meet need a greater measure of calmness in their lives. The best reason for pursuing tranquility ourselves is so that we can have a peaceful influence on those we love.

There is no possibility of being tranquil, however, if we look for it in the wrong places. It doesn't come from diets, exercises, self-help seminars, faddish lifestyles, or hip philosophies: *it comes from having characters that are aligned with true-north principles.* As La Rochefoucauld said, "When we are unable to find tranquility within ourselves, it is useless to seek it elsewhere." In a world of disturbing ups and downs, tranquility must come from truths that don't change.

To live in the presence of great truths and eternal laws,
to be led by permanent ideals — that is what keeps a man
patient when the world ignores him, and calm
and unspoiled when the world praises him.

HONORÉ DE BALZAC

CAUTION

Be cautious. Opportunity does the knocking for temptation too.

AL BATT

W HEN WE'RE CONFRONTED WITH DIFFICULT OR DANGER-
OUS CIRCUMSTANCES, WE NEED TO BE CAUTIOUS. There are
forces at work in the world that will destroy us and our loved ones if
we don't watch out. In the living of a human life, it pays to be careful.

It is possible, obviously, to be overly cautious, and if that's your
problem, today's reading may not be very helpful to you. But from
my observation, those with that problem are in the minority. The
swindlers of the world haven't reported any downturn in their business lately; you don't hear them complaining that people in general
have become too cautious. No, I think P. T. Barnum ("There's a sucker
born every minute") would be tickled to death if he were alive today.

We need to exercise caution in our beliefs. When we're forming our
basic beliefs, convictions, and even our opinions, we need to double-
check for accuracy. "Opinions should be formed with great caution
— and changed with greater" (Josh Billings). It's easier to verify the
truthfulness of our ideas and principles than it is to rebuild what we've
destroyed by acting on false information that we carelessly accepted.

We need to exercise caution in our relationships. Of all the damage
that carelessness can do, none is more heartbreaking than the damage we do to other people. To a greater or lesser extent, everything
we do impinges on someone else, and it's not sufficient, when we've
hurt someone, to brush the incident aside with a simple, "I just wasn't
thinking." That's the whole point, isn't it? We *should* have been thinking. We owe it to those around us to use caution in our conduct.

When we've been careless, we can't expect the laws of the universe to rescue us. Those laws operate with a terrible predictability:
the crop that we reap will always be the same one we sowed. If we sow
incautiously, it's foolish (and also a bit arrogant) to expect the "law of
the farm" to be set aside just for us, as if we could make poor choices
and still get the results that would have come from better ones. And
in the real world, poor choices can be disastrous, not only for us but
also for those who're affected by our actions. It pays to be careful.

The sower may mistake and sow his peas crookedly:
the peas make no mistake, but come up and show his line.

RALPH WALDO EMERSON

PARTICIPATION

> To say yes, you have to sweat and roll up
> your sleeves and plunge both hands into life
> up to the elbows. It is easy to say no,
> even if saying no means death.
>
> JEAN ANOUILH

LIFE CALLS US TO MAKE A DECISION: WILL WE PARTICIPATE IN IT OR MERELY OBSERVE? Will we take part in the great drama or be content to sit among the spectators? Quite a lot depends on our decision. If we choose to be active in the living of life, good things are more than likely to happen. If, on the other hand, we decide to remain passive and uninvolved, it's less likely that we'll enjoy life's goodness.

Whether we've studied philosophy or not, most of us understand the difference between "subjective" and "objective." Subjective things have to do with ourselves and the life that's "inside" us, while objective things are those that have their existence "outside" of us. Regarding the objective world, Paul Goodman has said this, "It is by losing himself in the objective, in inquiry, creation, and craft, that a man becomes something." Outside of our own minds and experience there lies a marvelous world to engage, to inquire after, and to be involved with. And we aren't really living a *human* life if we're not participating.

Going back to the analogy of life as a drama or play, isn't it true that each of us has some part, some role to play in the story? Surely we do, and the world loses some degree of goodness every time we back away from playing the part that we're uniquely equipped to play.

Does participating require more effort than being an observer? Yes, it does. Does it involve more risk? Without a doubt. That's why, as Jean Anouilh said, "It is easy to say no, even if saying no means death." But who wants death? It's worth whatever it takes to overcome our inertia, break the bonds of gravity, and say yes to . . . life!

The word "life" can be used in many different ways, and there is a sense in which the laziest, most passive person in the world is still "living." But in a greater sense, that person is not really living; he or she is doing no more than "being lived." And in the end, that kind of "life" has in it more to regret than to rejoice about.

> The notion of looking on at life has always been
> hateful to me. What am I if I am not a participant?
> In order to be, I must participate.
>
> ANTOINE DE SAINT-EXUPÉRY

STANDARDS

*Pray to God we may have the courage and the wisdom and the vision
to raise a definite standard that will appeal to the best that is in man,
and then strive mightily toward that goal.*
HAROLD E. STASSEN

LITERALLY, THE WORD "STANDARD" MEANS "RALLYING PLACE."
On the battlefield, a standard is a flag or banner which rallies the
troops to their cause. In ancient times, to be the standard-bearer was
an important responsibility: the flag could not be allowed to fall.

Then the word came to be used figuratively to mean an acknowledged measure of comparison, a criterion. Today, we often think of a
standard as an expected level of conduct or performance. We speak of
moral standards, ethical standards, business standards, and so forth.

A nation needs a worthy set of standards, and so do individual
people. If we have no rallying point in our lives and if there's no minimum level of honor to which we hold ourselves, then we're simply
adrift, and nothing very good will come from our activity. Living with
no standards produces more mediocrity than it does excellence.

We ought to be careful in selecting our standards. In the marketplace
of ideas, there are all sorts of standards to choose from, many with a
flashy appearance but little long-term value. It pays to be careful.

There ought to be some standards which we refuse to compromise.
There comes a time in life when we're tempted to barter with the
devil, so to speak. But there ought to be some things that are simply
not negotiable. We may back up and back up and back up, but eventually honor must assert itself and say, "No further!"

We need to be improving our standards constantly. Some of the best
work we ever do is that of upgrading our standards. None of us has a
perfect set of standards yet, and so we need to be working continually
on their quality, aligning them with principles of time-tested value.

In many homes there are two sets of dishes: one for everyday use
and another for special occasions. Most of us also have more than one
set of standards, and while meeting our highest standards may not be
possible every instant, those standards can certainly be met more than
once or twice a year. We should use our "good dishes" more often!

*You must regulate your life by the standards
you admire when you are at your best.*
JOHN M. THOMAS

COURAGE

I am tired of hearing about men with the "courage of their convictions."
Nero and Caligula and Attila and Hitler had the courage of their convictions
. . . But not one of them had the courage to examine their convictions
or to change them, which is the true test of character.

SYDNEY J. HARRIS

TODAY, AS WE CELEBRATE ABRAHAM LINCOLN'S BIRTHDAY, LET'S MEDITATE ON THE VALUE OF COURAGE. There can be little question that Lincoln's place in history was secured by the courageous coupling of his character and his well-informed conscience.

Courage is a quality of such basic importance that, from very ancient times, it has been counted as one of the four "cardinal" virtues: justice, wisdom, courage, and moderation. The word "cardinal" comes from the Latin *cardo* ("hinge" or "axis"), and these virtues are cardinal in that all the other virtues hinge on them. They're the necessary foundation on which all the other virtues must be built, and there is even a sense in which courage is the prerequisite for the other cardinal virtues. There are great difficulties in the practice of any good human trait, and it is courage that enables one to overcome these difficulties. Without courage, nothing else can be accomplished. As James Matthew Barrie put it, "Courage is the thing. All goes if courage goes."

And yet it should be equally obvious that courage must be balanced by other virtues or it becomes an evil thing. As Sydney J. Harris pointed out, many of the most sinister figures in world history have been persons of courage, but their courage was not informed by justice and equity. It is no great thing to act courageously if our actions are not governed by a conscience grounded in valid principles.

And so, as Harris suggests, what we need are folks with "the courage to examine their convictions," and also the courage "to change them, which is the true test of character." Abraham Lincoln was old-fashioned enough to believe that there are objective standards of right and wrong, and for all his courage, he also had humility. On more than one occasion, he took a position that varied from his previous policies, based on his growing understanding of the requirements of rightness for himself and for his nation. We're indebted to his example, and we need to be more Lincolnesque in the living of our lives.

Without justice, courage is weak.
BENJAMIN FRANKLIN

BREAKTHROUGHS

In life it is more necessary to lose than to gain.
A seed will only germinate if it dies.

BORIS PASTERNAK

A "BREAKTHROUGH" IS A MAJOR ACHIEVEMENT, ONE THAT OPENS THE DOOR TO MUCH FURTHER PROGRESS. It's important in life to take whatever steps we can take, however small, and we ought not to underestimate the value of ordinary progress. But isn't it exciting when a *big* step can be taken? On those occasions when some significant barrier or obstacle is overcome and we find ourselves in the presence of a whole range of new possibilities, that's when we're glad we kept going when it would have been easy to give up.

As can be seen from the word itself, "breakthroughs" involve "breaking through" limits. The limit might be what we think is possible. It might be what we've been able to do before. It might be what we presently know or understand. Or (and this is perhaps the most common limit of all) it might be what we feel in the mood to do. Limits come in many shapes and sizes, but they all have this in common: *they keep us from going anywhere but where we are right now.*

When we have a breakthrough, we burst out of our limits and move ahead into new territory. The barriers are broken, and we learn that what we previously were limited from doing, we now can do.

We'd all like to enjoy breakthroughs more often, but we don't because we're not willing to pay the price. Despite the fact that they hinder us, limits do provide a certain amount of comfort and familiarity. And people who're not willing to experience the discomfort of "breaking through" are doomed to stay where they are. We have to lose certain things in order to gain others, and the loss can sometimes be so dramatic that it feels like death. But we can't have it both ways at once. As Pasternak observed, "A seed will only germinate if it dies."

Perhaps that's why people with the pioneering spirit aren't very common. For all our talk about wanting progress, most of us are content to stick with what we've already got. But thank goodness for those who've got the courage to break through limits! Let's appreciate them for the scary, unsettling sacrifices they've been willing to make.

One doesn't discover new lands without consenting
to lose sight of the shore for a very long time.

ANDRÉ GIDE

ROMANTICISM

Life is a romantic business. It is painting a picture, not doing a sum;
but you have to make the romance, and it will come to the question
how much fire you have in your belly.

OLIVER WENDELL HOLMES

ROMANTICISM IS A SPIRIT THAT THE WORLD NEEDS MORE OF,
AND TODAY IS A GOOD DAY TO THINK ABOUT THAT. "Life is a
romantic business," as Holmes said, but too few of us approach it that
way. Too few of us see romance as anything more than the doing of
special things by sweethearts and spouses. In our daily lives, we fail to
feel the power of romanticism in the older, and more general, sense.

"Romance encompasses so much more than the spark of love
between sweethearts," wrote Thomas Kinkade. "[To be romantic] is
quite simply to allow yourself to fall in love with life — all of life —
and experience it fully, openly, passionately, and purposefully." I agree.
And to sweethearts, I would say this: if you find no evidence of romanticism in your lover's life outside of his or her interaction with you
personally, watch out. You've probably got an unromantic lover trying
to splash on a little romance just to win you over. It will pass!

But I digress. Let's get back to something more fitting for
Valentine's Day. It's a fact, isn't it, that we could do with a little more
romantic love. While there's more to the romantic spirit than the way
it expresses itself in love, we should try to keep love from being anything less than romantic. The thoughtful things we do today ought to
be spread out a little more evenly throughout the year. It takes work
to keep the romantic fires burning, but it's well worth it.

But to tell the truth, something else must be said. When a man
and a woman pledge their love in marriage, something deeper than
romantic love must guarantee the relationship. Romanticism may be
the icing on the cake, but the cake must be cooked with ingredients
that are delicious and healthful in their own right.

Love as distinct from "being in love" is not merely a feeling. It is a
deep unity, maintained by the will and deliberately strengthened by habit . . .
[Spouses] can retain this love even when each would easily, if they allowed
themselves, be "in love" with someone else. "Being in love" first moved them
to promise fidelity: this quieter love enables them to keep the promise.
It is on this love that the engine of marriage is run:
being in love was the explosion that started it.

C. S. LEWIS

PREDICTABILITY

Our peculiar dangers are those that surprise us
and work treachery in the fort.
HENRY WARD BEECHER

PREDICTABILITY IS ONE OF THE LEAST APPRECIATED OF ALL CHARACTER TRAITS. It's one of those virtues that operate below the surface, and as long as it's there, we tend to take it for granted. When someone conducts their relationship with us in such a dependable way that we never have to worry whether they'll do as we've come to expect, we may simply think that's the way life is supposed to be and fail to appreciate that we're actually being given a gift. It's not until we have to deal with someone who's erratic and unpredictable that we remember to give thanks for our more dependable friends.

Some of life's most difficult tests come as the result of unpleasant surprises sprung on us by other people. It's hard enough to exercise wisdom and strength when problems march up and challenge us in broad daylight. But, as Beecher said, it's even harder to deal with dangers "that surprise us and work treachery in the fort." And it's not only difficulty that is worsened by unexpectedness. Grief is that way too. "Unfamiliarity lends weight to misfortune, and there never was a man whose grief was not heightened by surprise" (Seneca).

So aren't you grateful for the "count-on-able" friends that you have? I am, and I try to thank them for this simple gift, the gift of predictability. Knowing what to expect takes a great deal of the stress out of life, and never having to worry that you're going to be harmed or hurt by the fluctuations in someone else's behavior is a blessing.

In short, then, predictability is a simple, but important, part of friendship. Spontaneity is a wonderful thing, to be sure, but the kind of things we want people to do spontaneously are *good* things. What we don't want are unfulfilled promises, broken commitments, frustrated expectations, and uncertain performance of duty. Life has enough ups and downs as it is; it will test us with enough surprises on its own. In the midst of these uncertainties, we need friends who're steady, those who are comfortably and confidently predictable. And since our friends also need that kind of friendship, it wouldn't be a waste of time for us to move our *own* predictability up a notch or two.

The shifts of Fortune test the reliability of friends.
CICERO

ELOQUENCE

The eloquent man is he who is no beautiful speaker,
but who is inwardly and desperately drunk with a certain belief.

RALPH WALDO EMERSON

NOT MANY ORDINARY PEOPLE WOULD SAY THAT ELOQUENCE IS A CHARACTERISTIC THEY DESIRE TO POSSESS. It sounds like something that would be of interest only to public speakers, but let's take a closer look at the word. The *American Heritage Dictionary* says that the "eloquent" person is "persuasive, fluent, and graceful in discourse." It seems to me that all three elements of this definition suggest some things we'd all do well to be interested in.

Persuasiveness. When you stop to think about it, a large part of the talk that any of us do on a given day consists of persuasion. From the big issues down to the little details of life, we spend a lot of time trying to influence others. So if eloquence helps us be more persuasive, then it's a thing we all can use. But the kind of eloquence that is most persuasive is not the "flowery" kind that we imagine "great speakers" using. As Emerson said, the eloquent person is the one who is "inwardly and desperately drunk with a certain belief." We'll all become more eloquent, and therefore more persuasive, when we start believing more deeply the things we say we want others to believe.

Fluency. Fluency is facility in the use of language. And isn't that something that we all ought to value? Language is a wonderful and powerful gift. We show appreciation for this gift when we take the time to learn how to use one or more languages easily and effectively.

Gracefulness. There is enough crudeness in the world already. Wouldn't it be nice if there were a little more gracefulness in the way we speak to one another? Pindar, the Greek poet, said, "A thing said walks in immortality if it has been said well." We do those who must listen to us a favor when we season our speech with a little grace.

"Eloquence," according to Richard Cecil, "is vehement simplicity." I like that definition. It suggests that we're eloquent when we know what we want to say, we believe it passionately, and we say it simply and straightforwardly. Eloquence, seen in this way, is not just for the orators among us. It's for everybody else too.

True eloquence consists in saying
all that should be said, and that only.

FRANÇOIS DE LA ROCHEFOUCAULD

ADVENTURE

Life is either a daring adventure or nothing.
To keep our faces toward change and behave like free spirits
in the presence of fate is strength undefeatable.
HELEN KELLER

WHAT DO WE DO WHEN WE'RE PRESENTED WITH SITUA-
TIONS THAT ARE STRANGE AND UNEXPECTEDLY DIFFI-
CULT? Do we back away from them? Like a lazy river meandering
down the course of least resistance, do we do that which is easiest?

There is a sense in which we can say that courage is the main
quality that life requires of us. The word "courage" comes from the
Latin *cor* ("heart"). To have courage is to have "heart," and that's
assuredly what we need. We need to be brave-hearted rather than
faint-hearted, willing to take life as it comes and deal with it honorably. Life holds little good for us if we're always retreating.

Courage, however, is a different thing than some people imagine.
The truly courageous are never foolhardy — that is, they don't throw
themselves unnecessarily into difficult spots. And when it comes to
true adventure (as opposed to recreation or entertainment), the wise
don't go looking for it. As Louis L'Amour wrote, "What people speak
of as adventure is something nobody in his right mind would seek
out, and it becomes romantic only when one is safely at home." Real
cowboys don't make a big deal about being "adventuresome."

But when adventure comes calling, we need to be ready to enter
into it openly and actively. Too often, we turn away from adventure
for no better reason than that it would be too much trouble to deal
with. We're comfortable in our familiar habits, and so we stay put. Yet
we miss much of the tang of life by our reluctance to be bothered. "An
adventure is only an inconvenience rightly considered. An inconvenience is only an adventure wrongly considered" (G. K. Chesterton).

There is nothing life can do to hurt us as much as we hurt ourselves by our unwillingness to embrace life and live it fully. There are
certainly times to be passive, but when the time to be active arrives,
we don't help ourselves or anyone else by defaulting and doing nothing. Lives that make a difference are lives that go forward!

Live venturously, plucking the wild goat
by the beard, and trembling over precipices.
VIRGINIA WOOLF

IMPARTIALITY

I am a great foe to favoritism in public life, in private life,
and even in the delicate relationship of an author to his works.

JOSEPH CONRAD

WHEN THE TIME COMES TO ACT FAIRLY AND JUSTLY, WE
SHOULD BE GUIDED BY IMPARTIALITY RATHER THAN
FAVORITISM. If a crime has been committed in the neighborhood,
for example, I may be eager for the criminal to be brought to justice.
But what if the criminal turns out to be my son? I should be no less
willing for the law to be applied in that case than if the culprit was
anybody else's son. What's fair is fair, regardless of who is involved.

Yet we sometimes veer off into misconceptions about impartiality. In these days of "tolerance," we sometimes think that everybody
should be treated the same regardless of whether they've done right
or wrong, and that, most assuredly, is not what impartiality is about.
Thomas Fuller said it well: "He is not good himself who speaks well
of everybody alike." Impartiality doesn't mean that the innocent and
the guilty should be treated alike. It just means that if two people
have done equally well, they should be equally praised — and if
they've done equally poorly, they should be equally blamed. When
right and wrong are opposed, justice not only allows us to take sides,
but it requires us to do so. Impartiality is not the same as indifference!

To be truly impartial, we must apply the same set of standards
to everybody. It takes courage to do that, but it must be done. When
called upon to make distinctions and render judgment, we're tempted
to apply a more lenient list of rules to our friends than to our enemies. And what's worse, we're tempted to apply an easier standard
to ourselves than to anybody else, even our friends. Nevertheless, the
temptation to play favorites has to be resisted.

As tough as it may be to look at things impartially, that's what
justice requires, and without justice, no society or community can last
very long. Yes, justice is willing to take extenuating circumstances into
account, and justice is also willing to extend mercy when that will
produce a greater good. But special cases like these notwithstanding,
fairness still demands that the same rule book be allowed to govern
the game, no matter who happens to be playing.

Justice is impartiality.

GEORGE BERNARD SHAW

February 19
SAFETY

Not a gift of a cow, nor a gift of land, nor yet a gift
of food, is so important as the gift of safety, which is declared
to be the great gift among all gifts in this world.

PANCHATANTRA

IF WE HAVE FRIENDS WITH WHOM WE ARE SAFE, WE HAVE ONE
OF THE MOST VALUABLE TREASURES IN THE WORLD. In relationships where we find safety, we're not only free to be the persons
we are right now, we're free to grow and to become more than the
persons we are now. Nothing is more liberating — or motivating —
than to have friendships that provide a safe harbor for our souls.

In safe relationships, there is no fear of betrayal. We don't have
to worry whether commitments will be kept. And neither is there any
fear that our private selves will be exposed to those outside the safe
confines of the relationship. We're free to be intimate, to peel back
even the deepest layers of our hearts, and to share the most sacred
parts of our inner world. We can do these things because we've been
made to feel secure. We're not haunted by the possibility of dismissal.

This kind of relational safety is a wonderful thing indeed, but
we shouldn't misunderstand what it means. Those with whom we're
safe won't hurt us, but that doesn't mean they won't hurt our feelings.
The more faithful a friend is, the more that person will be willing
to say what we need to hear, the bitter as well as the sweet. In a safe
relationship, painful tidings will be delivered gently, but they'll still be
delivered. "Faithful are the wounds of a friend" (Book of Proverbs).

What it boils down to is this: those with whom we're safe are
those who'll deal *wisely* with us — with our faults as well as our
finer qualities. The safety in which we rejoice doesn't mean that our
shortcomings will be condoned; it means that we'll be consoled and
encouraged and enlightened. When we fall, there'll be strong arms to
catch us and keep us from doing further harm. The very best will be
believed about us — and when we've done less than our best, safety
means that loving allowance will be made for our growth.

Oh, the comfort, the inexpressible comfort of feeling safe
with a person, having neither to weigh thoughts nor measure words,
but pouring them all right out, just as they are, chaff and grain together;
certain that a faithful hand will take and sift them, keep what is worth
keeping, and then with the breath of kindness blow the rest away.

DINAH MARIA MULOCK CRAIK

PRESENCE

Take care and say this with presence of mind.

TERENCE

PRESENCE OF MIND IS A HARD THING FOR BUSY PEOPLE TO ACHIEVE. The more we try to do, the less we think about our doings. Most days find us rushing through a crowded agenda, and we have little opportunity to concentrate. Our minds are pulled forward so urgently by the next thing that has to be done, they don't get a chance to dwell fully on the words and deeds of the current moment.

Consider Terence's statement quoted above: "Take care and say this with presence of mind." How much of what any of us have said in the last twenty-four hours has been said "with presence of mind"? Probably not more than a small fraction. Frankly, most of our words are said while our minds are on "automatic," and most of our deeds fall into the category of "going with the flow." If you don't have that problem, then you're living on a level that most of us haven't reached.

But what is "presence of mind"? Might it not mean that we not only *think* consciously about what we say and do, but also *savor* and *relish* these things as they are happening? Assuming that what we're doing is what we ought to be doing, we miss a great opportunity if, as we act, we don't consider and enjoy our actions, gratefully aware of (1) ourselves, (2) our deeds, and (3) those with whom we may be interacting. Life is made up of moments, and if we're not "present" in these as they pass by, then there is simply no other happiness we can enjoy.

When we fail in the matter of presence, one of the more tragic aspects of the problem is that others fail to receive from us the acknowledgment they deserve. In these days of multi-channel communications, it's rare to communicate with anyone, even face to face, and feel that you have a person's undivided attention. We're torn and divided. We're simply not present for one another anymore.

But try it, even once or twice a day, and see what a great difference it makes. As you interact with someone, honor that person by being fully and completely present for them. Say by the attention you devote to them, "I am aware of you. I am conscious of you. I am taking thought for you, and in this moment, I am at your service."

The greatest gift you can give another
is the purity of your attention.

RICHARD MOSS

February 21
GLORY

When I found I had crossed that line,
I looked at my hands to see if I was the same person.
There was such a glory over everything.

HARRIET TUBMAN

WE'VE ALL HAD THEM NOW AND THEN: THOSE EXPERIENCES IN WHICH EVERYTHING AROUND US CAME ALIVE AND SEEMED TO SHINE WITH A STRANGE AND WONDERFUL GLORY. Harriet Tubman, one of the great abolitionists of the Civil War period, described such an experience to her biographer, Sarah Bradford. When, in 1845, she first escaped from slavery and found herself in free territory, Tubman said she had to check to make sure she was the same person: "There was such a glory over everything."

In its literal sense, the word "glory" has to do with "brightness" or "brilliance." That which is glorious shines brightly. But we use the word figuratively to describe things that "shine" in that they possess "majestic beauty and splendor" (*American Heritage Dictionary*). Harriet Tubman, for example, experienced a joy that made everything around her seem more beautiful than she'd ever known it to be before.

It's no coincidence that the sun, which shines with visible glory, figures prominently in many of the situations that we later describe as glorious. In particular, the rising of the sun at dawn is a thing that we're moved by. "Full many a glorious morning I have seen" (Shakespeare). "Oft when the white, still dawn / Lifted the skies and pushed the hills apart / I have felt it like a glory in my heart" (Edwin Markham). And, to be fair, the moon has its own glory too. "Lo! the level lake / And the long glories of the winter moon" (Tennyson).

But whether it's some shining, shimmering thing in nature that touches us with glory, or, as in Harriet Tubman's case, it's some unusual event or circumstance, glory is a good thing to get a taste of. And like it or not, how often we're conscious of glory has more to do with us than with what happens to us. We're surrounded by glory almost all the time. But there are certain people who're more receptive to it than others. It may be the openness of their hearts or the eagerness of their outlook, but glory seems to be their frequent companion.

O what their joy and their glory must be,
Those endless sabbaths the blessed ones see!

PETER ABELARD

LEADERSHIP

He that would be a leader must be a bridge.

WELSH PROVERB

IT WOULD BE HARD TO THINK OF GEORGE WASHINGTON, WHO WAS BORN ON THIS DAY, AND NOT THINK OF LEADERSHIP. If it hadn't been for his ability to blaze a trail, both literally and figuratively, our nation might easily have been lost trying to find its freedom. We wouldn't have to stretch our imaginations much to believe that the availability of his leadership at that time was providential.

When history judges a person to have been a leader, that person is almost always someone who helped his contemporaries get through a time of change. And the more gut-wrenching the change, the more valuable were the services of the individual who led others through the transition. Great leaders don't waste time wishing for more favorable circumstances in which to demonstrate their skills or display their wisdom; they recognize that if circumstances were completely favorable, their services would scarcely be required. Hard work during hard times is what leadership is primarily about.

We are, unfortunately for our nation, quickly losing touch with the real-life facts of the Revolutionary War. Far removed from the bloody traumas of that period, comfortable in freedoms which have been the norm all our lives, and uninterested in reading our history books or honoring our heroes, we live as if things have always been the way they are now. We forget the horrifying chasm over which George Washington led us — from what once was to what now is.

But however valuable his service was, George Washington was not primarily interested in being remembered as an individual. He would not have wanted our freedoms to depend on any continuing influence by him down through the years. Like all great leaders, he wanted those whom he led to be enabled and empowered. He might have wanted to be remembered, but more than that he would have wanted us to move ahead, no longer needing his active assistance. And so, on his birthday, let's honor Washington wisely. Let's acknowledge with gratitude the bridge that he led us over, and then let's see if we can't find some chasms that our own neighbors need help crossing.

The final test of a leader is that he leaves behind him
in other men the conviction and the will to carry on.

WALTER LIPPMANN

DIVERSITY

The glory of creation is in its infinite diversity.

ANONYMOUS

IT'S HARD TO LOOK AT THE WORLD WE LIVE IN AND NOT BE INTRIGUED BY ITS INTRICACY. Rather than being one homogeneous substance throughout, it's made up of billions and billions of separate entities. This world's not a vanilla pudding; it's a tossed salad. And what a diverse salad it is! You could spend twenty-seven lifetimes studying the earth and not even list everything that's here, much less describe how every thing is different from every other thing. If variety's the spice of life, we're surrounded by spice, aren't we? And shouldn't we be grateful for it? The diversity of our world is a part of its strength and beauty, and meditating on that is a helpful exercise.

As persons, most of us would be stronger and more beautiful if there was more diversity in our character. There is a sense, of course, in which simplicity is beautiful, and we're not recommending here that any of us try to become complicated, difficult, or hard to figure out. Our point is just that variety can be a valuable thing, in ourselves just as it is in the world at large. Our characters will be better if they include various elements that reinforce one another and round us out.

One thing that can add diversity to our own characters, obviously, is to become interested in and respectful of other human beings who differ from us in significant ways. As Charles Dickens has one of his characters say in *Martin Chuzzlewit,* "Them which is of other natures thinks different." Our own thinking is strengthened when we learn how to view things from the perspective of people who stand at a different spot, and come at things from a different angle, than we do. This doesn't mean that every viewpoint is equally helpful or accurate; it just means that our thinking needs to be fertilized and enriched by input from sources outside our own present patterns of thought.

How many different kinds of people can you enjoy working with? How various are the situations in which you can be comfortable? How diverse are your tastes? Your habits? Your ideas? If your answer is, "Not very," you're missing out on much of the world's amazement. So jump into the tingling waters of diversity and go for a swim!

The heavens rejoice in motion, why should I
Abjure my so much lov'd variety.

JOHN DONNE

ADMONITION

A friend is one who warns you.

ARABIAN PROVERB

To "ADMONISH" IS TO REPROVE SOMEONE MILDLY OR KINDLY BUT SERIOUSLY. If a friend admonishes you, for example, that means that he or she cautions you or counsels you against a certain course of action. Because it has a distinctly "disciplinary" ring to it, admonition doesn't strike us as a particularly positive thing, but it's actually a better thing than most people give it credit for being. Success in this life often comes down to whether we're willing to be warned or not, and so being open to admonition is one of the key components of the good life. And as far as friends are concerned, a faithful friend will never fail to admonish us when admonition is in our best interest.

Receiving admonition is certainly not the most pleasurable thing we can imagine. And if we judge things merely by whether they give us pleasure, admonition may not rank very high. But the momentary pain of having it pointed out to us that we're headed down the wrong road is well worth accepting, simply because it helps us avoid a much greater, and perhaps disastrous, pain later on. As Shakespeare pointed out, "Better a little chiding than a great deal of heartbreak."

We need to work at being people who *receive* admonition in the proper spirit and *give* admonition in the right way. When we're being warned, we need to hear the admonition with openness, humility, courage, and an eagerness to act on every bit of truth we're hearing. And when we're doing the warning, we need to muster all the wisdom we've ever learned. It takes good judgment, honest love, and considerable skill to achieve a balance between courage and consideration, but without that balance, admonitions often go unheeded.

Yet whether we're fortunate to have friends who'll admonish us, we all have a conscience, and that's precisely what our conscience is supposed to do: warn us. We need to ensure that our consciences are well educated and that their warnings are based on reality. But more than that, we need to *listen* to our consciences. If we don't, the time will come when they'll give up. They'll quit trying to get our attention, and eventually, they'll abandon us. Let's not let that happen.

If conscience smite thee once, it is an admonition;
if twice, it is a condemnation.

NATHANIEL HAWTHORNE

FAVOR

A favour well bestowed is almost as great an honor
to him who confers it as to him who receives it.
RICHARD STEELE

FAVOR IS ONE OF THE MOST GRATIFYING THINGS IN LIFE.
Whether we think of it as an attitude or an act, it's always a
delightful thing. As an attitude, it's a gracious, kind, and friendly
way of thinking about somebody else. And as an act, it's a deed that
reflects such an attitude. When we "do a favor" for someone, we do
something that shows our "favor" for them personally. And as Richard
Steele suggests, a favor "well bestowed" (i.e., honestly, courteously, and
so forth) is "as great an honor to him who confers it as to him who
receives it." Favors, whether big or little, are a part of the grace of life.
Without them, this world would be infinitely more dreary.

It would be an honorable thing to develop a *basic disposition* of
"favor." That is, it would help us to learn to look on life "favorably."
Yes, there are things that have to be dealt with that cannot — and
should not — be looked upon with favor. In fact, there are many such
things, and it's foolish to pretend that they're better than they are. But
there is also much good in this world, and we have a choice to make
as to which we're going to spend the bulk of our time thinking about.
When we're determining our basic inclination or orientation, I believe
it's wise to decide that we're going to be *as favorable as possible.* It can
be our desire to think and to act as favorably toward others as wisdom
will allow. And when the evidence is ambiguous, we can give people
the benefit of the doubt. We can "favor" the more positive scenario.

We have it within our power, every day of the week, to show
kindness to other human beings, and by doing so, to show them favor.
We can live in such a way that doing a favor is more than a random
act that we engage in — favor can be an integral part of us. It can be
one of our principles, a part of the fabric of our character. When that's
truly the case, we'll find ourselves bringing a welcome happiness into
the lives of all who deal with us. And not only that, by having *gratitude* as a settled part of our character, we'll begin to appreciate how
much favor others show to us, and even the ordinary affairs of daily
living will be warmed with some colors that are quite wonderful.

How beautiful a day can be when kindness touches it.
GEORGE ELLISTON

USEFULNESS

A useless life is early death.

JOHANN WOLFGANG VON GOETHE

WANTING TO BE USEFUL IS AN IMPORTANT PART OF OUR NATURE. We may be easily distracted from that desire — and some folks seem to have suppressed the urge altogether! — but still it's true, we want to feel that we're of use to somebody. Times of enforced idleness, such as periods of illness or disability, are rarely the times we remember as the happiest points in our lives. "It is a great misfortune to be of use to nobody" (Baltasar Gracián).

In regard to this "misfortune," however, there is something we need to be aware of: it is never actually the case that we are "of use to nobody." We may *feel* useless sometimes, but that feeling is never entirely consistent with reality. My father, for example, who just celebrated his ninetieth birthday, struggles with feelings of uselessness from time to time. Physically, he's quite limited in what he can do, and it's often hard for him to see any real purpose for his continued existence in the world. Yet in truth, he continues to be useful to others in ways that he's not aware of. If nothing else, his example of steadfastness and good cheer is of great value to all who know him.

It's an obvious fact, of course, that our usefulness can be diminished by circumstances beyond our control. But usually, what is diminished is only our preferred and customary way of being useful. What we need to do is let go of the past and have the humility to switch gears. We need to adjust ourselves to *new ways of being useful* — ways that may be less congenial to us but are no less valuable to others.

In the real world, there will be few days when we can't do something that somebody else needs to have done. We can be useful if that's what we want to be, and it's a great thing to set that as our goal. An even greater goal, however, is to *combine usefulness with grace.* We can diminish the amount of drabness in the world by (1) doing what needs to be done, and (2) doing it in such a way that delights and encourages those whom we serve. Pragmatism and practicality are commendable qualities in their own right, but they're nothing short of astonishing when they're clothed with the added quality of grace!

The difference between utility and utility plus beauty
is the difference between telephone wires and the spider's web.

EDWIN WAY TEALE

SUFFICIENCY

No, 'tis not so deep as a well, nor so wide
as a church door; but 'tis enough, 'twill serve.
WILLIAM SHAKESPEARE

SUFFICIENCY IS NO SMALL THING! If what has been provided is "enough" or if it's "adequate," then we shouldn't look down on it or fail to be thankful. If we've gotten to the point where we feel that what is "sufficient" is somehow less than we deserve, then our affluence is probably hurting us more than it's helping us. And if, in our work, we feel insulted when someone describes our output as "sufficient," then we may have gotten too high-minded for our own good.

To be sure, excellence is a worthy ideal, and nothing said here should be taken as a recommendation for mediocrity. The person who is content to do less than his best needs to get off his derriere and start doing better. But if I've done my best and my best qualifies as sufficient, then I shouldn't see my effort as anything less than honorable. For all the talk done by those who promise excellence, the world could do with a few more folks who actually deliver sufficiency!

In my estimation, some of the greatest contributors to the world in which we live are those who quietly go about the business of supplying "sufficiency" in all their relationships. They don't have press agents. They don't get standing ovations. And they don't receive the awards. But they do what their more prominent peers often don't do: *they deliver the goods.* Adequately and dependably. Day in and day out.

Our talk of "excellence" is often a substitute for "sufficient" work. If you hear someone saying that they're too talented to work for the minimum wage, you'd expect that they might be making much more than that. All too often, though, that person has made less than the minimum-wage worker when all is said and done. As Aesop told us long ago, the tortoise often gets to the goal faster than the hare!

So how is it with us in our own lives? All of us have people (friends, family, coworkers, neighbors, etc.) whose lives are affected by what we do. Our relationship with these people is such that they depend on us to supply certain things that are needed. If we wish to supply more than what's "sufficient," that's fine — but our loved ones shouldn't have to worry about receiving any less than that either!

Enough is as good as a feast.
JOHN HEYWOOD

KEYS

Open sesame!

THE ARABIAN NIGHTS

LOCKED DOORS ARE MYSTERIOUS, AND THE KEYS THAT OPEN THEM HAVE A ROMANTIC AURA ABOUT THEM. I once came across a collection of keys on a brass ring in an antique store, and it was all I could do to keep from buying them. Even without knowing what doors they would have opened, I still found the keys fascinating. Keys are like that. They are powerful, and they are interesting.

The most important keys, of course, are not those that are physical; they are the intangible ones that unlock invisible doors: the doors that we all have to go through to get from one "room" in our lives to another. When we have trouble getting these doors open, it's nice to have a friend who can provide the key. And these keys come in many different forms, don't they? Sometimes it's *a word of encouragement* that opens the door, or perhaps *an insight* from our friend's thinking. It may involve *a recommendation* given by our friend to a third party. Often, it's simply *an act of kindness or service* by our friend that provides the key to progress. Each key is important in its own way.

Friendship also involves the mutual keeping of another kind of key. Close friends confide in one another in valuable ways, and in a faithful friendship, these special, private truths cannot be divulged without the permission of the other friend, who, in effect, holds the "key." In the words of Christopher Smart's poem: "'Tis in my memory lock'd / And you yourself shall keep the key of it."

Perhaps the most amazing kind of key, however, is the one that opens the door through which someone else discovers their real life! It's shocking to think about, actually, but we can sometimes assist other people in finding out who they are and where they should be headed. Looking back, most of us can identify friends who helped us in that way, and we should be willing to pass the favor along whenever we can. In fact, there aren't many higher things that we can aspire to. Simply being people who have the effect of "opening up" those around us, that is a character and a reputation worth working to maintain.

He opened us —
who was a key,
who was a man.

GWENDOLYN BROOKS

HANDS

> I have met people so empty of joy that when I clasped their frosty
> fingertips it seemed as if I were shaking hands with a northeast storm. Others
> there are whose hands have sunbeams in them, so that their grasp warms my
> heart. It may be only the clinging touch of a child's hand, but there is as much
> potential sunshine in it for me as there is in the loving glance for others.
>
> HELEN KELLER

OUR HANDS ARE MORE THAN JUST ANOTHER PART OF OUR BODIES. If our bodies are the instruments through which we do our work in the world, it's our hands, especially, that do that work. The Book of Ecclesiastes, for example, says, "Whatever your hand finds to do, do it with your might." Something that has been accomplished by an individual is that person's "handiwork." A disadvantage in our work is said to be a "handicap." And, of course, something that helps us do our work is described as "handy." No part of the body is more closely linked to the doings of human beings than the hands.

Have you ever noticed how much hands say about a person's character? The hands reveal hardly any less than the face. I once met an artist, in fact, who did nothing but hands. She sculpted hands, drew them, painted them, photographed them, and even wrote poems about them, as I recall. Children's hands and aged people's hands. Rugged hands and delicate hands. Friendly hands and hostile hands. The whole gamut of human feeling and experience was powerfully and beautifully portrayed by these hands, artistically rendered.

Most of us have clear memories of hands we've known in the past. Can't you remember your grandmother's hands? The hands of your piano teacher? Your baseball coach? These images should remind us: we're remembered for what we *do* and not just for what we *are*.

Having healthy, functional hands is not a thing to be taken for granted; it's a sober stewardship. With these physical extensions of our will we can do either good or evil, and we're responsible for the choices that we make. What we "hand" down to our descendants needs to be something that will invite thanksgiving rather than regret. And there is not a one of us who can't do this. No matter who we are, we can do worthy work. With our hands, we can work what is good and honorable and useful to those who are coming along behind.

> Enough, if something from our hands have power
> To live, and act, and serve the future hour.
>
> WILLIAM WORDSWORTH

SPORTSMANSHIP

Everyone admires a good loser — except his wife.
ANONYMOUS

FAILURE COMES IN MANY DIFFERENT FORMS. In any situation, there is more than one test we might fail, more than one way in which our conduct might fall below the level of acceptability. Today, let's think about the test of "sportsmanship." At first glance, you may not think "unsportsmanlike conduct" is one of the more serious crimes that a person might commit, but don't be so quick to dismiss it. If you'll just observe what happens around you for a few days, you'll see that a good bit of what causes friction among people comes down to a simple failure on somebody's part to play fair and to be a good loser or a good winner. Sportsmanship has to do with some fairly significant issues — such as justice, honor, and respect for others.

Playing fair. There would be a lot less stress in the world if we'd all remember what we learned on the playground about old-fashioned fairness. Despite our sometimes tortured legal arguments, it usually isn't all that hard to figure out what's fair. We may, for one reason or another, find it difficult to do what is fair, but knowing what a good sport would do isn't as complicated as we make it out to be.

Being a good loser. I once heard someone, probably a coach, say, "Don't criticize a poor loser — a poor loser's still a better opponent than any kind of a winner." Maybe so, but all joking aside, the problem of people acting dishonorably when they end up losing something they tried to gain is a very serious problem. And we're all guilty of it from time to time. If we wanted to make a positive contribution to the world, each of us could do that by resolving never again to act spitefully or vindictively when we've lost something we wanted to win.

Being a good winner. In a sense, being a good winner is harder than being a good loser. When we've lost, we have to be good sports to keep from being further shamed. But when we've won, it's hardly considered a sin if we indulge in a little well-earned gloating. So as winners, the incentive to good sportsmanship is simply our sense of *respect* for those on the other side. But what an incentive that should be! Without respect for others, our winnings aren't worth a dime.

Win as if you were used to it;
lose as if you enjoyed it for a change.
ANONYMOUS

AMAZEMENT

The true scientist never loses the faculty of amazement.

HANS SELYE

WE USE THE WORD "AMAZEMENT" IN A DIFFERENT WAY THAN IT WAS ORIGINALLY USED. In its older sense, amazement meant bewilderment or perplexity (the kind of feeling one has when lost in a "maze"). Shakespeare used the word this way in Act IV of *King John:* "I am amaz'd, methinks, and lose my way / Among the thorns and dangers of the world." Today, however, to be amazed means to be in a state of extreme surprise or wonder. Most of us already know that, but is there anything about this word that would make it a good word to meditate on? I think there is.

There is some value and some virtue in keeping our hearts open to the extent that we can be amazed. If we've seen so much, or perhaps grown so tired, that nothing amazes us anymore, then I believe we've suffered a sad loss. As far as the objective reality around us is concerned, there is very much in the world to be amazed about. Several times a day, most of us encounter something that should fill us with surprise and wonder. If our antennas are not up, however, the astonishing qualities of these things will be lost on us.

I would even go so far as to say that we are benefited by being amazed in the older sense, at least once in a while. Many of us have gotten so confident in our modernity that it would do us good to suffer some occasional bewilderment or perplexity. It's healthy to get lost in a "maze" sometimes — and to be reminded of our fallibility.

Amazement is certainly one of the keys to learning. As Hans Selye said, "The true scientist never loses the faculty of amazement." We need to keep our childhood curiosity and sense of wonder as long as we can. When we lose it, we quit learning new and useful things.

Beyond the learning value of amazement, however, we're simply healthier, more interesting people when there is some amazement in our lives. If I could choose only one life to live, I'd rather be a country bumpkin any day, easily and enjoyably amazed at the simplest of things, than to be a sophisticated man-about-town who's outlived his enthusiasm for the wonders of the everyday world.

As Tammie glow'red, amazed and curious,
The mirth and fun grew fast and furious.

ROBERT BURNS

REINFORCEMENT

What reinforcement we may gain from hope . . .
JOHN MILTON

NONE OF US IS SO STRONG THAT WE DON'T NEED SOME OC-
CASIONAL "REINFORCEMENT." In particular, we need the kind
of reinforcement that comes, as Milton suggests, from hope. As the
days come and go, our energies wane, our commitments weaken, and
our courage fails. Fairly frequently, we need to receive a reinforcement
of hope. We need to be buttressed with fresh strength.

But here is what I want you to think about: the best kinds of
reinforcement are those that add *a different kind of strength* than what
was already there. As in the physical world, the things that do the best
job of reinforcing are those that add strength *from a different angle.*

Older and younger. Do you want some serious reinforcement in
your life in a hurry? Just go find somebody whose chronological age is
very different from your own. Interact with them. Listen to them!

Men and women. A major part of the beauty and mystery of life
is the difference between the unique strengths of men and women.
To be truly strong, masculine strength needs to be reinforced by what
men can learn about strength from women, and vice versa.

Rich and poor. One reason for our weakness nowadays is that we
cut ourselves off from any real contact with anyone outside our own
social and economic niche. But "inter-niche" contact is reinforcing.

Each of us is a unique being, made up of strengths not found in
any other person in exactly the same combination. What that means
is that all of us have the ability to add reinforcing strength to other
people's lives. Because we're different, the strengths that we impart to
one another will always come from a different "angle" than what was
already in that person's life. And ultimately, that's why our gifts have
been given to us, whatever they may be. Our endowments are not for
our private enjoyment alone; they're meant to be used in the work of
reinforcement. And we use our various gifts best when we use them
"to charm, to strengthen, and to teach."

But the great Master said, "I see
No best in kind, but in degree;
I gave a various gift to each,
To charm, to strengthen, and to teach."
HENRY WADSWORTH LONGFELLOW

SELFLESSNESS

A man cannot enter into the deepest center
of himself . . . unless he is able to pass entirely
out of himself and give himself to other people
in the purity of a selfless love.

THOMAS MERTON

ONE OF THE GREAT IRONIES OF LIFE IS THAT WE FIND OUR-SELVES BY LOSING OURSELVES. If we're so obsessed with what we've accumulated for our own enjoyment that we won't let go of any of it for the sake of others, the result is not a richer life but a poorer one. (Think of Scrooge on Christmas Eve.) On the other hand, if we put less emphasis on what is ours and embrace the idea of sacrifice, what we find is that we've gained more than we've given away. (Think of Scrooge on Christmas morning.) We find what we're looking for only after we start looking for something else. We get a "self" not by self-*centered*-ness but — believe it or not — by self-*less*-ness!

If we haven't come to terms with it already, it's high time we recognized that we're happiest when we're giving ourselves away. That's just the nature of the reality that we happen to be a part of, and we can no more change it than we can amend the law of gravity. To try, as many do, to gain happiness by selfishness rather than selflessness is an effort doomed to failure. C. S. Lewis said it this way: "What is outside the system of self-giving is not earth, nor nature, nor ordinary life, but simply and solely Hell. Yet even Hell derives from this law such reality as it has. That fierce imprisonment in the self is but the obverse of the self-giving which is absolute reality." Selfishness is an assault on reality, and reality can't be successfully assaulted.

This doesn't mean that we have no self-interest at all. It would be an unhealthy person indeed who had no concern for his own wants and needs. But selflessness means that we're willing to *sacrifice* for the good of others and that our own desires are filled up only when we're willing to pour them out. There aren't going to be any good things in the world if somebody doesn't do some giving, and if we want a share of the goodness, we're going to have to participate in the giving. The world being as it is, there is no serious gain without significant loss!

Every man brings an egg and every one wants
an omelette — but without breaking his own egg.
That poses a most difficult situation.

FRANK MAR

CLARITY

Hold every moment sacred. Give each clarity
and meaning, each the weight of thine awareness,
each its true and due fulfillment.

THOMAS MANN

THERE IS TOO MUCH FUZZINESS IN MOST OF OUR LIVES. What should be sharp and clear is often indistinct and cloudy. We need to bring some clarity to the business of living — and also of loving.

Clarity in our thinking. Since our actions are the consequence of our thinking, we need to think clearly. Sometimes, however, we don't work very hard at doing this, even on important subjects. Alfred North Whitehead once spoke of a certain philosophy as "an adventure in the clarification of thought." If you know the philosophy of which he spoke, you may doubt whether it made things any clearer, but still, his expression, "an adventure in the clarification of thought," is interesting. How long has it been since you've embarked on an adventure like that? How recently has your thinking been clarified?

Clarity in our relationships. Sometimes our relationships lack quality because they're ill-defined. We haven't made the effort to know the other person clearly, and we haven't given them the chance to know us clearly — so things are a little foggy. How much better it would be if we clarified things with openness, humility, and courage!

Perhaps we find it difficult to think and speak and relate to others clearly because we don't experience things clearly ourselves. And maybe that's because so much of our experience now is "synthetic." Cut off from the clarity of things in the natural world, our minds are fed primarily by the flickering images on computer monitors, televisions, and movie screens. As wonderful as these media are, they can never present more than a vague representation of original reality. Out of touch with sharply defined reality itself, it's no surprise that our thinking loses a bit of focus. So we would do well to "clear up" our intellect and our imaginations more often by directly experiencing the creatures and creations that call to us outside our doors. Things that are clear in themselves can help keep our minds clear.

There is a poignancy in all things clear,
In the stare of the deer, in the ring of a hammer in the morning.
Seeing a bucket of perfectly lucid water
We fall to imagining prodigious honesties.

RICHARD WILBUR

INNOVATION

> We are more ready to try the untried when
> what we do is inconsequential. Hence the remarkable
> fact that many inventions had their birth as toys.
>
> ERIC HOFFER

DELIGHTFUL THINGS OFTEN OCCUR WHEN WE'RE WILLING TO TRY SOMETHING NEW. Perhaps that is why children's lives are so full of joy: their natural sense of playfulness encourages them to turn things upside-down and inside-out. Young people's lives fairly bristle with innovation, and the discoveries they make are often of benefit even to those much older and "wiser" than themselves.

As grown-ups, we often find it hard to get the right balance when it comes to innovation. Sometimes we go to the extreme of worshiping whatever is new, and we foolishly toss overboard anything that has any age or tradition to it. When we're in this mode, we need to be reminded that there's nothing inherently valuable about newness; it's value depends upon its context, and we need to think twice before we smash a tradition that can't be recovered once it's destroyed.

Yet we often go to the other extreme as well. We become so wedded to the status quo that we reject innovations that would be truly helpful. The apple cart becomes so sacred that we dare not touch it. Yet, as Frank A. Clark suggested, "Why not upset the apple cart? If you don't, the apples will rot anyway." It would be foolish to blindly apply that thinking to every situation, obviously, but there's no denying the value of the question itself: *why not upset the apple cart?*

Even in our personal relationships, there is a sense in which we need to be wholesomely innovative. No matter what the problem or project, if others can count on us to bring a fresh and helpful perspective to the undertaking, that's a very fine reputation to have.

Whatever may be our individual talents and abilities, these were meant to be used — energetically and even innovatively. If we're actively engaged with life, we'll make some delightful discoveries in the course of trying out new approaches to old problems. We'll be willing, at least once in a while, to experiment . . . just like the curious child who says, "I wonder what would happen if you did it *this* way?"

> I will work out the divinity that is busy within my mind
> And tend the means that are mine.
>
> PINDAR

INVENTIVENESS

The most gifted members of the human species
are at their creative best when they cannot have their way.

ERIC HOFFER

ONE OF THE MOST AMAZING THINGS ABOUT US IS OUR ABIL-
ITY TO FIND SOLUTIONS WHEN WE'RE FACED WITH PROB-
LEMS. Nearly every day we see evidence, either in our own lives or
those of others, that the old adage is true: "necessity is the mother
of invention." When our path is blocked, we find an alternate route.
When we're frustrated, we find a way to make progress. When no
tool exists that will serve our purpose, we invent a new tool. We're a
creative species, and it seems there is no end to our inventiveness.

Unfortunately, human beings have not always used their inventiveness to good ends. Many of the most harmful contrivances in the
world have been conceived by geniuses whose creativity was allowed
to run loose, unfettered by true principles or worthy values. And so we
need not think that inventiveness is a good thing all by itself. If true
goodness is to result from our ingenuity, our creative powers must be
harnessed and disciplined. When we answer the call to be inventive, it
must be in the pursuit of goodness only and never evil.

The world would be a better place, for example, if we would use
less of our inventiveness to get what we want for ourselves and more
of it to help supply the needs of those around us. If we could manage
to be even half as ingenious and clever in helping other people as we
are in helping ourselves, the world would be improved radically.

And speaking of our relationship to others, the most inventive
force in the world is *love*. Whatever it is that needs to be figured out
or accomplished, love will find a way. It doesn't really matter what the
hurdle is, if a person is in love, the hurdle is likely to be cleared!

Since the things and the people we love cause us to be so inventive, we need to be wise in deciding what those things are. Almost
inevitably, we move in the direction of our aspirations, creatively getting around every problem that stands between us and what we want.
So, as the old-timers used to say, we need to be careful what we want,
because we're apt to get it! Our inventiveness can be counted on to
get us to our goals; the only question is whether our goals are worthy.

Our inventions mirror our secret wishes.

LAWRENCE DURRELL

CREATIVITY

Man unites himself with the world
in the process of creation.

ERICH FROMM

WE'RE BORN INTO A PRE-MADE WORLD, BUT WITHIN THAT WORLD WE HAVE THE ABILITY TO MAKE MANY NEW THINGS OURSELVES. The cynic might say that we can't make anything really new; we can only do new things with the raw materials that were already here. But what wonderful reorderings of the raw materials we're capable of! Our creativity is a truly fascinating force.

Because it's so powerful, our creative urge needs to be carefully managed. Among those who're seriously involved in creative work, we often hear it said (by artists, musicians, writers, etc.) that the only reason for their work is to allow the creators to "express themselves." But in a world where we're all connected to one another, that should never be the case. Not everything that a person might "express" needs to see the light of day, and before I create anything, I need to ask myself the question: will this expression of myself make a *positive contribution* to those around me or will it *pollute* them? Will it *help* or will it *hurt?*

Our ability to create happens to have a rather serious stewardship attached to it, and in our present culture, there may be some doubt about whether we're handling that stewardship responsibly. "We live at a time when man believes himself fabulously capable of creation, but he does not know what to create" (José Ortega y Gasset).

When we take a wise approach to the creative act, however, magnificent things can be accomplished. Our creativity can bring a much needed freshness to our own lives and to those of others. And not only that, we have it within our power to create things that will continue to do good long after we're gone from this world. Few of us are going to be remembered by succeeding generations, but the question of what we're going to leave behind is still significant. We're at our best when we're using our creative powers to do lasting good. It doesn't matter whether the history books are going to give us the credit for it; it only matters that we've created something good that will continue to live.

Creativity is not merely the innocent spontaneity of our youth
and childhood; it must also be married to the passion of the adult
human being, which is a passion to live beyond one's death.

ROLLO MAY

WORK

Every man is a consumer, and ought to be a producer.
He fails to make his place good in the world unless he not only
pays his debt but also adds something to the common wealth.

RALPH WALDO EMERSON

TECHNICALLY, "WORK" IS SIMPLY TOIL OR LABOR — IT'S PHYSICAL OR MENTAL EFFORT OR ACTIVITY. But I'd like to suggest that we'd profit from thinking of work in a higher sense. The best concept of work is that which sees it as more than mere labor — it is labor that adds value to the world. When we're working, we're adding "something to the common wealth," as Emerson put it. We're repaying our debt to the world, first, by replenishing the resources that we've taken out of it and, second, by adding some value that wasn't there before. The result of our work is that something in the world has been improved in some way. Some worth has been created.

It's unfortunate that we so often limit the word "work" to the work that we're *paid* to do. When we speak of the "workplace," we usually mean the realm of money-paying jobs and careers. But the work that a human being does over the course of his or her lifetime involves a good bit more than that person's vocation. In fact, much, if not most, of the value that gets added to the world is added by the things that people do when they're not "at work," and we need to quit thinking that the only folks who're working are those who have "jobs."

In regard to our work, one of the best things we can do is dedicate it to one or more persons whom we love. It's no coincidence that writers usually dedicate their work to someone; great power comes from having a special someone "for" whom we're doing our work. But we don't have to be a writer to benefit from this power. Whatever work we're doing, we can see ourselves as doing it for someone else.

Good work is a blessing to be appreciated, not a burden to be resented. It's a privilege to have the opportunity to add value back to a world that has given us so much. And if we'll think of our work rightly, there's a good chance we'll want to enter into it appreciatively, enthusiastically, and energetically. *Adding value by giving honest effort* is a thing we'll find satisfying and, yes, even enjoyable!

Work! Thank God for the swing of it,
for the clamoring, hammering ring of it.

ANONYMOUS

RESTRAINT

Liberty exists in proportion to wholesome restraint.

DANIEL WEBSTER

IF WE THINK THAT FREEDOM MEANS THE ABSENCE OF ANY RESTRAINT, THEN WE'RE HEADED STRAIGHT TOWARD ONE OF LIFE'S GREATEST DISAPPOINTMENTS. It's nothing but naive to think that we can indulge every desire in any way we please, express ourselves with reckless abandon, disregard the rules of every game we play in, and still be remembered for having made a worthy contribution to the world. Listen to me: life doesn't work that way, and if we think it does, we're bound to have our hearts broken sooner or later.

It doesn't matter what kind of power is under consideration, whether in nature or in human relationships, power has to be restrained. Out-of-control power is never anything but destructive, and the greater the power is, the more damage it will do if it's not regulated, made to stay in bounds, and balanced by other forces.

If raw, unrestrained power did as much good as any other kind, a strong boxer could win every bout by simply rushing into the ring and throwing as many wild punches as possible. But as anybody knows who's ever been in a boxing match (or any other kind of difficult human situation), merely flailing away doesn't get the job done. To keep from getting your head knocked off, you've got to husband your strength, restrain your impulses, and keep punches under control.

In the living of a human life, there is no way around our need for restraint. We need some *external* restraints (laws, rules, requirements, etc.), and we need some *internal* restraints (training, discipline, self-control, etc.). We even need to have some *friends* who'll restrain us. We need these things, because without them we'd often go too far.

Rarely is it wise or beneficial to do, say, or think, all that might be done, said, or thought. More is not always better, and there's an undeniable beauty in things like reserve and understatement. So we need not only strength; we need wisdom. We need not only freedom; we need government. For those times when we can't see for ourselves that "enough is enough," we need the help of limits, those signposts of various kinds that simply say, "Here, but no further."

Ah, men do not know how much strength is in poise,
That he goes the farthest who goes far enough.

JAMES RUSSELL LOWELL

DEVELOPMENT

Those who won our independence believed that the final end
of the State was to make men free to develop their faculties.

JUSTICE LOUIS BRANDEIS

FREEDOM IS NOT GIVEN TO US FOR SELFISH INDULGENCE; IT'S
MEANT TO BE USED IN REACHING OUR POTENTIAL. This is as
much true of our civil freedoms as it is of those that are more personal
in nature. Even the laws under which we live are for the purpose of
creating conditions in which we can flourish and "develop [our] faculties," as Brandeis put it. Not many people realize that's what freedom
is for, and many who do realize it don't take full advantage of it, but
freedom is for the purpose of helping us grow. It's not about doing
whatever we want; it's about becoming all that we're capable of.

There is a sense in which human lives have to be "unfolded"
or "unpacked." They don't come already put together, and to say (as
the label always says on any product you need to use in a hurry) that
"some assembly is required" is a considerable understatement. So "development" is the word we often use to describe what has to happen
if a person's character is going to become all that it's capable of being.
It's as if many things are wrapped up in us that have to be unpacked.

Like many of the most worthwhile things, the development of
character takes time. It's not work that can be done in one day. In fact,
when we see it properly, we recognize that it's *a lifetime process.* No
matter how long we live, there's always some more unpacking to do!

But haven't we all seen a tendency in our lives to stop developing
at some point? It seems to me that the challenge of avoiding stagna-
tion is one of the major challenges that we face. It takes extraordinary
commitment and discipline to keep on developing and developing.

Rather serious issues are at stake, however. The choice that confronts us is, as someone has said, "Develop or die." Our endowments
are wonderful. Our resources are abundant. Our potential is so vast
that it seems unlimited. But none of these things can be neglected
without frightful consequences later on. If there's a law that's clearly
written on every page of nature's book, it is this: *use it or lose it.*

In every animal . . . a more frequent and continuous use of any organ gradually
strengthens, develops and enlarges that organ . . . while the permanent disuse
of any organ imperceptibly weakens and deteriorates it, and progressively
diminishes its functional capacity, until it finally disappears.

JEAN-BAPTISTE LAMARCK

SATISFACTION

He is well paid that is well satisfied.
WILLIAM SHAKESPEARE

MANY THINGS WE MAY NOT HAVE, BUT IF WE HAVE WHAT GIVES US SATISFACTION, WE CAN GIVE THANKS. No two of us are exactly the same, and so no two of us are going to be satisfied by the same things, but the world we live in is so wonderfully varied, there is something to satisfy everybody. What we need to do is make up our minds to be satisfied with our own satisfactions. Rather than being seduced by the advertisers and entertainers to want things that wouldn't really be satisfying even if we had them, we'd do better to bow our heads and give humble thanks for our own *real* satisfactions.

It's a common misconception that satisfaction is the same as apathy or indifference, but it's not. Genuine satisfaction doesn't mean complacency; it means contentment. Satisfaction still leaves room for growth, and it knows how to aspire to greater things. But it also knows how to enjoy and be honestly grateful for present benefits. What it comes down to is this: things don't have to be *perfectly* satisfying in order for them to be *pleasantly* satisfying.

It's an old suggestion, but it still contains a lot of good sense: simple things are often the most satisfying. As I am writing this, for example, the morning sun has just climbed above the horizon and warmed the waiting world with a golden glow. As I look up from my writing desk and take in the view outside my window, I see something that is satisfying in a simple way. Whatever else I may not have on this day in my life, I have enjoyed something that should content my soul.

But life isn't just about being satisfied; it's about giving satisfaction to others. It's not always possible to do that, of course, but when it is, we should be eager to do it, even if it means going the extra mile. Sacrificing to see that others are satisfied is one of life's privileges.

You may never have thought about it, but your own satisfaction is a contributor to the satisfaction of those around you. It's one of life's most refreshing joys to know and work with people who are at peace within themselves, and so we do everyone we deal with a favor when we choose to be satisfied. Not apathetic, mind you. But *satisfied.*

Let a man's talents or virtues be what they may, we only feel satisfaction in his society as he is satisfied in himself.
WILLIAM HAZLITT

TRUTH

The ideals which have lighted my way,
and time after time have given me new courage
to face life cheerfully, have been kindness, beauty and truth.

ALBERT EINSTEIN

TRUTH IS NOT A FIGMENT OF WEAK PEOPLE'S IMAGINATIONS; IT'S A STRONG AND NOBLE REALITY. Many of those who today think it's intellectually unsophisticated to talk about truth wouldn't be qualified to carry the briefcase of a man like Einstein, who not only talked about it, but honored it, sought it, and used it to noble ends.

We may as well admit it: we fight hopelessly if we fight against truth. Reality is unassailable. Yes, in the short term we may get away with operating on the basis of falsehood, but eventually the truth will assert itself. As Edgar J. Mohn colorfully said it, "A lie has speed, but truth has endurance." So philosophically, we ought to avoid untruth. But not only philosophically, we ought to avoid untruth *personally*. It simply does no good to deal in deceit. "Every time you try to smother a truth, two others get their breath" (Bill Copeland). So it seems smart to go ahead and commit ourselves to truth.

Doing that, however, requires more of us than we might think. Truth is not always easy to find, and the reason is one we may not like to confront. "We do not err because truth is difficult to see. It is visible at a glance. We err because this is more comfortable" (Alexander Solzhenitsyn). For every time when we haven't looked hard enough for the truth, there are hundreds of times when we've run away from truth that was in plain view. Our difficulty is not so much ignorance as it is cowardice. So a commitment to truth is a test of our bravery.

A fearless commitment to truth is one of the great components of moral human character. As far as I can see, it might even be the greatest of all. No matter what other virtues may adorn us, without a commitment to truth, everything else turns to the dust of death.

But we don't honor truth by paying lip service to it; we do it by submitting to it. That means that we must follow it, rather than try to lead it. There's just no calculating the good that can happen when we expend our energies in the service of truth — or the damage that can be done when we employ our powers trying to subvert the truth.

I have one request: may I never use my reason against truth.

ELIE WIESEL

LIFE

Life is a hard fight, a struggle, a wrestling with the principle
of evil, hand to hand, foot to foot. Every inch of the way is disputed.
The night is given us to take breath and to pray, to drink deep at the
fountain of power. The day, to use the strength that has been
given us, to go forth to work with it till the evening.

FLORENCE NIGHTINGALE

TO LIVE — THAT IS, TO BE FULLY *ALIVE* — IS A TEST OF THE
HIGHEST POWERS WITHIN US. The thing that can truly be
called "life" can't be reached by taking the course of least resistance. It
can only be enjoyed by those who're prepared to grasp it with decisiveness and determination. With anything less than that, we find that
we're not really living. We're just passive puppets who're "being lived."

Most of us can probably sympathize with Jules Laforgue's sentiment: "Oh, how daily life is!" It keeps coming at us, one day after
another, one moment after another. Continually, continually, continually these appear, as if marching to an inexorable drumbeat. One is
no sooner done with one than another presents itself before us. And
every single one of these days and moments asks to be used to a good
end or effect. If we default and do nothing (at least nothing worth
doing), the unused increments of our lives begin to pile up behind us,
creating a sad monument of negligence and lost opportunity.

So the gift of life — and it is a gift indeed — must be received
properly. We must appreciate it, certainly, but beyond that, we must
use it. It is to be employed as well as enjoyed. And the best employment of life is to use it defending and enhancing the lives of others,
helping them to have a greater measure of life in all its dimensions.

When we live responsibly, we live with a recognition of our connection to other people, and even to the other living creatures that
share our habitat. Except under rare circumstances, human life is not
a solo affair; it's a communal effort. We're living at our best when we
seek to relate ourselves rightly to the "unimaginable whole" of which
we are each a part. And what a delightful whole it happens to be!

Life is a roar of bargain and battle, but in the very heart of it
there rises a mystic spiritual tone that gives meaning to the whole.
It transmutes the dull details into romance. It reminds us that our only
but wholly adequate significance is as parts of the unimaginable
whole. It suggests that even while we think we are egotists
we are living to ends outside ourselves.

OLIVER WENDELL HOLMES JR.

DISCUSSION

No discussion between two persons can be of any use,
until each knows clearly what it is that the other asserts.

LEWIS CARROLL

WHEN WE DISCUSS THINGS, WE OFTEN ERR BY TALKING WHEN WE SHOULD BE LISTENING. Taking it for granted that we understand what the other person is saying, we're primarily concerned with whether they understand what we're saying. Understanding is not as important to us as being understood, and so our discussions often fizzle out ineffectively. What could have been a dialogue between two inquirers, and therefore an exercise in understanding, becomes a pair of monologues between two talkers, both of whom are in a defensive crouch rather than a learning posture.

Our English word "discuss" comes from a compound Latin verb: *dis-* ("apart") + *quatere* ("to shake"). It means, literally, to shake apart or break up. *But the thing "shaken apart" is not one's counterpart in the discussion — it's the subject being discussed!* To discuss something means to examine it closely by exchanging ideas and viewpoints. When two people discuss a matter, they speak to one another about it in an effort to ascertain truth or reach agreement. A discussion is a "talking over" of something. It's a *consideration* of a topic by means of *conversation*.

Discussion is a great help in clarifying our thinking. "Reading makes a full man, meditation a profound man, discourse a clear man" (Benjamin Franklin). We learn not just by thinking but by conversing, and most of us need to go through the give-and-take of a few discussions before we can see a subject clearly. "As iron sharpens iron, so a man sharpens the countenance of his friend" (Book of Proverbs).

But there is another, more important, reason why discussions are valuable: they help us along the path to *common* understanding. It is by discussing things that groups of people meld their visions into a shared vision, and their commitments into mutual commitments.

Discussions can sometimes turn contentious, as we all know, but they don't have to do so. And when they're conducted respectfully, as among friends, they are truly one of life's great joys. Debates and defenses have their place, no doubt, but discussions have theirs too.

The more the pleasures of the body fade away,
the greater to me is the pleasure and charm of conversation.

PLATO

PONDERING

First ponder, then dare.

HELMUTH VON MOLTKE

IT'S TRUE THAT MOST OF US NEED TO BE MORE ADVENTURE-SOME, BUT IT'S ALSO TRUE THAT WE NEED TO PONDER OUR DEEDS BEFORE WE DO THEM. As von Moltke says, the correct order of action is: "First ponder, then dare." And the more consequential the dare, the more profound should be the pondering that precedes it.

"Ponder" comes from the Latin *pondus* ("weight"). It means to consider something carefully. When we ponder, we "weigh" an idea in our minds, thinking how significant it is or, if the thought is one of action, what its outcome might be. Pondering is more than casual thinking — it is thinking with painstaking care and thoroughness.

There is no better way to build credibility than to be a person who ponders things. And in fact, we *shouldn't* have much credibility if we don't consider things carefully. If we're known to act rashly, we'll not be those whom our friends turn to in time of need or difficulty. Our carelessness will keep us from being as trusted as we'd like to be.

The notion that ideas can be "weighed" in our minds ought to be of more than passing interest. Contrary to what many seem to think nowadays, not all ideas are equal and interchangeable. Some have more weight than others; that is, some are more true, significant, helpful, beautiful, and so forth. The challenge in thinking is to discern, by pondering them, which ideas are weighty and which are not. When we're making decisions, we need to let the weighty ideas count for more, and pay somewhat less attention to the lighter-weight trivia. And the same principle applies when we're weighing our words!

Being a person who ponders things may sound pretty dull, as if that person never did anything but think. But the truth is, life is never dull when we're in a receptive state of mind. Those who take the time to ponder the world and its happenings find that surprises often break into their reveries. When we ruminate and meditate and cogitate, we open the doors of our minds to . . . who knows what?

Once upon a midnight dreary, while I pondered, weak and weary,
Over many a quaint and curious volume of forgotten lore —
While I nodded, nearly napping, suddenly there came a tapping,
As of someone gently rapping, rapping at my chamber door.

EDGAR ALLAN POE

ADVICE

Four eyes see better than two.
ANONYMOUS

IT'S A FOOLISH PERSON INDEED WHO DOESN'T APPRECIATE THE VALUE OF ADVICE. When we're looking at a situation that calls for a decision, not any of us sees every single thing that can be seen. We need the extra vision that comes from other sets of eyes, and to the extent that we let our viewpoint be enlarged and improved by other people's perspectives, our decisions will tend to turn out better.

There are some, no doubt, who go to the opposite extreme and take the advice of everyone they meet, without regard to whether the advice is good, bad, or mediocre. But the person who takes everyone's advice is just as foolish as the person who doesn't take anybody's. At some point, we have to take responsibility for our own choices, heeding good advice and disregarding that which is not so good.

But therein lies the trick! If we could always tell the difference between good and bad advice, we probably wouldn't need any advice. As John Churton Collins said, "To profit from good advice requires more wisdom than to give it." So each of us needs to grow in wisdom: the wisdom that's required both to recognize and to act on good advice.

The most common mistake we make is disregarding any advice that conflicts with our preferences and preconceived ideas. Whoever agrees with our preferred course of action is "wise" and his advice is "good," while the fellow who warns us that we're on the wrong road is usually written off as someone who "just doesn't understand."

But sometimes the best advice is that which is the most uncomfortable. And not only that, the best advice sometimes comes from unwelcome sources, perhaps even our enemies. Yet if we know what's good for us, we'll learn to profit from helpful advice, regardless of where it comes from or how little we may want to hear it.

In my experience, the best advice usually has to be sought out. It doesn't come looking for us; we have to take the initiative. Because they desire to be courteous, many of our wisest friends won't speak frankly about our circumstances unless we ask them to. And as we all know, asking for advice can be hard. But in the long run, we only hurt ourselves if we keep silent when we should be asking for help.

I not only use all the brains I have but all I can borrow.
WOODROW WILSON

QUIETNESS

True silence is the rest of the mind and is to the spirit
what sleep is to the body, nourishment and refreshment.
WILLIAM PENN

OUR NEED FOR QUIETNESS SEEMS TO INCREASE WITH EACH
PASSING DAY. It's a loud world we live in, in more ways than
one, and we can't stand loudness without some periods of relief.
Torturers have always known that it's possible to drive a human being
insane by subjecting him to incessant noise, even if it's no more than
the dripping of water. We have an irrevocable need for quietness: our
minds and hearts need stillness and silence in order to rest. And not
only that, but they need these things in order to *grow*. "I cannot be
the man I should be without times of quietness. Stillness is an essential part of growing deeper as we grow older" (Charles R. Swindoll).

Our need for quietness, however, shouldn't send us into the
woods or up to the mountaintop, there to live apart from any other
living being. Quietness, like physical sleep, is a necessity now and
then, but it's not the ultimate goal of life, and we can't allow our
enjoyment of things like meditation to detract from our responsibilities to others. As Morton Kelsey suggests, "What we do with our lives
outwardly, how well we care for others, is as much a part of meditation as what we do in quietness and turning inward."

Yet there's no denying that we need more quietness than we usually get in these days of urgent activity. The busier our lives become,
the more discipline it takes to eke out times of solitude and serenity.
It helps, I believe, to acknowledge the *virtue* of quietness. "Happiness
is the harvest of a quiet eye" (Austin O'Malley). We're too quick to
dismiss the ideal of quietness, and its twin ideal of simplicity, as being
outdated, and we need to get back to appreciating their goodness.

Quietness, to be frank, is an aspect of maturity — physically,
emotionally, and even spiritually. Both the perception of its value and
the discipline of its practice are things that require growth. And like
most forms of worthwhile growth, quietness calls for *commitment*.

If only I may grow
firmer,
simpler,
quieter,
warmer.

DAG HAMMARSKJÖLD

ENHANCEMENT

Good is all that serves life, evil is all that serves death.
Good is reverence for life . . . and all that enhances life.
Evil is all that stifles life, narrows it down, cuts it to pieces.

ERICH FROMM

FEW THINGS, IF ANY, GET BETTER ALL BY THEMSELVES. To the contrary, most things deteriorate unless somebody does something now and then to enhance them. To enhance means to augment something for the better, to make its value or its beauty greater. And that, really, is what our work in this world is all about. It's not just maintenance; it's enhancement. By the work that we do, we have the privilege of improving the things that we deal with. And it's a fine thing to be known as individuals who enhance whatever we touch.

Appreciation for improvement. One of our major goals for personal growth ought to be the acquiring of a character that appreciates improvement. We must learn to see the value of working toward betterment. We must gain a greater vision of what can happen when we commit ourselves to adding value to all we deal with, little by little.

Enhancement of everything. With an appreciation for improvement, we then must be active enhancers. It's more than an attitude; it's an active endeavor. We might even say that it's a way of life. In this way of life, we don't merely walk past that piece of litter on the sidewalk; we pick it up and place it in the nearest trash can.

Gratitude for grace. The people who're the most active enhancers are usually those who're possessed of a deep sense of gratitude for the grace that has been shown to them personally. And that's no coincidence. In the end, that's the great motive for helping others: the realization that we ourselves have been helped beyond our merits.

Sometimes, it's surprising what enhances life. Just as certain herbs and spices only release their full zest when they're crushed or rubbed together, we may find that the flavor of life is enhanced by events that may, at first, seem to be only irritants. When we view life with a basically appreciative attitude and respond to those around us with grace and respect, even our differences can make life more zestful. But then, it's not life that's being enhanced — it's we who are.

[My wife and I] sometimes had those little rubs which
Providence sends to enhance the value of its flavors.

OLIVER GOLDSMITH

POTENTIAL

There are admirable potentialities in every human being.

ANDRÉ GIDE

POTENTIAL HAS TO DO WITH POSSIBILITIES. It means that we are capable of growing, developing, and learning to use powers that are, at present, only latent within us. And the fact is, every human being has some potential. That's true because no human being is presently using all of the powers that he or she is capable of using. We all have room to grow, and we need to be encouraged by the fact that our potential for growth is greater than we've ever imagined.

There is a sense, of course, in which it's better to have as little potential as possible. If we define potential as unused ability, then it would be a compliment if someone said we had very little of that!

But most of us do have at least a few powers that we've not yet learned how to use, and so one of the most important items of business in life is reaching forward to the realization of our potential. In fact, the quality of our lives depends more on this than it does on the enjoyment of things we've already accomplished. There is always some impulse within us that's wanting to make *progress*. Apathy, indifference, complacency, and the like are deadly enemies of ours, and we're not happy, really, unless we're striving toward our full potential.

And yet, there's a consideration even more important than our own growth, and that would be the growth of those whom we love. We never use ourselves more worthily than when we do things that assist our loved ones in reaching their potential. Indeed, we do them a great favor when we even help them to *see* their potential more clearly. And there aren't many joys in life greater than watching someone reach a potential that we've helped them to see and develop.

The fulfillment of potential, whether it's our own or somebody else's, almost always requires sacrifice. The weightlifter's motto, "No pain, no gain," is pertinent to far more than physical training. There is nothing worth having in life that doesn't have a price tag, and the cost of realizing our potential often consists of letting go of the comforts of our present condition. We can't have tomorrow and today too. So either we pay the price and grow, or we stay stuck right where we are.

The important thing is this: to be able at any moment
to sacrifice what we are for what we could become.

CHARLES DUBOIS

SEASONS

Sing a song of seasons!
Something bright in all!
ROBERT LOUIS STEVENSON

JUST AS THE YEAR FALLS INTO FOUR NATURAL DIVISIONS —
SPRING, SUMMER, AUTUMN, AND WINTER — IT IS GOOD FOR
US TO LEAD LIVES THAT ARE "SEASONAL." Nowadays many of us
are cut off from any significant contact with nature and its recurring
periods, and if we're not careful, we will fall into the habit of doing
the same thing all of the time, twelve months a year. But just as nature
does a different kind of work in the spring than it does in the fall, we
need to vary the pattern of our living. Our human years need to be
characterized by seasons, so that we enjoy some rhythm and variety.

To begin with, it would help us to recover our appreciation of
the natural seasons. The qualities that distinguish the four seasons
are truly refreshing. Yet if we even notice these qualities, it is often
only to complain: if it is hot or cold, dry or rainy, we speak as if these
variations were undesirable. But they're not undesirable; they're the
changes that can give structure and pattern and texture to our lives.
We need to taste the seasons more consciously and appreciatively.

Taken as a whole, our lives also fall into seasons. There is the
spring of youth, the summer of early adulthood, the fall of late adulthood, and the winter of old age. All of these present special opportunities and challenges. Each is to be enjoyed and used wisely.

But young or old, it's good to follow the natural seasons each
year, enjoy them, and adapt to their differences. If we'll lead a sum-
mer-like life in the summer, a winter-like life in the winter, etc., we'll
find ourselves not only relishing life more but also being more productive. Respecting the seasons is a good way to get more out of life.

Today, it's good to be reminded that spring is the "first" season.
It's a time of new beginnings and new growth. As greenery starts to
emerge from the gray of winter, who can help but be reminded of the
opportunity this gives us to renew our commitment to life? So whatever good thing you can begin — or renew — today, let it *live* in you!

In our hearts those of us who know anything worth knowing know
that in March a new year begins, and if we plan any new leaves,
it will be when the rest of Nature is planning them too.
JOSEPH WOOD KRUTCH

EXAMINATION

Before we set our hearts too much upon anything,
let us examine how happy those are who already possess it.

FRANÇOIS DE LA ROCHEFOUCAULD

MANY OF LIFE'S REGRETS COME FROM NOT HAVING LOOKED AT THINGS CAREFULLY ENOUGH. It frequently happens that we acquire possessions or become involved in activities that end up bringing us more grief than happiness, and it would have been relatively easy to see where they would lead if we'd examined them beforehand. That boat you thought you had to have, for example. Did you even ask anyone how much time it would take to maintain it? As La Rochefoucauld points out, before letting ourselves be disturbed by desire for something, we ought to "examine how happy those are who already possess it." We ought, in other words, to look before we leap.

"Fine print" is usually boring to read, but it's often helpful to read it anyway. And the more important the contract, the more wise we are to read the fine print. But we don't often do that, do we? We assume too much. We take too many things for granted, without *examining* them, and then later, when we realize what we've gotten ourselves into, we wish we'd inspected the situation a bit more carefully.

As little as we examine some things, however, there are others that we examine too much. For instance, most of us spend far too much time inspecting and analyzing business that is not our own. A "busybody" is a person who meddles or pries into the affairs of others, and that's exactly what we catch ourselves being and doing some-times. In fact, I have a friend who, based on his observation of human nature, has formulated the following rule: our interest in any topic is inversely proportional to that topic's bearing on our own conduct.

A far more productive use of our time would be to engage in *self-examination*. When Socrates said that "the unexamined life is not worth living," he wasn't talking about making someone else's life more worthy by examining it! Our progress in life depends on our being willing to scrutinize ourselves. The flaws are there waiting to be seen, and they are correctable — but only if we submit to self-scrutiny.

When we see men of worth, we should think of becoming
like them; when we see men of contrary character,
we should turn inward and examine ourselves.

FRANÇOIS DE LA ROCHEFOUCAULD

POLITENESS

Manners are the happy way of doing things.

R A L P H   W A L D O   E M E R S O N

IF SOMETHING MAY BE DONE IN MORE THAN ONE WAY, POLITE-
NESS MEANS CHOOSING THE MORE GRACIOUS WAY OF DOING
IT. Nearly everything we do has an impact on somebody else, and
being polite is simply one way of making our impact as pleasant as
possible. For example, the act of chewing one's food can be accomplished with one's mouth open or closed. But the inside of the human
mouth, especially when there's food in it, is not a very attractive sight,
and so to make our table mates' experience more pleasant, we spare
them the sight of our open mouth. George Washington, who learned
early about how human influence works, wrote this in his copybook
when he was sixteen years old: "Put not another bite into your Mouth
till the former be Swallowed, and let not your Morsels be too big for
your Mouth." That's a "happy way" of doing things at the table!

The rules of etiquette are not arbitrary, and before we discard
them, we might do well to consider that these are time-tested ways
that have been proven to have some value. The fact that some people
carry them too far doesn't mean that they have no usefulness at all.

Some people who flout the conventions of politeness do so
because they think their rudeness projects a certain kind of strength
or bravado. But the truly strong don't need to be impolite. As Eric
Hoffer observed, "Rudeness is the weak man's imitation of strength."

Nor is politeness insincere or pretentious. "Politeness is the art of
selecting among one's real thoughts" (Madame de Staël). Not everything we truly think needs to be spoken out loud, and even when
tough truths need to be communicated, politeness will make us want
to balance our courage with a healthy measure of consideration.

The bottom line is this: politeness looks out for the other person's
best interests. It wants the other person to have as pleasant an experience as possible. So good manners are just a way of showing courtesy
and kindness to those around us. And while the difference between
the polite and the impolite may sometimes seem too small to be significant, that's not an argument for discarding the idea of politeness.
In fact, it may be the little acts of politeness that matter the most.

Never come between anyone and the fire.

W A B A S H A

CHOICE

You choose, you live the consequences. Every yes, no, maybe,
creates the school you call your personal experience.
RICHARD BACH

EACH TIME WE MAKE A CHOICE, TAKING ONE FORK IN THE ROAD RATHER THAN ANOTHER, AN INTERESTING THING HAPPENS. On the one hand, our lives expand. As we move forward along the path we've chosen, new elements are added to our experience that weren't there before. But on the other hand, our lives contract. The path that we didn't take is no longer a possibility. Whatever might have been if we'd chosen that option is something we've now let go of. Some similar choice might open up in the future, but it will be a different choice, at least slightly. Once choices have been made, those exact choices never come to us again. When we choose our path, we open our hands to certain things and we let go of others.

None of us is happy with every choice we've ever made. Now and then, we all make decisions that yield unexpected consequences. But there are two points to keep in mind about that. One is the point made by Richard Bach above: "Every yes, no, maybe, creates the school you call your personal experience." The wonderful variety in life — the exquisite "particularity" of each individual — comes largely from the combination of all our choices, both the painful and the pleasant. Not many of us have complexions that are flawlessly perfect, and we don't have a personal track record that's perfect either. In both cases, we must learn how to be comfortable in our own "skin."

But the second point is that we should have the maturity and discipline to act with honor concerning our choices. The man who says, "I'll honor this contract as long as it doesn't stand between me and something else I might want in the future" is probably not a fellow we'd want to go into business with. We all want to deal with people who honor their choices, and we need to do the same ourselves. In the end, it helps to know that life is made better, not worse, by things like trust and honor. We can't always be hedging our bets, running away from risk, and trying to get out of inconvenient arrangements. *Choices made and promises kept are the stuff of life!*

Life does not give itself to one who
tries to keep all its advantages at once.
LÉON BLUM

EFFICIENCY

There can be no economy where there is no efficiency.

BENJAMIN DISRAELI

BY DEFINITION, EFFICIENCY REDUCES WASTE, AND FOR THAT REASON IT'S AN ESSENTIAL HABIT TO ACQUIRE. When our resources are scarce, it's obviously important to minimize waste, but when they're abundant, as they are for most of us nowadays, it's no less important to use those resources efficiently. When we're plentifully supplied with raw materials to do our work, it's harder to see the need for carefulness, but abundance is never an excuse for waste, and we ought always to get the most good that we can out of every moment, every dollar, and every ounce of our strength.

I would suggest that the area where efficiency and good stewardship are most critical is the area of personal talents and abilities. Since these are intangible qualities, it may be harder to see them as "resources," but that's exactly what they are. Think, for example, about a trait like intelligence. The more intelligent a person is, the more that person should use his or her intelligence efficiently, that is, wasting as little of it as possible on unworthy pursuits. "Be pleased, O God, to grant unto me that great freedom of mind that will enable me to . . . manage the common affairs of life in such wise as not to misemploy or neglect the improvement of my talents" (Susanna Wesley).

It is often pointed out today, by teachers like Stephen R. Covey, that "efficiency" must always be governed by "effectiveness." We may climb life's ladder with all the efficiency in the world (good technique), but if, when we get to the top, we find that we've had our ladder leaning against the wrong wall (wrong vision), we're in trouble.

Working efficiently and effectively requires the old-fashioned quality of wisdom. There's no shortcut to it — except our willingness to listen and learn from the wisdom of those who've gone before us.

The thing to remember is that we're only here for a short time. We have only a limited number of days to make the contribution that we were put here to make. And so it's common sense, at the very least, to work as efficiently as we can. If by working efficiently, we can reach the end of our lives having done more good than by working any other way, that's a pretty sound argument for learning how to be efficient.

The possession of efficiency — the power to do.

NICHOLAS MURRAY BUTLER

FASCINATION

Youth, large, lusty, loving — youth, full of grace,
force, fascination, do you know that old age may come
after you with equal grace, force, fascination?

WALT WHITMAN

NO MATTER WHO WE ARE OR WHERE WE MAY BE ON LIFE'S
PATHWAY, FASCINATION SHOULD CHARACTERIZE US. We
should, on the one hand, be people who enjoy being fascinated by the
assortment of wonders around us, but on the other hand, we should
take such an approach to life that our lives end up having a little
fascination of their own. "Being fascinating" doesn't qualify as one of
the major goals in life, obviously, but the fact remains, if a human life
is well lived, fascination will be one of its by-products.

If something "fascinates" us, what does that mean? It means that
it holds our interest with intense attraction. It spellbinds us. Think of
the snake charmer using music and movement to hold the unbroken
attention of a cobra. Think of the hypnotist mesmerizing his subject
or the orator enthralling his audience. That which fascinates us intrigues us. It does more than pique our interest; it rivets our attention.

But what is it that really fascinates us? I like Calvin Miller's
suggestion: "Joy intrigues." Isn't that it? Aren't we most powerfully
intrigued by those who, despite the ups and downs and the occasional
unhappiness of life, drink deeply of a joy that seems to be theirs no
matter what? I think we are, and I think our fascination with joy is a
significant clue to many of the greater mysteries of the human spirit.

So we don't become fascinating by imitating the ways in which
other people are fascinating; we do it by entering deeply and enthusiastically into the experience that happens to be our own. One of the
most fascinating people I've ever met was a lady who lived in the same
retirement center as my father for a while. She was 104 years old, had
never been married, and had been retired from her job as a school
teacher for over forty years. Her fascination came not from having
done anything offbeat, but from having wholeheartedly lived the life
that was hers to live. And so the question is not what we've done; it's
how joyously we've let our years be used up, whether many or few.

There's a fascination frantic
In a ruin that's romantic;
Do you think you are sufficiently decayed?

SIR WILLIAM SCHWENCK GILBERT

EXPECTATION

Expect people to be better than they are;
it helps them to become better. But don't be disappointed
when they are not; it helps them to keep trying.

MERRY BROWNE

OUR EXPECTATIONS ARE POWERFUL FORCES THAT ACT ON OTHER PEOPLE'S LIVES. High expectations pull people upward; low expectations drag them downward. So it behooves us to be careful what we expect of others. What we expect is very often what we get.

But the suggestion that we should expect the best in those around us is often met with cynicism, if not outright mockery. "It's naive to expect the best," some would say. I well remember a teacher in college who told me, "Gary, nobody ever went broke underestimating the ignorance of the human race." He said it humorously, tongue-in-cheek, but I'm afraid there are a number of people who would say that and not be joking at all. In fact, most people seem to think cynicism is the safest path to follow: "Expect the worst, and then if anything better than that takes place, you can be pleasantly surprised."

Whatever "safety" there may be in cynicism, however, I know of no world-class performers in any field who take that approach. Can we imagine, for example, a Vince Lombardi ever telling his football players, "Now, guys, I don't really expect that you're going to play up to your potential, but if it turns out that you do, that'll be okay. I'll take it as a pleasant surprise"? No, high achievers around the world have always expected the best of themselves and of everybody else too.

In fact, it's not naive to expect the best of others. The best that others can offer may not be flawlessly perfect, but whatever their best is, they're capable of offering that, and it's not unrealistic to expect it.

"Great expectations" (to borrow Charles Dickens's phrase) motivate us. They give us energy to "go for the good stuff." And so it makes a lot of sense to do three things: (1) nourish high expectations of ourselves, (2) surround ourselves with friends who'll help us keep our expectations high, and (3) influence others to expect higher things for themselves. In every possible way, it's wise to encourage *hope* in the hearts of our fellow travelers. It's among the greatest of all gifts.

A master can tell you what he expects of you.
A teacher, though, awakens your own expectations.

PATRICIA NEAL

APPRECIATION

It takes a heap o' livin' in a house t' make it a home,
A heap o' sun an' shadder, an' ye sometimes have t' roam
Afore ye really 'preciate the things ye lef' behind,
An' hunger fer 'em somehow, with 'em allus on yer mind.

EDGAR ALBERT GUEST

I T'S SAD HOW LITTLE WE APPRECIATE SOME THINGS UNTIL WE'VE LOST THEM OR THEY'VE BEEN LEFT BEHIND. By deferring our appreciation until we've been deprived, we miss out on so much of the day-to-day enjoyment of appreciation. It would be so much better if we paid the price to gain a sense of gratitude right now.

Appreciation is the last link in a chain that starts with the *conscious effort to count our blessings*. It has never been said better than in the words of that old hymn: "Count your many blessings, name them one by one." This means consciously focusing our minds on the things that are valuable to us. And though this sounds simple, it is no small task in these busy days. We rarely have the time to leisurely and luxuriously reflect on each of the good things in our lives — but we need to take the time to do so. When we do, it's likely that we'll be struck by how sadly our lives would be impoverished if we didn't have these things, and that awareness then leads to the last link in the chain — *appreciation*. So remember the sequence: (1) meditation on our blessings, (2) awareness of their importance, and (3) appreciation of their value.

Out of all the things we ought to appreciate, of course, the greatest are the people around us. In the words of psychologist William James's famous statement, "The deepest principle of human nature is the craving to be appreciated." In our heart of hearts, we all know that this saying contains a great insight. And if we know how much we appreciate being appreciated, that's all the more reason for us to go out of our way to appreciate others. They need it as much as we do.

Disliking things is easy, isn't it? It requires little effort and little character. But finding worthy things to like and then fully appreciating them requires more of us. That being true, let's set ourselves a goal: *let's aspire to be people who're defined by both the goodness of the things we love and the depth of our appreciation for every one of them.*

The question is not what a man can scorn,
or disparage, or find fault with, but what
can he love and value and appreciate.

JOHN RUSKIN

MORALE

Morale is faith in the person at the top.
ANONYMOUS

IN MOST OF THE GROUPS THAT WE'RE MEMBERS OF, GREAT THINGS DEPEND ON THE MORALE OF THE GROUP. If those who make up a group are collectively discouraged, depressed, negligent, and unwilling to work, it's not likely that good things are going to result. But if they're confident, cheerful, disciplined, and eager to contribute, then there aren't many goals that can't be accomplished by the group. In all collective endeavors, very much depends on morale.

Leaders need to understand and accept the fact that morale among the "troops" is largely a matter of whether the troops believe the leaders know what they're doing. Great morale comes from leadership being trusted — trusted to lead successfully in the direction of goals that are held by all to be good and important.

But if "morale is faith in the person at the top," many people would say, "Morale is not my responsibility; I'm not the person at the top." If we think that way, we're probably taking a somewhat limited view of our lives. We're probably only thinking of one or two of our relationships, such as work or school. But in the larger reality, all of us are members of dozens of different relationships, and every one of us has the responsibility for leadership in at least some of these.

Think of a relationship, however small, in which others look to you for leadership. How is the morale? Is the relationship encouraged or discouraged? Could you make a difference by leading differently?

Sometimes without realizing it, the thing that we share with others is our fear, rather than our courage. But folks usually have enough fears of their own. So Robert Louis Stevenson gave good advice when he said, "Keep your fears to yourself, but share your courage."

We need to value good morale enough to promote it and protect it. And doing that often doesn't require the taking of big steps; it only requires that we take small steps in the right direction. Those who're following us just need to know that genuine *progress* is being made.

When enthusiasm is inspired by reason; controlled by caution;
sound in theory; practical in application; reflects confidence; spreads
good cheer; raises morale; inspires associates; arouses loyalty,
and laughs at adversity, it is beyond price.
COLEMAN COX

EAGERNESS

We act as though comfort and luxury were the
chief requirements of life, when all that we need to make
us happy is something to be enthusiastic about.

CHARLES KINGSLEY

RUNNING OUT TO MEET LIFE EAGERLY IS A WISE AND BENEFI-
CIAL THING TO DO. Whatever we do, we do it better when we
do it eagerly rather than reluctantly. Obstacles are overcome more
easily, cooperation from others is gained more freely, and satisfaction
is experienced more deeply when eagerness is a part of our approach.

If we take an honest look at our lives, however, many of us will
have to admit that we've let the daily forces grind down our eagerness
to the point where there's little left of it. Perhaps we're not yet at the
point of despair or outright rebellion, but we find ourselves merely
tolerating life rather than living it. We're "going through the motions."
As G. K. Chesterton remarked, "There is a great deal of difference between an eager man who wants to read a book and the tired man who
wants a book to read." Just so, there is a big difference between the
person who has a life to live and the one who merely has to live life.

But we can do better, can't we? We can rebuild our reserves of
enthusiasm and eagerness. It may take time to get back in touch with
the principles that produce excitement, but it's worth working on,
starting today. And one of the best reasons for doing so is that we
honor others by being eager. Our general attitude toward life comes
through in our dealings with those around us, and when we're living
our lives eagerly, others experience that eagerness as a welcoming,
enthusiastic approach to them personally. It's like giving them a hug!

Deep down, eagerness is always a product of *gratitude*. Those
who're enthusiastic are those who appreciate the gift of life. Without
diminishing their difficulties, eager people put the emphasis on their
opportunities — and they show thankfulness for these opportunities
by *embracing* them. With each new day, we get a chance to recharge
our attitude and take another run at life's requirements. While some
folks greet the rising sun with a groan, others are rarin' to go. When
we decide which it'll be, we make a very important choice.

Wake up with a smile and go after life . . .
Live it, enjoy it, taste it, smell it, feel it.

JOE KNAPP

JUSTICE

The just hand is a precious ointment.

LATIN PROVERB

ONLY THOSE WHO'VE BEEN TREATED WITH SERIOUS INJUS-
TICE CAN FULLY UNDERSTAND WHAT A "PRECIOUS OINT-
MENT" JUSTICE IS. Frankly, there aren't many things in life more
valuable than the simple treasure of fairness. And no matter who we
are, we'd do well to examine ourselves honestly from time to time, and
make a new commitment to this virtue, which is one of the greatest.

But when we're meditating on justice, which is the more profitable question to ask: whether we've received adequate justice from
others or whether we've done adequate justice to others? In a culture
where we almost compete against one another for the status of "greatest victim," we seem to be concerned mainly that others haven't given
us what we deserve. But if our lives as a whole were to be taken into
consideration, would we really want what we deserve? Before we say
yes, we should probably reconsider. "Use every man after his desert,
and who should scape whipping?" (Shakespeare). If we ever really
got what we should get, most of us would prefer to go back to the
unfairness that we thought was so intolerable. H. L. Mencken was
right when he said, "Injustice is relatively easy to bear; what stings is
justice." To tell the truth, what most of us want is mercy, not justice.

So perhaps we should spend a greater portion of our time ques-
tioning our own doing of justice. Here, most of us ordinary folks will
find lots of room for improvement, especially when we consider that
we may do injustice as much by what we leave undone as by what we
do. A few days' trial of Benjamin Franklin's rule ("Wrong none by
doing injuries, or omitting the benefits that are your duty") will show
us how challenging it is to make a real-life commitment to justice.

Above all, however, we must be careful not to limit our defense
of justice to those who make a favorable impression on us. If we have
a most-common failing in the matter of justice, it's probably that we
show favoritism in dispensing it. But to be true, justice must be "blind,"
in the honorable sense. Everybody deserves to be treated fairly.

Do justice to your brother (you can do that, whether you love
him or not), and you will come to love him. But do injustice to him
because you don't love him, and you will come to hate him.

JOHN RUSKIN

AMUSEMENT

Anyone without a sense of humor
is at the mercy of everyone else.

WILLIAM ROTSLER

ON THIS DAY EVERY YEAR, PRACTICAL JOKES ARE TRADITION-ALLY ACCEPTED, AND EVEN ENCOURAGED. Today of all days, "anyone without a sense of humor is at the mercy of everyone else."

Some of us need more than one such day a year. We tend to take ourselves too seriously, like Queen Victoria of England, who would cut off anyone guilty of being humorous in her presence with the stiff reply, "The Queen is not amused." Thus the Victorian Age, for which she is known, is remembered for some good things, but amusement is not one of them. The Queen, apparently, was not a comedienne.

Not many of us would like to find that we have a reputation for being a "stuffed shirt." We like people who have the ability to be amused, and we'd prefer to be thought of that way ourselves. Too often, however, we let the weighty issues of life drag us down into a place where there is no amusement. So we need a day once in a while, like today, when a bit of humor is forced upon us. "Humor," as Jan McKeithen said, "is a hole that lets the sawdust out of a stuffed shirt."

The ability to be amused and to amuse others are abilities worth cultivating, if they're not a part of our character right now. It may seem contradictory to talk about "working on" our amusement, but that may, in fact, be what we need to do. We may need to make some conscious decisions to loosen up and learn how to be both the amuser and the amusee. Doing so pays great dividends. The breaking-in period may be uncomfortable, as with a new pair of shoes, but eventually the capacity for genuine, healthy amusement will be worth acquiring.

Amusement is a part of what makes for rich relationships with other human beings. If we want our relationships to be multi-layered and many-dimensioned, we need to aspire to having more than one kind of influence. We need, certainly, to work on being able to teach, to inspire, to encourage, and so forth. But, personally, I also want to be able to amuse. And those whom I count as my dearest friends are those whom I know I can amuse now and then. How about you?

We cherish our friends not for their ability to amuse us,
but for our ability to amuse them.

EVELYN WAUGH

ANTICIPATION

There is something new every day if you look for it.
HANNAH HURNARD

ONE OF OUR MOST REMARKABLE ENDOWMENTS IS THE ABILITY TO FORETASTE PLEASURE. The literal meaning of "anticipate" is to "take before," and we have it within us to look ahead (at least a little way) and take enjoyment from our experiences before they arrive. To make this choice and welcome the future with joy is an act of courage. It is also an act of considerable wisdom.

Not everything about the future will be pleasant, of course. But even so, anticipation is a wise choice. As a positive character quality, anticipation gives us a more constructive outlook. By believing the best and acting on our hopes, we find a better future than if we expected the worst. For this reason, Albert Schweitzer, who spent his adult life dealing with life's rough edges, said, "My knowledge is pessimistic, but my willing and hoping are optimistic."

How then can we heighten our anticipation and relish our future? Although it seems contradictory, the primary thing we can do is pay more attention to what happens in the present moment. As I write these lines, for example, it is early spring and the trees outside my window are beginning to bud and blossom. It would be difficult to look at these things thoughtfully and not anticipate (or "take before") the greater, more fully developed beauty they'll have tomorrow morning. So whatever death and decay there may be, let's also see the evidence that many good things in the world are moving, growing, and reaching forward. If we "taste" deeply the present truth about these things, our minds will tingle with anticipation for what lies ahead.

Even when we have no idea what will happen tomorrow, there are still reasons for us to anticipate it. The intriguing mystery of it all — the very possibility that tomorrow's path may take a surprising turn — ought to energize us. If life could be completely planned and programmed, we would be safe perhaps, but in our hearts we know that we want more than safety. Like the inquisitive, once-upon-a-time children that we used to be, we want to learn more than we know and do more than we've done. There's a bit of the adventurer in all of us.

Still round the corner there may wait,
A new road, or a secret gate.
J. R. R. TOLKIEN

PEACEFULNESS

In our rough-and-rugged individualism, we think of gentleness as weakness,
being soft, and virtually spineless. Not so! . . . Gentleness includes such
enviable qualities as having strength under control, being calm and peaceful
when surrounded by a heated atmosphere, emitting a soothing effect on those
who may be angry or otherwise beside themselves.

CHARLES R. SWINDOLL

PEACE IS ALMOST UNIVERSALLY PRAISED, BUT THE PEACEFUL-
NESS THAT LEADS TO PEACE IS NOT ALWAYS ADMIRED. People
who have adopted the character trait of peacefulness are often seen as
being weak rather than strong. But genuine peacefulness is anything
but weak. In fact, conflict is an easy thing compared to constructive-
ness. Bridges are much easier to blow up than they are to build.

To be sure, if a person were to pursue peace *at any price,* that
would not only be weak but weak in the very worst possible way.
There is no honor in sacrificing our principles merely to appease an
enemy, and Dag Hammarskjöld, who served an illustrious career as
Secretary-General of the United Nations, was correct when he gave
this advice: "Never 'for the sake of peace and quiet' deny your own
experience or convictions." But whether we're honest enough to admit
it, it's often not our principles that have to be sacrificed to establish
peace — it's merely our personal preferences and privileges.

The real test of whether we have a peaceful character is not how
well we deal with adversaries who have cooperative attitudes, but how
diligently we work with those who don't. Peacefulness requires more
than the ability to reconcile with a dear friend after a minor disagree-
ment. As Yitzhak Rabin once said, "Peace is not made with friends.
Peace is made with enemies." And so, as Thomas à Kempis said, "To
be able to live peaceably with hard and perverse persons, or with the
disorderly, or with such as go contrary to us, is a great grace."

It should be obvious that if peacefulness is to characterize us,
we're going to have to learn patience. Establishing constructive, if not
friendly, relations with those with whom we have serious disagreements calls for the highest and best that's within us. And we can't let
ourselves be discouraged when our efforts don't yield immediate results. Peacefulness is costly, and the cost spreads out over many years.

Peace is a daily, a weekly, a monthly process, gradually changing opinions,
slowly eroding old barriers, quietly building new structures.

JOHN F. KENNEDY

EXPEDIENCY

No man is justified in doing evil on the ground of expediency.
THEODORE ROOSEVELT

EXPEDIENCY IS AN UNUSUAL WORD IN THAT IT'S OFTEN USED IN TWO DIFFERENT SENSES, ONE NEGATIVE AND THE OTHER POSITIVE. In addition to their denotation, or explicit meaning, many words also have a connotation, a more indirect meaning consisting of a positive or negative "aura" or "atmosphere" that surrounds the words. "Expediency" has two basic meanings, but these two meanings have two different connotations. One is negative, and the other is positive.

The first meaning of "expedient" is "serving to promote one's interests," and this meaning does not give us a good feeling. This kind of expediency is the kind that we associate (whether rightly or wrongly) with politicians. Pontius Pilate, for example, apparently decided to go ahead and have Jesus of Nazareth executed because it was politically expedient. But as Theodore Roosevelt argued, "No man is justified in doing evil on the ground of expediency." And with regard to this kind of expediency, William Morley Punshon summed it all up this way: "Cowardice asks, Is it safe? Expediency asks, Is it politic? Vanity asks, Is it popular? Conscience asks, Is it right?"

But the second meaning is "appropriate to a particular end or purpose," and this meaning not only has a positive connotation, but it contains an idea that's very valuable for us to think about. Used this way, the word "expedient" means that which is fitting, proper, beneficial, or helpful. And in this sense, we ought to consider the expediency of every action that we contemplate engaging in. Whatever the decision, the crucial question for an honorable person is not simply "Is this permissible from a legal standpoint?" but more important, "Will this help? Will it do good? Is this the very best that I can do?"

Laws are important, and we can't do without them. But laws are no more than a minimum standard for us to go by — within the law, we must also be concerned with what is expedient. The fellow who is willing to do "anything the law allows" is not the fellow you want for a next-door neighbor. But our neighbor shouldn't have that kind of neighbor either! So we've always got to ask, "Is this beneficial?"

"All things are lawful," but not all things are helpful.
"All things are lawful," but not all things build up.
FIRST LETTER OF PAUL TO THE CORINTHIANS

CONSCIENCE

Conscience . . . is the impulse to do right
because it is right, regardless of personal ends.

MARGARET C. GRAHAM

NOT A DAY GOES BY THAT OUR CONSCIENCE DOESN'T TEST US. Some of the tests are big while others are little, but we are always having to ask the question, "Will I do what my conscience is telling me is the right thing to do, or will I do something else, something perhaps that will be easier or more pleasant?" These tests, however insignificant they may seem, are important for two reasons: (1) they demonstrate what kind of character we presently have, and (2) they move our character even further along the path of goodness or evil. Every time we say 'yes' or 'no' to our conscience, we add a little more evidence to the record that will eventually be our legacy.

Joy. If you've never experienced the joy that comes from saying 'yes' to your conscience, you really ought to try it. "A good conscience is a continual Christmas" (Benjamin Franklin). I've lived in the world long enough to have enjoyed many of its pleasures, but I've yet to find one that compares to the good feeling of going to bed at night knowing that you've done, that day, what your conscience said was right.

Stability. There is no way to tell what any of us will have to deal with before our lives are over. If we haven't already done so, some of us may experience significant and unexpected hardship, and we may think we can't find anything steady to hang on to. But a clear conscience is an amazingly stable thing, despite the twists and turns of life in this vale of tears. "There is one thing alone that stands the brunt of life throughout its course, a quiet conscience" (Euripides).

We admire those who, in the great moments of history, have taken a heroic stand based on conscience. Most of us will never stand in the spotlight of history, however, and even if we did, our moment there might not be the most accurate measure of our character. What is more telling, perhaps, is whether we listen to our conscience in our quiet, private moments. The thing that we want to do in those moments is simply and purely what is *right.* Just because it's right.

I cannot and will not recant anything, for to go
against conscience is neither right nor safe. Here I stand.
I can do no other, so help me God. Amen.

MARTIN LUTHER

CONSTITUTION

[Our nature] is constituted for the practice of what is good.

MENCIUS

IF MOST NATIONS HAVE A CONSTITUTION, SO DO EACH OF US PERSONALLY. In its most literal sense, the word "constitution" means the composition of a thing, and when it's used in reference to a human being it usually means that person's physical makeup, as in the phrase "a man with a strong constitution." I'd like to use the word in a broader sense, however, and suggest that all of us have some sort of general constitution. Thinking not just of our bodies but also our characters, all of us have come to have some kind of constitution. If we said, for example, "She's made out of pretty strong stuff," we wouldn't just mean the physical components of that person's body. We'd mean that she had a strong character. So at this point in your life, what kind of constitution do you have? And what kind do I have?

We start out in life with a number of good things going for us. Potentially, we all have the makings of a strong constitution, and I agree with Mencius's statement that our nature "is constituted for the practice of what is good." Along the way, however, most of us have let some less-than-desirable "stuff" get into our constitutions, and not only that, we have failed to develop the good potential that was there all along. So we need to be encouraged to be careful about our constitutions. They need to be cared for, protected, and enhanced.

Even physically, we need to adopt lifestyles that contribute to a stronger, rather than a weaker, constitution. Socrates, for example, said, "A man should inure himself to voluntary labor, and not give up to indulgence and pleasure, as they beget no good constitution of body nor knowledge of mind." There happens to be an intricate relationship between character and physical condition, and we need to nurture both sides of our makeup so that they interact healthily.

When you compare yourself to others, you may think you don't have a very strong constitution. But if you were suddenly thrown into the midst of certain circumstances, you might surprise yourself. All of us are made of stronger stuff than we realize. It pays to be grateful.

By my physical constitution I am but an ordinary man . . . Yet some great events, some cutting expressions, some mean hypocrisies, have at times thrown this assemblage of sloth, sleep, and littleness into rage like a lion.

JOHN ADAMS

FAIRNESS

Fair play is primarily not blaming others
for anything that is wrong with us.
ERIC HOFFER

FAIRNESS CAN'T BE SEPARATED FROM PERSONAL RESPONSI-
BILITY. It would be unfair of me, for example, to blame you for
something that was my responsibility. In fairness, I can't ask you to
accept any more responsibility than is actually yours. And, of course,
the converse is also true: I can't ask you to accept any less responsibility than is yours. Fairness and personal responsibility go hand in hand.

We all prefer to live in nations, communities, and neighborhoods
where justice prevails, but large-scale justice will never prevail in those
areas if ordinary, small-scale fairness doesn't prevail in our everyday
dealings with those around us. "A man who deals in fairness with his
own, he can make manifest justice in the state" (Sophocles). So it's a
helpful exercise to ask ourselves from time to time: if everyone in the
world treated people exactly as I do, what would the world be like?

Out of all the things we might want to be known for, fairness
would be one of the most admirable. Whatever else might come to
people's minds when they think of us, if they think of fairness, that's a
reputation we should be glad to have. In fact, if we ever had to choose
between being loved and being respected (for things like fairness),
being respected would be the better choice. If those who know us can
take it for granted that, come what may, we can be counted on to do
what's fair, then that ought to give us a very good feeling.

In the long run, it's foolish to deal unfairly with anyone. Doing
so is morally wrong, of course, and that ought to be reason enough to
keep us away from it, but the fact remains, unfairness is also foolish.
It doesn't work. Eventually, it always proves to be ineffective. We may
take advantage of somebody today and think we've gotten away with
it, but sooner or later that person will realize that we've been unfair,
and the repercussions at that time will outweigh any short-term benefit we may have received from our injustice. In the matter of fairness,
as in all others, the law of the farm rules. We reap what we sow.

Since nothing is settled until it is settled right,
no matter how unlimited power a man may have,
unless he exercises it fairly and justly his actions
will return to plague him.
FRANK A. VANDERLIP

GODLINESS

The difference between worldliness
and godliness is a renewed mind.
ERWIN W. LUTZER

IF IDEAS HAVE CONSEQUENCES, AND THEY CLEARLY DO, THE MOST CONSEQUENTIAL OF ALL OUR IDEAS IS THE IDEA OF GOD. Once we choose how we're going to deal with this idea, a very different kind of life begins to unfold than any that would have unfolded from any other choice. Nowhere does life ask us any more basic question than when it asks us what we're going to believe about God.

Today, think with me about the concept of "godliness" as a character trait. Let's attempt to set aside our personal preferences and predispositions, and ask what would really be involved in this trait.

(1) Openness to the idea of God. "The finest fruit of serious learning should be the ability to speak the word 'God' without reserve or embarrassment" (Nathan M. Pusey). The godly mind is receptive to the possibility that God may be more real than we've ever thought.

(2) Commitment to the truth about God. 'A' can't be 'A' and 'Not A' at the same time. Either it's true that God is an objective reality or it's not true. If God is, in fact, an objective reality, then rightly understanding the nature of that reality should matter to us greatly.

(3) Adoption of the virtue of godliness. Godliness will certainly show up outwardly, but it's primarily an inward matter, a matter of the heart. Godliness means seeing all worldly things from a godly perspective. It means that God is our basic frame of reference.

Among the people I know, the person who demonstrates the trait of godliness with the greatest integrity is a woman whose "renewed mind" is nothing short of a marvel. Independently and against daunting odds, she has chosen to open herself honestly to the idea of God. She is not only passionate in learning what's true about God, she follows whatever facts she discovers with a you-can-count-on-it dependability almost unheard of in this day of convenience and compromise. Because of her godliness, I trust her . . . I learn from her . . . I love her.

Thy soul was like a star, and dwelt apart;
Thou hadst a voice whose sound was like the sea:
Pure as the naked heavens, majestic, free,
So didst thou travel on life's common way,
In cheerful godliness.
WILLIAM WORDSWORTH

INSTRUCTION

Learn from others what to pursue and what to avoid,
and let your teachers be the lives of others.

DIONYSIUS CATO

IT'S A SIMPLE THING, BUT IT'S VERY HARD TO ADOPT: THE
WILLINGNESS TO BE INSTRUCTED. If any instruction needs to
take place, it's more satisfying to our pride to be the instructor than
the instructee. Most of us would agree that straightening out someone
else is far more comfortable than being straightened out ourselves.

But if we don't adopt the willingness to be instructed, we cut
ourselves off from most of the learnings that can make our lives useful
and enjoyable. "Learn from others what to pursue and what to avoid,"
Dionysius Cato said, and his advice is good. When others try to share
with us the wisdom they've learned from the mistakes they've made,
common sense says that we ought to be "instructable." We need to
learn from the mistakes of others because, as the old saying goes, none
of us is going to live long enough to make them all ourselves.

There certainly are times, however, when our own experience can
be a powerful teacher, and at such times, we need to be just as open to
instruction as we are when someone else is teaching. That's especially
true when our experience is the painful kind. "Those things that hurt,
instruct," said Benjamin Franklin. But too much of the time, pain's
lessons are lost on us, and we have to repeat those lessons later.

If someone pointed out to us how many times a day we're in the
position of either instructing or being instructed, we'd probably be
surprised. The fact is, much of life consists of these two interactions,
and so the more we can learn about what makes a good *instructor* and
a good *instructee,* the more advantage we have in many ways.

When was the last time you willingly let yourself be instructed?
If the honest answer is that it has been a long time, you may be older
than you realize . . . or you may simply have let your *mind* grow old
before its time. We may not want to hear it, but instructability (or the
lack of it) is one prime indicator of how much life we've got left in us!

Every act of conscious learning requires the willingness
to suffer an injury to one's self-esteem. That is why young
children, before they are aware of their own self-importance,
learn so easily; and why older persons, especially if vain
or important, cannot learn at all.

THOMAS S. SZASZ

RECOGNITION

Recognition of the individual affirms respect
for human dignity and the uniqueness of each person.

CHARLES COLSON

IT'S A DELIGHTFUL THING TO BE A PERSON WHO "RECOGNIZES" OTHER PEOPLE. Contrary to the thinking of the chronically competitive, it doesn't take anything away from us to acknowledge others and their accomplishments. We don't lose anything by the recognition of those around us; we gain a great deal — almost as much, in fact, as those whom we recognize. "Appreciation is a wonderful thing: it makes what is excellent in others belong to us as well" (Voltaire).

Basically, recognition means that we "notice" someone, but when we use the word, we usually mean the *favorable* noticing of that person. When we give recognition, we're acknowledging that we're aware of, and we appreciate, the good qualities of another person. And shouldn't it be obvious that that's a good thing to do? As Charles Colson reminds us, recognizing another individual is an affirmation of our "respect for human dignity and the uniqueness of each person."

One of the most universal of human traits is the need to be appreciated. Some individuals, of course, allow that need to become obsessive, and their lives turn out to be no more than a quest for approval and praise. But even the most emotionally healthy among us need some appreciation. We need to know that there's at least someone who recognizes our individuality and our efforts to do good works.

Nowhere is recognition more important than in the marriage relationship. Oliver Goldsmith wasn't overstating the case much when he said, "All that a husband or wife really want is to be pitied a little, praised a little, appreciated a little." It's such an easy, enjoyable thing to honor our mates with recognition, but it's often neglected.

Yet whether in marriage or in other relationships, few things are more *motivating* than recognition. When specific praise is given to someone in a way that is thoughtfully appropriate to them personally, great good comes from that, almost without exception. So let's recognize one another. Let's do it thoughtfully. And let's do it regularly!

If you want people to understand that you value their contributions
and that they are important, the recognition and praise you provide
must have meaning that is specific to each individual.

TOM RATH

RESPECT

When I approach a child, he inspires in me two sentiments:
tenderness for what he is, and respect for what he may become.

LOUIS PASTEUR

NONE OF US HAS EVER MET A HUMAN BEING WHO DIDN'T DE-
SERVE SOME RESPECT. Faults and foolish decisions shouldn't be
respected, of course, and evil character can't be condoned. But our desire should be to give as much respect as we can. In the case of almost
everybody, what they are, even right now, should be met with some
"tenderness," and when we consider what they may become, "respect"
is not too strong a word to describe what we should feel for them.

Respect means showing regard for and esteeming others. To respect
other people is to hold them in honor and to treat them accordingly.
As C. S. Lewis liked to say, there is no such thing as an "ordinary"
human being. No human being ever existed who didn't have unimag-
inably glorious possibilities, and that fact ought to elicit our respect.

Respect means not violating or interfering with others. Whatever
closeness may develop between human beings, it's still true that individuals have boundaries that need to be respected. Respect means not
violating another person's privacy or interfering with their free will.

There will be occasions when we're not sure how much respect
to extend to a particular person. There's no denying that the offering of respect requires wisdom and good judgment. But if we err,
wouldn't it be better to err on the side of extending too much respect
rather than too little? In the grand scheme of things, it does much less
harm to respect a person more than he or she deserves than it does to
withhold respect that is due. Indeed, most of us know from our own
experience that having someone love us, trust us, and respect us more
than we know we deserve is a powerfully motivating thing. It makes
us want to rise to meet the expectations of those who respect us.

We probably underestimate how much depends upon respect in
our relationships with others. It's valuable in every relationship, and
absolutely essential in some. And it's exceedingly hard to replace if it's
ever lost. So we dare not take it for granted. We dare not act in ways
that make respect more difficult, either for us or for those around us.

He removes the greatest ornament of friendship
who takes away from it respect.

CICERO

COMFORT

Let me come in where you are weeping, friend,
And let me take your hand.

GRACE NOLL CROWELL

L IFE IS HARD, AND IF WE HAVE THE EYES TO SEE, WE SEE ALL AROUND US PEOPLE NEEDING COMFORT. The sources of discomfort are as numerous and varied as the people who're hurting, but the end result is much the same: *people need comfort*. Considering the vastness of the need, it may be discouraging to think how little difference for good any of us can make in alleviating the suffering that's in the world. But the vastness of the need may not be the thing we need to concentrate on. Wouldn't it be better to concentrate on those few individuals whom we *can* comfort? In their lives, at least, we can make a difference, and they deserve that we give it our best effort.

Grief. Many of those who need our comfort are those who're grieving the loss of something valuable to them. Whether it's a loved one they've lost, or something else (such as a relationship, a hope, or a dream), it hurts to lose things. Grieving people need our comfort.

Hardship. If there are sorrowful things in the world, there are also difficult things that have to be dealt with. And while the need for comfort during hardship may not be as poignant as the same need during grief, it's no less real. Struggling people need our comfort.

Fear. When people don't know what's going to happen, but they suspect that it's not going to be good, fear is the emotion that results. And fear, in its many forms, can be one of life's most debilitating, dehumanizing experiences. Frightened people need our comfort.

Our word "comfort" comes from the same root as the word "fortify." Its literal meaning is "to strengthen." I believe it does us good to recognize the strengthening, fortifying power of comfort. To comfort someone is a truly remarkable thing. When we comfort, we often do no less than pull the comforted one back from the brink of despair, or even of death. It's a doable thing, and we need to do it more often.

Those who can sit in silence with their fellowman, not knowing
what to say but knowing that they should be there, can bring new life
in a dying heart. Those who are not afraid to hold a hand in gratitude,
to shed tears in grief, and to let a sigh of distress arise straight from
the heart can break through paralyzing boundaries and witness
the birth of a new fellowship, the fellowship of the broken.

HENRI J. M. NOUWEN

April 13

AFFIRMATION

Speak the affirmative.

RALPH WALDO EMERSON

TO AFFIRM SOMETHING IS TO SAY "YES!" TO IT. The opposite of a denial, in which we state what we don't believe, an affirmation is a positive, firm declaration of what we do believe. When we affirm things, we maintain that they're true. And I want to "affirm" that maintaining what we believe is something we should do more often than refuting what we don't believe. In debating terms, we should find ourselves more often in the affirmative than in the negative.

Affirmation is constructive, while negation is reactionary. When we're denying things, we're reacting against a position that someone else has taken, and to a certain extent, that means that we're merely responding to someone else's agenda. It's much more proactive to affirm things that we ourselves believe are worthy of belief.

Certainly, some negation is necessary in life. Only a very naive person would think otherwise. But every moment we spend having to deny falsehoods is a moment lost from the more important work of building up the positive contribution that we want to make in the world. Like some household chores, negation is work that occasionally has to be tended to, but those with an affirmative outlook on life will always be eager to get back to the business of saying "Yes!"

There are at least two things that we should want to affirm as often as we can. In the realm of ideas, we should take delight in affirming things that are *true*. And in the realm of personal relationships, we should take delight in affirming things that are *positive*. Whatever falsehoods need to be refuted, it should bring us great pleasure to declare *truthful concepts* and *admirable qualities in others*.

When we engage in the act of affirmation, we are saying "Yes!" to life and all the good things that are in it. And even in a broken, imperfect world, there are still many such things that should claim our attention. Yes, there are some things in life to be against, but the things that we can be for are far greater. Let's not fail to affirm them!

Affirmation of life is the spiritual act by which man
ceases to live unreflectively and begins to devote himself
to his life with reverence in order to raise it to its true value.
To affirm life is to deepen, to make more inward,
and to exalt the will to live.

ALBERT SCHWEITZER

April 14
RELAXATION

You will break the bow if you keep it always bent.
GREEK PROVERB

IN A WORLD WHERE "MANAGING MULTIPLE PRIORITIES" HAS BECOME A SURVIVAL SKILL, WE FIND OURSELVES CEASELESSLY BUSY. Rarely do we relax, and even when we do, we book a time slot for it in our day planners, as if relaxation were simply another item to check off on our agendas. Plainly, we are a driven people. But what is it that drives us? Whatever it is (and truthfully, there are dozens of different possibilities), we need to be exceedingly careful these days. Unrelieved activity will kill us. The bow will break if it's always bent.

Is it productivity that we're concerned about? There are doubtless many good things to be doing nowadays, but those who know the most about real productivity understand the need for adequate downtime. Relaxation doesn't take away from our productivity; it adds to it. Winston Churchill said, "I found I could add nearly two hours to my working day by going to bed for an hour after luncheon."

Do we feel guilty when we're doing nothing? I remember a conversation years ago with the girl who ended up graduating with the highest academic average in our college class of several thousand. She had dropped by my apartment one afternoon, and greeted me with the usual, "Hi, whatcha doing?" When I said, "Nothing," she was aghast! "Don't you feel guilty?" she said. "Not at all," I replied, and I went on to introduce her to the concept of "creative inactivity." I believed then, and I still believe today, that we need to get over the idea that relaxing by doing nothing is morally wrong. Having worked, we need to relax!

It's certainly true that doing something *different* is often the best way to relax. Anatole France went so far as to say, "Man is so made that he can only find relaxation from one kind of labor by taking up another." I'm not sure we can only find relaxation by taking up another kind of labor, but even so, France's general point is well taken.

I'm still confident, however, that there are times when it's not only not wrong to do nothing, but nothing's the most beneficial thing that we can do. And if we can't ever — at any time, under any circumstance — bring ourselves to do that, we need to ask ourselves, "*Why?*"

He does not seem to me to be a free man
who does not sometimes do nothing.
CICERO

LAWFULNESS

The law is the last result of human wisdom acting
upon human experience for the benefit of the public.
SAMUEL JOHNSON

IF WE EVER GOT TO THE POINT WHERE WE THOUGHT OF "LAW"
AS A TOTALLY NEGATIVE WORD, THAT WOULD BE UNFORTU-
NATE. The fact is, "law" is not a bad word. We need to rehabilitate the
idea behind it and think of the entire subject more appreciatively.

The principle of law can be abused, of course, and when it comes
to specific laws, there will always be some that need to be repealed.
But as a basic concept, law ought not to be despised. All things
considered, it's good to have laws. We're better off with them than
without them, even when keeping them is inconvenient or expensive.

Sometimes we ask too much of law. Forgetting that the purpose
of law is limited, we try to make it do things it can't do. Disappointed
with the results, we then become cynical about the value of law.
Yet we're too quick to be critical. Martin Luther King Jr. was right:
"Morality cannot be legislated, but behavior can be regulated. Judicial
decrees may not change the heart, but they can restrain the heartless." Law can't be the only tool we use to build a good society, but it's
certainly one tool, and it's foolish to try to do without its help.

People who have made lawfulness a part of their character are a
pleasure to work with and to live next door to and to be friends with.
A willingness to be bound by the rules makes a person dependable. We
tend to trust those who can be counted on to honor the law's restraints;
with them, the possibility of unpleasant surprises is much less fearful.

So if we appreciate this trait in others, we need to adopt it ourselves. We need to steer clear of the arrogance and unpredictability
of lawlessness and develop a genuine appreciation for legal limits.
As noted above, those aren't the only limits we need, but all of us do
need them to some extent, and we ought to appreciate them as far as
they go. In one way or another, most of us would like the world to be
"a better place." The rule of law can help bring about that result, but
we'll enjoy little of its benefit if we ourselves don't obey the law.

I sometimes wish that people would put a little
more emphasis upon the observance of the law
than they do upon its enforcement.
CALVIN COOLIDGE

GOODWILL

People don't care how much you know
until they know how much you care.

ANONYMOUS

IT TAKES A PERSON OF UNUSUAL HONESTY TO CONFRONT THE QUESTION OF GOODWILL. It's easy to say we care about people and that we have goodwill toward all, but it's a rare person who can say those things and not be twisting the truth. Aren't there a few individuals whom it would give us some secret pleasure to see hurt? Not a lot, of course, just a little bit . . . just to give them a taste of their own medicine . . . just to see that justice is done. It would, after all, be "for their own good," wouldn't it? Because we "care" about them.

The unvarnished truth is this: most of us ordinary folks have at least a trace of *malevolence* ("ill will") in us. Where there should be *benevolence* ("good will"), there is too often a residue of spite or vindictiveness. We say we "don't mean anybody any harm," but we harbor the thought that harm is exactly what some people have got coming to them — and it wouldn't hurt our feelings much to see them get it.

It's my considered opinion, however, that ill will is not a way of thinking that's natural to us. It's a perversion, a warping of our better instincts. I agree with Václav Havel, who said, "Time and time again I have been persuaded that a huge potential of goodwill is slumbering within our society. It's just that it's incoherent, suppressed, confused, crippled, and perplexed." So we need to be honest about it when we see that our goodwill has been "suppressed, confused, etc.," and be relentless in rooting these interferences out of our hearts.

Whether our will toward others is good or ill, will is something we can change. If we've gotten into the habit of thinking hurtful thoughts about others, it may take some practice, but we can change our "ill will" into "good will." We can determine to be benevolent.

But as we work on our goodwill, let's make it better by making it more specific. Generic goodwill toward the human race is of relatively little use. What we need is an active, practical, small-scale goodwill toward those whom we actually have to deal with every day!

You cannot add to the peace and goodwill
of the world if you fail to create an atmosphere of harmony
and love right where you live and work.

THOMAS DREIER

April 17

PROGRESS

Were it not for the nonconformist, he who refuses to be satisfied
to go along with the continuance of things as they are and insists upon
attempting to find new ways of bettering things, the world
would have known little progress indeed.

JOSIAH WILLIAM GITT

COMMITTING OURSELVES TO CONSTANT PROGRESS IS ONE OF THE BEST GIFTS THAT WE CAN GIVE TO THOSE WHOM WE LOVE. Right now, not a one of us is everything we ought to be, and our loved ones suffer, to some extent, from our shortcomings. They would be delighted to see day-to-day evidence that we're making progress in becoming the persons that we're capable of being. But not only that, they'd be delighted to see evidence of a commitment on our part to make everything we touch at least a little better, if we possibly can.

A commitment to progress involves a certain amount of risk, however. It will probably make us somewhat of a nonconformist. As Josiah William Gitt notes, little progress would have been made in the world up to now if it weren't for that out-of-step fellow who "refuses to be satisfied to go along with the continuance of things as they are and insists upon attempting to find new ways of bettering things." If all we want is comfort and familiarity, progress will probably not be the result of our efforts. "Progress always involves risks. You can't steal second base and keep your foot on first" (Frederick B. Wilcox).

When it comes to something better than the status quo, most of us could do with a little more *desire*. Things don't usually get better, at least significantly better, unless someone really wants them to, and so we need to lose our fear of words like *aspiration* and *passion*. In a healthy sense, we need to be discontent with the progress that has already been made — and *eager* for the progress that's still ahead.

Whether the need for improvement is in our inward character or the outward things we deal with, a commitment to progress is an act of both faith and hope. In defiance of those who say, "It's no use," we must trust what we know about the possibility of progress. Going forward isn't easy, and setbacks are sure to be suffered along the way, but faith and hope say, "What *needs* to be improved, *can* be improved."

Progress begins with the belief
that what is necessary is possible.

NORMAN COUSINS

UNITY

There can be no unity, no delight of love,
no harmony, no good in being, while there is but one.
Two at least are needed for oneness.

GEORGE MACDONALD

OUR CONCEPT OF UNITY IS OFTEN QUITE SUPERFICIAL. We tend to equate unity with identity or sameness. We envision "oneness" as an environment where everybody walks, talks, and even thinks alike. But real unity, that is, unity between or among *persons*, is never that bland. Clones might do some things, but clones can't enjoy unity. "Two at least are needed for oneness," as MacDonald says.

The first thing we need to see about unity is *the power for good that comes from being unified.* It's nothing short of astonishing to behold the potency of ordinary people who stand together. As Homer remarked in the *Iliad,* "Not vain the weakest, if their force unite."

But the second thing we need to see is *the seriousness of the consequences of disunity.* When Ben Franklin, at the signing of the Declaration of Independence, reminded his fellow signers, "We must all hang together, or most assuredly, we shall all hang separately," he spoke a more universal truth than he may have realized. There are, in fact, many ways to "hang separately" in the world, and many of them are the sad result of people not having the sense to "hang together."

But unity, whether in families, neighborhoods, or nations at large, is not the instantaneous product of a moment of enlightenment; it's a goal that we gradually, and sometimes painfully, work our way toward. It's the fruit of honest commitment and long-term investment.

In any relationship where we don't presently have the unity that we'd like to enjoy, the answer is not merely to try harder (although most of the time we certainly need to do that). We must change not only the quantity of our effort but the quality of our thinking. Our perspective must be altered, preferably by being elevated, so that we can see how things look "from the balcony." And before we blame all of the alienation on the other people in the relationship, let's stop to remember that, as somebody said, "it takes two to tangle." It's not just the other people's thinking that needs adjusting. Our own does too.

We can find common ground
only by moving to higher ground.

JIM WALLIS

April 19

FRANKNESS

The Macedonians . . . had not the wit
to call a spade by any other name than a spade.

DESIDERIUS ERASMUS

FRANKNESS IS OFTEN A VIRTUE, BUT IT'S ONE THAT CAN EAS-
ILY BE PERVERTED. When it's important that clear communication takes place, plain speaking is to be preferred over any other kind,
and Benjamin Disraeli was right when he said, "There is no wisdom
like frankness." But how many of us have this wisdom? How many of
us have the skill to speak candidly and straightforwardly without losing control of our words and speaking rudely, or even cruelly?

Like many other similar traits, frankness is only good if certain
conditions are met, and in this case, the first condition that must be
met is *truth*. Anytime anything less than truth is being communicated, then frankness loses a bit of its luster, to say the least.

But a second condition that must be met is *kindness*. Confucius
said, "Straightforwardness, without the rules of propriety, becomes
rudeness." The courage that drives us to be candid must be balanced
with the kindness that makes us courteous. We should speak frankly,
yes, but we should also be considerate of those who have to listen to
our communications. We need to be strong enough to be tactful.

It's one of the commonest things in the world for unkindness
to be excused as mere candor. Tennessee Williams said, "All cruel
people describe themselves as paragons of frankness." And Marshall
McLuhan echoed that thought when he said, "It is the weak and confused who worship the pseudo-simplicities of brutal directness."

So we need to check not only our techniques but also our motives
— honestly and without self-deception — when we speak frankly. It
may sound like an overstatement, but I believe it's true: *love is the only
healthy reason for telling the truth*. Frankness will only be commendable
in us when we use it to convey truth with charity and good judgment.

But finally, what about those times when we are the recipients of
someone else's frankness? What if they speak rudely and with a lack
of love? Well, in that case, as long as what we're hearing is truth, we
need to profit from it, regardless of the source or the delivery method!

An enemy who tells the truth contributes infinitely more
to our improvement than a friend who deludes us.

LOUIS FORTIN

DESIGN

> . . . He stops upon this threshold
> As if the design of all his words takes form
> And frame from his thinking and is realized.
>
> WALLACE STEVENS

HAVE YOU CONSIDERED HOW MUCH OF THE QUALITY OF YOUR LIFE DEPENDS ON YOUR "DESIGNS"? Think for a moment about the meaning of the word. Apart from its more common use, "design" can mean "a reasoned purpose, an intention." It's often used in a negative sense ("He has designs on his neighbor's wife"), but it can also be used positively. Our designs are our intentions with regard to the future, and, as I say, much that is important to us depends on these designs. High-quality lives don't come from inferior designs.

What happens outwardly in our lives is the manifestation of what is going on inwardly. Just as a house is the manifestation of what was on the blueprint from which it was made, which in turn was the manifestation of a design in the mind of the architect, our lives are the outworkings of our inward values and goals. If we're unhappy with what has been manifested in our lives, we can always change our designs, and when we do, other things will begin to be manifested.

We owe it to those around us, especially our loved ones, to be more purposeful in our designs. Those who've entrusted themselves to us in friendship and love need to know that we've carefully considered the alternatives and made wise choices in our designs. Haphazard living doesn't just hurt us; it hurts others too. So we need to be careful.

Ultimately, our designs will turn out to be useless if they run counter to the principles of goodness and honor. We can't operate from selfish or destructive intentions and expect our outward lives to be blessed by abundant joy and satisfaction. We do not live unto ourselves alone, and the laws of human behavior and interaction can't be ignored with impunity. Our designs — that is, what we plan to be and do — must harmonize with the good of those around us, and even with the overarching purposes of the whole creation of which we're a part. If they don't, our designs are doomed to be inconsequential.

> Direct, control, suggest, this day,
> All I design, or do, or say,
> That all my powers with all their might,
> In Thy sole glory may unite.
>
> THOMAS KEN

April 21

COLLABORATION

Collaborating in the very private way of love
or the highest kind of friendship . . .

ELIZABETH HARDWICK

O
NE OF THE MOST DELIGHTFUL THINGS ABOUT INTIMACY IS
THE COLLABORATION THAT IT MAKES POSSIBLE. When individuals draw close to one another, they not only enjoy *being* together,
but they enjoy *working* together. Good work is pleasurable enough on
its own, but it's even more pleasurable when it's the result of collaboration. Laboring with congenial coworkers is one of life's real treats.

Not everyone, however, is equally good at collaboration. There
are lots of people who can *operate*, but they can't seem to *co-operate!*
Collaboration is, in fact, a higher skill. It takes a stronger, wiser person
to participate productively in joint undertakings and collective efforts.

Yet when a group is made up of those who know how to collaborate, the "synergy" that results multiplies the effect of the work exponentially. Working in the spirit of true collaboration, two people can
produce far more than twice what either of them could do alone. And
not only that, there's a good chance their combined work will be more
valuable than it would have been as the solo project of either one.

Some types of work are more suitable for collaboration than
others, of course. The *Mona Lisa,* for example, could not have been
produced by a committee. Yet even in the realm of artistic endeavor,
teams of workers are often helpful, and even essential. When was the
last time you heard the director of a great movie win an Oscar and not
have a list of people to thank? The fact is, very few works of any kind
are able to be completed in the real world without collaboration.

I believe that most of us want to collaborate. Some of us may
work a bit better on our own than we do with other people, and some
of our projects may require less help than other projects do. But deep
down, we're social creatures who thrive on togetherness. We experience a fundamental satisfaction when we collaborate. And I believe
we enjoy the "together" aspect of work because we realize we're connected to a reality that's bigger than any of our individual works.

A democratic society presupposes confidence and candor in the relations of
men with one another and eager collaboration for the larger ends of life
instead of the pursuit of petty, selfish, or vainglorious aims.

FELIX FRANKFURTER

April 22

METHODICALNESS

You know my methods, Watson.

SIR ARTHUR CONAN DOYLE

WE MAY NOT CARE TO BECOME AS METHODICAL AS
SHERLOCK HOLMES, BUT MOST OF US COULD STAND TO
BE A BIT MORE METHODICAL THAN WE ARE. Especially when dealing with the more important matters in life, we need to have trained
ourselves how to proceed in a careful, orderly manner. In most of the
more significant areas of life, there is just no way around the fact that
being somewhat methodical is conducive to getting better results.

Ralph Waldo Emerson observed, "There is always a best way of
doing everything, even if it be to boil an egg." But the best way to do
something isn't always apparent to the casual observer, and so if being
methodical helps us to find the best way, then the more important the
activity is, the bigger the benefit we get from being methodical.

But while there's some virtue in being methodical ourselves,
there's a danger in being too judgmental of other people's methods.
None of us likes to be micromanaged ("directed or controlled in a de-
tailed, and often meddlesome, manner"), and when someone has been
given a job to do, we're wise to let them choose their own methods for
getting the desired result. Each of us works in a somewhat different
way, and what may seem like a foolish lack of method to us may turn
out to be more methodical than we thought. Shakespeare's line may
be appropriate: "Though this be madness, yet there is method in't."

All of those who have to deal with us from day to day deserve
the very best that we can give them. And if being at least a little more
methodical would help us give them our best, then that's a trait we'd
do well to adopt. This is true, especially, of heads of households, it
seems to me. Who wants to live in a household where the head of it is
totally chaotic, never knowing what's going on or what comes next?

The human mind is an amazingly ingenious instrument. It can
not only see what *needs* to be done; it can figure out a method by
which it *can* be done. We need to appreciate the creativity and me-
thodicalness of our minds and use these qualities carefully. If "madness" is the norm for us, we might try introducing a little "method."

While Honey lies in Every Flower, no doubt,
It takes a Bee to get the Honey out.

ARTHUR GUITERMAN

RECREATION

People who cannot find time for recreation
are obliged sooner or later to find time for illness.
JOHN WANAMAKER

WITHOUT SUFFICIENT "RECREATION" OF THE RIGHT KIND, WE EXHAUST OUR ABILITY TO SERVE AND CONTRIBUTE TO OTHERS. It's a fine thing to want to give ourselves to good works that benefit those around us, but we don't have an infinite supply of energy and motivation. These things have to be replenished on a fairly regular basis, and if we don't take care of that, we sicken and die.

Perhaps it would help us to consider the meaning of "recreation." As the spelling of the word indicates, recreation is a *re-creation* of ourselves. When we've been used up, recreation is that which "makes us over again." It rejuvenates us, sending us back to our work refreshed.

But although the above sounds simple, it involves a sobering thought. So much that passes for recreation these days is anything but refreshing. Sometimes, we pursue it with such a frenzied obsession that it leaves us more drained than when we began. But quite frankly, even in moderation, some of the things we call recreation today are destructive. They drag us through the sewer of human experience and leave us, not uplifted and invigorated, but diminished and degraded.

Thoughtful observers have long argued that there's a link between recreation and character, both on the individual level and that of society, and I, for one, agree with the statement of Lin Yutang: "We do not know a nation until we know its pleasures of life, just as we do not know a man until we know how he spends his leisure. It is when a man ceases to do the things he has to do and does the things he likes to do, that the character is revealed. It is when the repressions of society and business are gone and when the goads of money and fame and ambition are lifted, that we see the inner man, his real self."

The irony is that we defend our recreational imbalances as an effort to "enrich" our experience in the world. Yet enrichment takes place only up to a certain point, after which the law of diminishing returns sets in. Whether it's unrelieved work or unworthy recreation, what we get back is not enrichment — it's impoverishment.

A poor life this if, full of care,
we have no time to stand and stare.
WILLIAM HENRY DAVIES

PRAISE

The acknowledgment of effort has to be tailor-made. People pick up on
canned compliments, especially if they hear the same things being said to
other people. Nothing is more effective than sincere, accurate praise, and
nothing is more lame than a cookie-cutter compliment.

BILL WALSH

PRAISE IS POTENT. It's productive. It makes a difference for good.
And while it's true that our words to others must take the form of
criticism now and then, when it comes to sheer power, criticism is no
match for praise. "Praise can give criticism a lead around the first turn
and still win the race" (Bern Williams). And yet, as Bill Walsh's comment reminds us, if praise is to be of any benefit, it must meet certain
criteria. Our praise of others must be "tailor-made" for them.

Specific. When was the last time you felt really encouraged by a
compliment that you knew the giver had handed out to four other
people in the room in the exact same words in the last ten minutes?

Accurate. When was the last time you felt really encouraged by a
compliment that you knew, and maybe the giver knew, was false? If
you're a liar, does it make you feel good to be praised for honesty?

Sincere. When was the last time you felt really encouraged by a
compliment that you knew was an attempt to butter you up by somebody trying to get on your good side? To be of benefit, praise must not
be a "technique." It must truly be "about" the recipient, not the giver.

When the power of praise is being discussed, however, it never
fails that some individuals will say this: "Well, yes, I know that praise
in general is powerful, but personally, I don't matter enough to anybody that my praise would make any difference." But if we think that,
we need to think again. Even if there was not a single human being
who knew us enough to want to hear our praise in particular (and
the truth is, most of us have far more than one or two such people),
we ought not to underestimate the good that can be done by prais-
ing those with whom we have no special relationship. Even with total
strangers, "random acts of praise" can be truly remarkable, both for the
recipient and the giver. Just try it and see. Find something that you
can *specifically, accurately,* and *sincerely* praise about the next person
you meet in public today, and see what happens. It'll be good!

The applause of a single human being is of great consequence.

SAMUEL JOHNSON

April 25
INTROSPECTION

If we hope to move beyond the superficialities
of our culture — including our religious culture — we must
be willing to go down into the recreating silences,
into the inner world of contemplation.

RICHARD J. FOSTER

MANY OF US SUFFER FROM AN INSUFFICIENT AMOUNT OF SELF-EXAMINATION. We don't engage in "introspection" often enough; that is, we don't "look within" ourselves — or if we do, we don't consider very carefully what we see there. It's an amazing fact, actually, that we can not only think, but we can think about our thinking. We can stand at a distance and observe our own thought processes. And that's a wonderful ability which we ought to use more often. So today, let's turn our thoughts inward and "introspect."

Paying attention. The first way we can be introspective is simply to pay attention to what we're thinking. That sounds simple and it is, but we don't often do it. We plow through our daily agendas so furiously that our thoughts run here and there without our giving them any more than passing notice. And as a result, all manner of unhelpful and unworthy "stuff" sneaks in and takes up residence in our minds.

Listening. It's a rare moment that we're not talking, either verbally to someone else or inwardly to ourselves. But great good comes from learning how to turn off the chatter and just listen. In particular, we need to listen to our consciences. Often, our consciences have crucial things to say to us, but we can't hear them because there's too much noise. We desperately need to acquire the habit of listening.

Correcting. Paying attention to our thoughts and feelings, and even listening to our conscience, is not enough, however, if we don't make the corrections in our thinking that these exercises indicate need to be made. One of our greatest endowments is the freedom that we have to make deliberate adjustments in the way we think. This freedom is a marvelous gift, and we ought not to waste it or lose its benefit.

In truth, there's no substitute for introspection. Without it, we're lost. And mark it well: if we're not examining ourselves inwardly, being busy is no excuse. That just means we need to do it all the more.

Half an hour's listening is essential except
when you are busy. Then a full hour is needed.

FRANCIS DE SALES

April 26
ABSTINENCE

Discipline is the basic set of tools
we require to solve life's problems.
M. SCOTT PECK

SOMETIMES IT IS BOTH WISE AND BENEFICIAL TO SAY NO. Not everything we might have the urge to do can be done with honor, and when a deed can't be done honorably, those who know how to abstain enjoy a distinct advantage over those who don't.

In most people's minds, abstinence is what prudish people practice when they refrain from sexual activity or the consumption of alcohol. Certainly those who choose to be temperate in these areas are being abstinent (and there might be many reasons for doing so, some better than others), but these are only two examples of abstinence. Abstinence means the all-around ability to discipline ourselves and subordinate our urges and appetites to the priority of our principles. We need to get beyond the mocking, condescending stereotype that some folks have of this concept. It involves a good deal more than prudishness, and it's a much stronger and more valuable practice than many people seem willing to admit. Without the ability to abstain, we're hopelessly adrift on the sea of life, at the mercy of whichever hormonal wind happens to be blowing at the moment.

Not only will there be things that we ought to say no to as a matter of principle, there are at least two other times when we might consider abstinence. One is when we're faced with a choice between good, better, and best. There is nothing silly or uptight about abstaining from one course of action because we want to pursue a path that's relatively higher. That's where *excellence* comes from! But the second is when we abstain from something simply to exercise our self-discipline muscles. Just as it's a good idea now and then to do something we don't want to do — simply to stay in practice — it's a healthy exercise once in a while to abstain from something we really want to do.

Our emotions and our appetites are good things. They can serve us well and contribute to the quality of our lives. But these things don't serve us well unless they've been *trained* to do so. Much that is good about life in this world depends upon freedom, and there is no freer person than the one who has learned how to use the word "no."

Rule your mind or it will rule you.
HORACE

THRIFT

Men are divided between those who are as thrifty
as if they would live forever, and those who are as extravagant
as if they were going to die the next day.

ARISTOTLE

TO BE "THRIFTY" IS TO "THRIVE." In fact, the two words come
from the same root. Thrifty is what we must be if we ever hope
to thrive, and in a sense, thriving may be defined as the quality of life
that we, in fact, enjoy when we're thrifty. The word "thrifty" has to
do with the careful management of money, time, and other resources,
and it specifically denotes the person who is industrious, saving, and
otherwise diligent in conserving the means at his disposal.

As Aristotle remarked, we tend to go to extremes in the matter of
thrift: either we're obsessed with it and turn ourselves into misers, or
we're careless about it and spend our resources without any conservation at all. When the question is whether to spend or to save, balance
is hard to achieve, as it is in most things. But we can at least improve
our balance in this area, and to that end, here are two basic ideas:

(1) Economy. Thrift comes down to the question of managing
the raw materials that we have to work with in life. If we're not good
stewards of these resources, we won't be able to do as much good with
them as we otherwise would. So we need to be economical: in other
words, we need to learn self-denial and restraint, we need to avoid
waste, and we need to practice the principles of wise conservation.

(2) Wise economy. As good as it is, economy is not the ultimate
good in life, however, and so we need to strive for *wise* economy. If we
don't, our thriftiness will actually result in a diminishing of the good
that we're capable of doing. Especially in the matter of love, our primary concern ought not to be conservation. Love is often extravagant,
and expressions of love shouldn't be rationed out as if they were in
limited supply. Love takes great delight in spending and being spent!

The essence of thrift, then, is the wise conservation of resources.
Concerned about more than the selfish desires of the present moment, thrift takes thought for the needs of others, both now and later
on. Thrift's primary motive is to do as much good as it can today —
and if possible, it wants to do even more good tomorrow.

It is thrifty to prepare today for the wants of tomorrow.

AESOP

AMENDS

Little said is soon amended.

MIGUEL DE CERVANTES

THE ONLY WAY TO AVOID HAVING TO MAKE AMENDS IS TO DO NOTHING. If we're actively involved with life, doing our best to do as we should, we're going to make some mistakes, and when we do, amends will have to be made. Looking at it one way, the less we say and do, the fewer apologies we'll have to make. "Little said is soon amended," as Cervantes said, and there is definitely some wisdom in that. But on the other hand, life is about more than the negative avoidance of mistakes; in a larger sense, it's about the positive use of our abilities to accomplish as many good results as we can. We can't give up or stop trying. Making amends is just one of life's necessities.

In its most basic sense, to make amends is to "mend" a situation that has been "broken" by an error that we've committed. And, of course, to "mend" something is to "repair" it. Thus the *American Heritage Dictionary* defines "amends" as "reparation or payment made as satisfaction for insult or injury." So when we make amends, we "repair" what we've damaged, making "reparation" for our wrongdoing.

To make amends honorably, we must do a good bit more than offer an apology, though that's the obvious starting point. Even at the level of apology, we must do more than express regret that someone's been hurt. We must (a) acknowledge the *wrongfulness* of what we've done, (b) commit ourselves to *change* (that is, promise that we would never do the same thing again, even in the same circumstances), and then (c) make *restitution* for the damage done, to whatever extent that may be possible. Obviously, many wrongs do damage for which no perfect restitution can be made, but we should never fail to try. If we've gotten out of the blaming mode and into the amendment mode, the question we'll always ask is, *"What can I do to make it up to you?"*

Making amends is one of the most difficult things in life, but it's also one of the most important. If we can't do it eagerly, we can at least do it willingly. And just as important, the making of amends is something we should do regularly. Timely amendments are a part of the maintenance that keeps our relationships working. If we value these relationships, we'll spare no effort to fix them when they break.

Keep your friendships in repair.

RALPH WALDO EMERSON

SOURCES

If there is but little water in the stream,
it is the fault, not of the channel, but of the source.

JEROME

OUR "SOURCES" ARE THE SINGLE MOST IMPORTANT DETER-
MINANT OF OUR LIVES. Whether we like the quality of life that
we have right now or not, the quality of our lives is no mere coincidence; it's the result of a sequence of things that can be traced back to
certain sources. And if there's anything about our lives that we'd like
to change, going all the way back up the line and reexamining our
sources is the most productive, and responsible, thing we can do.

Although it's true that external circumstances have a bearing on
our happiness, our real quality of life is produced, not by our circumstances, but by our character. To whatever extent circumstances hurt
us or help us, character hurts us or helps us even more. But our individual characters didn't just happen to us; they've come, as we've said,
from certain sources. Consider three of the most important of these:

Principles. Our principles are the ultimate sources from which
our characters flow. Consider, for example, this principle: "All human
beings are answerable to an objective moral law that rules the universe." It makes a gigantic difference whether that principle is true or
false. Surely all would agree that it's important to decide whether or
not a principle like that would make a good source for our thinking.

Values. Our values are the things we appreciate more than others,
and here again, our decisions are important. For example, which do
we like more: beauty or ugliness? Which would make a better source?

Goals. Our principles and our values usually produce some goals
that we want to reach. Good lives can't come from any source other
than good goals. So it's vital that we select goals of the highest quality.

Whatever the sources of our individual characters are, it is to
be hoped that we've chosen these sources carefully. If we have, then
these are sources, no doubt, that we believe are good. And if that's
true, then we need to value our sources and honor them. Above all, we
need to live with consistent *integrity* to our sources — so that the excellence of "where we're coming from" will radiate to those around us.

... showing them a light that is so lovely
that they want with all their hearts to know the source of it.

MADELEINE L'ENGLE

PERSUASIVENESS

The persuasion of a friend is a strong thing.
HOMER

PERSUASION IS AN ACTIVITY THAT WE ENGAGE IN MORE OFTEN THAN WE MIGHT THINK. Indeed, much of what we do on an average day consists of persuasion in one form or another. Anytime we say or do anything to try to influence someone else's thinking or acting, we're engaging in persuasion. When a politician makes a campaign speech or a salesman makes a sales presentation, they're obviously trying to persuade, but so is the schoolboy who's trying to get a pretty little girl to "like" him. In truth, there's not much we do that doesn't involve at least some element of persuasion.

Most of us have far more influence than we think we do. We persuade others sometimes without even realizing that we're doing so. And since our influence can have far-reaching consequences, we ought to give some careful thought to the matter of our persuasion.

If we want to influence others, I believe the single thing that adds the most to our persuasiveness is this: *we must be honestly and deeply persuaded ourselves.* Cicero, the great Roman orator, said, "There is no better way to convince others than first to convince oneself." It's a waste of time to try to persuade someone else to a belief that we ourselves accept only halfheartedly. Passion is what persuades!

But close behind our convictions is our character. Even if our convictions are passionately held, if our character is out of sync with those convictions, our hypocrisy will be evident and people won't be persuaded. What we are speaks every bit as loudly as what we say.

There are all kinds of ways to persuade people, some of which, unfortunately, play upon motives that are less than honorable. It may be tempting to use whatever works, but I believe most of us would rather appeal to the highest and best instincts within those around us. "We must approach them on their noble side," as Henri Amiel said.

When it comes to persuasion, perhaps it's best to concentrate on quality rather than quantity. Both in the content of our persuasion and the methods that we use, let's not fritter away our influence on trivia. To persuade someone to another viewpoint is a serious thing. We need to pick our battles wisely. And when we persuade, let's *persuade!*

One thought driven home is better than three left on base.
JAMES LITER

REMINDERS

The older we grow, the more we find things hard to forget
and the less we find things easy to remember.

ANONYMOUS

OF ALL THE AMAZING THINGS ABOUT OUR MEMORIES, ONE OF THE MOST AMAZING IS THEIR SELECTIVITY. Some things we remember, but others — indeed, most others — we forget. Who has ever been able to explain the difference? As Oliver Wendell Holmes observed, "Memory is a net; one finds it full of fish when he takes it from a brook; but a dozen miles of water have run through it without sticking." But although so many things will inevitably be forgotten, there are some things so important that we dare not forget them. And for that reason, reminders are an essential part of life.

But why is it so important to remember some things? Well, give some thought to this statement by Michel de Montaigne: "Memory is a wonderfully useful tool, and without it judgment does its work with difficulty." We need to remember some things because without our memory of those things, our wisdom and judgment are impaired. Every day that we live we're called upon to make decisions based upon our judgment, and some of these decisions are of profound consequence. We will err in making the judgment calls that come our way if our minds can't remember the things in the past (both the good and the bad) that would impart wisdom to our decision-making.

A journal is a good place to write down things that you don't want to forget: just bits and pieces of anything that you know you need to remember in order to be more wise in the future. Another good place for reminders is a calendar. On my calendar, for example, I record the days when anything personally important happens, so that I can always go back and remember those days. There is a Chinese proverb that says, "The palest ink is better than the best memory." So whatever needs to be remembered, it's a good idea to write it down.

The most valuable things to remember, of course, are the things that form the foundation of our character: *our principles.* You'd think a person would never forget his principles, but the fact is, we sometimes do — if we haven't made provision to be reminded of them. So do whatever it takes, in the way of reminders, to keep a grip on yourself.

Remember who you are!

LEWIS CARROLL

VIGOR

Iron rusts from disuse; stagnant water
loses its purity and in cold weather becomes frozen;
even so does inaction sap the vigor of the mind.

LEONARDO DA VINCI

A VIGOROUS MIND IS AN ASSET. To see why that's true, we need to understand what the word means. It comes from a Latin verb which meant "to be lively," and it conveys the idea of active strength. When we say that a person is vigorous physically, we mean that he or she is energetic and agile in the exercise of their strength, and similarly, when we speak of a person's mental vigor, we refer to the active use of their mind. A vigorous mind is a lively mind! It's one that is eager to work and inquisitive and courageous. A mind like that is an asset, and it needs to be nourished and kept active.

Think with vigor! We often get poor results from our thinking because we're so lazy about it. Not having been fed properly and exercised regularly, our minds have lost their childhood vigor. But that's a problem that can be corrected. We can start thinking more actively.

Speak with vigor! Whether it's written or spoken, language often has to be used vigorously in order to be effective. Yes, there is a time and place for soft words, but I would say that our communications fail more often from being too bland than from being too vigorous.

Live with vigor! I wholeheartedly agree with Justin Wilson, the Louisiana comedian and cook, who is known for saying that everybody ought to live with "great vigorosity," and also with Emeril Lagasse, another great Louisiana cook, who's always urging us to "Kick it up!" As we pass through this world, we don't want, as somebody said, to fail to taste the fruit for lack of courage to shake the tree.

None of us has an infinite supply of vigor, however, and so we have to make some choices. We can't say a vigorous "Yes!" to some things if we haven't said a definite "No!" to other things. And maybe that's where a good part of vigor comes from anyway: the ability to focus and the willingness to make a choice. If we're going to follow Justin Wilson's advice and live with "great vigorosity," we're going to have to make up our minds who we are and what we won't do.

Men must be decided on what they will
not do, and then they are able to act with vigor
in what they ought to do.

MENCIUS

May 3
RELEASE

Courage is the price that life exacts for granting peace.
The soul that knows it not, knows no release
From little things;
Knows not the livid loneliness of fear,
Nor the mountain heights where bitter joy can hear
The sound of wings.

AMELIA EARHART PUTNAM

ALL OF US NEED RELEASE FROM CERTAIN THINGS. We find ourselves enslaved to harmful habits. We are hindered by limitations and problems that block our path to progress. We're oppressed by anxieties and insecurities. All of these things, and many more, tie us down and keep us from exercising our freedom to live as we should. And it's likely true, as Amelia Earhart Putnam wrote, that, because of our lack of courage, the "little things" bind us the most. The greater things can't be enjoyed as long as we hold on to these little ones.

Release is a powerful concept. If we could think more often in terms of that metaphor, or paradigm, we'd probably be more effective. Think of an undesirable habit, for example. Which would probably have the greater chance of helping you in the short term: thinking of the task of "gaining" something difficult that you don't have right now (a better habit, a virtue that you need, etc.) or thinking of the freedom that would come from "letting go" of the thing that you don't want? In my own mind, I try to envision the things I'm attempting to get rid of in my character as a "big bag of rocks." It's both easy and exciting to think of just putting down the bag of rocks and not carrying it around anymore. That's "release" — and it's really quite wonderful!

But let's get the focus off of ourselves. Wouldn't it be a fine thing to be people who serve the role in other people's lives of helping them to enjoy more freedom? Surely it would, and that's one of the best gifts we can give to those around us. Often, all it takes to help others find release is an encouraging word. "A positive word releases positive energy and becomes a creative force" (Robert Harold Schuller).

Whether in our own lives or those of others, release often comes down to the difference between faith and fear. So let's be people who choose faith over fear, and also help others to make that bold choice.

It is cynicism and fear that freezes life;
it is faith that thaws it out, releases it, sets it free.

HARRY EMERSON FOSDICK

PURPOSEFULNESS

The great and glorious masterpiece
of man is to know how to live to purpose.
MICHEL DE MONTAIGNE

PURPOSEFULNESS INCLUDES TWO DIFFERENT, BUT EQUALLY IMPORTANT, IDEAS. First, the purposeful person is one who is guided by deliberate intentions and goals, rather than the impulses of the moment. But second, the purposeful person follows his or her intentions with determination and perseverance. In other words, if we're purposeful, we plan our work (deliberate intent) and then work our plan (determination). Both of these parts of purposefulness are essential. Neither can be left out if we expect to get good results.

The beauty of purposefulness is that it gives us something good to work toward. Although most of us spend a good deal of time trying to move away from certain things, there really is a greater power that comes from having something positive that we passionately want to move toward. And purposefulness gives us that something. It identifies the thing that we most deeply want to say "Yes" to, and then helps us move in the direction of that vision. Purposeful people aren't just against things; they're for things — and they're *powerfully* for them!

To be helpful, however, purposefulness must balance two traits that are sometimes hard to balance: steadfastness and flexibility. We need to pursue our purposes with determination, certainly, but we also need the wisdom to know when to modify our intentions, or even to change them altogether. Purposefulness shouldn't make us pigheaded.

William Arthur Ward listed the following as the *Four Steps to Achievement:* "Plan purposefully, prepare prayerfully, proceed positively, and pursue persistently." Something like that four-step program will have to be adopted if we're ever going to contribute in a worthy manner to the world in which we live. In the absence of purposeful planning and execution, we're at the mercy of our external circumstances. If we don't live deliberately and intentionally, we can't expect much more than to be tossed back and forth by every breeze that happens to blow. Those around us should be able to expect more of us than that. They should find us to be people who know what our destination is and are purposefully moving toward it.

The secret of success is constancy to purpose.
BENJAMIN DISRAELI

PARADIGMS

But whether they shift us in positive or negative directions,
whether they are instantaneous or developmental, paradigm shifts move us
from one way of seeing the world to another. And those shifts create powerful
change. Our paradigms, correct or incorrect, are the sources of our attitudes
and behaviors, and ultimately our relationships with others.

STEPHEN R. COVEY

SOME OF OUR BELIEFS ARE MORE BASIC THAN OTHERS. The larger and more important the subject, and the more fundamental the concept, the more a belief falls into the category of a "paradigm." Paradigms are beliefs that constitute the "lens" through which we see the world. They form our worldview, our basic perspective on what kind of reality we're living in and how that reality works.

For example, some people work from the perspective that we've been created by a God to whom we're accountable, while others work from the viewpoint that there is no such God. Our belief on that subject is one of our most important paradigms. Or consider another example. Some people believe that we're capable of exercising freedom of will in our actions, while others accept the perspective that everything that happens was already determined before we were born. Whichever position we take, that position is one of our paradigms.

Few of us are probably aware of the extent to which we've unthinkingly picked up our paradigms from other people. To say that we've gotten a paradigm from someone else is not necessarily to say that the paradigm is untrue. But we do need to be careful, don't we? If, when it comes to our most basic beliefs, we tend to just "go with the flow," we'd better make sure that we're in a pretty good flow!

The main thing is not where we got our paradigms, but whether they're true. At all costs, we must do our best to bring our perspectives into alignment with reality. Quite fortunately, we're not stuck with the set of paradigms we have right now; we can exchange them for better ones. And doing this — *improving our paradigms* — is a part of the main business of life. It's also a very powerful thing to do!

In the words of Thoreau, "For every thousand hacking at the leaves
of evil, there is one striking at the root." We can only achieve quantum
improvements in our lives as we quit hacking at the leaves of attitude and
behavior and get to work on the root, the paradigms from
which our attitudes and behaviors flow.

STEPHEN R. COVEY

DOING

Things won are done;
joy's soul lies in the doing.

WILLIAM SHAKESPEARE

OUR NATURE IS SUCH THAT WE DERIVE A DEEP SATISFACTION FROM "DOING." We are workers, and despite our occasional complaints to the contrary, we basically enjoy the act of working. It's not just that we enjoy the accomplishment of "having done" certain things, and it's not just that we enjoy the rest and recreation that come after we've engaged in "doing" — we actually enjoy the doing itself, at least under normal circumstances. There is a deeply felt, wholesome sense of rightness that comes from being in the midst of *doing*.

The joy of doing, however, depends to a large extent on whether we're doing our best. The old saying that "anything worth doing is worth doing well" is a reminder that there is some worth or value in well-doing, and a part of the worth is the joy that comes from it. Simply put, it feels good to be actively involved in high-quality work.

Yet even doing our best is not enough. It's also important to inquire whether what we're doing is good and right. As Gore Vidal commented, "There is nothing more debasing than the work of those who do well what is not worth doing at all." So we must make sure our doing is aligned with principles of proven worth. Unprincipled work, no matter how high the quality, is much better off left undone.

But, as Montaigne said, "Saying is one thing and doing is another." In the present age of information, we are inundated with words. Talk is everywhere. But as someone long ago said, "Talk is cheap," and we need to be careful not to let talk substitute for doing. The joy of doing comes not from promising to do but from doing what we promise, so we need to follow through and do what we say.

If there's another problem that's characteristic of our age, however, it's that we often rush through our doing so hurriedly that we lose out on any enjoyment that it might provide. How much better it would be if we did our "doings" more thoughtfully. If we'd take the time to "taste" the things we do, we'd often find them very gratifying.

Let us, then, be up and doing,
With a heart for any fate;
Still achieving, still pursuing,
Learn to labor and to wait.

HENRY WADSWORTH LONGFELLOW

PROVIDING

He that can work is a born king of something.

THOMAS CARLYLE

To CONTINUE LIVING IN THE WORLD, CERTAIN BASIC THINGS HAVE TO BE PROVIDED: FOOD, CLOTHING, AND SHELTER. When we do honest work to provide these things for ourselves and our loved ones, we do an honorable thing. And though it's been a long time since the daily necessities had to be grown, caught, or made by very many of us with our own hands, it can hardly be denied that there is still an elemental satisfaction in doing these things personally and directly. "There is," in the words of Marianne Moore, "no pleasure subtler than the sensation of being a good workman."

In the 1940s, Harlan Hubbard and his wife, Anna, left the elite social life of Cincinnati and took to the Ohio River. Eventually, they settled in a little cove called Payne Hollow, building a house with the rocks and timbers they found there and living forever afterward by what they could provide with their own hands. Theirs was no experiment, like Thoreau's sojourn at Walden Pond, but a committed way of life from which they never looked back. On May 7, 1999, I had the privilege of visiting Payne Hollow. The artist to whom the Hubbards gave the property when they died still lived there, single-handedly maintaining a working homestead as Harlan and Anna would have wanted. Payne Hollow is to me a wonderful symbol, a monument to the wholesome pleasure of working and . . . providing.

Jacques Barzun said, "Work is something that engages the heart and the mind as well as the hand, something that involves the surmounting of difficulties for results that are deemed important to the worker." When we work to provide for our own needs, and especially when we use materials that we've garnered from our own surroundings, we come into contact with a satisfaction that's as old as our oldest ancestors. And we're the losers for not enjoying it more often.

Work itself is not a curse, and manual labor is a far better thing than most people suppose. "Thou, O God, dost sell us all good things at the price of labor" (Leonardo da Vinci). Today, let's reconsider the quality of our own work. Let's recall the pleasure of providing.

No race can prosper till it learns there is as much
dignity in tilling a field as in writing a poem.

BOOKER T. WASHINGTON

MOTHERLINESS

When God thought of mother, he must have laughed
with satisfaction and framed it quickly — so rich, so deep, so divine,
so full of soul, power, and beauty was the conception.

HENRY WARD BEECHER

SOME HUMAN ATTRIBUTES ARE TYPICALLY FOUND IN WOMEN
MORE OFTEN THAN IN MEN, AND "MOTHERLINESS" IS ONE
SUCH TRAIT. Indeed, motherliness is so closely associated in our
minds with the feminine disposition that it stands as one of the defining characteristics of femininity. The natural tendency to love and
cherish, to nourish and nurture, and to encourage and support are so
bound up with being a woman that these skills are usually thought to
come as part of a woman's "original equipment."

But notice carefully the word we're meditating on today: it's not
just "motherhood," but "motherliness" that we want to think about.
Motherhood is the biological fact of being a mother, and it may or
may not be accompanied by motherly attitudes and actions. Usually
it is, but not always. And so we properly pay tribute to those women
who've not only borne children, but having done so, have also given
their children (and perhaps others) the great gift of motherliness.

Motherliness is not just a trait; it's a virtue. It's something to
be admired and praised. Yes, it does come naturally to most women,
but the actual following of motherly instincts on a day-to-day basis
requires choice. It requires work. And it requires no small measure of
sacrifice. Those mothers who have gone beyond motherhood into the
realm of real motherliness are to be honored in the very highest way.

In some parts of the world, May is the month when "Mother's
Day" comes around. This is a day to remember our mothers for their
greatness — and if they're still living, to express our appreciation to
them personally. Fortunately, greatness as a mother doesn't require a
woman to have achieved many of the things that the world admires;
"success" (at least in the usual sense) is simply not necessary. And
that's a good thing because not many of our mothers had any realistic
chance to make a mark that the world would notice. But oh, how they
loved us! And if today we had little else in life but the love our mothers gave up their lives to give us, we'd still be wealthy, wouldn't we?

A rich child often sits in a poor mother's lap.

DANISH PROVERB

MASTERY

Let no one or anything stand between you and the difficult task;
let nothing deny you this rich chance to gain strength by adversity,
confidence by mastery, success by deserving it. Do it better each time.
Do it better than anyone else can do it. I know this sounds
old-fashioned. It is, but it has built the world.

HAROLD H. CURTICE

MASTERY GIVES US A SATISFACTION THAT MEDIOCRITY CAN NEVER PROVIDE. Yet too few of us have tasted the joy of mastery. We've dreamed about hundreds of things. We've dabbled in many things. And maybe we've even progressed to the intermediate level in several things. But few of us have paid the price to gain the level of mastery in any single realm of endeavor. We've not invested the years of patient sweat and sacrifice that it takes to reach the state of consummate skill and genuine expertise. But those who have done so enjoy a gratification that is truly one of life's special treats.

Mastery doesn't mean pride. When Curtice suggests that we do something "better than anyone else can do it," what he's talking about has nothing to do with arrogance, competition, or prideful self-sufficiency. He's just urging us never to be content with anything less than improvement. In any activity, mastery means the constant desire to increase the excellence of the art, craft, science, or whatever it may be. If how we do a particular thing is no better than it has already been done (by anyone, including ourselves), then we've probably not done it as excellently as it *might* be done. Mastery is always pushing the limits.

Mastery doesn't mean perfection. In the world as we know it, it's not possible to achieve absolute perfection in any endeavor. But that doesn't mean that mastery is not possible. Flawlessly perfect houses can't be built by anybody, but that doesn't keep us from distinguishing people who've become master carpenters from those who haven't.

The most important kind of mastery, however, is *self-mastery.* We needn't think that, just because we've mastered our job, our work, or our craft, there is no need to master ourselves, for therein lies the real mastery, and without it, no other mastery will be found praiseworthy.

We should every night call ourselves to an account:
What infirmity have I mastered today? What passions opposed?
What temptation resisted? What virtue acquired? Our vices will abate
of themselves if they be brought every day to the judgment.

SENECA

LONGINGS

There is not a heart but has its moments of longing,
yearning for something better, nobler, holier than it knows now.

HENRY WARD BEECHER

ALL OF US HAVE LONGINGS, BUT NOT ALL OF US ACKNOWL-
EDGE THEM OR HONOR THEM. We may not think about it very
often, and even when we do, we may not be able to put our feelings
into words, but every one of us has a "strong, persistent yearning or
desire" (*American Heritage Dictionary*) for circumstances more perfect
than those that presently surround us. And it's not only better circumstances that we long for; I believe we also long for a more perfect
character. Whether we look outside ourselves or inside, what we see
leaves much to be desired. And so we desire to improve, longing for
what we've seen so far only in our dreams and aspirations. Wouldn't it
be wise, then, to acknowledge our longings and even to honor them?

Many of the things that motivate us to do worthy work stem
from our longings. For instance, even our intellectual curiosity, our
desire to understand the nature of what is real, is a form of longing.
"Philosophy," wrote Plato, "is a longing after heavenly wisdom."

In *Antony and Cleopatra*, Shakespeare had Cleopatra say, "I have
immortal longings in me." The notion of "immortal longings" is one
that has occurred to many of the wisest people who've ever lived. It
does, in fact, seem reasonable that our yearnings are a hint of our true
nature, a suggestion that we're connected to a larger, more enduring
reality than the one that we experience in space-time with our physical senses. The writer of the Book of Ecclesiastes affirmed that we've
been created by a God who "has put eternity in [our] hearts."

If we had no longings, we'd be an impoverished people. We'd
be flatter, duller, and less capable of significant contribution. After
all, a major part of what we have to offer others is our aspiration, our
yearning to move forward. So our longings are not to be regretted or
avoided. Although they may sometimes be so poignant as to be painful, they're usually pulling us in a direction that we need to go. There
is a certain beauty to our wistfulness, and good things often come
from letting our longings be felt — and even allowed to grow.

I long to be filled with longing;
I thirst to be made more thirsty still.

A. W. TOZER

PURSUIT

Look round the habitable world: how few
Know their own good, or knowing it, pursue.

JOHN DRYDEN

TWO QUESTIONS TEST OUR CHARACTER AT ITS DEEPEST LEVEL. Marcus Aurelius was not mistaken when he said, "The true worth of a man is to be measured by the objects he pursues." So it's important at regular intervals to ask ourselves these two questions: *What are we pursuing?* and *How are we pursuing it?*

The "what" of our pursuit. Some things are wrong to pursue, morally and ethically, and these endeavors can't be made worthy by any amount of excellence in the manner or method of their pursuit. Yet even within the realm of what's right, we need to be careful about what we try to achieve. The "good" is often the enemy of the "better" and the "best," and we ought to care enough about the quality of our lives to pursue the very best that we can. Even more important, however, we need to be cautious in the criteria by which we judge what is good, better, and best. By some criteria, for example, it would be better to pursue becoming a doctor than becoming a nurse, but by other (equally valid) criteria, the person who has become a nurse has pursued a goal no less praiseworthy than that of the doctor, despite the doctor's higher social and economic profile. To be completely accurate, we'd have to say that a person's true worth is measured not only by the objects he pursues but also by the reasons for which he pursues them.

The "how" of our pursuit. Even with admirable pursuits, we need to make sure that we pursue them in a principled way. Contrary to popular belief, the end does not justify the means, and we are never excused from wrongdoing simply because we had an honorable objective. And not only should the pursuit of our goals be principled; it should also be passionate. "The roots of true achievement lie in the will to become the best that you can become" (Harold Taylor).

It's needful, then, for us to pay attention to our pursuits. Not many good goals can be reached by merely "going with the flow." It takes deliberate, conscious choice to keep ourselves pointed in the right direction — and in whatever direction it's right for us to be pointed, it takes character to fire up our pursuits with principle and passion.

Every calling is great when greatly pursued.

OLIVER WENDELL HOLMES

SEEING

A fool sees not the same tree that a wise man sees.
WILLIAM BLAKE

THERE ARE FEW OF US WHO WOULDN'T BE HELPED BY AN IMPROVEMENT IN OUR VISION, OUR ABILITY TO SEE. Too often, we see (i.e., experience) things without learning anything. We see them, but their importance escapes us. We notice them, but their wonder is wasted on us. There may be nothing wrong with our eyesight, but truly, "a fool sees not the same tree that a wise man sees."

Depth of vision. At times, we don't see deeply enough, that is, we don't take the time to look below the surface. And not taking the time is really the heart of the problem, as anyone knows who has wrongfully judged another person by making a hasty assessment on the basis of a first impression or a superficial acquaintance.

Breadth of vision. When we don't see what we need to see, sometimes the problem is not so much incorrect seeing as it is insufficient seeing. John Ruskin wrote, "Not only is there but one way of doing things rightly, but there is only one way of seeing them, and that is, seeing the whole of them." Factors like perspective and scope are critically important. Just as there are times when we need to look more deeply, there are times when we need to back up and take a wider view. It's often amazing what can be seen from a distance!

If we need to see more deeply and more broadly, one of the best ways to learn to do so is to listen attentively when other people tell us what they see. One reason the fool doesn't see the same tree as the wise man is that the fool won't pay attention when the wise man is describing what he sees. The fool never learns a deeper, broader vision because he's ignorantly content with what little he sees on his own.

In the end, it's a combination of *motive* and *experience* that allows us to improve our seeing. We have to want to see more than we do right now, but even with that desire, we have to have our understanding prepared by certain experiences before we can be struck by the full significance of the things that we encounter. The longer we live, the more we're able to recognize certain truths that have been "right before our eyes" for many years. That's one reason that life in this remarkable world is such a never-ending adventure in seeing.

People only see what they are prepared to see.
RALPH WALDO EMERSON

INDEPENDENCE

Nothing is more desirable than to be released from an affliction,
but nothing is more frightening than to be divested of a crutch.

JAMES BALDWIN

INDEPENDENCE, PROPERLY DEFINED, IS A STATE WORTH STRIV-
ING FOR, BUT FRANKLY, IT REQUIRES MORE COURAGE AND IN-
TEGRITY THAN WE MIGHT NOW POSSESS. Desiring "to be released
from an affliction" is easy, as Baldwin suggests, but "nothing is more
frightening than to be divested of a crutch." Independence involves
not only an enjoyable freedom but also a sobering responsibility.

One popular misconception of independence is that it means
complete self-sufficiency, without the need to depend on anyone else
for anything at all. But if that's what independence is, then none of us
will ever experience it. In the real world, nobody is self-sufficient, and
we need to have the humility to confess that fact. If we can't see how
often in the past we've had to be helped by other people, we're either
blindly arrogant or arrogantly blind. Like it or not, we all have needs
that can't be supplied by the unassisted work of our own hands.

Another misconception is that independence means absolute au-
tonomy or self-rule. But again, in the real world this kind of independence is impossible. If we're looking for a life in which we don't have
to be subordinate to the authority of any other person in any role or
relationship whatsoever, we'll probably be looking for a long time. In
the many different relationships in which we find ourselves participating, sometimes we have to lead and sometimes we have to follow.
Truly independent people have the ability to follow as well as to lead.

Independence simply means *taking personal responsibility for the
quality of our lives.* As we grow beyond dependence, we quit expecting
others to hand us happiness on a silver platter, and we begin paying
more attention to our character than our outward circumstances. This
kind of independence is a huge step in the right direction for us. And
yet, as desirable as independence is, and as preferable as it is to unhealthy dependence, independence is not the *summum bonum* of life.
Tomorrow, we'll talk about an even higher goal that calls us.

True independence of character empowers us to act rather than be acted upon.
It frees us from our dependence on circumstances and other people and is a
worthy, liberating goal. But it is not the ultimate goal in effective living.

STEPHEN R. COVEY

INTERDEPENDENCE

Extreme independence is as destructive
to a relationship as total dependence.

JAMES C. DOBSON

INTERDEPENDENCE IS A HIGHER VALUE THAN INDEPENDENCE.
If we can't see that, perhaps we've been confused more than we realize by the various misconceptions of independence that are so much
in vogue today. Yet misguided independence can hinder us every bit as
much as the unhealthy dependence which we're so eager to avoid.

Interdependence is a cooperative relationship in which individuals yield some of their independence to others in a relationship for
the purpose of achieving a mutual goal or realizing a shared vision.
It involves trust, commitments, and collaboration, and it's based on
the understanding that the great challenges of life call for a bit of
"together" work now and then. Interdependence produces what has
been called "synergy," an effect produced by the joint action of two or
more people which each would be incapable of producing individually.
One person brings to the work certain qualities or abilities, others are
supplied by another person, etc. — and in the end, a result is reached
that marvelously multiplies what any of the parties could have created
alone. So interdependence goes beyond independence. To the courage
of independence, interdependence adds this element: the humility to
recognize when we can do more together than we can do separately.

Interdependence, as many have noted, is a choice that only
independent people can make. It requires a strength of character not
possessed by those who're still bogged down in blaming and evasion
of responsibility. So if we've outgrown *dependence* and come to see the
value of *independence,* that's good. But it's even better if we've come to
appreciate the synergistic power of *interdependence.* Indeed, one of the
major measures of our personal maturity is the extent to which we've
learned to live and work interdependently. If we're not there yet, we
should at least make sure that we're growing in that direction!

On the maturity continuum, *dependence* is the paradigm of *you* — *you* take
care of me; *you* come through for me; *you* didn't come through; I blame *you* for
the results . . . *Independence* is the paradigm of *I* — *I* can do it; *I* am responsible; *I* am self-reliant; *I* can choose . . . *Interdependence* is the paradigm of *we*
— *we* can do it; *we* can cooperate; *we* can combine our talents and abilities
and create something greater together.

STEPHEN R. COVEY

FANTASY

Fantasy is a natural human activity. It certainly does not destroy or even insult Reason; and it does not either blunt the appetite for, nor obscure the perception of, scientific verity. On the contrary. The keener and the clearer is the reason, the better fantasy will it make. If men were ever in a state in which they did not want to know or could not perceive truth (facts or evidence), then Fantasy would languish until they were cured.

J. R. R. TOLKIEN

IT IS TOO BAD THAT "FANTASY" IS SO OFTEN USED AS A DE-ROGATORY TERM. As a category of literature, it is looked down upon and considered unworthy of the effort of any truly gifted writer. And as an intellectual activity, it is almost laughed at, as if those who enjoy fantasy (whether of someone else's making or of their own) are somehow suffering from a case of arrested development. Yet fantasy is not only a legitimate intellectual and artistic endeavor, the ability to enjoy it is one of our most delightful human endowments. It's one of the channels through which joy comes to us: joy in the high, pure, otherworldly sense. Those who've never had their hearts pierced by the sharp, sweet joy of the "perilous realm," have missed one of life's most ennobling pleasures, and one of its most refreshing experiences.

Eudora Welty made a helpful observation about fantasy when she said, "Fantasy is no good unless the seed it springs from is a truth, a truth about human beings." Those who say they prefer stories that are "true," need to understand that the power of fantasy comes from nothing less than its truth. For all its strangeness and wonder, the genuinely fantastic rings true — *exactly* true — to what we know is in our hearts, both the good and the bad. But it does not stop at the truth of what is; it beckons us to believe in the bright truths of what can be. It suggests that what we experience in the mundane world is not all that will ever be, and it's not all there is to reality even now!

Of the many gifts that have been given to us, fantasy is one of the greatest. That it's not always used well or wisely is obvious, but that is no more than can be said about any of our other powers. Rather than relegate fantasy to the nursery, we would do better to honor it as adults and school ourselves in the wisdom of its joy. Like education, fantasy is much too good to limit to the young!

I now enjoy the fairy tales better than I did in childhood: being now able to put more in, of course, I get more out.

C. S. LEWIS

WILL

"Where there is a will, there is a way," says
the proverb. That is not entirely true; but it is true
that where there is no will, there is no way.

THOMAS S. SZASZ

WITHOUT A SUFFICIENTLY STURDY WILL, WE CAN'T BE EF-
FECTIVE IN ANY WORTHWHILE ENDEAVOR. If our intellect
and our emotions are the "legislative" parts of our minds, then our
will is the "executive" part. It executes our decisions. It carries out the
dictates of our conscience. It even brings into being the creations of
our imagination. And if, for some reason, our will is lazy or not strong
enough to do these things, then all the finest thinking, discerning, and
desiring that we might do would amount to very little in the end.

We often speak of our will as being "free," and there are some
important senses in which that is true. In a strict sense, however, our
will is not absolutely free. It is always attached to an object or purpose
that is determined by the other parts of our minds. As Joyce Cary put
it, our will "is simply the engine in the car — it can't drive." Or to go
back to our government analogy, the will doesn't make the laws; it
just carries out the instructions that have been given to it. It should
be obvious, then, that we need to be careful what instructions we give
to our wills. If our thinking is carefully maintained, then our wills can
serve us well. Otherwise, great damage is likely to be done.

Most of us know that the will doesn't always come through for
us. Yes, it can be very strong when the choice is "what I want vs. what
you want," but it can be amazingly weak when the choice is "what I
ought to do vs. what I want to do." When my alarm goes off at five
in the morning, and it's time to get up and write, I wonder where the
strong will is that showed up so quickly when I "discussed" matters
with the idiot who cut ahead of me in the line at Starbucks.

The fact is, if we don't deliberately *train* our wills, they won't be
helpful. If undisciplined, our wills will be too strong in some areas and
too weak in others. So training and conditioning our wills to help us
is one of the most important parts of becoming mature, and Anatole
France was certainly right when he wrote, "An education that does
not cultivate the will is an education that depraves the mind."

The will to do, the soul to dare.

SIR WALTER SCOTT

HUMOR

There's nothing like a gleam of humor
to reassure you that a fellow human being
is ticking inside a strange face.

EVA HOFFMAN

LIGHTHEARTEDNESS AND LAUGHTER ARE PRETTY GOOD
SIGNS THAT THERE IS SOME LIFE IN US. Our exteriors may be
buttoned-up and businesslike, but a little humor cracks the façade and
lets it be known that there's a little impish vitality in there after all.

"Humor is the sunshine of the mind" (Edward Bulwer-Lytton).
In the physical world, of course, sunshine is not the only kind of
weather that we need, but isn't it wonderful when we happen to have
the benefit of it? Similarly, in the emotional world, we take a special
delight in the "sunshine of the mind." Isn't it pleasing when humor
breaks through the clouds of a "rainy" set of circumstances? Isn't it
agreeable when something funny is said, when something hilarious
happens, or when something comical catches us by surprise?

It would be hard to overestimate the value of the gift that we give
when we show others "a gleam of humor." For most people, life can be
a bit difficult, and without a dash of funniness once in a while, it can
be almost impossible. So it doesn't matter who the folks are who have
to deal with us regularly; they would enjoy, if not some laughter, at
least a little pleasantness coming from our side of the relationship.

It might be a mistake, however, to suddenly decide that we're
going to start being "humorous." If that hasn't been our habit in the
past, it might be more beneficial simply to start being more *obser-
vant* of the things that happen around us that are comical. Genuine
humor can rarely be planned or programmed. As Erma Bombeck
said, "Humor is a spontaneous, wonderful bit of an outburst that just
comes. It's unbridled, it's unplanned, it's full of surprises."

Ordinary life contains all the humorous sunshine that any of us
needs, if only we have eyes and ears to receive it. Indeed, professional
humorists get their best material by just watching and listening as the
"mad, mad, mad, mad world" goes by. And I'm guessing, if something
funny didn't happen to you today, you just weren't paying attention.

There is one word in America that says it all,
and that one word is, "You never know."

JOAQUÍN ANDÚJAR

INQUIRY

*Free inquiry, if restrained within due bounds, and applied
to proper subjects, is a most important privilege of the human mind;
and if well conducted, is one of the greatest friends to truth.*

THÉODORE-AGRIPPA D'AUBIGNÉ

PEOPLE WITH HIGH-QUALITY LIVES TEND TO BE THOSE WHO
(A) ASK GOOD QUESTIONS, AND THEN (B) WORK HARD TO
FIND THE ANSWERS. Inquiry is a conspicuous habit of almost all successful people. There is really no substitute for it. Either we "inquire"
or we "expire" without having learned what we needed to know.

Carefulness in our inquiries. It's not enough to ask questions; we
need to ask good questions. Contrary to what the "enquiring" tabloids
seem to think, some questions are a waste of time. Just as there is junk
food, there is also such a thing as junk knowledge. And not only that,
but some things are simply none of our business. So we need to be
careful in deciding what the things are that we'd like to inquire about.

Diligence in our inquiries. Assuming that our questions are worth
seeking an answer to, we also need to understand that hard work and
persistence may be required of us. Accurate answers to our questions
are not always easily found or quickly understood. So if there's something worth knowing and we say that we want to know it, we need to
be willing to pay the price. Inquiries take time and energy.

Charles Sanders Peirce said, "Do not block the way of inquiry."
If we don't watch out, we may find ourselves doing that, either for
ourselves or for others. There is something a little frightening about
new knowledge, and we're often tempted to resist inquiries that may
lead in disturbing directions. But truth, even uncomfortable truth, is
always preferable to untruth. We have every reason to be courageous.

A healthy measure of old-fashioned inquisitiveness can add
immense value to our lives. Curiosity may have killed the cat, and, as
we've suggested, there are things we ought to have the good sense not
to inquire into. But even so, we shouldn't fail to recognize the good
that can come from good inquiries. There are vast treasuries of knowledge waiting to open their doors to us. All we have to do is . . . ask!

*I keep six honest serving-men
(They taught me all I knew);
Their names are What and Why and When
And How and Where and Who.*

RUDYARD KIPLING

ILLUMINATION

> There are very few human beings who receive the truth,
> complete and staggering, by instant illumination. Most of them
> acquire it fragment by fragment, on a small scale, by successive
> developments, cellularly, like a laborious mosaic.
>
> ANAÏS NIN

To be "illuminated" means to be "enlightened." In our
language, light is very often used as a metaphor for knowledge or
understanding; so when we speak of "illumination," we are saying that
someone has "seen the light." A previously unrecognized truth has
"dawned" on them. What was dark is now "as clear as day."

Illumination is a more important thing than we sometimes give
it credit for being. If our character accumulates from our conduct,
and our conduct grows out of our thinking, then it's a matter of great
importance whether our thinking is accurate or not. If we're "in the
dark," we may imagine that we "see" some things that are not actually
there. Even a little "enlightenment" can help us to see what is really
there and what is not — and once we accurately judge the nature of the
reality we're dealing with, our actions can be appropriate to that reality.

But as important as it is for our minds to receive illumination,
most of us find that gaining greater light on significant subjects is a
gradual, and sometimes painstaking, process. On very rare occasions,
we may get some tremendous flash of insight that opens up entire
vistas of understanding all at once. But more often, our understanding
grows slowly. Most of us get a more accurate view of reality, as Anaïs
Nin suggests, "fragment by fragment, on a small scale." The process is
well worth it, however, even when it seems unbearably slow.

Whether big or small, those moments of illumination — someone has called them "A-ha!" experiences — are delightful when they
occur. They happen to be some of life's happiest turning points. It isn't
really possible to plan when these moments are going to take place,
but we can certainly make a difference by being open to illumination.
If we have an honestly receptive mindset, life's experiences will prepare us for moments of understanding, when the time is right. As the
saying goes, "When the student is ready, the teacher will appear."

> What in me is dark
> Illumine, what is low raise and support.
>
> JOHN MILTON

CONFESSION

It is not wrong actions which require courage to confess,
so much as those which are ridiculous and foolish.
JEAN-JACQUES ROUSSEAU

EVERY TIME WE'RE FACED WITH THE NEED TO MAKE A CON-
FESSION, WE FIND OUT TWO THINGS: HOW MUCH WE VALUE
TRUTH AND HOW MUCH COURAGE WE HAVE. When we've done
a wrong deed or made a mistake, a confession is simply an acknowl-
edgement that the error is ours and that we take full responsibility for
it. If the truth is that we made the mistake, a decision not to confess
the error is a decision to give untruth a higher priority than truth. So
in deciding whether to confess, we find out how much we value truth.
But even if we've decided to tell the truth, it still takes courage to do
that. So our courage is tested as well as our commitment to truth.

Some confessions take more courage than others, of course.
Certain mistakes might be considered so understandable that we
would almost gain a greater standing in other people's eyes by con-
fessing them. Other things we might do, however, as Rousseau suggests, would be viewed as being so "ridiculous and foolish" that other
people's estimate of our character would be adjusted downward in
ways that we would find very painful. Confessions that get us sympathy are comparatively easy to make; it's the ones that get us well-de-
served shame that take both courage and a commitment to truth.

As long as we're engaged in the business of living, we're going
to have to make confessions from time to time. As Daniel Webster
remarked, "There is no refuge from confession but suicide; and even
suicide is a confession." Once done, a deed can never be undone, obviously, but the honest confession of our faults restores to us a virtue
and an integrity that are the only honorable substitutes for innocence.
Having done wrong, we can at least do what's right about our wrong!

Most of us would say that we prefer reality to illusion or deception. Yet by covering up or excusing our mistakes, aren't we saying
that we prefer others to have a favorable impression of us, even if
it's inaccurate, rather than an unfavorable impression that's based on
truth? Wouldn't it be better to come clean and take a stand for reality?

For him who confesses, shams are over
and realities have begun.
WILLIAM JAMES

ALTRUISM

If I am virtuous and worthy, for whom
should I not maintain a proper concern?
CONFUCIUS

W E'RE NOT FULLY HUMAN IF WE DON'T RECOGNIZE OUR
CONNECTION TO OTHER HUMAN BEINGS. There is a sense
in which the human race can be thought of as a family, and family
members have important reasons to treat one another unselfishly and
with benevolence. For one thing, family members are attached to one
another in such a way that whatever one does affects all the others. In
the human family, we need to recognize that each of our own actions
has some impact on our siblings. If nothing else, we have to share the
same living space, the same habitat. To misuse the world which is our
home or to take too much out of it, just for our own indulgence, is to
be shamefully selfish. To fail to help the helpless is to withhold good
things from the family of which we ourselves are a part. Connected as
we are, how can we not be concerned about one another?

"Altruism" means selflessness. It's an active concern for the wel-
fare of others. When we choose to be altruistic, we're making a choice
to be humane and helpful. "A man of humanity is one who, in seeking
to establish himself, finds a foothold for others and who, desiring at-
tainment for himself, helps others to attain" (Confucius).

There is a danger, however, in saying that we "love humanity." That kind of sentiment can be so vague and general that, for all
practical purposes, it's useless. Dostoevsky said, "In abstract love of
humanity one almost always only loves oneself." We'd do better to
love *actual persons* — real ones, like those who live in the house next
door or work in the office down the hall — rather than "humanity."

If we're not as altruistic as we should be, we need to start growing
in that virtue. Yet there's no denying that it's hard. It demands a great
deal of us. Just because we don't think we're doing any harm to anybody, that doesn't mean we're doing the good that we should do. In the
words of Roy Masters, "Loving what is right is different from hating
what is wrong and feeling right about it." And frankly, the more affluent we are, the more we need to be warned: altruism isn't a philosophy
— it's a lifestyle that results in the positive blessing of other people.

To hoard is worse than to steal.
JEWISH PROVERB

TEAMWORK

The human body is probably the most amazing example of teamwork anywhere. Every part needs the other. When the stomach is hungry, the eyes spot the hamburger. The nose smells the onions, the feet run to the snack stand, the hands douse the burger with mustard and shove it back into the mouth, where it goes down into the stomach. Now that's cooperation!

JONI EARECKSON TADA

TEAMWORK IS THE RESULT OF PEOPLE DOING THINGS THAT COMPLEMENT, OR COMPLETE, ONE ANOTHER'S WORK. It doesn't matter whether a group is formally organized and called a "team" or not; the identifying characteristic is still the same: *people do things, each helping the other, that accomplish a common goal.* Joni Eareckson Tada's analogy of the parts of a human body working together to get a hamburger is apt. Something similar to that always takes place when individuals pool their talents and function as a team.

Teamwork requires maturity. We won't function well on a team if we haven't grown up enough to get past selfishness and "itsy-bitsy thinking." If our skill set contains only two responses to frustration — fight or flight — then we aren't yet mature enough for teamwork.

Teamwork is difficult. The benefits of teamwork are amazing, but they aren't free. There is a price to be paid. We have to determine that we'll learn how to cooperate and work through difficulties and challenges to the team. Patience and perseverance are absolutely essential.

Teamwork requires humility. Teamwork isn't for prima donnas or peacocks. It's for people who have enough humility to contribute to a worthy endeavor in whatever way they can, whether they're in the spotlight or not. Teamworkers are content for the team to get the credit.

In moments of success, we dare not forget that what has been accomplished has been, almost always, the result of collaboration. Rarely do we bring any project to completion without the help of some kind of team, whether large or small, and acknowledging that fact ought to be something we're eager to do. Teamwork happens to be a good thing. It's a privilege to be part of something bigger than our solitary selves.

Success is a ruthless competitor for it flatters and nourishes our weaknesses and lulls us into complacency. We bask in the sunshine of accomplishment and lose the spirit of humility which helps us visualize all the factors which have contributed to our success. We are apt to forget that we are only one of a team, that in unity there is strength and that we are strong only as long as each unit in our organization functions with precision.

SAMUEL JONES TILDEN

FINALITY

Great events, we often find,
On little things depend,
And very small beginnings
Have oft a mighty end.

ANONYMOUS

BEGINNINGS ARE OFTEN GOOD, BUT ENDINGS ARE SOMETIMES BETTER. Especially when "small beginnings" turn out to have a "mighty end," we should be grateful. Finality shouldn't be something we shy away from. It's a better idea than many people think.

We need to be people who appreciate the value and importance of finality. Yes, there is an excitement about new undertakings, and no, we don't want to rest on our past achievements. But let's not be afraid of the old saying that "all good things must come to an end." Most good things are begun for the very purpose of reaching some end. If the end is honorable, should we be sad about reaching it?

There is a sense in which finality is a virtue, and both our character and our conduct need to possess that virtue. When our friends think of us, for example, they need to be able to think of finished things, not things begun and hastily abandoned. They need to know that we're well acquainted with the concept of closure.

Similarly, our agreements and commitments need to have a certain finality about them. No matter how great our potential may be, indecisiveness can diminish, if not destroy, the service that we have the opportunity to render. Our friends need to know what they can expect from us. They need to know that we can be counted on.

Each of our lives is moving toward an ultimate finality — death. Any evaluation or verdict that might be passed upon our work right now would only be an interim report; it's only when "finality" has been reached that the true tale can be told about any of us. So it's wonderful if we started out with great advantages, and it's delightful if we're enjoying great blessings in the present. But what matters most is whether we follow through and complete the work that is ours to do in the time that's allotted to us. If the final chapter of our personal history is disappointing, the rest of it will be seriously lacking in value.

Every advantage in the past is judged
in the light of the final issue.

DEMOSTHENES

MODERATION

Whatever is enough is abundant in the eyes of virtue.

S E N E C A

W E'VE ALL HEARD THAT "ENOUGH IS ENOUGH." And yet, properly appreciated, enough is a good bit more than enough. Just the right amount of a thing (think of salt in your gravy) can do far more good than either too little or too much, and so "enough" is not simply something to accept; it's something to be thankful for. As Seneca said, "Whatever is enough is abundant in the eyes of virtue."

"Moderation" is the trait of avoiding extremes. That which is moderate is just right, neither too much nor too little. And so, to return to the cooking illustration, the moderate chef is the one who has both the knowledge and the discipline to put just the right amount of each ingredient in the pot to produce the best of all possible results. When he sees that he's about to put too much or too little pepper in the gumbo, he moderates his actions, not because he's weak or cowardly or colorless, but because he knows that the right amount will be much more delicious than any other amount. Moderation is an act of grace!

Some things, of course, should never be moderated. You can't put too much integrity into your life, for example. When something is a matter of principle, moderation is indeed a sign of weakness. And so Thomas Paine was quite correct in this observation: "Moderation in temper is always a virtue; but moderation in principle is always a vice."

That said, it is true that principles have to be balanced with one another, and balancing our principles does involve a certain kind of moderation. Moderation will teach us how to balance courage and kindness, decisiveness and patience, strength and gentleness, etc.

If we're honest, however, most of us know that we need to learn moderation in regard to some things we have trouble controlling, such as "speaking our mind" and "using physical force." A certain measure of these things is necessary sometimes, but used excessively or ill-advisedly, they can do great harm. If we had no ability or inclination in these areas, being moderate about them would be automatic. But the fact is, we do have the ability — and because we're free to choose, we have to learn the valuable, but hard to master, skill of moderation.

Moderation is a virtue only in those
who are thought to have a choice.

H E N R Y K I S S I N G E R

SPIRITUALITY

*I am certainly convinced that it is one
of the greatest impulses of mankind to arrive
at something higher than a natural state.*

JAMES BALDWIN

SPIRITUALITY STARTS FROM THE PREMISE THAT TOTAL RE-
ALITY CONSISTS OF MORE THAN THE TANGIBLE, MATERIAL
PHENOMENA THAT WE EXPERIENCE WITH OUR FIVE SENSES. Of
course, this idea may be right or wrong, accurate or inaccurate, but in
any event, this is where spirituality starts: with the belief that physical
reality is not all there is — there is also a spiritual reality that surrounds or pervades us. And not only is there a spiritual part of reality,
but most spiritually minded people believe that the spiritual part is
more enduring and should be given greater priority than the physical.

The question posed by spirituality is no trivial question. If reality
does have a spiritual dimension, ignoring or dealing irresponsibly with
that reality would be foolish at least, and quite possibly disastrous.
Spirituality deserves quite careful consideration and also, if we deem
it to be valid, a wise decision as to what we're going to do about it.

These days, we often hear people speak, with obvious satisfaction, of being "spiritual but not religious." What about that possibility? For some, the phrase simply means that they don't participate in
"organized" religion, and in that case, Jonathan Swift's remark may be
appropriate: "What religion is he of? Why, he is an Anythingarian."
But there is a deeper issue, and it has to do with whether there's any
substance or validity to religion of any kind at all. If true religion
(whether "organized" or not) consists of dealing rightly with God,
then the question of whether to practice it depends on whether one
believes there is any God to be dealt with. If God does, in fact, exist,
then it would seem hazardous to leave religion out of our spirituality.

These daily readings are not spiritual. They're simply about positive words and worthy character traits. Yet any list of positive words
that left out "spirituality" would be incomplete, wouldn't it? When
it comes down to it, few of us are card-carrying materialists. In our
hearts, we believe in spiritual realities — and we're the nobler for it.

*Great men are they who see that
the spiritual is stronger than any material force.*

RALPH WALDO EMERSON

RELIGION

Religion . . . is in essence the response
of created personalities to the Creating Personality, God.

A. W. TOZER

SOME DEFINITIONS OF RELIGION ARE SO ALL-ENCOMPASSING
THAT THEY'RE USELESS. A definition that includes everything
actually includes nothing, so for today's reading let's work with
something like the traditional definition of religion, summarized well
enough by the *American Heritage Dictionary:* "belief in and reverence
for a supernatural power recognized as the creator and governor of the
universe." Religion, in other words, consists of the thoughts, words,
and deeds that go into *a person's relationship with God.*

This definition leaves room for the possibility of false religion. If
God does not exist, for example, then a person's "relationship" to that
non-existent God would have little point. But even if God does exist,
a person might misapprehend the nature of that God or otherwise fail
to properly relate to God's being, in which case that person's religion
would be based on unreality. So it doesn't always happen, but ideally,
religion is what we do when we're *rightly* relating ourselves to God.

There couldn't be a weightier issue than the question of God.
Considering the consequences of being mistaken, "religion" deserves
our best thinking, certainly no less than the concept of "spirituality."
When we're faced with the need to do some hard thinking, however,
it's tempting to dodge the issue and wave religion aside as a matter
of mere tradition, as if one tradition were as useful as another. But
traditions are not simply interchangeable. Many of us, for example,
hold the tradition that all human beings are equal. Is that tradition
no more accurate or useful than its rival tradition, that some races are
superior to others? By the same token, after we've described a certain
religion as a tradition, we've still got work to do to determine if that
tradition is based on fact or fiction, realism or delusion, honor or error.

Alexander Chase said it well: "More and more people care about
religious tolerance as fewer and fewer care about religion." Isn't it time
to start caring about this thing that we seem to need so desperately?

Religion that is merely ritual and ceremony can never satisfy.
Neither can we be satisfied by a religion that is merely humanitarian and
serviceable to mankind. Man's craving is for the spiritual.

SAMUEL M. SHOEMAKER

FACILITY

All things are difficult before they are easy.

THOMAS FULLER

EASE SHOULD NEVER BE THE PRIMARY THING WE SEEK IN LIFE, BUT IN A LIMITED SENSE, IT'S A GOOD THING AND ONE THAT'S WORTH STRIVING FOR. "Facility" is the quality of ease. When we do something with facility, that means we do it effortlessly, with little difficulty. The world-class figure skater, for example, has spent thousands of hours practicing her skill and can now perform feats of immense difficulty with an ease and grace that are beautiful to behold. Consider three words that have to do with this kind of ease:

Facile. Though this word can sometimes be used with a negative connotation, it can also be used positively to mean that something is done "in a relaxed manner." Isn't that something worth working for? I believe it is. As a public speaker, I work at that difficult craft in order to be able to speak to my audiences in a way that is "facile" or easy.

Facilitate. To "facilitate" is to make a process easier, and a "facilitator" is one who removes the difficulty from an activity. I suggest that we should all equip ourselves to become facilitators in one way or another. It's a high compliment when someone says, "Thanks for your involvement; the work went much more smoothly with your help."

Facility. Those who have acquired "facility" in a given work are those who have gained aptitude or fluency in it. It is "ready skill derived from practice or familiarity" (*American Heritage Dictionary*). If, as the saying goes, anything worth doing is worth doing well, then working with facility ought to be our goal in whatever we do.

When we run into obstacles in our various and sundry pursuits, we often make matters worse, rather than better, by acting in frustration. When a screwdriver doesn't seem to be working, we often pick up a hammer . . . and use it in anger! But while it's quite natural to want our work to be easily done, we need to understand that a difficult apprenticeship often has to be served first. As Thomas Fuller said, "All things are difficult before they are easy." Facility, fluency, and effortlessness in our work are good goals that contribute to quality results, but they usually mean learning to work smarter as well as harder.

When you encounter difficulties and contradictions,
do not try to break them, but bend them with gentleness and time.

FRANCIS DE SALES

FARSIGHTEDNESS

Rashness succeeds often, still more often fails.
NAPOLEON BONAPARTE

WHEN WE FAIL TO LOOK AHEAD, WE OFTEN MAKE DECISIONS THAT DO HARM — AND THEY'RE APT TO BE HARMFUL TO OTHERS AS WELL AS TO OURSELVES. To avoid the problems of rashness, we need to acquire a bit of "farsightedness," the quality of thoughtfulness with regard to the future. None of us has a crystal ball that's completely accurate, but that doesn't mean we can't look a little distance beyond the present moment and adjust our conduct accordingly. It's simply a fact that those who consider the likely consequences of their actions have less trouble in life than those who don't.

One aspect of farsightedness is planning prudently for the future. This simply means doing what Harvey Mackay suggested in the title of one of his books: *Dig Your Well Before You're Thirsty.* Some people may go to an extreme here, obsessing about the future and refusing to spend any resource they fear they may need later. But many of us have the opposite problem. We make no effort to anticipate future needs and provide for them in advance. We're not as "provident" as we should be, and the quality of our lives suffers as a result.

You may not have thought of it, but one way to foresee the future is to take a long, hard look at the consequences of certain actions in other people's lives. In the long run, none of us can beat the odds. When we see the law of cause and effect operating in someone else's life, it's foolish to think we'd get any different harvest if we sowed the same kind of seed. None of us is exempt from the law of the farm.

Laurence J. Peter liked to say, "If you don't know where you're going, you're probably going to end up somewhere else." Often, it takes no more than pausing to "stop and think" to see that where we're going is not where we want to go. We don't have to be fortunetellers or perfect prognosticators of the future to foresee that some actions are inadvisable. We just have to learn to press the "pause button" once in a while and consider the question of consequences. For every person who suffers from too much caution and too much conservatism, many more of us suffer from too little foresight. We need to become people who are known to be wise, shrewd, judicious, and thoughtful.

The prudent man looks where he is going.
THE BOOK OF PROVERBS

RESULTS

The wise man, knowing how to enjoy achieved results
without having constantly to replace them with others,
finds in them an attachment to life in the hour of difficulty.

ÉMILE DURKHEIM

IT'S GOOD NOT ONLY TO WORK TOWARD BETTER RESULTS IN THE FUTURE, BUT ALSO TO FIND HAPPINESS IN RESULTS THAT WE'VE ALREADY REACHED. We should certainly value the getting of actual results (as opposed to merely talking, for example), but we shouldn't be so preoccupied with the future that we forget to relish the results that are already ours to enjoy. There's much left to do, but after all, some things have been done and we should enjoy them.

In fact, there is a sense in which we should be willing for others to judge us on the basis of the results we've achieved up to now. The real evidence that demonstrates our character is not our "shoulda, woulda, couldas," but our established, accomplished, and verified *results.* If we're "selling" anything else, we're just selling "vaporware."

In the real world, it's worth striving to be people who get results. Talk is cheap, as we've often been reminded, and so we must do more than talk about what needs to be done — we must do what needs to be done. I like the way the irrepressible Pat Croce put it. He said, "Neil Armstrong is not remembered for having circled the moon, although he did that; he's remembered for having *landed* on the moon."

It may be true that we get so few results today because we've been conditioned to be so impatient. Having come to expect quick fixes and thirty-minute solutions in the world of entertainment, we have a dangerous tendency to insist on instant results in everything we do. "[Television] has spread the habit of instant reaction and stimulated the hope of instant results" (Arthur Schlesinger Jr.). Yet few worthwhile things in this world come quickly . . . or easily.

If we're willing to work, however, we can work in faith — not faith in ourselves, but faith in what we know about the reliability of true-north principles. If (a) our principles are correct, and (b) we work with diligence, then the results are surely going to be worthwhile.

It is only by risking our persons from one hour
to another that we live at all. And often enough our faith
beforehand in an uncertified result is the only thing
that makes the result come true.

WILLIAM JAMES

TOGETHERNESS

> Something there is that doesn't love a wall,
> That wants it down.
>
> ROBERT FROST

THERE IS A "TOGETHER" INSTINCT IN NEARLY ALL OF US. Some people may be able to tolerate being alone more than others, but very few can say they have no need whatsoever for the experience of togetherness. We're communal birds — and we tend to flock together.

Yet in these days of radical individualism, some folks shy away from togetherness, fearing that it will smother their individual identities. But while some forms of togetherness might do that, authentic togetherness never obliterates the individual. Kahlil Gibran wrote, "Let there be spaces in your togetherness," and that's good advice. It's the rhythm of togetherness and separateness that makes life exciting.

It also needs to be said that the best kind of togetherness is outward-looking rather than inward-looking. "Love," said Antoine de Saint-Exupéry, "does not consist in gazing at each other, but in looking outward together in the same direction." The more "together" we are, the more we'll derive pleasure from things that are external to the relationship. There is no self-centeredness or self-infatuation when people are truly together. Their combined vision simply gives them a better view of all that can be experienced and enjoyed "out there."

Togetherness takes character, maturity, and hard work. Although our instincts seem to run in that direction, we find that the practice of togetherness is not something that comes naturally. It requires conscious effort to build wholesome relationships and then to enjoy them healthily. Like all other valuable things, togetherness has a price tag.

The main thing togetherness requires, of course, is love. By love we don't mean the silly, sentimental thing that masquerades as love nowadays, but a solid, enduring commitment to the highest good of those around us. This kind of love has affection as one of its ingredients, but it also includes some other things: a desire to give rather than get, a willingness to sacrifice, and a readiness to go the extra mile for the sake of those with whom we're together. If togetherness is the dough that makes the bread, love is the yeast that makes it rise.

> Love puts the fun in together . . . the sad in apart
> . . . the hope in tomorrow . . . the joy in a heart.
>
> ANONYMOUS

May 31
HOSPITALITY

What is there more kindly
than the feeling between host and guest?

AESCHYLUS

HOSPITALITY MEANS THAT WE WELCOME GUESTS WITH
WARMTH AND GENEROSITY, AND HOSPITABLE MEANS THAT
WE MAKE A HABIT OF SHOWING HOSPITALITY. Both "hospitality"
and "hospitable" come from the Latin word for "host." When a host
receives a guest with friendliness, something special happens. There is
nothing "more kindly than the feeling between host and guest."

It is possible, of course, to be hospitable anywhere at any time,
but there's no denying that the most special kind of hospitality is that
in which we welcome guests into our own homes. And not only that,
the highest form of hospitality is when we welcome into our homes
those who are strangers. Indeed, the ancient Greek word for hospitality was *philoxenia*, which meant "love of strangers." Almost anyone
can be hospitable to friends, but it takes more character to show the
same welcome and kindness to those who aren't well known to us.

But hospitality, whether at home or elsewhere and whether toward
friends or strangers, is always an outgrowth of benevolence, which
means "good will." It is an outward practice, certainly, but it begins
on the inside, with a heart inclined to show kindness. "Where there is
room in the heart there is room in the house" (Danish proverb).

Few things are more discouraging than to be "welcomed" into
a home when the host's heart is closed to us. So we need to guard
against that inconsistency and receive our guests with *genuine* hospitality. "It is nothing won to admit men with an open door, and to
receive them with a shut and reserved countenance" (Francis Bacon).

Real, down-home hospitality does have a way of being inconvenient. It's no surprise that those who love their lifestyles more than
they love their neighbors find it to be a bother to share their homes.
But for those who know that it's "more blessed to give than to receive," hospitality is well worth the sacrifice that it usually requires.

Hospitality is a test for godliness because those who are selfish
do not like strangers (especially needy ones) to intrude upon their
private lives. They prefer their own friends who share their lifestyle.
Only the humble have the necessary resources to give of themselves
to those who could never give of themselves in return.

ERWIN W. LUTZER

June 1
MANNERLINESS

Good manners are the technique of expressing
consideration for the feelings of others.
ALICE DUER MILLER

SHOWING CONSIDERATION FOR OTHERS IS EASIER WHEN WE
HAVE SOME PRECEDENTS TO FOLLOW. If, for example, someone
did us a favor and we had never in our lifetime seen or heard anyone else respond considerately to a favor being done, we might have
trouble figuring out how to respond appropriately ourselves. In such
a situation, it's a big help to know that saying "thank you" has been
proven over a long period of time to be a considerate response. Being
able to fall back on a useful precedent is a great relief. So in the final
analysis, that's what good manners are: ways of "expressing consideration for the feelings of others" that time has proven to be valuable.

Mannerliness amounts to making others as comfortable as possible in our presence. But making others comfortable requires that we
be comfortable within ourselves, and so Alexander Pope wrote, "True
politeness consists in being easy one's self, and in making everyone
about one as easy as one can." True mannerliness is always an outgrowth of personal integrity, principled behavior, and peace of mind.

Most worthwhile things take learning and practice, and mannerliness is no exception. If, as Alice Duer Miller writes, good manners
are the technique of expressing consideration, that technique needs
to be acquired. Good intentions are not enough — we have to learn
what are the time-tested ways of showing our good intentions.

Going to the trouble to learn and practice mannerly ways is one
way to say "I love you" to those around us. Especially when we're in
a country or a culture different from our own, it takes extra effort to
find out how consideration can best be shown in that environment,
but making that extra effort is how we show that we truly care.

In a busy world, we need to make sure that things like good
manners don't become casualties of our busyness. In fact, it can be
argued that the busier and more stressed out we are, the more we need
to be mannerly. The "technique of expressing consideration for the
feelings of others" is a skill that we should never be too busy to use.

Life is not so short but that
there is always time for courtesy.
RALPH WALDO EMERSON

June 2
TESTS

Is life worth living?
Aye, with the best of us,
Heights of us, depths of us,
Life is the test of us!

CORINNE ROOSEVELT ROBINSON

NOT MANY DAYS GO BY THAT DO NOT PRESENT US WITH SOME KIND OF TEST, WHETHER LARGE OR SMALL. Once in a while, the tests are quite large indeed. And then, perhaps two or three times in our entire lives, we find ourselves meeting the biggest tests of all, the ones where our characters are assayed in the hottest fires they'll ever experience. Do we resent life's tests and resist them? Wouldn't it be better if we welcomed the feedback they give us?

One of the interesting aspects of our lives is that we can't always tell which tests are the biggest ones. Many of the most significant trials of our character don't seem like any big deal at the time. It may be years before we can see that the way in which we made a certain choice (or failed to make it) was the passing or failing of an important test. The school of life is no ordinary school: we often don't know which are the quizzes and which are the final exams . . . until later.

Could I give you a little friendly advice? *Pay big attention to the little tests!* You'll do better on the big ones later if, up until then, you've been doing right by the little ones. Don't save up your willpower for the conspicuous occasions when you think everything is on the line; spend it freely on the daily choices that, in their cumulative effect, will either make or break your character. For most of us, the first test of the day arrives when the alarm clock goes off. Pass that test, and you'll be well on your way to handling the rest of the day's decisions, whatever they may be. Fail it, and you'll find your bigger choices being harder than they have to be. So take the little tests seriously.

What tests demonstrate, of course, is whether we're strong or weak. One good thing about them is that in the very act of being tested we can grow stronger. But we ought to be careful about the kind of strength we aspire to. The strength to serve, more than the strength to get our own way, ought to be our aim. That's the real test.

What we can do for another is the test of power;
what we can suffer for is the test of love.

B. F. WESTCOTT

TRAINING

Meekness is love in school,
and temperance is love in training.

DWIGHT LYMAN MOODY

IT TAKES "TRAINING" (1) TO BE GOOD AT WHAT WE DO, (2) TO ENJOY WORTHWHILE PLEASURES, AND EVEN (3) TO EXERCISE HONORABLE CHARACTER TRAITS. Love, for example, seems to be a fairly spontaneous thing, but even it has to be schooled and trained. As Moody says, meekness is its school and temperance is its training.

The word "training" is actually an interesting word. Its basic idea is that of following. A railway "train" is a succession of cars that follow one another in a line, the "train" on a wedding gown follows wherever the bride goes, and so forth. So to "train" something is to teach it to follow obediently. The difference between a concert pianist's fingers and mine is that by long discipline and government hers have been taught to follow the dictates of her mind very precisely. I might hear the same notes in my mind and even order my fingers to play them — but my fingers are unruly. They haven't been taught to follow.

Much more important than any kind of physical training is the training of our minds and spirits. To be constructively useful, these helpers have to be trained. Specifically, they have to be trained to serve the interests of our principles and our conscience. And really, that's what life consists of, isn't it? It's a training ground where we learn the disciplined use of our endowments. As C. S. Lewis said, "If you think of this world as a place intended simply for our happiness, you find it quite intolerable: think of it as a place of training and correction, and it's not so bad." And on this point, I also like what Aldous Huxley said, "Of the significant and pleasurable experiences of life only the simplest are open indiscriminately to all. The rest cannot be had except by those who have undergone a suitable training."

But whether or not we recognize it, we *are* training ourselves. By our habitual practices, we are ingraining certain traits within us, for better or worse. And mark it well: if it's by nothing more than negligence and laziness that we're training ourselves, we need not think that we'll eventually enjoy the benefits of a better kind of training.

A man can seldom — very, very seldom — fight
a winning fight against his training.

MARK TWAIN

PLANTING

To own a bit of ground, to scratch it with a hoe, to plant seeds,
and watch their renewal of life — this is the commonest delight
of the race, the most satisfactory thing a man can do.

CHARLES DUDLEY WARNER

THERE IS AN ELEMENTAL, AGE-OLD JOY THAT COMES TO US IN THE ACT OF PLANTING. No matter how urbanized our culture becomes, it's not likely that we'll ever outgrow the pleasures that were a part of our ancestors' agricultural way of life. Getting our hands into the soil, planting seeds, watering them, and nurturing the greenery as it begins to grow, these are joys that have a rich heritage in our hearts. Planting is almost pure happiness, and we need to do more of it.

Planting is an act of faith and trust if ever there was one. No one would ever plant anything if he or she weren't willing to take a risk. Planting is based on the confidence that there are things we can do today that will make a difference for good tomorrow, and anytime we plant a seed, we make a statement about the future: we may not know many things about it, but we've chosen to point ourselves in that direction, and we believe the future's worth making an investment in.

By far the best planting we ever do, however, is not agricultural but personal. When we make new beginnings with other people, either by entering into new relationships or doing things that reinvigorate old ones, we are "planting" in the very highest sense. And we should enjoy this to the extent that it becomes an observable part of our character and conduct. We should want to be people who're known to do a lot more planting than we do uprooting!

The exciting thing is that it's never too late to do some planting. We may have done little of it in the past. We may even have blighted things that were planted by someone else. But the more life has gone badly for us in the past, the more it's "planting time" right now.

The results that can come from planting good things in our relationships with others are truly amazing. A bountiful harvest can come from even modest plantings, if the seeds are sown in love. The soil doesn't even have to appear particularly promising. We just have to believe that the timeless laws of growth have not yet been repealed.

Plant a word of love heart-deep in a person's life.
Nurture it with a smile and a prayer, and watch what happens.

MAX LUCADO

DEVOTION

*Devotion is not a thing that passes, that comes and goes,
as it were, but it is something habitual, fixed, permanent that
extends over every instant of life and regulates all our conduct.*
DOUGLAS V. STEELE

DEVOTION AND LOVE ARE CLOSELY RELATED, BUT DEVOTION ADDS AN IMPORTANT ELEMENT THAT'S NOT ALWAYS FOUND IN LOVE. Both love and devotion have to do with attraction and attachment, but in contrast to love, devotion tends to be more selfless and more settled. In situations where love might fluctuate, based on whether it was getting what it wanted, devotion would remain steady. As Douglas V. Steele says, it's "something habitual, fixed, permanent."

The joy of dedication. Giving oneself to a particular end, not just in affection but in dedication, is one of the most intensely joyful experiences open to us. But when was the last time you pledged yourself to pay close and loyal attention to some honorable "devotion"?

The joy of fidelity. Hardly less than the happiness that comes from dedication is that which comes from fidelity or faithfulness. If you haven't tried it lately, try devoting yourself to something with steadfastness and allegiance. Be someone somebody else can count on.

One of the saddest things in life is to see people who've never learned the joy of being devoted to something outside of themselves. Yet our culture is sometimes so self-centered we find ourselves having to fight that tendency. We become so engrossed in getting the world to operate as we want it to that we pay less and less heed to the larger concerns of life. So we need to be warned. As George MacDonald said, "There is one kind of religion in which the more devoted a man is, the fewer proselytes he makes: the worship of himself."

But even when we do practice a little devotion, there is another tendency we have nowadays, and that is to devote ourselves more to ideas and abstractions than to real, flesh-and-blood people. There is nothing wrong with being devoted to a worthy cause, of course, but it takes more character, and it should be a higher priority, to be devoted to some actual persons, whether many or few. Causes can surely be helped by our devotion, but people can be literally transformed!

*There is a difference between devotion
to principles and devotion to a person.*
OSWALD CHAMBERS

INITIATIVE

This one makes a net while that one stands and wishes.
Would you like to make a bet which one gets the fishes?
CHINESE RHYME

I ONCE HEARD INITIATIVE APTLY DEFINED AS "DOING WHAT'S RIGHT WITHOUT HAVING TO BE TOLD." The word "initiative" comes from the Latin *initium* ("beginning"). To "initiate" something means to begin it, and to show "initiative" means to begin it without a lot of external prodding and persuasion from other people. When it comes to doing what's right, those with initiative don't sit back and wait for someone else to lead — if need be, they lead the way themselves. Consider that there are at least three elements in initiative:

Enterprise. People who show initiative are first of all enterprising, that is, they're able to envision worthwhile endeavors and then undertake these ventures eagerly. They're imaginative and creative, but more than that, they're energetic in getting started and enthusiastic carrying out their plans to completion. Initiative and enterprise, then, are the qualities of the true "adventurer," the person willing to "venture."

Determination. Nothing very good comes from initiative if those who show it don't have the determination to persist and persevere. There aren't many significant ventures that don't encounter at least a few obstacles, and so initiative must include the ability to keep going in the face of discouragement. Perhaps we need another word to express this concept: we need not only initiative but . . . finishiative!

Self-motivation. The last element of initiative is the quality of self-motivation. For every person who can carry out quality work under the influence of someone else's motivation, there are relatively few who can motivate themselves. But this, in the end, is the main ingredient of initiative. Initiative means that we're powered by a fire within our own hearts, one that burns brightly from the inside out.

If initiative is not a part of our character (or if it is, but we're just too lazy to show it), the consequences can be more damaging than we might think. It may seem a small thing to see a worthy opportunity and just do nothing, but that's exactly how things in our lives start to get dilapidated. I have forgotten who said it, but it's true: *taking the course of least resistance is what makes both men and rivers crooked.*

Seize opportunity by the beard, for it is bald behind.
BULGARIAN PROVERB

VICTORY

*The spiritual life is indeed a life of struggle; but it is also
a life of well-grounded hope. Hope is grounded in freedom,
and freedom is grounded in all the high purposes and powers of spirit,
human and divine. The last word of spirit is Victory.*

EDGAR SHEFFIELD BRIGHTMAN

IT'S NOT HARD TO FIND FORCES THAT WOULD DISCOURAGE US AND DEFEAT US, IF WE LET THEM. These forces are everywhere around us, and sometimes it's hard to keep from giving in. But one of the marvelous things about human life is that we are personal beings blessed with spirits and wills that are free. *We don't have to give in!*

No matter what happens, it's always within our power to act on the basis of conscience. There is no external force strong enough to make us violate our conscience, and when we deliberately choose to act with honor, basing our thoughts and words and deeds on the best principles we know, then we're victorious in the highest sense of the term. No matter what the circumstantial outcome, if we've courageously put first things first, then the victory is ours! Whatever it was that threatened us, that force has failed to break our integrity.

It would be hard to overstate the importance of *decisiveness* in doing what's right. In all the things that matter, victory depends on being able to make radical choices . . . and make them stick.

Those who demonstrate the quality of decisiveness are valuable to us as examples. We need more of them! Those who show us that life's hardships can be overcome by the maintenance of integrity are "encouraging" to the rest of us. To "encourage" means to "impart courage to," and that's what people do for us when they refuse to compromise their own integrity for any foe: they give us courage.

Perhaps you've heard someone of strong character described as having an indomitable spirit. Isn't that what we all really want, deep down? We want to have minds and hearts that are so fixed on our principles and ideals that we can't be beaten by any foe that bars our way. And the truth is, we can have exactly that kind of spirit. Any of us can. We just need to have something to reach out for — some "cathedral" to build that we would sooner die than give up building.

*He who bears in his heart a cathedral to be built
is already victorious. He who seeks to become sexton
of a finished cathedral is already defeated.*

ANTOINE DE SAINT-EXUPÉRY

APPROVAL

> Adapt yourself to the things among which your
> lot has been cast and love sincerely the fellow creatures
> with whom destiny has ordained that you shall live.
>
> MARCUS AURELIUS

IT'S WORTH MAKING AN EFFORT TO APPROVE AS MANY THINGS AS POSSIBLE. There is a time to approve and a time to disapprove, no doubt, but we ought to have characters such that we derive a greater joy from approving than disapproving. We ought to be on the lookout for things that are praiseworthy, eagerly searching them out so that we may affirm them. Disapproving of things only when there's no honorable alternative, we ought to jump at the chance to approve everything in our experience that we possibly can.

Granted, there are some things that can't be approved without sacrificing our principles, and nothing here should be taken to imply that we should do that. That being said, however, I think it's true that many of the things we find ourselves disapproving on an average day are things we haven't taken the time to understand. Too many of our rejections are based on superficial investigation, insufficient aware-ness, and snap judgments, and so we often need to listen and learn a good bit more before we decide either to approve or disapprove. "Understanding," as André Gide said, "is the beginning of approval."

If there's something worse than hasty disapproval, however, it's the demon of excessive, insincere, or unmerited approval. I, for one, don't believe B. F. Skinner was mistaken when he wrote some years ago, "The simulated approval and affection with which parents and teachers are often urged to solve behavior problems are counterfeit. So are flattery, backslapping, and many other ways of 'winning friends'."

But where are you and I? Chances are, we're at the other extreme: we fail to approve that which *should* be approved, rather than vice versa. If we're imbalanced on one side or the other, it's probably on the side of criticism. So we need to work on approving the things that are, in fact, excellent. And not only that, whatever the things are of which we may approve, we need to work on *expressing* our approval!

> Do not keep the alabaster box of your love and tenderness
> sealed up until your friends are dead. Fill their lives with sweetness.
> Speak approving, cheering words while their ears can hear them
> and while their hearts can be thrilled by them.
>
> HENRY WARD BEECHER

STABILITY

Flash powder makes a more brilliant light than the arc lamp,
but you can't use it to light your street corner because it doesn't last
long enough. Stability is more essential to success than brilliancy.

RICHARD LLOYD JONES

IN THE LONG RUN, STABLE PEOPLE DO MORE GOOD IN THE
WORLD THAN THOSE WHO'RE UNSTABLE. If we waffle and waver,
we won't accomplish anything of any significance, even though we
have the best of intentions. As they say down South where I grew
up, *"Mean to" don't pick no cotton.* So we need a good dose of stability added to our characters: we need to resist frivolous or unhelpful
change, we need to be constant and steadfast in our purposes, and we
need to be dependable enough that others won't hesitate to rely on us.

Intellectual stability. It's a fine thing to be open-minded. But our
minds are like our mouths: we open them in order to close them on
something solid. If after a lifetime of study, we still don't know anything for certain, then we've probably taken the wrong approach.

Volitional stability. Intellectual stability ought to lead to volitional
stability, or stability of the will. At some point, we must become
people who know how to make decisions and make them stick. A
stable will is absolutely vital; without it, we can't keep commitments.

Emotional stability. Our feelings can be expected to fluctuate,
and indeed, it would be a much less interesting world if they didn't.
Nevertheless, we do need to be stable enough that our emotions don't
overthrow our convictions or keep us in a constant state of doubt.

As you can see, all of the above are types of *inward* stability.
This is, by far, the most important kind. "It is not the outward storms
and stresses of life that defeat and disrupt personality, but its inner
conflicts and miseries. If a man is happy and stable at heart, he can
normally cope, even with zest, with difficulties that lie outside his
personality" (J. B. Phillips). What we seek in life is not the absence
of any storms that would batter us from the outside; we seek inward
characters that are grounded in stable, trustworthy principles. And
make no mistake: our principles are a matter of our own choice.

Those who are the happiest are not necessarily those for whom life
has been easiest. Emotional stability is an attitude. It is refusing to yield to
depression and fear, even when black clouds float overhead. It is improving
that which can be improved and accepting that which is inevitable.

JAMES C. DOBSON

MOMENTUM

Hope is an adventure, a going forward
— a confident search for a rewarding life.

KARL MENNINGER

AS WE TRY TO GO FORWARD IN LIFE, IT HELPS TO HAVE A LITTLE "MOMENTUM" — AN IMPELLING FORCE OR IMPETUS THAT FILLS OUR SAILS WITH WIND AND PROMOTES OUR PROGRESS. Momentum is the thrust that comes from hope. It's the energy and enthusiasm that are generated when it begins to appear that our actions may have an exciting, desirable outcome after all.

Momentum is one of the most helpful, and delightful, things in life. Athletes, for example, know how powerful it can be. In a critical contest, to have momentum on your side is to be almost unstoppable — and to know that momentum is on your opponent's side is to be in a difficult position indeed. In a similar way, we can be helped tremendously in all of our everyday affairs by the power of momentum.

Most of us interact with other people regularly, and we're involved in a number of collective endeavors where people have to work together to accomplish shared goals. In these kinds of interactions, we need to strive to be individuals whose involvement lends positive momentum to whatever activities we attach ourselves to. We can be people whose presence in any group helps to give hope and positive energy to that group's undertakings, whatever they may be.

Momentum, whether in our private lives or in group endeavors, is not simply something we have to sit passively and wait for. It's not something that happens to us as much as it's something we create by our own decisions. Yes, external events do sometimes impart a welcome momentum to our projects, but more often than not, it lies within our power to water the soil out of which momentum grows.

The best momentum creator, as most of us have experienced, is *action*. When there's an unpleasant thing to be done and we feel the wind blowing against us, we have only to *get started* and suddenly we feel the wind at our back, helping us. "It is only when I dally with what I am about, looking back and aside instead of keeping my eyes straight forward, that I feel these cold sinkings of the heart. But the first broadside puts all to rights" (Sir Walter Scott). Try it and see!

Action is the antidote to despair.

JOAN BAEZ

June 11
Approachableness

> The main motive for "non-attachment" is a desire
> to escape from the pain of living, and above all from
> love, which, sexual or non-sexual, is hard work.
>
> GEORGE ORWELL

BECAUSE IT SOMETIMES HURTS TO LET OTHERS "APPROACH"
US, MOST OF US HAVE A TENDENCY TO MAKE OURSELVES
SOMEWHAT DIFFICULT TO GET TO. Often, escape seems easier than
engagement, and so we withdraw. Call it protectiveness, unwillingness
to work, or even lack of love, the result is much the same. We forfeit
the opportunity to be of service to those who share our space.

Thoreau wrote, "For an impenetrable shield, stand inside yourself." To keep others away, we don't have to erect any artificial barriers; all we have to do is "stand inside ourselves." There are none more
unapproachable than the self-oriented, the self-absorbed, and the
self-serving. So for the sake of approachability, we need to extend our
vision and our concern to include the needs of those around us.

Given the ever-present possibility of rejection, it's always hard
for people to approach others, even under the best of circumstances.
Making any kind of significant overture to another human being is
scary. So when someone needs to approach us, we ought not to make
the matter any more difficult or daunting than it has to be. We ought
to be receptive to the overtures of others and make their approach as
easy as it can be. Wouldn't we want them to do the same for us?

Connections to other human beings, and the communication
that must be a part of those connections, are important. They're worth
opening ourselves up to. Whatever dangers may go along with being
approachable, the downside of being unapproachable is even greater.
When we make it hard for others to reach out to us, we lose the personal connections that we need in order to live lives of service.

The best motive for making ourselves open and approachable is a
simple, and yet powerful, quality of character: *grace*. No one who ever
approaches us is perfect, and no one ever approaches us in a perfect
manner. But are we ourselves so perfect that we've forgotten our own
need for grace? The last time we needed to approach someone, have
we forgotten how glad we were that they showed us compassion?

> To be social is to be forgiving.
>
> ROBERT FROST

EXPLORATION

Originality is unexplored territory.
You get there by carrying a canoe
— you can't take a taxi.

ALAN ALDA

EXPLORATION IS INCONVENIENT. To see, to experience, or to do that which is original, we have to go to places that aren't always easy to get to. Consequently, many people don't make the effort. They may enjoy reading *National Geographic,* and they may even dream of what it would be like to be an explorer, but basically, they're willing to leave the blazing of new trails to bolder, more romantic souls.

Yet there's a sense in which we should all be explorers, and in fact, the day we cease to be explorers is the day we begin to die. Our minds need to be stimulated and invigorated by the regular infusion of fresh information. We need to expand the borders of our knowledge. Fairly often, we need to feast our eyes on some new territory.

But it doesn't do any good to explore new territory if we don't let the significance of what we see sink in and make us more wise. We have eyes, but unfortunately, we don't always see. We have ears, but sometimes we don't hear. So we'd do well to ponder the words of Marcel Proust: "The only real voyage of discovery consists not in seeking new landscapes but in having new eyes."

Explorers have a reputation for being restless people, never content and never satisfied. But exploration isn't necessarily incompatible with contentment. We can, and should, derive deep satisfaction from the sights we've seen many times and still tingle with excitement when we catch our first glimpse of things that are strange to us.

At this late date, there's very little unexplored territory left in the world, at least from a physical standpoint. But most of us would have to say that we've left a great deal of territory unexplored "in here," inside our very selves. This is valuable territory, and its exploration yields rich treasures and rare delights. It's the final frontier, really. But discovering terrain we've never seen within ourselves before — and more important, doing what's right about our discoveries — calls for the finest courage that any human being is capable of showing.

Explore thyself. Herein are
demanded the eye and the nerve.

HENRY DAVID THOREAU

June 13

ALLOWANCE

Unless you make allowances for your
friend's foibles, you betray your own.
PUBLILIUS SYRUS

IF NOBODY MADE ANY ALLOWANCE FOR ANYONE ELSE, IT
WOULD BE A TENSE WORLD, WOULDN'T IT? Mistakes are a fact
of life, and if every one of them had to be fully rectified, life would
soon grind to a miserable halt. None of us can stand up to a zero-
tolerance audit of our performance. We need there to be some ease,
some slack, in our relationships. We need others to make a reasonable
allowance for our less-than-perfect efforts to get things right.

Making allowance for others doesn't mean that we condone
wrongdoing or that we're indifferent to matters of excellence and
quality. It doesn't mean that we're neutral as to whether things turn
out for the better or the worse. Allowance is not the same as apathy.

Neither does making allowance mean that we're weak. Quite
to the contrary, it takes extraordinary strength and self-discipline to
make the kinds of allowances that need to be made. People who never
make allowances are not strong; they're weak in the worst sort of way.

What allowance does mean is that *there is more to any situation
than we are aware of.* When what appears to be a mistake has been
made, there is almost always more than one possible explanation
for what has happened. When we make allowance for others, we're
willing to give them the benefit of any possible doubt, both as to
what happened and why. Until the facts make it impossible for us to
maintain a more positive view, we put *the best possible interpretation on
the facts as we know them.* And even when the facts demand a negative
verdict on someone else's conduct, making allowance for them means
showing *as much mercy as wisdom will let us show.* Allowance means
safety: it means that we make it safe for those around us to stumble.

But we need not only to allow for others' less-than-desirable
traits — we should also "allow" those that are praiseworthy. In fact,
"allow" comes from the Latin *allaudare,* which meant "to give praise
to," and the older meaning of "allow" was to honor or praise. So think
about this: if we want others to allow (in the modern sense) for our
bad deeds, shouldn't we allow (in the older sense) for their good ones?

He deserved to have his merit handsomely allowed.
SAMUEL JOHNSON

June 14

HISTORY

To understand a man, you must know
his memories. The same is true of a nation.

ANTHONY QUAYLE

EVERY INDIVIDUAL IS A UNIQUE COMBINATION OF MEMO-
RIES OF THE PAST, ACTIONS IN THE PRESENT, AND HOPES
FOR THE FUTURE. Each of these is important in its own way, but
let's think for a moment about the significance of our memories. A
person's history can't be changed any more than a nation's can, but it's
still important to pay attention to it. "History is the ship carrying living memories to the future" (Stephen Spender). The living memories
of our personal past need to be cared for and kept alive.

Unfortunately, we tend to neglect the facts, stories, objects, and
images that have gone into our personal archives. We don't study
these things as we should. If we did, we'd have a better understanding
of who we are — and a better grasp of what our role is in the world.

But if there are those of us who neglect our personal histories,
there are many more of us who neglect the history of our country and
the history of the world. Will Durant, a man who certainly earned
the right to comment on the value of history, said, "Most of us spend
too much time on the last twenty-four hours and too little on the last
six-thousand years." This shortsightedness costs us dearly. We not
only lose the humility that comes from seeing the larger reality of the
world; we also lose the wisdom. People who never get outside of their
own experience in the present moment make many needless mistakes.

We should be aware that when we give ourselves to others, we
are giving them a person with a past, a history. It's an even better gift
when we give them a person who *appreciates* the past.

If we haven't lived so that our personal histories are rich and
good and worth remembering, we need to start doing that. Today, we
can begin building histories that will be a joy to be connected to later
on. But for most of us, there are already many things in our past that
can enrich us when we remember them. These are things we should
meditate on from time to time, humbly and respectfully. Lest we lose
touch with our roots, we need to remember where we came from,
from whom we came, and what we've done in getting to the present.

A people without history is like wind on the buffalo grass.

SIOUX PROVERB

FATHERLINESS

Becoming a father is easy enough,
but being one can be rough.

WILHELM BUSCH

JUST AS IT'S POSSIBLE TO BE A MOTHER WITHOUT BEING MOTHERLY, IT'S POSSIBLE TO BE A FATHER WITHOUT BEING FATHERLY. Fatherliness is a set of attitudes and actions that most men find themselves inclined toward, but this inclination has to be accepted, disciplined, and put to good use. Being a good father is not something that happens automatically. It's a matter of choice.

Frankly, the present age is a tough age in which to be a father. No longer are there any social norms that tell a father what to do. Many fathers are disoriented and discouraged. And not only that, but now that it's somewhat easier for a mother to survive economically without the assistance of a husband, the role of the father in a family is coming to be thought of as unessential, if not altogether undesirable.

But if it's a difficult time, that doesn't mean it's a time for complaining. When the going gets tough, the tough get going. We need to accept responsibility for the fact that, to a large extent, we men have created the present situation by our failures in the past, and rather than resent today's challenge, we need to rise to meet it. As painful as growth can sometimes be, whatever provokes us in that direction should be seen as a good thing, not a bad one.

Words like "responsibility" and "accountability" are of key importance. In the past, we have wanted the benefits of fatherhood without the responsibilities of fatherliness. We've checked into and out of our families' lives so often that it's no wonder our children have questioned whether we loved them dependably. In our "manly" strength, we've spoken so thoughtlessly that any objective observer might question whether we're familiar with the word "consequences."

But words and deeds do have consequences, and we need to take responsibility for them. Yes, our wives and our children are often forgiving, and they'll probably survive our carelessness. But why can't we live so that some really *positive* consequences are set in motion? Why can't we give our children the gift of honest-to-goodness *fatherliness?*

What a father says to his children is not heard
by the world, but it will be heard by posterity.

JEAN PAUL RICHTER

BUILDING

> There is no past we can bring back by longing for it.
> There is only an eternal now that builds and creates
> out of the past something new and better.
>
> JOHANN WOLFGANG VON GOETHE

W E CAN'T LIVE IN ANYTHING BUT THE PRESENT MOMENT, BUT THE PRESENT MOMENT OUGHT TO BE USED BUILD-ING THINGS THAT WILL HAVE SOME VALUE IN THE FUTURE. Specifically what is to be built will differ from person to person, depending upon the interests, abilities, and opportunities of each individual, but in one way or another, all of us need to be engaged in the work of building. It's hard work, of course — much harder than tearing down. But building is what we ought to be busy doing.

Actually, building is an activity from which we instinctively derive satisfaction. The world in which we live is such that a certain amount of building has to be done by us, even for our bare survival, and our natures are such that this necessary work is something that we find joy in doing, if we think about the matter rightly. Whether or not we acknowledge the fact or do anything worthwhile about it, most of us have a deeply ingrained tendency or need to be building something. And no small part of our happiness depends on whether we have a healthy means of satisfying our building impulse.

To be builders, however, we have to rise above cynicism. Defying those who say that nothing we do will make any difference, we have to believe that at least some of the building we're capable of doing in this world is worth the effort. Despite short-term discouragements, we have to trust that, in the long run, it does some good to do good.

And not only that, but we must be willing to build for the benefit of others. "The fate of the architect is the strangest of all," wrote Goethe. "How often he expends his whole soul, his whole heart and passion, to produce buildings into which he himself may never enter."

But finally, think about this: of all the things any of us can build, none is more beautiful, or important, than *love*. Even if in the past we've torn down more than we've built up, today can be well spent if we build a bigger love in our hearts than has ever been there before.

> And ruin'd love, when it is built anew,
> Grows fairer than at first, more strong, far greater.
>
> WILLIAM SHAKESPEARE

ORDERLINESS

*Sure there is music even in the beauty, and the silent note
which Cupid strikes, far sweeter than the sound of an instrument.
For there is a music wherever there is a harmony, order, or proportion;
and thus far we may maintain the music of the spheres.*

SIR THOMAS BROWNE

WHO WOULD DISAGREE THAT THERE IS A "MUSIC" MADE
BY THINGS LIKE HARMONY, ORDER, OR PROPORTION? We
don't have to be neurotically obsessed with neatness to appreciate the
beauty — and even the value — of balanced efficiency and harmoni-
ous arrangement in the world around us. Freedom and spontaneity are
wonderful things, but none of us would want to live in a world where
total confusion and unpredictability were the norm. The marvelous
spontaneity that we so deeply enjoy in nature is supported and made
possible by a larger pattern of orderliness. So most of us are glad to
live in a *cosmos* (from the Greek *kosmos,* which meant "order") rather
than a *chaos* (from the Greek *khaos,* which meant "emptiness").

Our habitations. Deep down, wouldn't most of us rather live and
work and play in spaces that are made more comfortable by a reasonable amount of order? Surely we would, and the work that's required
to maintain a little orderliness in our habitations is worthy work.

Our lifestyles. Just as unmaintained spaces become chaotic and
uninviting, so do our lifestyles when we default on our "housekeeping"
chores. It doesn't take long for the chaos to creep in. So what about
your manner of life? Is it overdue for some serious reordering?

Our characters. Since other people see our lifestyles, we may try
to keep them somewhat orderly. But our characters, like our back
yards, can't be seen so easily, and there, we may not be as careful. But
in truth, our "back yard" speaks volumes about who we really are, and
nothing is sadder than a run-down character, rank with "weeds."

Nowadays, we ought to make up our minds that we're simply not
going to let words like "orderliness" have a negative connotation to us.
Orderliness doesn't do away with spontaneity; it's the very thing that
makes freedom such a delightful possibility. As in nature, so it is in
our own lives: order is what gives us a playground on which to play!

*Some people regard discipline as a chore.
For me, it is a kind of order that sets me free to fly.*

JULIE ANDREWS

SUBORDINATION

Subordination tends greatly to human happiness.
SAMUEL JOHNSON

BEING SUBORDINATE TO SOMEONE ELSE ISN'T NECESSARILY SOMETHING TO RESENT OR TO BE EMBARRASSED ABOUT. In life there happen to be many hierarchies, and as we live and work within these arrangements, it's no disgrace to occupy a lower rank than someone else or to be subject to the authority of someone else. Being subordinate may be more or less difficult, depending on how both we and those to whom we're subordinate conduct ourselves in a given relationship, but there's nothing inherently wrong with the principle of subordination itself. Our social world is no different than the natural world in that hierarchies are necessary: the normal operation of living systems can't occur without them. So we need to work our way toward a healthy, wholesome concept of subordination.

We ought to make life as pleasant as possible for those to whom we're subordinate. By the manner in which we relate to those whose leadership we are to follow, we can make their lives either heaven or hell. Anyone can carp and criticize those who have the duty of decision-making. That's easy. But it takes more character to be helpful to those who have to make the decisions, and that's what we ought to aim for.

We ought to make life as pleasant as possible for those who're subordinate to us. There may be many relationships in which we're under someone else's authority, but sooner or later, we're going to end up in other relationships in which we are in the lead and others will be subordinate to our role. When that happens, we need to govern our attitude and our behavior in such a way that others find it a pleasure to carry out their responsibilities under our leadership.

In whatever relationships we find ourselves, our goal always ought to be to give subordination a good name, rather than a bad one. Doing that requires hard work, and it requires more strength and self-discipline than many of us have right now. It's not going too far to say that one of the major tests of our character is whether we're willing, with the right attitude, to be subordinate to others. If we're so power-hungry that we demand no less than equal authority in every relationship, then we've disqualified ourselves from any true leadership.

No man is safe above but he that will gladly be beneath.
THOMAS À KEMPIS

HAVENS

> ... then we learn that the storms of life have driven us,
> not upon the rocks, but into the desired haven.
>
> GEORGE MACDONALD

SOME OF THE HAPPIEST "HAVENS" IN LIFE ARE THOSE THAT WE WOULD NEVER HAVE FOUND HAD NOT SOME "STORM" DRIVEN US THERE. If necessity is the mother of invention, it's also the mother of discovery. When we have to, we find out where there is refuge, safety, and sanctuary. At other times, we're in desperate need of finding a haven and we have no idea where to look, but the very haven we need appears anyway. Either way, storms are not to be regretted if they result in our finding a pleasant port that we never knew about before.

We need to appreciate the extent to which other people have provided rest and refuge for us. There aren't many of us who're not indebted to friends who've given us shelter in the midst of some storm, sometimes at significant personal sacrifice. The worst thing we could do would be to take those havens for granted — and the best thing we could do would be to provide for others what has been provided for us.

For a human being, the ideal haven would not be a place of inactivity and indolence. And when it comes to relationships, those that provide the most helpful havens for us in troubled times aren't necessarily those where everybody agrees with every word we say, strokes our ego, and tells us to just sit back and relax. Even when we're in pain, there are times when we need to be confronted with honest truths that can cause us to grow and make progress. A true haven provides safety, yes, but the safety should be used constructively. Repairs need to be made, and then our ship needs to put back out to sea!

Wherever we are, in whatever "place" we may find ourselves, we need to see our circumstances as some sort of a haven. We may think our present situation is undesirable. We may worry that it leaves us open to certain dangers. But whatever difficulties it may be our lot to experience, it's almost always the case that those difficulties protect us from some other, perhaps more dangerous, difficulties. In the real world, contentment often comes down to seeing and appreciating the haven-like aspects of our current condition, whatever that may be.

> All places that the eye of heaven visits
> Are to a wise man ports and happy havens.
>
> WILLIAM SHAKESPEARE

June 20

INSTANCY

The keen spirit
Seizes the prompt occasion —
Makes the thought
Start into instant action, and at once
Plans and performs, resolves and executes.

HANNAH MOORE

INSTANCY IS URGENCY OR IMMEDIACY IN OUR ACTIONS. It is, as Hannah Moore tells us, the thing that "makes the thought start into instant action." It's not only planning but performing, not only resolving but executing. And what a powerful virtue instancy is! It takes dreams, kind intentions, and loving impulses off the drawing board and injects them into real life, where they can do some good.

Not everything should be done instantly, of course. Some things should not be done at all, and we need to guard against the rashness that would do right now what, on later reflection, would clearly be seen as foolish. But even when something needs to be done, wisdom often indicates that now is not the best time to do it. So there is a time to be instant and a time to wait. We can't let our lives be tyrannized by the pressure of all those things that are only superficially urgent.

Nevertheless, when we know full well that the time to do a certain thing is now, instancy needs to be the quality that our character demonstrates. It's an exceedingly dangerous thing to ignore our conscience when it's urging us to act. Every time we say "no" to our conscience, we make it that much harder to say "yes" to it in the future.

But instancy, or the lack of it, not only has consequences for us; it also affects those around us, especially our loved ones. We probably have no idea how many difficulties we create for others when we put off doing things that should be done instantly. Instancy, then, is a great gift that we can give to those who have to live and work with us.

There is a beauty possessed by instancy that delay can never hope to attain. Our lives are made up of moments, or "instants," and when we use these well, we honor them. Acting with integrity in each moment of choice, we express appreciation for the gift of life — and we show by the use of our free wills that there are things worth pursuing.

But with unhurrying chase,
And unperturbèd pace,
Deliberate speed, majestic instancy . . .

FRANCIS THOMPSON

June 21

CYCLES

What is so rare as a day in June?
Then, if ever, come perfect days;
Then Heaven tries the earth if it be in tune,
And over it softly her warm ear lays.

JAMES RUSSELL LOWELL

A "CYCLE" IS A PERIOD OF TIME DURING WHICH A SERIES OF REGULARLY REPEATING EVENTS OCCURS. There is, for example, a cycle that takes place as our hearts beat. First one thing happens, then another, then another, etc. — all in an orderly sequence, until the cycle is finished, at which time the cycle repeats itself. This happens over and over and over again as long as we live.

As the spelling of the word indicates, "cycle" is closely related to "circle." Cyclical things are circular: their ends are connected back to their beginnings, and they go around and around. Some of the cycles that we invent are tedious and tiresome, but those in the world of nature should never grow old to us. They are marvelous.

If you live in a climate where there is a marked change of seasons, be glad. The cycle of spring, summer, autumn, and winter is a thing of wonder, and its wonder ought not to be lost on us.

There are many things in the world, like the seasons, whose enjoyment stems mainly from the fact that we don't have them all of the time. To enjoy something, not have it for a while, and then see it come around again is one of life's most pleasant experiences. As the seasons cycle through their yearly round, we are refreshed, replenished, and reminded of things that we'd forget if we didn't have the seasons.

Today, of course, it's in our thoughts that summer has come around again. Here is a season that most of us find it easy to enjoy, and this, it seems to me, is because summer is tied in so many of our minds to the intense happiness of childhood. I, for one, couldn't agree more with Edith Wharton, who said, "Summer afternoon — summer afternoon; to me those have always been the two most beautiful words in the English language." In the cycle of the seasons, summer will come around again next year, just as it did last year. But on this day of this year, summer's just beginning. Let's welcome it with high spirits.

In those vernal seasons of the year, when the air is calm and pleasant,
it were an injury and sullenness against Nature not to go out, and
see her riches, and partake in her rejoicing with heaven and earth.

JOHN MILTON

MEDITATION

Only in quiet waters things mirror themselves undistorted.
Only in a quiet mind is adequate perception of the world.

HANS MARGOLIUS

IT TAKES A CERTAIN AMOUNT OF QUIETNESS AND STILLNESS FOR IMPORTANT TRUTHS TO MAKE AN IMPRESSION ON OUR MINDS. But modern life, much to our detriment, tends to make us fidgety and frantic. Neither quiet nor still, our minds are usually racing, moving at full throttle from one item on our agenda to another, or from one interesting entertainment to another. We think about many, many things, but rarely do we think about any of them meditatively. We don't give ourselves a chance to reflect and ponder and consider. And as a result, a number of important thoughts pass through our brains without any real chance to take up residence there.

To "meditate" means to think about something quietly and at length. "Meditation," as William Grimshaw said, "is the soul's chewing." Indeed, one of the synonyms for meditate is "ruminate," which means to "chew" something over in our minds. But sometimes, we meditate by just quietly reflecting, without any words or mental action at all. Often, this is the most helpful kind of meditation. It's a beneficial thing simply to grow quiet and . . . *listen.* We can be powerfully reminded of important principles when we are receptively still.

Meditation is important because that's where we usually see the meaning and significance of what we know. Without meditation, we may have much information in our minds, but there'll be little wisdom in our hearts. It takes meditating on matters to move from the question "What?" to the more important question "So what?"

But we can't have the benefits of meditation without making the sacrifice that meditation requires. For one thing, genuine meditation requires a discipline that has to be learned. But not only that, it takes being willing to let go of some of our activities in order to have the time to meditate. We can't have it both ways, and it's foolish to try.

If, like the lake that has the boon
Of cradling the little moon
Above the hill,
I want the Infinite to be
Reflected undisturbed in me,
I must be still.

EDNA BECKER

REVERENCE

Does not every man feel that he is himself made
higher by doing reverence to what is really above him?

THOMAS CARLYLE

IS THERE ANYTHING "ABOVE" US? Are we answerable or accountable to any power or personal supremacy that it would be right
for us to give "reverence" to? Historically, most human beings have
thought so, but it's not a question that ought to be answered on the
basis of tradition alone. It's an issue for each individual to confront,
and it's the most crucial question, by far, that anybody ever asks.

The fact that we have the capacity for reverence is an interesting
thing in itself. No other flesh-and-blood creatures have this power.
Only we can admire and be in awe, or extend honor and esteem. Only
we can *worship* — lovingly and purely. And these qualities are no
small gift: of all the things that set us apart from the lesser creatures,
the capacity for reverence is the most distinctive. "Without feelings of
respect, what is there to distinguish man from beasts?" (Confucius).

If we wish to deepen the quality of reverence in our lives, I would
like to suggest that we look first at our speech. Reverence resides prin-
cipally in the heart, of course, but it's a fact that we can sometimes
encourage our hearts to change by adjusting external things like our
words. We live in a time when reverential, or even respectful, speech
has become almost old-fashioned, even among religious folks. We've
become shockingly rude. I believe we'd gain some good things in our
lives if we'd recover a certain modesty and reserve when we feel the
urge to speak of things above us, and I agree with Nietzsche's opinion:
"Concerning great things one should either be silent or speak loftily."

Yet in the end, it's obvious that reverence must be more than
words, or even feelings or sentiments. Reverence is a right orientation
to, and a real-life relationship with, all that is above us. If, for example,
there really is a God, then reverence would be a worshipful manner of
actually dealing with that objective reality. So let us reconsider the concept of reverence. Let us learn again the wholeness that can only come
from humility toward that which is higher and greater than we are.

Let knowledge grow from more to more,
But more of reverence in us dwell;
That mind and soul, according well,
May make one music as before.

ALFRED, LORD TENNYSON

ESSENTIALS

Make it clear. Make it simple.
Emphasize the essentials.
CHARLES R. SWINDOLL

SOME OF OUR GREATEST IMPROVEMENTS IN LIFE COME FROM CUTTING THROUGH THE CLUTTER AND GETTING BACK TO THE ESSENTIALS. In the round of daily ideas and activities, some things matter much more than others, and it's important to give the best of our time and energy to the deeds that are going to make the most difference for good. But that's hard to do. Trivia creeps into our lives at an astonishing rate, and it takes more discipline than most of us possess to keep the clutter at bay and stay focused on our priorities. So now and then, we're greatly helped by a good "housecleaning" — one in which we get rid of "things" we don't really need.

If something is essential, that means we have to have it. We can't do without it. The real difficulty in life, however, is being honest enough to identify what's essential and what's optional. It takes a person of uncommon honesty to see the difference between what he really needs and what he merely wants. If we want something badly enough, it's fairly easy to convince ourselves that we have to have it.

Yet even when we're willing to be honest and courageous, we need to understand that what we think is essential depends on what our standards are. Our standards come from our principles and our values, and the truth of the matter is, we're sometimes dangerously careless in deciding these things. We casually pick up our principles, and the standards that go along with them, from the media, the popular culture, and the people around us. As a result, we find ourselves defining the "essentials" as cars, clothes, cologne, and Caribbean cruises, and we spend 90% of our time on things that are 10% essential to real life.

Life can be complicated. The surface appearance of some things can be deceiving, and as long as Hollywood and Madison Avenue are with us, there's going to be some confusion over what matters in life and what doesn't. So fairly often we need to call a halt to the commerce. We need to slow down and listen. If we'll listen, our hearts and our consciences will tell us what the essentials have always been.

It is only with the heart that one can see rightly;
what is essential is invisible to the eye.
ANTOINE DE SAINT-EXUPÉRY

NOURISHMENT

Any deep relationship to another human being requires
watchfulness and nourishment; otherwise, it is taken from us.
PAUL TILLICH

Things that are physically alive need nourishment or else they die. Most of us, somewhere along the way, have neglected a houseplant or two and seen the sad results. But there are some intangible things that need nourishment too, such as our relationship with those around us. Your relationships with other people may not need physical nutrients (although there's a lot to be said for eating good food with good friends), but they do need emotional and spiritual nourishment. And the consequences of malnourished relationships are far sadder than the loss of any physically living thing.

Relationships need to be fed huge helpings of love and appreciation and concern. They also need the nourishment that comes from time and energy and service. And above all, of course, love itself needs to be nourished. "Love is a tender plant; when properly nourished, it becomes sturdy and enduring, but neglected it will soon wither and die" (Hugh B. Brown). The love, however, that usually needs to be nourished is not the love that others have for us but our love for them. It's a selfish mistake to make our relationships totally dependent on the quality of love that other people show to us. Without being condescending or patronizing, we can grow better relationships by nourishing the love we show to them. Amazing transformations in relationships can take place when we feed the affection that's in our own hearts (or even used to be there), regardless of the immediate response.

Wouldn't it be a fine thing to be known as somebody who nurtures and nourishes, rather than somebody who depletes and destroys? Indeed it would, and in truth, that's a reputation that's within the reach of every person on the planet. Many things we may not be able to do, but we can be people who nourish our friends and neighbors.

Nourishment never goes out of style. There'll never be a time when it's not needed. The more we nourish those who cross our paths, the more they'll enjoy being nourished. It's an everyday opportunity, really, and a lifelong privilege. Let's not miss the pleasure of it.

The more the heart is nourished
with happiness, the more it is insatiable.
GABRIELLE ROY

THINKING

As soon as a man does not take his existence for granted, but beholds
it as something unfathomably mysterious, thought begins.

ALBERT SCHWEITZER

IT'S HARD TO SEE — I MEAN REALLY *SEE* — THINGS AND NOT
BE MOVED TO *THINK* ABOUT WHAT WE SEE. Observation naturally leads to contemplation. What is this thing that I see? Is there
more to it than appears at first glance? How did this thing come to
be? What is its purpose? Is it to be used? Enjoyed? Learned from?
What is there about this thing that I should be glad to know?

The world in which we live is so wondrously and brilliantly
multifaceted, one lifetime is too short a time to see and think about it
all. Every day that the sun comes up, we're surrounded by things that
beckon us to observe them gratefully and consider them thoughtfully.
If we ever catch ourselves being bored, there can be only one explanation for that: we're simply not paying attention to what's around us.

The ability to think about things is one of our unique endowments. Of all the species in the world, we alone can think rationally
about the nature and significance of what we experience. And this
ability to think about what we experience adds a whole new depth
to our enjoyment of the world. "Thinking," as Lord George Noel
Gordon Brown described it, "is the magic of the mind." Not only can
we enjoy things, we can enjoy the fact that we are enjoying them!

Unfortunately, we often miss the benefit of thinking by trying to
bypass the work that's involved in it. But there aren't any shortcuts to
the enjoyment of a fully human life. It takes thinking, and "no amount
of energy will take the place of thought. A strenuous life with its eyes
shut is a kind of wild insanity" (Henry Van Dyke).

Because we have the gift of language, we also have it within our
power to *share* the good things that come from thinking. Our less-
than-honorable thoughts should not be shared, of course; they're usually better off left unexpressed. But once in a while, most of us have a
good thought, a helpful thought, a beautiful thought. And we never
give a better gift than when we share the best of what we've thought.

If, instead of a gem or even a flower, we could cast
the gift of a lovely thought into the heart of a friend,
that would be giving as angels give.

GEORGE MACDONALD

COACHING

[The best coaches] pay great attention to providing
real-time feedback on their players' performance . . .
Without immediate and precise feedback, the learning
process ends and mediocrity is sure to emerge.

JAMES M. KOUZES & BARRY Z. POSNER

IF WE'RE SERIOUSLY INTERESTED IN IMPROVEMENT, COACH-
ING IS ONE OF THE MOST VALUABLE THINGS WE CAN OBTAIN.
Whatever the activity may be in which we're trying to improve, none
of us sees enough to see our own doings objectively. Even if I were to
watch a videotape of my own golf swing, for example, I could not see
all the flaws in that swing that a skilled coach could see. I would need
the eyes of a coach to help me see the things I need to do differently.
In a word, I need the *feedback* that only a coach can provide.

Feedback is uncomfortable to receive, of course, and so many of
us avoid being coached. We struggle along, trying to improve without
any outside help. And that's unfortunate because there are almost
always people available to us whose feedback would be quite valuable.

Do you aspire to be a person who can coach others? If you do,
that's a noble aspiration. But be advised that coaching is one of the
hardest things in the world to do well. To start with, you'll never be a
good coach if you don't have the humility to be coached yourself. But
beyond that, you'll need knowledge, wisdom, good judgment, common sense, compassion, fairness, gentleness, firmness, respect, trust,
and many other hard-to-acquire qualities. Perhaps no job in the world
requires more different, and more demanding, skills than coaching.

In the end, coaching comes down to teaching, and there's far
more to teaching than simply imparting information. Anyone can impart information, and anyone can tell other people what they should
do. But not everyone can teach, and not everyone can coach. Both of
these, by means of accurate feedback, help others to see what it's so
hard to see with our own eyes: how we can perform to the best of our
ability in ways that best serve the goals of the team.

I believe effective leaders are, first and foremost, good teachers. We are in the
education business. Whether in class or on the court, my job was the same: to
effectively teach those under my supervision how they could perform to the
best of their ability in ways that best served the goals of our team. I believe
the same is true for productive leaders in any organization.

COACH JOHN WOODEN

BENEVOLENCE

That best portion of a good man's life,
His little, nameless, unremembered acts,
Of kindness and of love.

WILLIAM WORDSWORTH

REAL GREATNESS OFTEN GOES UNRECOGNIZED. The standards by which greatness is judged are often such that individuals with nothing more than a bit of outward glitter make the headlines while others with deeper, more enduring qualities are written off as nobodies. Benevolence, for example, is one of the time-honored qualities of truly great character, but because it's usually quiet and unassuming, benevolence doesn't usually land people in the spotlight of greatness. It's a great quality, but its greatness often goes unrecognized.

In its most literal sense, benevolence means "good will." It's the opposite of malevolence, which means "ill will." But in practical terms, benevolence means more than simply wishing someone well. It's an active thing that moves us to go ahead and do the helpful thing that we feel inclined to do. The benevolent person is not the one whose heart is warmed by generous feelings for the human race, but rather the one who gets up and actually does a good deed for that member of the human race who lives next door to him!

The major components of benevolence are *compassion* and *kindness,* and these qualities are sorely needed in the broken old world that we live in, are they not? Against the rising tide of indifference, cynicism, and non-involvement, we need to hold on to hearts that can be moved by the sufferings of other people, and we ought to learn how to help others in the gentlest, kindest way possible.

If we're going to be benevolent, we're going to have to *choose* to be so. As Mencius said, "Benevolence, righteousness, propriety, and knowledge are not infused into us from without." These things are virtues that we deliberately decide to include in our character.

Learning to be benevolent requires practice, and not many days go by that don't present us with opportunities to do that. What are we waiting for? The good that comes from showing goodwill is too good to save up for the big situations. Benevolence is an everyday quality!

Do not wait for extraordinary circumstances to do
good actions; try to use ordinary situations.

JEAN PAUL RICHTER

June 29

NEIGHBORLINESS

The love of our neighbor in all its fullness simply means
being able to say to him: *What are you going through?*

SIMONE WEIL

NEIGHBORLINESS INVOLVES BOTH AN ATTITUDE AND AN
ACTION. It is both a spirit and a state of living. When we live
neighborly lives we recognize that we are, for better or worse, connected to those around us, and we honor that connection by being
willing to share one another's sorrows and joys. To be a neighbor is to
be able to say, as Simone Weil suggests: *What are you going through?*

Our neighbors are not simply those for whom we'd like to have
a fond feeling, and they're not just those whom we'd prefer to deal
with if we could arrange our circumstances to suit ourselves. No, our
neighbors are the folks with whom we're called upon to deal in our
actual circumstances. George MacDonald said it succinctly: "Your
neighbor is the man who is next to you at the moment, the man with
whom any business has brought you into contact." These are the real
people who are sorrowing and rejoicing around us. They are the ones
to whom we must be able to say: *What are you going through?*

Neighborliness has to be shown by us personally. We can't hire
it done, and, worst of all, we can't expect the government to do it.
Hubert H. Humphrey, who as a politician believed that government
should spend great sums to cure social ills, knew as a human being
what all of us should know: "The impersonal hand of government can
never replace the helping hand of a neighbor." As tempting as it is to
let society take care of our neighbors, that's our job as individuals.

Angelus Silesius said, "What you wish for your neighbor, that
you ask for yourself. If you don't wish his good, you ask for your own
death." We can't neglect others without hurting ourselves, but neither
can we help others without uplifting ourselves. Somewhere deep inside, most of us know this to be true. We just need to act on what we
know. We need to renew our appreciation of the old-fashioned virtue
of neighborliness. *What are you going through?* has always been one of
life's most important questions. Let's learn to ask it every single day.

While the spirit of neighborliness was important on the frontier
because neighbors were so few, it is even more important now
because our neighbors are so many.

LADY BIRD JOHNSON

NEWNESS

How endless is that volume which God hath written
of the world! Every creature is a letter, every day a new page.

JOSEPH HALL

O UR EVERYDAY WORLD PRESENTS US WITH UNLIMITED OP-
PORTUNITY TO EXPERIENCE NEWNESS. The list of new things
awaiting our discovery is endless, and the supply of fresh wonders
is inexhaustible. When we grow stale and tired of our lives, it's not
because we've exhausted the opportunities that are available to us; it's
because we've ceased to see the newness of each day as it comes to us.

New things are refreshing to us, of course. Even a new perspective on something old can give us fresh courage and determination.
But newness is not an inherent, unqualified good. A thing is not
good simply because it's new, and we need to guard against the sort
of obsession with newness that some folks seem to have. These folks
want nothing but "the latest thing," and they have no use for anything
that's old or traditional. For them, all that they need to know about
something is that it's new. But that's an unfortunate, and even dangerous, way to live. Those who worship newness as if it were a god lose
the time-tested value of many things that are no longer new, and they
become guilty of what C. S. Lewis called "chronological snobbery."

That said, however, there are plenty of things that are both new
and good, and it does us good to discover them. Our families and
friends find us to have a more refreshing influence on them when
we're energized by the frequent discovery of things we never knew or
appreciated before. We do those around us a favor when we stay fresh.

But we shouldn't just look for new things to experience; we
should also work on the renewal of ourselves. In a sense, we need to
become new people each day. And that takes work. Concerning love,
for example, Ursula LeGuin said, "Love doesn't just sit there, like a
stone; it has to be made, like bread; remade all the time, made new."

Newness often surprises us. When we are the tiredest and we feel
that everything has grown drearily old, something delightfully new
can break through the gloom. Make a habit of watching for it!

When old words die out on the tongue, new melodies
break forth from the heart; and where the old tracks are lost,
new country is revealed with its wonders.

RABINDRANATH TAGORE

REFORMATION

> I've never met a person, I don't care what his condition is, in whom
> I could not see possibilities. I don't care how much a man may consider
> himself a failure, I believe in him, for he can change the thing that is wrong in
> his life any time he is ready and prepared to do it. Whenever he develops the
> desire, he can take away from his life the thing that is defeating it. The
> capacity for reformation and change lies within.
>
> PRESTON BRADLEY

WHEN WE LOOK HONESTLY AT OURSELVES, WE OFTEN SEE THE NEED FOR SOME REFORMATION. So far, we may have made some progress in becoming the people we aspire to be, but for most of us, there's still plenty of room for improvement. Some things about us may be so much out of their proper shape that they need to be "re-shaped" or "re-formed." In some of our personal characteristics, we may need a drastic makeover . . . or a radical "reformation."

One of the most wonderful things about this world is that reformation is always a possibility for us. Change for the better is always within our reach, and as long as life lasts, we'll never face a situation in which there's not some step we can take to improve our character.

Unfortunately, we lose many of our best opportunities for reform by thinking of it primarily as something that other people need to be concerned about. Mark Twain spoke for a lot of us when he said, "Nothing so needs reforming as other people's habits." Ask most people to name the world's greatest reformers and they'll name historical figures who have led society to change, but while we're certainly grateful for reformers like that, I think there's another kind of reformer who deserves some credit: the individual who has seen the need to change himself and has seized the opportunity to do that. The humble self-reformer may not be extolled in the history books, but I'll wager that his or her influence on the world is nothing less than great.

It's often frightening to reform ourselves, and that's probably why we don't do it more often. But maybe we need to rethink our concepts of safety and security. These things don't come from staying with the status quo. They come from bravely shaping ourselves in the likeness of true-north principles — and then reforming ourselves as often as we need to, as we learn to see those principles more clearly.

> Only in growth, reform, and change, paradoxically
> enough, is true security to be found.
>
> ANNE MORROW LINDBERGH

SURVIVAL

A nation without the means of reform
is without the means of survival.

EDMUND BURKE

WHETHER WE'RE CONSIDERING NATIONS OR INDIVIDU-
ALS, THERE IS NO SURVIVAL WITHOUT THE ABILITY TO
CHANGE. None of us has figured out how to get things exactly where
they need to be and then how to keep them there forever afterward.
We might think we'd like it if no changes had to be made ever again,
but like it or not, the real world presents us with the constant need to
change. If we couldn't do that, we wouldn't survive for very long.

Our English word "survive" is a colorful word. Literally, it means
"to remain alive," and it comes from the Latin verb *supervivere*, which
was formed from *super* ("over") and *vivere* ("to live"). If we've survived
something, that means we've lived "over" it — that is, we've continued
to live despite the thing that threatened to extinguish our life.

But these days, there is, I think, an interesting irony with regard
to survival. Unlike our ancestors who had to work the land diligently
to provide food, clothing, and shelter, we have the technology to
provide these things with a minimum of physical labor on our part.
But as Guy Frégault said, "Mere survival is an affliction. What is of
interest is life, and the direction of that life." And ironically, the less
attention we have to pay to the sweat-of-the-brow survival issues of
our ancestors, the more our own survival, in the deeper sense of real
life, seems to be in doubt. I agree with Charles Lindbergh who wrote,
"I believe that for permanent survival, man must balance science with
other qualities of life, qualities of body and spirit as well as those of
mind — qualities he cannot develop when he lets mechanics and
luxury insulate him too greatly from the earth to which he was born."

So will we survive? Will we live? Will we grow? Well, whether
we're thinking of bare physical survival or survival in some greater
sense, we won't survive if we don't decide to. Life is tough, and the real
survivors are those who're possessed of enough stubbornness that they
refuse to be defeated. Every day's a test. And most days, it's do or die.

Victory at all costs, victory in spite of all terror,
victory however long and hard the road may be;
for without victory there is no survival.

WINSTON CHURCHILL

July 3
CONSIDERATION

Quaker to a burglar: "Friend, I would do thee no harm
for the world, but thou standest where I am about to shoot."
ANONYMOUS

IS THERE EVER A TIME WHEN IT WOULD BE OUT OF PLACE TO
BE CONSIDERATE? Well, perhaps. Consideration means that we try
to avoid hurting the feelings of others, and as important as that often
is, there are some occasions when feelings shouldn't be the primary
concern. For example, a person who would refuse to do justice because
he didn't want to hurt anyone's feelings would have a confused set of
values. Nevertheless, it's probably true that we err more often in the
opposite direction. Even when it is in order, we fail to be considerate.

Actually, the word "consideration" can be used in two ways. First,
it means to "consider" something, to give careful thought to it or ponder it. But second, we speak of "showing consideration" to someone,
and by that we mean being courteous or kind to them. Yet doesn't the
second kind of consideration grow out of the first? When we show
consideration to those around us, isn't that because we've thought
about them? Yes it is, and that's why consideration is so greatly appreciated. It's an action by which we say, "You matter enough to me that
I have *thought* about you. I have taken the time to *consider* you."

Emerson said, "Consideration is the soil in which wisdom may
be expected to grow." I think that's true in both of the senses above.
Obviously, *thoughtful concentration* is where one kind of wisdom
comes from, but listen: there's also a wisdom (maybe a better one) that
comes from *thoughtful concern* for the people that we're connected to.

But just as being considerate gives us wisdom, it takes wisdom to
show consideration. It's a mistake to think that having generous feelings toward someone is enough to tell us how to treat them. Charles
Seymour wrote, "Consideration is not merely a matter of emotional
goodwill but of intellectual vigor and moral self-sacrifice. Wisdom
must combine with sympathy." So the ideal is both wise consideration
and considerate wisdom, and these are truly wonderful traits to learn.

Your greatness is measured by your kindness —
Your education and intellect by your modesty —
Your ignorance is betrayed by your suspicions and prejudices —
Your real caliber is measured by the consideration
and tolerance you have for others.
WILLIAM J. H. BOETCKER

July 4
DEMOCRACY

Man's capacity for justice makes democracy possible,
but man's inclination to injustice makes democracy necessary.
REINHOLD NIEBUHR

WHAT IS DEMOCRACY? It's government by "the people," and its operative principles are social equality and respect for the individuals within a community. In a democracy, the people choose who will govern them, as opposed to monarchies, dictatorships, etc., where the leaders come to power by inheritance or brute force.

Reinhold Niebuhr's comment, quoted above, should be carefully considered. It's the ability of human beings to act justly that makes democracy possible. But it's the likelihood that some rulers will turn out to be unjust that makes democracy necessary. It's the best safeguard against tyranny. In the real world, it's certain that some citizens are going to undermine the common good, but if these folks are public officials, in a democracy "the people" can turn them out of office.

Equality, of course, is one of the central tenets of democracy. Over the years, millions have emigrated to the United States longing to live in a land where they would be given a fair chance to get ahead in life and where their voice would be heard right alongside anyone else's. We rightly treasure this freedom and this equality.

But I fear that our concept of equality needs to be refreshed and reconnected to its meaning in the minds of our forefathers. Equality means that every person has *an equal right to be heard* — it does not mean that *any one idea is as true as any other,* and it certainly doesn't mean that *all ideas are equally helpful to society.* Democratic societies give their citizens the equal freedom to speak; it does not, however, protect them from speaking foolishly. So the freer we are, the harder we need to work at speaking wisely . . . and then acting responsibly.

Democracy is a bold experiment, without a doubt. It's based on faith, and faith's always dangerous because it allows for some pretty serious disappointments in the short run. But democracy believes, rightly it seems to me, that more good than harm will come — in the long run — from trusting the common folks with a voice and a vote. Today, we celebrate the good that has come from that trust!

Democracy assumes that there are extraordinary
possibilities in ordinary people.
HARRY EMERSON FOSDICK

July 5
CALMNESS

The idea of calm exists in a sitting cat.
JANE PAULEY

IT'S HARD NOT TO ENVY THE CALMNESS OF A CAT. Crazy things may be going on in the immediate area, but a cat can look upon the entire scene with an aloofness and imperturbability that are amusing and marvelous. If we had some of that calmness, wouldn't it be nice?

For most ordinary folks, calmness doesn't come naturally. Our tendencies seem to run in the direction of anxiety and agitation, so the quality of calmness probably won't be ours unless we cultivate it. There are principles we'll have to learn and disciplines we'll have to practice. Bit by difficult bit, we'll have to gain the ability to be calm.

We live in a distinctly uncalm age, and when people nowadays see the need for more calmness, they often have no idea where to look for it. Stewart L. Udall had some good advice for us all when he wrote, "If you want inner peace, find it in solitude, not speed, and if you would find yourself, look to the land from which you came and to which you go." It may be hard to find any solitude now, at least the kind that contributes to calmness, and we may have little time to appreciate where we've come from or to ponder where we're going, but these things are vital. They're vital not only to our calmness but to our strength and our ability to withstand the stress of constant change.

Calmness is one of the best gifts that we can give to others. You may think that you have little to offer to others, but if you'll work on acquiring a calm spirit, the example of that will be a powerful influence on those who know you. In this troubled world, we need more people who've paid the price to acquire some calmness. Calmness can preach a powerful sermon even when few words are spoken.

Calmness, of course, shouldn't be the highest value in a human life. There are times when honor calls us to lay aside quietness and enter into struggle and conflict. But if calmness is not the *summum bonum* of life, that doesn't mean it's not important at all. As Matthew Arnold said, "Calm's not life's crown, though calm is well." Balanced and complemented by other values, calmness is one of life's very good things. It's a good thing to have — and a good thing to give away.

He is a first-rate collector who can,
upon all occasions, collect his wits.
GEORGE DENNISON PRENTICE

TIMELINESS

How many things by season seasoned are
To their right praise and true perfection!
WILLIAM SHAKESPEARE

WE PROBABLY UNDERESTIMATE THE EXTENT TO WHICH THINGS ARE EITHER HELPED OR HURT BY THEIR TIMING. The old adage "timing is everything" may be an exaggeration, but it's certainly true that timing is critical. At exactly the right time, a certain thing may prove to be powerful, popular, or productive — while at any other time, the very same thing would fall noticeably flat. So what are some ways we could profit from pursuing timeliness? What does this quality mean when it's applied to our character and conduct?

Timeliness means being prompt. Two identical thank-you notes, one written within twenty-four hours and the other written six weeks after the fact, will have two very different effects on the recipient. Why do we let procrastination drain the goodness out of so many of our well-intended actions? Promptness pays huge dividends.

Timeliness means being punctual. Two of your employees are very similar in most ways, but one is always at work on time while the other is chronically late. Which one are you going to think of as being more mature and responsible? Two of your friends are very much alike, but one frequently keeps you waiting past the agreed-upon time. Which one are you going to describe as being more courteous?

Timeliness means being predictable. It's not enough to get the job done, and it's not enough to deliver the product — the job needs to be done on schedule, and the product needs to be delivered on time! Those on whom our actions impinge need to know what to expect from us; they need to be able to depend on our timeliness. So predictability, as simple as it seems, is a great gift that we can give to others.

In nothing, however, is timeliness more important than in our words. Whatever needs to be said, it usually takes some wisdom to know when to say it, and if we don't exercise that wisdom, the encouraging benefit of our words may be lost on those to whom we speak. It's one of life's greatest challenges to learn timeliness in our speech, but when we do, once in a while, say precisely the right thing at exactly the right time, what a marvelous thing of beauty it is to enjoy.

A word spoken in due season, how good it is!
THE BOOK OF PROVERBS

PRUDENCE

No one tests the depth of a river with both feet.
ASHANTI PROVERB

PRUDENCE MEANS BEING CAREFUL. It means using wisdom, good judgment, and common sense in deciding one's course of action. When the harmful consequences of a plan's failure would be greater than the helpful consequences of the plan's success, prudence will say, "Don't do it." In the game of Russian roulette, for example, a person has a five-out-of-six chance of winning. But that sixth chance is so dire that a prudent person would not play the game at all. It's prudence that keeps us from "courting disaster," as the saying goes.

Some other less-than-desirable traits often masquerade as prudence, of course. "Prudence is no doubt a valuable quality," wrote Robert Cecil, "but prudence which degenerates into timidity is very seldom the path to safety." So whenever we say we're being prudent, it's often worth asking whether we're being that or just plain timid.

And not only that, there are many times when prudence should not be the governing factor. From the standpoint of common sense, doing the right thing is often very imprudent, and many of the noblest deeds in the history of the world would never have been done had their doers allowed prudence to decide the question. Robert Hall summed it up nicely in this way: "In matters of conscience, first thoughts are best; in matters of prudence, last thoughts are best."

But properly understood and wisely exercised, prudence is a very good thing indeed. It would be a coward who never considered anything but the counsels of prudence, but it would be a fool who never consulted prudence at all. Prudence should always be given a seat at the table when significant matters are being decided.

In the end, I think the best way to look at prudence is to see it as something that helps us in the areas of restraint and reserve. In this age of uninhibited excess, we need to get reacquainted with some things like simplicity and understatement. It may be trite, but it's also true: less is sometimes more. Prudence can help us to get that "more" by putting the brakes on our runaway trains of thought.

Tell not all you know,
believe not all you hear,
do not all you are able.
ITALIAN PROVERB

MARRIAGE

A wedding anniversary is the celebration of love, trust, partnership,
tolerance, and tenacity. The order varies for any given year.

PAUL SWEENEY

IT TAKES MANY KINDS OF CHARACTER STRENGTH TO MAKE A
MARRIAGE WORK, NOT THE LEAST OF WHICH IS COMMITMENT.
In any given marriage, the combination of character traits is blended
differently; some marriages have a greater portion of love, some of
partnership, and some of tenacity. But all successful marriages are
built from the raw materials supplied by *character*. Personality may
have gotten the thing started, but character is what keeps it going.

A good marriage is no accident, and when one has been built,
it's a thing of admirable beauty. Love stories are always refreshing,
of course, but the most refreshing are those that have stood the test
of time. Think of your grandparents, for example. Without knowing them, I'd venture to guess that they were married for quite a long
while, despite difficulties that had to be overcome, and that their
relationship is something you find it encouraging to think about.

It's not stretching the truth to say that an effective marriage is
one of the highest achievements that a human being is capable of.
Those who've paid the price to be worthy marriage partners have
done something that requires far more substance than it would take to
win the World Series or the Nobel Prize. If you know someone who
has helped to build a good marriage, let them know that they're a bigger hero in your eyes than those who usually make the evening news.

Marriage is what we might call a dynamic relationship: within
it, things move and change and shift. You can't be in the marriage
relationship without being changed — and without changing the
person you're married to. The question is not whether we'll grow, but
whether we'll make that growth positive rather than negative. So may
we commit ourselves, today and every day, to two important things:
(1) growing toward greater health in our own character, and (2) growing toward a more healthful influence on the spouse to whom we
promised ourselves, the one who's being affected by everything we do.

You don't marry one person; you marry three: the person you think
they are, the person they are, and the person they are going to become
as the result of being married to you.

RICHARD NEEDHAM

STORIES

God made man because he loves stories.
ELIE WIESEL

ALL OF US ARE WRITING STORIES, AND WE'RE SURROUNDED
BY STORIES THAT OTHER PEOPLE ARE WRITING TOO. As
Thoreau said, "Wherever men have lived there is a story to be told."
Our stories may not be written down with pen and ink, but even so,
we're all engaged in events that, were they to be written, would constitute quite a chronicle. The tales that we're telling by the unfolding
of our human lives are immensely and endlessly interesting.

In its most basic sense, a "story" is a sequence of events. To have
a story, you must have more than an idea, a truth, a theme, or a thesis.
You must have some events, some happenings, and these must be successive: that is, they must be linked together, one leading to another.
But the truly fascinating thing about stories — and it's the reason why
we like stories so much — is that the telling of a sequence of events
can often reveal to us (or remind us of) ideas and truths that are outside our limited world of time and space. A plot is a powerful thing!

C. S. Lewis, who was very wise when it came to the magic of
stories, said it this way: "In life and art both, as it seems to me, we are
always trying to catch in our net of successive moments something
that is not successive. Whether in real life there is any doctor who can
teach us how to do it, so that at last either the meshes will become
fine enough to hold the bird, or we be so changed that we can throw
our nets away, and follow the bird to its own country, is not a question
for this essay. But I think it is sometimes done — or very, very nearly
done — in stories. I believe the effort to be well worth making."

So we should love stories. We should love to hear them, read
them, and tell them. And as for those stories that we ourselves are
living, we should be careful about them. Nothing is sadder in old age
than to look back on a life that, if a truthful storyteller were to tell it,
would be a hurtful story, an embarrassing story, or a shameful story.

But if our own stories are important, we should also be interested
in other people's stories. The tales that are unfolding around us every
day are well worth paying attention to. You just never know when
somebody's else's tale might be better than any you've heard so far . . .

But that is another story.
RUDYARD KIPLING

COMPENSATION

> There are comforts and compensations that one
> who has not suffered knows nothing of — like the lamps
> that nobody sees till the tunnel comes.
>
> A. W. BARBOUR

IN MANY WAYS BIG AND SMALL, LIFE HAS A WAY OF MAKING UP FOR THE THINGS THAT HAVE BEEN TAKEN AWAY FROM US. We hardly ever suffer loss in one area without finding that our capacity for joy has increased in another area. It's the bitterness of loss that allows us to savor the taste of other things, and like "the lamps that nobody sees till the tunnel comes," we see certain joys more clearly.

It's good for us to learn to appreciate life's compensations. To some extent, we all do appreciate the touches of grace that make up for our losses, but we need to appreciate them more *consciously.* If you've been wiped out financially but still have your health, don't take it for granted. Enjoy your health! Savor it! Don't let a drop of it go to waste!

It's also good for us to find ways to be a part of life's compensation to others. If your next-door neighbor has suffered some misfortune, you may be absolutely helpless to do anything about that misfortune, but your neighborliness may be a part of the way in which life is going to compensate them for their loss. Almost certainly, there is going to be something you can do, in some other area, to brighten their life.

And finally, it's good for us to compensate others for the generous things they do for us, or at least to try to do so. Granted, some people shower us with such kindness that we could never repay them adequately, but it's still a good idea to try. If we put our minds to it, we can almost always find some means of saying, "Let me make it up to you." My father, for example, was a watchmaker. He repaid many a kindness by fixing somebody's watch, free of charge, the next time it quit running.

We need to respect the fact that our world is governed by moral laws as well as physical ones. In the long term, if not in the short, wrongs tend to be righted. If we've been so foolish as to mistreat those around us, justice will eventually stand up and defend those who've been our victims. They will be compensated — and so will we. The medicine that we dispense to others had better have a good flavor, because sooner or later, we're going to get a taste of it.

> This is a world of compensations.
> ABRAHAM LINCOLN

July 11
FAMILIARITY

That song is best esteemed
with which our ears are most acquainted.

WILLIAM BYRD

THERE IS A WONDERFUL DELIGHT THAT COMES FROM THINGS THAT HAVE GROWN FAMILIAR. New things are delightful too, of course, but with new things, it takes a while to get to know all of their nooks and crannies so that we can enjoy them fully. In the case of familiar things, however, knowing them well allows us to enjoy them at a deeper and richer level. For example, I've enjoyed many books the first time I read them, but I wouldn't take anything for the great books that have become *familiar* to me. Each time I read them again, I love them even more. I "get" things that could never have been appreciated on the first (or even the second or third) reading.

To my way of thinking, there is a down-home kind of goodness that attaches itself to familiar things. E. B. White, who was a master at describing ordinary, everyday things, said, "Familiarity is the thing — the sense of belonging." Even with inanimate objects, there is a rich sense of rightness in handling things that we've grown accustomed to through long usage. This morning, I fried my breakfast bacon and eggs in my favorite cast-iron skillet. I've used it thousands of times. I know every little scratch on its surface. Its handle fits my hand as if it were made for it. And while a new skillet might have its own attractions, it would take a long time to love it as I love this old one. As Shelley said, "Familiar acts are beautiful through love."

It's tempting to let our eyes roam here, there, and everywhere in a never-satisfied quest for the extraordinary. But while it's good to be excited by the new from time to time, most of our attention needs to be paid to the familiar. Let's not despise or overlook the value of the commonplace things in our lives: all the objects, the events, the places, and the people who are well known to us. I've been around a little bit, and I can tell you, there is nothing in this world any better than "the old familiar faces" (Charles Lamb). Familiarity need not breed contempt — in the grateful heart, it can breed great contentment.

I embrace the common, I explore and sit at the feet of the familiar, the low.
Give me insight into today, and you may have the antique and future worlds.
What would we really know the meaning of? The meal in the firkin; the milk
in the pan; the ballad in the street; the news of the boat.

RALPH WALDO EMERSON

July 12
WHOLENESS

Not only is there but one way of doing things rightly,
but there is only one way of seeing them, and that is,
seeing the whole of them.

JOHN RUSKIN

WITH MOST THINGS, YOU CAN THINK OF THE WHOLE OR YOU CAN THINK OF THE PARTS. Sometimes it's necessary to identify and examine the parts, but that analysis doesn't do much good if we forget the whole situation that the parts are a part of. The "trees" may be interesting, but it's dangerous to lose sight of the "forest."

As finite beings with limited powers of observation and understanding, we're not going to see the complete whole of anything that we deal with. But even so, there's great wisdom in always trying to see as much of reality as we can. Many, if not most, of our mistakes come from taking into account only a part of the truth, so we help ourselves greatly when we take the time to understand more of the subject, to hear more of the evidence, and to see more of the picture.

Not only should we try to see more of the whole of things, but wholeness itself is a characteristic worth valuing. We should appreciate it, honoring and giving thanks for things that are whole and healthy. We should aspire to it, making wholeness in all things one of our ideals. And we should contribute to it, playing a positive role in making the things around us more whole rather than tearing them apart.

Wholeness is even something we should seek within ourselves, and "integrity" is the word that describes this kind of wholeness. Integrity is oneness or unity between our character and our conduct. When our outer practice is in harmony with our inner principles, then we experience a wholeness that is one of life's best possessions.

But in the most important sense, personal wholeness does not come from trying to integrate or unify the various parts of ourselves; it comes from taking our rightful place in relation to the larger reality of the world outside of ourselves. There is no wholeness without a peaceful conscience, and there's no peacefulness of conscience without doing our simple, individual duty to the world that is our home.

You exist but as a part inherent in a greater whole.
Do not live as though you had a thousand years before you.
The common due impends; while you live,
and while you may, be good.

MARCUS AURELIUS

MOMENTS

We do not remember days; we remember moments.

CESARE PAVESE

IN OUR MEMORIES ARE THE SNAPSHOTS OF MANY MAGICAL MOMENTS. I don't know how many moments can be stored in one person's memory, but I know it's a lot. My father, who at this writing is ninety years old, has a mental photo album that contains enough snapshots to entertain him long past the point when he will need to be entertained! And his has not been an unusual life. Like all of us, he has simply lived in a world where, as the days go by, there are lots of likable, "momentary" things to save up and enjoy later.

Good moments are things to savor. Occasionally, we're aware "in the moment" that something special is happening, and we should consciously taste every drop of the event as it unfolds. More often, though, it's only later that we recognize a moment's goodness, and when we do, we ought to enjoy that memory's taste with zest and gratitude. The memory may be of a private moment or of one shared with others. Either way, good moments are meant to be relished.

One of the most thoughtful things we can do for others is to make a few moments for them. While it's true that the best moments in life are often unplanned, spontaneous occurrences, it's also true that, if we're on the lookout, we can sometimes find an opportunity to make a moment memorable for someone else. It doesn't always have to involve a grand gesture or a costly gift; it just takes doing something that says, "I'm aware of you. I acknowledge you. I honor you." Extraordinary moments, in fact, tend to be made out of very ordinary materials: ice cream cones and park bench kisses, midsummer walks and late-night thunderstorms — things like these are what moments are made of. We don't have to look far; we just have to look.

The truth is, moments, and the memories that bring them back to us, are windows that look out onto another world. Bound as we are by time, our lives come to us sequentially, one moment at a time. But with each moment, especially the ones that bring intense joy or sorrow, we get a glimpse of something beyond the walls of the workaday world, something that calls to us. Our best moments, then, are those in which we answer the call . . . to dream, to grow, and to live.

Eternity was in that moment.

WILLIAM CONGREVE

THERAPY

> Fortunately [psycho] analysis is not the only way to resolve
> inner conflicts. Life itself still remains a very effective therapist.
>
> KAREN HORNEY

NOWADAYS, THE WORD "THERAPY" SUGGESTS NO MORE TO THE AVERAGE PERSON THAN "PSYCHOTHERAPY" OR PROFESSIONAL COUNSELING. But the word "therapy" is too good a word to limit to clinicians and counselors. To engage in therapy simply means to give help that is healing or curative in nature, and that's something that every one of us needs to be busy doing from time to time.

By the time our lives are finished, each of us will have become one or the other: a helper or a hurter. As far as our peers are concerned, there's not much in between. So it's good to aspire to being a helper. If others can say they find us to be good "therapy," we will have been paid a high compliment indeed. It's worth preparing our character and our conduct so that such a thing can truthfully be said.

The ability to help heal people when they've been hurt is not acquired accidentally. Healing is an art that requires skill, wisdom, and compassion, among other things. So if we want to be able to help those around us, we need to elevate therapy to the status of a goal in our lives. We need to start learning the tools of that worthy trade.

The therapeutic power of *words* is nothing short of amazing. Of all the things that human words can do, none is more impressive than their ability to heal. Sometimes even very serious emotional wounds can be helped by a seemingly simple balm: a word of encouragement, an expression of appreciation, or a suggestion of hope and confidence.

But if the words of others can be therapeutic — and they surely can be — then our own words can have that effect too. There may be times when someone we know needs to see a professional "therapist," and at times like that, we may feel we don't have much to offer in the way of help. But for every time when a friend needs professional help, there are many more times when a friend will need to hear the healing words that we can speak to them. Yes, it takes wisdom, and wisdom requires work, but we can learn to use the gift of language in such a way that those who hear our words are helped — and even healed.

> Words of comfort, skillfully administered,
> are the oldest therapy known to man.
>
> LOUIS NIZER

July 15
EASE

He flies through the air with the greatest of ease,
This daring young man on the flying trapeze.
GEORGE LEYBOURNE

HAVING LEARNED HOW TO DO SOMETHING EASILY IS ONE OF LIFE'S MOST WONDERFUL SATISFACTIONS. Especially when the thing was very difficult or awkward to begin with, there is a wholesome gratification that now comes from being able to do it easily. And not only do we enjoy what we ourselves can do easily, but we enjoy the ease with which others can do difficult things. Just last evening, I watched again the amazing performance of Michael Flatley and his troupe in *Lord of the Dance*. Irish step dancing is no easy thing, but Flatley and his friends do it with such joyous, exuberant ease that the result is enthralling, especially to those who know how hard it is.

In each of our lives, there are a number of helpful things we need to be able to do, and we should be willing to pay the price (in terms of discipline, sacrifice, and hard work) to do these things graciously and easily. Most good things are hard before they're easy; that's just the way the world works. So we have to persevere through our various apprenticeships and not give up until we've gained the mastery.

When the word "ease" is mentioned, however, many people think not of learning to do difficult things easily but of avoiding difficulty altogether! Some seem to envision a "life of ease" as a life where nothing difficult or unpleasant ever has to be done. And unfortunately, our culture seems to be headed in the direction of worshiping that kind of ease. But as W. Somerset Maugham said, "Any nation that thinks more of its ease and comfort than its freedom will soon lose its freedom; and the ironical thing about it is that it will lose its ease and comfort too." That's just as true for individuals as it is for nations.

But properly defined, ease is something we should pursue. We'll probably do more of the things we ought to do when they've become easy for us. But when we see people who can do those things easily right now, it would be foolish to want their skill without accepting the work that went into getting that skill. The "life of ease" is not one of lazy leisure but one of easy action — a life where good deeds aren't as difficult as they used to be. Getting to that point is anything but easy.

A life of ease is a difficult pursuit.
WILLIAM COWPER

RELIABILITY

Life is like a game of cards. Reliability is the ace,
industry the king, politeness the queen, thrift the jack.

EDWARD HOWE

SIMPLE RELIABILITY IS A FAR MORE VALUABLE, AND POWER-
FUL, TRAIT THAN MANY PEOPLE REALIZE. It may well be the
ace in life's game of cards, as Edward Howe says. If people can't safely
and consistently rely on us, then whatever other admirable qualities
we may possess, they won't be of much use in the long run. Reliability
is a major ingredient in the glue that holds everything else together.

Fact. Those who have to deal with us should be able to count on
our reliability in matters of fact. That is, they should be able to take it
for granted that we'll deal truthfully with them, whether in word or in
deed. It takes many years of honesty to build up a reputation for that
kind of reliability, but there's no more worthy goal we could have.

Follow-through. For every person who says he'll do something,
there aren't many who can be relied upon to do it, come what may.
These days, absolute dependability in the performance of one's commitments is a rare quality. Everywhere we turn, people are making
excuses for a failure to honor their obligations. But if follow-through
is rare, that only means it will be more valuable when we acquire that
trait. "Doing what we say" will distinguish us as being different.

Friendship. There have probably been few friendships that have
not been tested at some point by adversity or conflict, and friendships that can stand the test are both refreshing and strengthening.
Wouldn't it be good to give our friends the gift of reliability? Wouldn't
they appreciate knowing that they can count on our friendship?

As Edward Bulwer-Lytton suggests in the quotation below, those
who are "of consequence" in the world are those who can be relied
upon. It's true, just being reliable won't win you the Nobel Prize, and it
won't get you nominated for "Person of the Year" at any of the major
magazines. But being honest in what you say and do, reliable in the
performance of your duty, and faithful in each of your friendships will
make you a great person in most of the ways that matter very much.

A man is already of consequence in the world when it is known that we can
implicitly rely upon him. Often I have known a man to be preferred in
stations of honor and profit because he had this reputation: when he said he
knew a thing, he knew it, and when he said he would do a thing, he did it.

EDWARD BULWER-LYTTON

July 17
STEADINESS

FOR EVERY TIME WHEN WE NEED TO CHANGE, THERE ARE MANY MORE TIMES WHEN WE NEED TO HOLD STEADY. And for every person who is hurting himself by being unadaptable, there are many more who are hurting themselves by being unsteady.

The main ingredient in steadiness, obviously, is self-control. No matter what course we've charted for ourselves, it's inevitable that some contrary winds are going to blow against us somewhere along the way. Without a certain amount of self-control, we're simply not going to make it to our destination. To keep fluctuations, deviations, and vacillations from undoing us, we have to be able to enforce the dictates of our will. Our "self" must be governed and controlled.

A lack of self-control, and therefore steadiness, is what keeps most people from getting where they ought to go. They may know how to "talk the talk," they may have occasional flashes of inspiration and bursts of energy, they may even have enormous intelligence and talent — but without steadiness, they won't have many actual accomplishments to their credit when all is said and done. Despite all they could have done, they will have done less than the plodding good ol' boy who may not have known many things, but he knew how to keep putting one foot in front of the other, steadily. But that's not a very new insight, is it? In the fable of *The Tortoise And The Hare,* Aesop tried to teach us long ago that "slow and steady wins the race."

If you have a few friends who possess steadiness, you have one of life's genuine treasures. Those who are "steady of heart, and stout of hand" (Sir Walter Scott) deserve our highest esteem. But we ought to do more than just want steady people around us; we ought to be steady people ourselves. The steadiness that comes from being able to control ourselves will help to steady the lives of those who deal with us. We may never know exactly how, but holding a steady course in our own "little" lives really does help the bigger world around us.

Be his my special thanks, whose even-balanced soul,
From first youth tested up to extreme old age,
Business could not make dull, nor passion wild:
Who saw life steadily and saw it whole.
MATTHEW ARNOLD

July 18
PITY

Pity melts the mind to love.

JOHN DRYDEN

A S FEELINGS AND ATTITUDES GO, PITY IS A BIT ODD. We're not sure whether we think it's a good thing or a bad one. In general, we'd say that pity is a virtue, but it's a virtue with a mixed reputation.

If we heard someone being described as "pitiless," we wouldn't think the person had received a compliment, and if someone said, "Don't just stand there — for pity's sake, help him," we wouldn't see that as anything but an honorable appeal. But when we're on the receiving end, pity's not always something we appreciate. As Balzac said, "The response man has the greatest difficulty in tolerating is pity, especially when he warrants it." But should we resist or resent pity? Is it anything more than pride that keeps us from appreciating the pity that a caring friend (or even an honest enemy) might extend to us?

Pity is not condescending, or at least it doesn't have to be. If our present situation is one which another human being might naturally respond to with concern and regret, it really doesn't matter whether that person is "above" us or "below" us. When pity is a reasonable response to some circumstance of ours, we ought to receive it humbly and gratefully. And when someone else's circumstance calls for our pity, we ought to feel that honorable sentiment without any condescension. If you're suffering today, I'll probably be the one suffering tomorrow. It's a waste of time to ask who is "superior" to whom.

Most of us understand, however, that in order to be genuine, pity must be more than a feeling; it must involve real, active compassion. "We may have uneasy feelings for seeing a creature in distress without pity; for we have not pity unless we wish to relieve them," said Samuel Johnson. So authentic pity is a sorrow for someone else's condition that urges us to help them, if we can. In the New Testament, James, the brother of Jesus, wrote, "If a brother or sister is naked and destitute of daily food, and one of you says to them, 'Depart in peace, be warmed and filled,' but you do not give them the things needed for the body, what does it profit?" So today, if there is any pity to be shown, let's make sure it's the kind that serves as well as sympathizes.

What value has compassion that
does not take its object in its arms?

ANTOINE DE SAINT-EXUPÉRY

RELIANCE

It's a vice to trust all,
and equally a vice to trust none.
SENECA

IF IT'S IMPORTANT TO BE RELIABLE, IT'S ALSO IMPORTANT TO BE RELIANT. Although we need to be wise in choosing people to rely on, we need to be willing to rely on those whom we choose. Never trusting anyone at all would not be a virtue. It would be a vice.

To be sure, our ultimate reliance should not be placed in any human being or group of human beings. In the larger sense, Asher Ben Jehiel was giving good advice when he said, "Don't rely on the broken reed of human support." God alone should be our final trust.

And not only that, there is another clarification that needs to be made: reliance on other human beings doesn't mean that we're naive about the possibility of being disappointed by them. We can make allowance for human error and still not be as cynical as H. L. Mencken, who, true to his usual form, said, "No man is worthy of unlimited reliance — his treason, at best, only waits for sufficient temptation." People don't have to be perfect for us to rely on them. We know that mistakes will be made and, yes, even that treason will be committed, but relying on others can still be a wise thing to do. For one thing, it multiplies the amount of work that can be accomplished.

When we make the choice to rely on somebody, we give them a gift. By trusting them to do something, knowing in advance that the result may be far from perfect, we say to them: "I am willing to rely on you. I am willing to make myself vulnerable to you. I hope you'll venture boldly in your effort to get the job done, knowing that if you make mistakes, I'll help you fix them. Even if you fail me seriously, that won't be the end of the world. I accept the risk of trusting you."

So can we not set ourselves the goal of being both reliable and reliant? Can we not make the voluntary choice, occasionally, to rely on the help of our friends and neighbors and coworkers? There's no doubt that relying on others is going to hurt us now and then, but even so, there's more to be gained by reliance than by refusing to rely. In this world, things don't always turn out as we expect, but even in an imperfect world, I believe reliance is still a gift worth giving.

Love all, trust a few.
WILLIAM SHAKESPEARE

July 20
RIGHTEOUSNESS

To be individually righteous is the first of all duties, come what may
to one's self, to one's country, to society, and to civilization itself.
JOSEPH WOOD KRUTCH

IN TODAY'S READING, I WANT TO ASK YOU TO RECONSIDER
YOUR CONCEPT OF A VERY IMPORTANT WORD: RIGHTEOUS-
NESS. The popular concept of this word is that it is a religious word
meaning little more than *self-righteousness*. If someone said they were
striving to be righteous, most people would think they were in danger
of developing a holier-than-thou attitude. But as the spelling and the
etymology of the word suggest, righteousness ("right-wise-ness") has
to do with what is *right*. To pursue righteousness is to set oneself the
goal of thinking and acting rightly in all of one's dealings. And this, as
Joseph Wood Krutch reminds us, is "the first of all duties."

Actually, the core concept of righteousness is *justice*. And what
is justice? It's doing what is fair — and the fairness is judged not by
our own opinions but by the objective standards of equity that people
have held to throughout history. I like Benjamin Disraeli's definition:
"Justice is truth in action." When we act with justice, we're acting in
concord with timeless truth. And to do that is to act righteously.

We need to have more faith in the ultimate victory of righteousness. To act against what's right is to fight against reality, and to do
that is to doom ourselves to failure. Sooner or later, right will predom-
inate; nothing can prevail against it. "God's mill grinds slow, but sure"
is the way George Herbert put it. And so Abraham Lincoln spoke
wisely when he said, "Let us have faith that right makes might, and in
that faith let us to the end dare to do our duty as we understand it."

These days many of us live in affluent societies. As far as the
"creature comforts" are concerned, we have much to be thankful for.
But prosperity (and even the opportunity to become prosperous) has
a dangerous tendency: it nudges us in the direction of a self-centered,
materialistic view of life. In the mad rush to enjoy ever more of the
possessions and pleasures of this world, the importance of things like
righteousness may be left behind. So we need reminders — I need
them as much as you do — that in the final tally of all our deeds, the
only thing that will matter is whether we did what was *right*.

God takes notice of clean hands, not full hands.
LATIN PROVERB

TRANSFORMATION

The future enters into us, in order to transform
itself in us, long before it happens.

RAINER MARIA RILKE

A REN'T YOU GLAD THAT WE CAN CHOOSE TO BE CHANGED? If
we couldn't envision a better future and then decide to do things
that result in a transformation from one quality of life to another, we'd
be stuck right where we are. It's a marvelous ability, this ability to undergo change. We ought not to (a) underestimate the extent to which
we can be transformed, or (b) underappreciate the decision-making
ability that can set those changes in motion.

The positive transformations that take place in our lives are good
not only for us but for our loved ones. Right now, none of us has a
finished character, and we need to be changing and growing in the
direction of realizing our full potential. When we submit ourselves to
positive change, and even actively seek it out, we are showing one of
the highest kinds of love to the other human beings who know us.

The importance of emotion. Carl Jung argued that there "can be
no transforming of darkness into light and of apathy into movement
without emotion." I believe he was right. Real transformation must involve the heart as well as the head. In particular, we must learn to look
ahead and "taste" the joy that will come from making good changes.

The importance of solitude. One reason we rarely experience any
significant transformation nowadays is that we spend too little time
alone. "Solitude," said Henri J. M. Nouwen, "is the furnace of transformation." We'd open the door to positive change more often if we'd
get away from the crowd and go someplace conducive to reflection.

Don't discount the possibility that before this day is done something you think, something you do, or something that happens to you
will trigger a large transformation in your life. Will the change be for
the better or for the worse? Well, that depends on what you choose to
think, what you choose to do, and how you choose to respond to what
happens to you. Although I don't know you personally, I do hope that
the ways in which you allow yourself to be transformed will be truly
and lastingly good, not only for you but for those around you.

Even a thought, even a possibility,
can shatter us and transform us.

FRIEDRICH WILHELM NIETZSCHE

POWER

All power is of one kind, a sharing of the nature of the world.
The mind that is parallel with the laws of nature will be in the
current of events, and strong with their strength.
RALPH WALDO EMERSON

IF WE WISH TO BE POWERFUL (AT LEAST IN THE GOOD SENSE),
THERE IS SOMETHING THAT WE MUST UNDERSTAND. Power
comes from having our character and our conduct aligned with true-
north principles. Over the long haul, the "laws of nature," as Emerson
referred to them, can't be safely defied or successfully ignored. Both
our goals and our means of getting to our goals must respect what is
real. They must be in sync with truth and reality: the way the world
really works. If they're not, our "power" will prove impotent sooner or
later. No human being is a law unto himself. We're each connected to
and surrounded by a larger reality of people, things, and forces. When
our actions rightly relate us to the world in the larger sense, we gain
power; but when our actions put us at odds with the world that we're
a part of, we lose power. It's pretty simple, actually.

Responsibility. To be aligned with reality, we must accept this
fact: the power that comes from rank is weak if it doesn't accept the
responsibility that goes with rank. Authority is a trust, a stewardship.
It must always exercise its power for the common good.

Passion. If we don't care deeply about the things we care about, we
ought not to be surprised at our lack of power. John Stuart Mill said,
"One person with a belief is a social power equal to ninety-nine who
have only interests." So which do you have: beliefs or mere interests?

Humor. It may seem ironic, but we lose power when we take
ourselves too seriously. I've always liked Eric Sevareid's observation:
"Next to power without honor, the most dangerous thing in the world
is power without humor." We're more effective when we can chuckle.

The most powerful power, of course, is the power that *serves.*
There is far more power in the open hand than in the clenched fist.
So let's appreciate the concept of power. Let's gain it for the right reasons and use it in the right ways. Some kinds of power may corrupt,
but *principled* power doesn't do that. It ennobles those who possess it.

In every community, there is work to be done.
In every nation, there are wounds to heal.
In every heart, there is the power to do it.
MARIANNE WILLIAMSON

PLANNING

Our lives are not totally random.
We make commitments, we cause things to happen.
WENDY WASSERSTEIN

THINGS DON'T ALWAYS TURN OUT AS WE PLAN, BUT IF WE DON'T PLAN, WE DOOM OURSELVES TO NOTHING MORE THAN DRIFTING. Planning is the process in which we decide what we're going to do and how we're going to do it. If we couldn't do that, we'd be the helpless victims of circumstance. But the truth is, we can plan. It's a marvelous thing to consider, but we really can alter the course of events in this world. By thinking and making commitments, we can, as Wendy Wasserstein says, "cause things to happen."

There is a sense in which the planning is the hardest part of any project. The construction of a high-quality house may have its own difficulties, but conceiving the plan for that house is likely to have been harder. Once things are well planned, the planning makes their accomplishment easier. As Samuel Johnson said, "Many things difficult to design prove easy to performance." We'd often make our work easier if we'd go to the trouble of planning it wisely and creatively.

Most of us sell ourselves short. We rarely make plans that are big enough to fire our imaginations. We'd be moved to greater effort if our plans were on a grander scale. So Daniel Hudson Burnham said, "Make no little plans; they have no magic to stir men's blood."

But the fact of the matter is this: we often don't accomplish our goals because we don't follow through on our plans. Speaking of strategic planning in the business world, Peter Drucker said, "What makes a plan capable of producing results is the commitment of key people to work on specific tasks." If that's true in the world of commerce, it's probably even more true in the ordinary world of everyday activities. A good theoretical plan having been made, we need to commit ourselves to the specific steps ("tasks") that will turn the abstract plan into something concrete, something real. There's a Persian proverb that says, "Thinking well is wise; planning well is wiser; but doing well is the wisest and best of all." We ought to plan our work, and we're fools if we don't. But eventually, we've got to work our plan.

Plans get you into things,
but you've got to work your way out.
WILL ROGERS

GIFTS

When the hand ceases to give,
the heart ceases to pray.
IRISH PROVERB

EVENTUALLY, WE ALL COME TO BE SEEN BY OUR PEERS AS BEING ONE OR THE OTHER: GIVERS OR TAKERS. If we're givers, we'll sometimes do some taking, of course, and if we're takers, we might do a little giving once in a while. But by the time we've lived a few years, other people can usually tell which trait is our predominant one. We're creatures of habit, and if we don't adopt the habit of giving, then the habit of taking will be the one that people will know us for.

The giving of gifts is one of the most important things we ever do. And if those around us rarely receive any gifts from us, that is a dangerous and hurtful situation indeed. In the words of the proverb quoted above, "When the hand ceases to give, the heart ceases to pray." We can make no rightful claim to things like reverence and gratitude if there is no evidence of giving in our lives. Nor can we say we care about other human beings. As Frank Clark said, "You may give gifts without caring — but you can't care without giving."

Not many days will go by in which we can't find an opportunity to give someone a gift. We ought to be eager to seize these opportunities — and creative in the ways in which we take advantage of them. Whether large or small, our gifts should always involve the giving of some portion of *ourselves*. That's the very thing that makes a gift so meaningful and important. A true gift always says, in effect, "I value you enough to give up a part of my very self for you." Measured by that standard, the best gifts are those in which we devote our minds and hearts to others. In fact, Richard Moss may be right when he says, "The greatest gift to another is the purity of your attention."

We ought not to underestimate the value of the gifts that we're able to give. We may not be in a position to give gifts of any great monetary value, but those aren't usually the most beneficial gifts anyway. What about the helping hand that we could give? Or the encouraging word? Or the smile or the friendly handshake? We dare not despise these good gifts or fail to give them whenever we can.

Give what you have. To someone it may
be better than you dare to think.
HENRY WADSWORTH LONGFELLOW

COMPLIMENTS

It is a great mistake for men to give up paying compliments,
for when they give up saying what is charming,
they give up thinking what is charming.

OSCAR WILDE

BECOMING A PERSON WHO FREQUENTLY PAYS COMPLIMENTS TO OTHERS IS ONE OF THE HEALTHIEST THINGS THAT ANYONE CAN DO. Just as our thinking has an effect on our behavior, it's also true that our behavior, including our speaking, has an effect on our thinking. When we speak words of praise to other people, complimenting their good points, the effect on us is healthy — it's refreshing, energizing, and uplifting. Granted, we don't give out compliments primarily because it makes us feel better, but the fact remains, it does make us feel better. We'll come a lot closer to thinking of others as we should when we find ourselves speaking to them as we should.

To be sure, compliments must be sincere and unselfish in order to be healthy. The other person may receive some benefit from a compliment that is selfishly motivated on our part, but the exercise is hardly healthy for us. Indeed, flattery is one of the most corrosive things imaginable. When we compliment someone for the primary purpose of getting them to take more notice of us, we're doing a despicable deed. By our compliment, we're pretending to say, "I am aware of you," when in reality what we're saying is, "I want you to be aware of me." So the deed is not only despicable; it's also dishonest.

When we're on the receiving end of a compliment, however, it's a waste of time to wonder what the other person's motives might be. In general, it's a good idea to accept others' compliments humbly and gratefully, giving them the benefit of whatever doubt there may be as to motive. "A compliment is a gift not to be thrown away carelessly unless you want to hurt the giver" (Eleanor Hamilton).

Compliments are powerful gifts that we can give to those around us. They're powerfully encouraging and powerfully strengthening. And not only that, when they're genuine, they bring welcome joy and delight, both to the giver and the receiver. Given the ease with which compliments may be enjoyed, it's a wonder that we don't indulge in them more often. Don't we see how much good a good word can do?

A compliment is verbal sunshine.

ROBERT ORBEN

PROFESSIONALISM

A professional is someone who can do
his best work when he doesn't feel like it.

ALISTAIR COOKE

ARE YOU A PROFESSIONAL? The *American Heritage Dictionary* defines a profession as "an occupation or vocation requiring training in the liberal arts or the sciences and advanced training in a specialized field." By that definition, medicine and law would be professions. There is, however, a more general kind of professionalism that can apply — and should apply — to almost every one of us.

Standards. Professionals hold themselves to higher standards of excellence than amateurs. They're never content to do mediocre work, and even when they have the knack of doing excellent work easily, they're not content until the work is the very best that they can make it, within the time that's available. Professionalism means working at the highest level, constantly learning and continually improving.

Ethics. In a world where it sometimes seems that corruption and unfairness have crept into every corner of the workplace, we need to be reminded that it's only the amateurs who cheat. The true professional is governed by the strictest ethics of his profession. He never bends the rules for personal advantage. "The essence of a genuine professional man is that he cannot be bought" (H. L. Mencken).

Self-discipline. Basketball great Julius Erving once said, "Being a professional is doing all the things you love to do on the days when you don't feel like doing them." In my line of work, for example, a writer who can't write except when he's in the mood is, at least in that respect, still an amateur. Professionalism means that we learn how to put mind over matter. It means training the flesh to follow the spirit, rather than allowing the flesh to run (and often ruin) the show.

We don't have to make our living in one of the recognized professions to get the benefit of professionalism in our work. Whatever we do, we can do it with the attitude of the professional rather than the amateur. We can hold ourselves to higher standards, finer ethics, and better self-discipline than those who are content to just get by.

If your work is worth doing, it's worth doing with excellence. At the end of the day, you wouldn't want it any other way, would you?

Never let it be said of you that you lived an amateur life.
ANONYMOUS

VERVE

> One of the final challenges for human beings is to get old
> with as much verve and gumption as possible. Old parents who
> keep on being interested in life give a subtle kind of sustenance
> to their children; they are givers of hope and affirmers of life.
>
> ALISON JUDSON RYERSON

VERVE AND GUMPTION. How much of these are you going to have left by the time you get old, if you haven't already gotten there? Do you have any verve and gumption right now? These may not be life's most important character qualities, but they're valuable in their proper place and we should appreciate them for what they are.

Verve is a colorful word. Its sound almost gives away its meaning: the expression of one's ideas with energy and enthusiasm. Think of old Red Skelton, for example. He never said anything profoundly new or radically unique, but whatever he said, he said with verve. And as a result, people listened — with engagement, interest, and delight.

If you and I don't have much verve anymore (as we naturally did when we were children), it's worth wondering why. We might blame it on circumstances that have beaten us down and sapped our energy. But real verve doesn't come from being surrounded by fortunate circumstances; it comes from *giving ourselves enthusiastically to the tasks that are ours to take care of.* "Satisfaction," wrote Nikolai Berdyaev, "is felt not by those who take and make demands but by those who give and make sacrifices. In them alone the energy of life does not fail."

People who live their lives and do their work with verve tend to have a more powerful impact for good on the lives of others. So we'd probably give our friends and family a gift worth giving if we started expressing ourselves with a bit more energy and enthusiasm.

On the other hand, few things in life are sadder than to see someone who no longer has any verve left. "The worst bankrupt in the world is the man who has lost his enthusiasm" (H. W. Arnold).

Some of the things we need to do in life aren't very effective if they're not done with verve (such as saying "thank you" or "I love you"). Too many of us fall below the level of effectiveness because our words and deeds are little more than lukewarm. Wouldn't it be better, really, if we decided to do life's good things with a little more zip?

> It don't mean a thing, if it ain't got that swing.
>
> ELLA FITZGERALD

July 28
FAVORITES

I know what I like.
HENRY JAMES

O UR "FAVORITES" ARE THE THINGS, THE OCCASIONS, AND
THE PEOPLE WHOM WE REGARD WITH SPECIAL FAVOR. Like
Henry James, most of us know what we like, and our favorites are the
things we like especially well. To have favorites is simply to have, as
Henry David Thoreau put it, "a sincere love for some things."

The amazing variety that characterizes the human race is due,
in part, to the fact that we each have a unique set of favorites. "There
are," as Horace wrote, "as many preferences as there are men." Our
likes and dislikes may overlap with those of our closest friends to
some extent, but no two of us have exactly the same set of favorites.
And that's good. It would be a much less interesting world if we all
regarded everything in life with exactly the same degree of favor.

It seems to me that we should take the time to consciously appreciate our favorite things more often. If there is something that
delights me in a special way, I ought to relish that thing and savor
its enjoyment intentionally. And if there is something that uniquely
pleases you, you ought to drink its enjoyment down to the last drop. It
does us a down-home kind of good to have familiar, favorite things —
and it does us even more good to appreciate them mindfully.

Nowadays, we hear a lot about "equality," and that may cause
us to feel a little uncomfortable with the concept of favoritism. But
having favorites is not unjust, and it's no infringement on equality. It's naive to think that we can like everybody and everything
without showing any partiality at all. In fact, if we tried to do that, it
would take much of the value out of bestowing favor on anything. As
Moliére wrote, "Esteem must be founded on some sort of preference.
Bestow it on everybody and it ceases to have any meaning at all."

What would be wrong, of course, would be to *limit* ourselves to
our favorites. Having favorites is fine, but we need to deal rightly with
things (and especially people) that we don't like as well. And not only
that, we need to be willing to experiment. Who knows? There may be
some really good things out there that could become favorites if we
ever got outside of our preferences and gave them a chance.

Let us prefer, let us not exclude.
JOSEPH ROUX

PRESERVATION

*The fundamental idea of good is thus: that it consists in preserving life,
in favoring it, in wanting to bring it to its highest value; and evil consists
in destroying life, doing it injury, hindering its development.*

ALBERT SCHWEITZER

AS WE LIVE AND WORK FROM DAY TO DAY, THE RESULT OF
OUR ACTIVITY OUGHT TO BE THE PRESERVATION, OR SAVING,
OF SOME THINGS WORTHY OF BEING SAVED. We don't always think
clearly about what is worth preserving, and our efforts at preservation
aren't always successful, but it would be sad if nobody could say, at the
end of our lives, that there was any good thing that we had preserved.

Few of the good things in the world can remain unless somebody expends some effort to preserve them. And so when we lend our
energies to the work of preservation, we're doing worthy work. "To
preserve and renew is almost as noble as to create," said Voltaire.

Life is full of change, of course, and never more so than in these
modern days. There are times when things need to be replaced,
removed, or gotten rid of. But the purpose of these changes is not
merely negative. Ideally, we set aside some things in order to have
better things which can be preserved. Thomas Babington was correct when he said, "Reform, that you may preserve." Reformation and
preservation don't have to be enemies; they can be allies.

Specifically what it is that we preserve depends, of course, on
our values, so there is much to be said for refining and improving our
values. Most of us know what it's like to look back and see things that
we discarded in the past that should have been preserved. So we're
wise if we work on improving our powers of judgment and discrimi-
nation. We should want to be, in the well-known words of Abraham
Lincoln, "honorable alike in what we give and what we preserve."

Are you a "preservationist"? Are there any good things that, by
your help, are being saved from destruction? If not, there may be some
little deeds you could start doing right now that would help preserve
the most important thing of all: the *hearts* of your fellow human beings. You have it in your power to help hold back the ruinous forces
that your friends and family members are struggling against. *So do it!*

*Life is made up, not of great sacrifices or duties,
but of little things, in which smiles and kindness and
small obligations win and preserve the heart.*

HUMPHRY DAVY

July 30
INTIMACY

> The great gift of family life is to be intimately
> acquainted with people you might never even introduce
> yourself to, had life not done it for you.
>
> KENDALL HAILEY

INTIMACY IS THE ACT OF TWO PEOPLE MAKING THEMSELVES KNOWN TO ONE ANOTHER IN A VERY DEEP WAY. Sexual intimacy immediately comes to mind, of course, and there is certainly a sense in which that kind of intimacy involves the deepest knowing that is possible between two human beings. But there are other kinds of intimacy that are hardly less important. As Kendall Hailey humorously suggests, there is even an intimacy among extended family members that we should learn to be thankful for.

It's sad to contemplate the fact that some people never allow themselves to be known intimately by anybody. Even those who are married sometimes fail to make themselves known — genuinely, honestly, and deeply — to their spouses. Rollo May said, "Intimacy requires courage because risk is inescapable. We cannot know at the outset how the relationship will affect us." Yet if it is fear that keeps us from the generous joys of intimacy, we need to overcome that fear.

Perhaps it should go without saying, but we'll say it anyway: *we shouldn't be intimate with just anybody and everybody.* Historically, the major codes of morality in the world have always indicated that our sexual intimacy should be limited to one person. But even with the intimacy of close friendship, we shouldn't give that private gift to any but a few, and those few should be chosen with great wisdom.

A healthy human life requires some intimacy and also some aloneness. Depending on our personalities, some of us need more of one than the other, but to some extent we all need a balance between making our personal selves known to others and keeping some distance between ourselves and others. On some other day, you may need a reminder of the healthfulness of independence, but today, let's be reminded of the goodness of intimacy. Though it requires a courage that sometimes seems beyond us, intimacy — with a few individuals, carefully chosen — is one of life's great privileges. Don't miss it.

> Our daily existence requires both closeness and distance,
> the wholeness of self, the wholeness of intimacy.
>
> JUDITH VIORST

CONSTANCY

No virtue can be great if it is not constant.

ALFONSO MILAGRO

IN A WORLD WHERE THE PACE OF CULTURAL CHANGE IS QUICK-ENING, WE SHOULD MAKE SURE THAT OUR CHARACTER AND OUR COMMITMENTS DON'T CHANGE AS OFTEN AS OUR OUTWARD CONDITIONS DO. Whatever virtues we may possess today, these will be of little value in the long run if they don't remain constant.

Constancy is a truly amazing gift when it's given to others. Until you try it, you may not believe the difference it will make when you let those around you know that, from now on, they can count on you. No matter what the relationships may be, when those who have to deal with you find out that they no longer have to guess what you're going to do, there will quickly be a change for the better in those relationships. When (a) your character is constant, (b) your commitments are kept, and (c) your actions are "count-on-able," you will start getting thank-yous from people who appreciate what you've given them.

John Calvin said, "The word 'hope' I take for faith; and indeed hope is nothing else but the constancy of faith." It may be that this statement sums up the major challenge before us these days: to maintain the constancy of *faith*, that is, to hold on to the things that we believe in, based on trustworthy evidence, when the momentary appearance of things seems to call our confidence into question.

There is one kind of constancy that may seem to be inconstant, and that is the constancy of *growth*. If we're true to our principles, constancy may sometimes require changes that have the appearance of inconsistency. But there is no better constancy than holding fast to conscience — making whatever changes are necessary as our conscience gets a better grip on the reality of right and wrong.

Perhaps above all, though, we need the constancy of *love*. Most of us are at least a bit moody, and even if we're not moody, we're subject to the pressures of our changing circumstances. Can't we make it a point of honor to be constant in our love for those who have a right to expect love from us? Try giving that gift and see what happens!

There are two sorts of constancy in love: the one comes from the constant discovery in our beloved of new grounds for love, and the other comes from making it a point of honor to be constant.

FRANÇOIS DE LA ROCHEFOUCAULD

CONCERN

It is your concern when your neighbor's wall is on fire.
HORACE

OFTEN, WE HAVE A DANGEROUSLY NAIVE CONCEPT OF WHAT IT IS THAT WE NEED TO BE CONCERNED ABOUT. When it comes to the truly big issues of life, we can be shockingly unconcerned, and at the same time, we can be enormously concerned about things that are little more than trivia. In general, of course, we tend to be too self-centered in our concerns, but even there, we can be naive. We often fail to see how we hurt ourselves in the long run by being so unconcerned about our fellow human beings in the short run. As Horace said, "It is your concern when your neighbor's wall is on fire."

What would be a fair measure of how concerned we are about a particular thing? Well, many people judge the level of their concern by their thoughts. That is, they believe that they are concerned about a thing if they think about it a lot, or even if they intend to think about it a lot at some point in the future. But the genuineness and greatness of our concern aren't measured by emotional intensity alone, although that's a part of it. It's measured also by action. The things that we're concerned about are the things that we're doing something about.

So, in a sense, we need to give more consideration to our actions than to our thoughts. It is true that our actions grow out of our thoughts, and in that sense, we need to be primarily concerned with our ideas and principles. But having striven to have right thoughts, we must then be even more concerned to carry out those thoughts in right actions. Planning is crucially important, as all wise people know, but for every person who fails for lack of planning, many more fail for lack of execution. For that reason, then, we need to give a greater share of our concern to the actual, day-to-day conduct of life. "Conduct is three-fourths of our life and its largest concern" (Matthew Arnold).

We rarely, if ever, honor our friends and family any more than when we show concern for them. And although concern is a gift of great value, it's a gift that all of us can give, whether we're rich or poor. It would be good if we gave it more often — with less worry about what we have to do and more interest in what is good to do.

Grace refuses to put a ceiling or a floor
on concern for the neighbor.
JOSEPH FLETCHER

August 2

NURTURING

Countless times each day a mother does what no one else can do quite
as well. She wipes away a tear, whispers a word of hope, eases a child's fear.
She teaches, ministers, loves, and nurtures the next generation of citizens.

JAMES C. DOBSON

WHEN SOMEONE ENGAGES IN AN ACT THAT HAS A NURTUR-
ING EFFECT ON ANOTHER PERSON, ONE OF THE MOST
WONDERFUL THINGS IN THE WORLD TAKES PLACE. Nurturing is
wonderful both in its beauty and its benefit. It's beautiful because it's
an act of grace, and it's beneficial because it makes the difference between life and death. Nurturing is among the highest of human acts.

Although women often have a more natural aptitude for nurturing than men, nurturing is not just a female responsibility. Just as
with other responsibilities, the responsibility to nurture is not limited
to those who find it naturally easy. Whether we're male or female, or
young or old, we all have some duty in the matter of nurturing others.

"Nurture" comes from the same root as the words "nutrition"
and "nourish." In its most basic sense, it means to provide that which
is needed for another person to survive and thrive. None of us is so
independent that we can do without sustenance from anyone else.
People need to be nurtured — and they need to nurture one another.

But like people, relationships also need to be nurtured. You can't
nurture a relationship, of course, without nurturing the people who
are in it, but it's helpful to think of relationships themselves as "persons" who need to be taken care of and given the proper nutrition.

Too much of the time, we're interested in whether others are
nurturing us and not in whether we're nurturing them. The quality of
our lives would be improved if we reversed this emphasis and started
being more concerned about nurturing those around us. Being a nur-
turer — or at least being a good one — requires work. To provide the
things that others need, we have to grow. We have to equip ourselves
with the abilities that are necessary to nurture and to nourish. But if
this work is important, it's also satisfying. Indeed, there aren't many
things in this world more nourishing than to nourish someone else.

Just as we are learning to value and conserve the air we breathe,
the water we drink, the energy we use, we must learn to value and conserve
our capacity for nurture. Otherwise, in the name of human potential we will
slowly but surely erode the source of our humanity.

ELAINE HEFFNER

IMMEDIACY

Each day provides its own gifts.

MARTIAL

L IVING WITH A SENSE OF "IMMEDIACY" MEANS THAT WE DEAL RIGHTLY WITH WHAT IS DIRECTLY IN FRONT OF US. If something is "immediate," that means there is nothing between us and it. The present moment is immediate: there are no intervening moments that we have to live through to get to it. It is "right here, right now." Consider the wisdom of gaining a measure of immediacy in our lives:

The value of immediacy. Doing right now the thing that is best suited to our immediate situation is the only way to taste the goodness of life in its fullness. As Martial reminds us, "Each day provides its own gifts." Whatever tomorrow's gifts may be, there is a span of time between us and those gifts. Today's gifts have already arrived, however. They are immediate, and their goodness shouldn't be despised.

The importance of immediacy. If we don't use a particular moment to its best advantage, then we lose that moment, and it can never be gotten back. The present is a precious commodity; it's all that we have. And so to default, procrastinate, or otherwise throw away the immediate point in time is to throw away the only thing that truly belongs to us in life. "Remember," wrote Marcus Aurelius, "that the sole life which a man can lose is that which he is living at the moment."

The power of immediacy. Learning to live in the immediate moment is a powerful thing to do. If you've never tried it, you'd probably be amazed at the good momentum it can set in motion in your life. But not only that, it also increases our influence on others. The folks who have a positive impact on other people aren't usually guilty of procrastination; they know that the time to act is almost always now.

There are few resolutions we can make that will make any greater difference for good than resolving to live with a sense of immediacy. Enjoying each moment as it passes, doing each moment's duty as it confronts us, and gaining the influence that comes from living immediately — these are things that we'd be foolish not to do. It's worth the effort to deal promptly and thankfully with what is immediate, even when it's difficult — and *especially* when it's difficult.

The difficult we do immediately.
The impossible takes a little longer.

UNITED STATES ARMY

August 4
TASTEFULNESS

Men, generally, going with the stream, seldom judge
for themselves, and purity of taste is almost as rare as talent.
FRANÇOIS VOLTAIRE

MENTION THE WORD "TASTE," AND YOU'RE LIKELY TO GET AN ARGUMENT GOING. Some folks believe that "there's no accounting for taste," and that one person's tastes are as valid as anyone else's. Others go to the opposite extreme and assume that their own tastes are the infallible standard by which everybody else's ought to be judged. Extremes and confused notions aside, however, there is something to be said for the idea of "good taste." There really is such a thing, and most of us would do well to learn a bit more about it.

"Taste" is the ability to discern what is excellent or appropriate and what is not. The fact that judgment has to be exercised doesn't mean the process is meaningless, nor is the process nullified simply because people sometimes use poor judgment. Some things are important to attempt even though our attempts may be imperfect, and acquiring the habit of tastefulness is one of them. Distinguishing between the excellent and the inferior is a virtuous thing to try to do.

We owe it to ourselves to sharpen our taste and live life as tastefully as possible. Not many days go by that we don't face some choices between the tasteful and the not-so-tasteful. Having a good conscience requires, in part, that we pursue what good taste would say is best.

But we also owe it to those around us to act tastefully. One part of taste is knowing what is seemly or least likely to give offense in social situations. Isn't that a good thing to know? And if we avoided acting in bad taste around others, wouldn't that be a good gift to give them?

While there is obviously a subjective element in the enjoyment of many things, concepts like "beauty" and "joy" aren't totally subjective. We miss the best part of life when we fail to acquire a taste for that which is enduringly beautiful and everlastingly joyful. It's one of life's great challenges to learn to approve the things that are excellent, but when we rise to meet that challenge, we find that life has a depth and a richness that we never knew before. And not only that, but when we live tastefully, our friends will enjoy being around us more too.

Beautiful things, when taste is formed,
are obviously and unaccountably beautiful.
GEORGE SANTAYANA

August 5
DESTINY

If thou follow thy star, thou canst not fail of glorious heaven.
DANTE ALIGHIERI

EACH OF US HAS A "DESTINY" IN THIS WORLD — MAYBE YOU'D LIKE TO CALL IT A "DESTINATION" — THAT IS UNIQUE TO US. Although as human beings we have a good many things in common, we also have some things that set us apart, and among the most important of these are our dreams and goals: the things that we want to accomplish while we live. Leaving aside for the moment the question of our eternal destiny, let's consider the value of seeing that we have (or at least that we can have) a destiny to move toward in this world.

To begin with, destiny doesn't mean determinism. It doesn't mean that what's going to happen in our lives is inevitable or that any specific path is the only one we're meant or allowed to take. No, in any realistic view of destiny, we see that both our destination and our path are matters of choice. Almost always, the abilities and opportunities that have been granted to a particular person can be used honorably in more than one way, and out of all the possible scenarios that would be right from a moral and ethical standpoint, we're free to choose. Unfortunately, many people don't choose. They just drift.

Let me put it this way: *your destiny is the thing that will result if you use your life in the way that is best suited to the unique person that you are.* Sometimes it's hard to figure out what our goals should be in that regard, and I agree with Jean de La Fontaine, who said, "A person often meets his destiny on the road he took to avoid it." But when a person finally does lock in on whatever is the best possible thing they can do to contribute to the world, the motivation that results from that is so powerful it feels like the force of an irresistible fate.

Our destiny, therefore, is determined by the ways in which we choose to think, day by day. Orison Swett Marden said it pointedly: "Our destiny changes with our thought; we shall become what we wish to become, do what we wish to do, when our habitual thought corresponds with our desire." We can't think one way and then somehow arrive at a completely different destination. So you need to be careful about your thinking, don't you? If you keep on thinking as you have today, what kind of destiny is that going to lead you to?

Destiny is simply the relentless logic of each day.
JEAN GIRAUDOUX

ENDURANCE

To endure is greater than to dare; to tire out hostile fortune;
to be daunted by no difficulty; to keep heart when all have lost it;
to go through intrigue spotless; to forego even ambition when
the end is gained — who can say that is not greatness?

WILLIAM MAKEPEACE THACKERAY

GREATNESS, AS THACKERAY REMINDS US, OFTEN COMES DOWN TO ENDURANCE. Not everything that is honorable to aim for is easy to achieve, and so we need to be able to hold up under the hardship of worthwhile effort. If we can't endure long enough to "tire out hostile fortune," then little good will come from our lives.

Resistance is simply a fact of life, and Catherine of Siena was probably not exaggerating when she said, "Nothing great was ever done without much enduring." Having a long list of things that we can do easily doesn't make us a success in life. What counts is being willing to do important things that we find difficult to do.

Sydney Harris made an interesting comment on endurance when he said, "We can often endure an extra pound of pain far more easily than we can suffer the withdrawal of an ounce of accustomed pleasure." If true, that's a good argument for being careful about our attachments. Our ability to endure can be seriously impaired by our unwillingness to let go of things that have to be relinquished.

Don't we owe it to those around us to be more enduring? Many, if not most, of the stresses in our personal relationships come from giving up too soon in the face of difficulty. So if not for our own sake, then for the sake of others, we should learn to hold up and hold out.

But I think we should keep in mind that endurance is more than grim determination. Although grim determination is something we should be capable of when all else fails, most of the time endurance is a finer thing than mere resignation to unpleasant reality. It's a positive character quality, one that enables us to bear our adversities with grace and gratitude. At times, endurance can even be a gentle thing. "A profusion of pink roses bending ragged in the rain speaks to me of all gentleness and its enduring" (William Carlos Williams). When we endure, then, we bear hardness with a purpose that transforms us.

Endurance is not just the ability to bear
a hard thing, but to turn it into glory.
WILLIAM BARCLAY

August 7
ORIGINALITY

The courage to imagine the otherwise is our
greatest resource, adding color and suspense to all our life.
DANIEL J. BOORSTIN

POTENTIALLY, EACH OF US CAN MAKE THE WORLD A DIF-
FERENT AND BETTER PLACE THAN IT WOULD BE IF WE HAD
NEVER LIVED HERE. No two of us are exactly alike. We've each been
endowed with a unique combination of personal qualities, and those
special endowments, coupled with the freedom of our will, make it
possible for us to (a) imagine good things that have never been in the
world before, and then (b) work to bring those new ideas to fruition.
When we do that — that is, when we make the unique contribution
to the world that we're capable of making — we're being original.

There is no value, of course, in being different just for the sake of
being different. But the fact is, each of us has a separate, distinct role
to play in the world, and we ought not to be afraid to play it.

Despite our sometimes naive talk about being non-conformists,
most of us avoid any real originality as if it were the plague. Deep
down, we know that originality will not only distinguish us from the
establishment, it will also make us different from our peers, those
individuals with whom we desperately want to fit in. As Lorraine
Hansberry remarked, "Eventually it comes to you: the thing that
makes you exceptional, if you are at all, is inevitably that which must
also make you lonely." We can't have it both ways — we can't be original and also be surrounded by people who understand our experience.
So originality takes courage. "To go against the dominant thinking of
your friends, of most of the people you see every day, is perhaps the
most difficult act of heroism you can perform" (Theodore H. White).

But if there were no such thing as human originality, the material
world would soon tire us out. It's the courage of at least a few folks to
be original that adds interest and intrigue to life. So we ought to appreciate the value of genuine originality (as opposed to the pretended
or superficial kind). Now and then, we need to break out of the safe
confines of what "everybody else is doing." The person who never
considers what anybody else is doing is a fool, obviously — but we'd
be equally foolish if all we ever did was what others have done before.

You don't get harmony when everybody sings the same note.
DOUG FLOYD

TENDERNESS

Tenderness is passion in repose.

JOSEPH JOUBERT

TO BE TENDER, WE DON'T HAVE TO BE WEAK. True tenderness doesn't indicate a lack of strength or character — it simply shows that a person's strength has been trained and is under control. When we choose to deal tenderly with someone, we are disciplining our strength, holding it in reserve, and applying it gently, with a genuine desire to help as much as possible and hurt no more than is necessary.

Nor does tenderness indicate a lack of color in our convictions or passion in our personality. "Tenderness is," as Joubert described it, "passion in repose." A person can be quite full of fire, but that fire doesn't always have to be blazing out in every direction. When we're being tender, our passion is resting peacefully, so to speak.

For every time when we fail to be tough enough, there are probably ten times when we fail to be tender enough. Of the two extremes, most people err more often on the side of too little tenderness. And there's a good reason for that: although being tough may be a bit hard sometimes, it's easy compared to the challenge of being tender. In fact, it takes more strength to be tender than it does to be tough. Those who brag about "telling it like it is," regardless of anyone else's feelings, are advertising their weakness, not their strength.

A failure to be tender is actually a failure to be thankful. When we show too little tenderness to someone else, we're demonstrating our lack of appreciation for the many times when others have shown tenderness to us, despite the fact that we didn't deserve it. And not only that, we show a lack of understanding that we're going to need the tenderness of others in the future. So Bob Goddard's advice is good: "Resolve to be tender with the young, compassionate with the aged, sympathetic with the striving, and tolerant with the weak and the wrong. Sometime in life you will have been all of these."

Tenderness is a test of our character. If we can be tender toward those who are tender, that's good — but almost anyone can do that. The real challenge is to be tender toward those who are not tender.

The last, best fruit which comes to late perfection, even in the kindliest soul, is tenderness toward the hard, forbearance toward the unforbearing, warmth of heart toward the cold, philanthropy toward the misanthropic.

JEAN PAUL RICHTER

CONVERSION

The whole secret of the teacher's force
lies in the conviction that men are convertible.

RALPH WALDO EMERSON

WHEN YOU THINK ABOUT IT, PROBABLY TWO-THIRDS OF EVERYTHING WE DO INVOLVES SOME KIND OF EFFORT TO GET SOMEBODY TO TURN IN A DIFFERENT DIRECTION THAN THEY'VE BEEN GOING. Persuasion, in all its many forms, is one of the main activities in most of our lives. A teacher tries to get students to go in the direction of understanding a subject. A salesperson tries to get a customer to go in the direction of buying a product. A lawyer tries to get a jury to go in the direction of a particular verdict. A mother tries to get a child to go in the direction of coming to the supper table. Every day, in almost every way, we're all trying to influence the "direction" of the other people with whom we come in contact.

If human beings weren't capable of choosing to change their actions, all such efforts would be meaningless. Nearly every interaction that we have with one another presupposes the possibility of change. Whether we've ever studied psychology in school or not, we all sense that the human mind is comprised of three faculties: *intellect* (the "knowing" part), *emotion* (the "feeling" part), and *will* (the "choosing to change" part). To say that we have a free will is simply to say that we're capable of choosing to change — voluntarily and deliberately.

The word "conversion" is not necessarily a religious word. It just means changing direction. "Conversion simply means turning around" (Vincent McNabb). And isn't it a wonderful thing that human beings are convertible? Aren't we glad that we can turn when we need to?

You've probably noticed that the greatest turnings in your life have come at times when your past and present circumstances were lined up in such a way that you were ready to be changed. William James, the psychologist, said, "When the fruit is ripe, a touch will make it fall." And Thomas Paine said, "Time makes more converts than reason." Surely, we need to take this truth into account in our efforts to influence others. But in all honesty, which should we pay the most attention to: turning other people around or turning ourselves?

It is so easy to convert others.
It is so difficult to convert oneself.

OSCAR WILDE

August 10

EMPOWERMENT

Programs should attempt to empower people to soar, to sail, to step
bravely into the unknown, being guided more by imagination than memory,
and ultimately to reach beyond their fears and past failures.

STEPHEN R. COVEY

THE WORD "POWER" CAN SOMETIMES HAVE A NEGATIVE CON-
NOTATION, BUT THE BASIC IDEA OF POWER IS NOT AT ALL
NEGATIVE. In terms of human relationships, power is simply the abil-
ity to act. If the action is good, the power to do it can't be all bad.

In our day, much has been written about "empowerment." The
concept has become somewhat of a fad. But empowerment is too important to be dismissed as a passing trend. One danger of fads is that
we may hear about a concept nearly every day for a while and still not
grasp its real importance. Empowerment is a truly "powerful" concept. While the motivational speakers and seminar leaders have been
talking about it, have we really been listening? Do we really see how
important it is to empower the people who are around us each day?

When the University of Texas defeated the University of
Southern California in the 2006 Rose Bowl and won the national col-
legiate football championship, their star player, Vince Young, was an
immensely talented athlete with a "free spirit" — he could be exasperating, to say the least. But when Mack Brown, his coach, was asked at
what point Young's abilities began to help the team, he said, "When
we quit nagging him and started supporting him." I like that a lot.

Both at home and in the workplace, we all need to do a better
job of empowering others. We ought to want them to succeed at their
highest level, even if their achievements eclipse our own. And while
working wisely to help them overcome their weaknesses, we ought to
exert a greater effort to bring out other people's strengths. Usually, our
job is to help supply them with the knowledge and skills they need —
and then step back and give them the freedom to do their thing!

Sadly, we sometimes do the exact opposite: we disempower people. But are we blind? Everybody would benefit if we learned to foster
environments in which people could do their best. Isn't that obvious?

Your role, your assignment, your responsibility, your stewardship
is to create the conditions that allow people to flourish.

BLAINE LEE

August 11
CURIOSITY

> I am often amazed at how much more capability
> and enthusiasm for science there is among elementary
> school youngsters than among college students.
>
> CARL SAGAN

OH, THAT WE COULD KEEP THE CURIOSITY WE HAD WHEN WE WERE CHILDREN! It's such a shame to lose that sense of wonder, that eagerness to open doors and peek into new worlds. Would that we could somehow hang on to that openness to new life.

Curiosity can be unwisely exercised, of course. Some things are none of our business and other things would be detrimental for us to know. But tempered with a little good judgment, curiosity is a good thing. Uncurious people may be safe, but they're also ignorant.

Truly curious people are proactive when it comes to learning. The things we need to know, or could profit from knowing, don't usually track us down and impose themselves on our thinking; we have to get up and go look for them in likely places. Curiosity requires a bit of energy. It's not for the lazy or the indifferent. "Be curious always! For knowledge will not acquire you; you must acquire it" (Sudie Back).

When we lose our curiosity, we stagnate. We become stale, uninteresting, and uninviting to our loved ones. "Curiosity," as William A. Ward said, "is the wick in the candle of learning." So for the sake of those around us, if not for our own sake, we need to keep ourselves curious. Daily, we need to inquire into things that can make us grow.

The moment we quit growing, we begin to die. That's as true in the mental, spiritual, and emotional realms as it is in the physical. The old adage warns us that "curiosity killed the cat," and it's certainly true that foolish curiosity can get us into trouble. But wisely inquisitive people tend to live longer and remain stronger. And it's not hard to guess why that's true: curious people tend to be active. They're folks who are reaching forward — using their muscles, stretching their capabilities, and invigorating themselves with fresh information whenever they can. So while a cup of oatmeal each morning may be a good idea, a cup of new knowledge every day is probably even better.

> In spite of illness, in spite even of the archenemy sorrow,
> one can remain alive long past the usual date of disintegration
> if one is unafraid of change, insatiable in intellectual curiosity,
> interested in big things, and happy in small ways.
>
> EDITH WHARTON

PROTECTION

Woodman, spare that tree!
Touch not a single bough!
In youth it sheltered me,
And I'll protect it now.

GEORGE POPE MORRIS

IT'S A FACT: THERE ARE SOME THINGS THAT DESERVE TO BE
PROTECTED. Some of these things are physical, but others are
less tangible. Whatever worthy thing there may be whose safety is
jeopardized by forces that would harm it unjustly, that thing needs to
be shielded and safeguarded. And when something needs to be protected, we can't always expect someone else to see that it gets done.

Of all the things that need protection from time to time, people
are the most important. In the world as it is, there are all manner
of harms and hurts that threaten people. Whenever we can do so
without causing a greater harm, we need to defend one another. We
should offer to stand between other human beings and the things that
would hurt them, willing to take the hit ourselves, if need be.

A word of caution is in order, however. Although our intentions
are no doubt good, these days we're often tempted to protect people
from experiences that, while difficult, would still be good for them to
deal with. A parent, for example, who "protects" his or her child from
any difficulty or unpleasantness (such as work, responsibility, or the
consequences of bad behavior) is not creating a safe child but rather an
emotional cripple. No, the things we need to defend people against are
not difficulty or unpleasantness, but rather danger, injustice, and evil.

Protecting people certainly involves risk. Often it involves serious
self-sacrifice. Now and then, it may cost the very life of the one doing
the protecting. But if we're not willing to protect others, we shouldn't
expect to be protected when our time comes, as it surely will.

There is no more worthy work in the world than that of protection. Do you long to be significant? Do you want your life to matter,
to count for something? Then render the simple, but great, service of
offering protection. Any of us can do that. Even the least of us.

Small service is true service while it lasts:
Of humblest friends, bright creature! scorn not one:
The daisy, by the shadow that it casts,
Protects the lingering dewdrop from the sun.

WILLIAM WORDSWORTH

LISTENING

The older I grow, the more I listen to people who don't talk much.
GERMAIN G. GLIDDEN

WHOM DO YOU FIND IT EASY TO LISTEN TO? The dynamic public speaker? The fascinating celebrity? The person with plenty of personality and the gift of gab? Well, unfortunately, those who are the easiest to listen to don't always have anything that's worth listening to. And so Germain G. Glidden's comment is a wise one: "The older I grow, the more I listen to people who don't talk much."

I doubt if there is a greater gift that we can give to others than simply to listen to them — sincerely, openly, and respectfully. It's been said that imitation is the sincerest form of flattery, but I have a hunch that listening may be an even greater form. Those who deal with us every day are paid a huge compliment when we just listen to them.

But if some people are easier to listen to than others, some truths are also easier to listen to. Samuel Johnson said, "In order that all men may be taught to speak truth, it is necessary that all likewise should learn to hear it." The truth, particularly the truth about character flaws that we need to correct, is not always easy to hear. If we have friends who care enough to tell us the truth that we need to hear, we should count ourselves blessed. And we should listen when they speak.

"While language is a gift, listening is a responsibility" (Nikki Giovanni). There is a sense in which listening requires more effort than speaking. It doesn't seem to come naturally to us; we have to choose to do it. Although a certain kind of listening may be easy, the kind that really matters is active listening: the engaged, involved listening that grows out of an intent to learn. That kind of listening takes discipline and practice. (And it requires the character trait of humility, which isn't in very plentiful supply in our culture.) But when we learn the discipline of listening, we're changed for the better in many ways.

While talking (or writing) may be a learning experience some of the time, few of us learn as much when we're talking as we do when we're listening. It can hardly be a coincidence that we have two ears but only one mouth, and that ratio makes a point that we ought to ponder. There is a time to talk, obviously. But there is also a time to shut up and listen — lest we fail to hear words that we need to hear.

Listen, or your tongue will keep you deaf.
NATIVE AMERICAN PROVERB

PROMPTNESS

During a very busy life I have often been asked,
"How did you manage to do it all?" The answer is very
simple: it is because I did everything *promptly*.

SIR RICHARD TANGYE

T HERE MAY NOT BE ANY OTHER HABIT YOU COULD ADOPT
THAT WOULD PAY BIGGER DIVIDENDS THAN THE SIMPLE
HABIT OF PROMPTNESS. Doing things (both the big and the small)
at our earliest opportunity is a practice that renders nearly everything
we do more effective than it would be otherwise. Promptness is a
powerful lever that increases our ability to lift much more weight in
our daily activities. When we practice the habit of promptness, we
find ourselves improving in almost every department of life.

You might be surprised to learn how much a reputation for
promptness increases other people's confidence in you. In the business
world, for example, nothing inspires trust in a person any more powerfully than delivering the goods on time, every time — and nothing
sabotages a person's reputation any quicker than always being behind.
And in other areas of life, the same thing is true: people trust people
who do things promptly, not just occasionally but all of the time.

When we fail to act promptly, it's usually because we're avoiding
something that is (a) unpleasant, (b) difficult, or (c) both unpleasant
and difficult. But avoidance only makes matters worse. If an enemy
has to be met, it's much better to take the initiative and march out to
meet him head-on, rather than cowering behind walls of postpone-
ment and procrastination. To use the analogy in Brian Tracy's great
little book *Eat That Frog!*, if you have to eat a frog, the earlier in the
day you eat it, the better you'll feel about yourself the rest of the day!

But like most habits, promptness has to be learned. It's a matter
of discipline and training. If we've gotten into the rut of procrastination, we have to unlearn that habit gradually. We have to start small,
make some progress, and then build on our progress incrementally.

When we begin to act promptly in our dealings, what we find is
that the gift of promptness adds to the delightfulness of every other
gift we give to those around us. Whatever we're able to give, giving it
at the earliest opportunity adds a powerful measure of grace to it.

He gives twice who gives promptly.

LATIN PROVERB

FEELINGS

It is as healthy to enjoy sentiment as to enjoy jam.

G. K. CHESTERTON

WE DO A GOOD THING FOR OUR FRIENDS AND LOVED ONES WHEN WE ALLOW OURSELVES TO FEEL THINGS DEEPLY. However tempting it may be at times to avoid the feeling of certain things, it's usually better to feel them, at least for a while. People who feel are simply more enjoyable to relate to than those who don't.

It's important not only to feel things but also to express our feelings. Unexpressed feelings aren't nearly as beneficial as those that are shared. We may not feel adequate to express our feelings wisely or well, but the effort is still worth making. Usually, our good intentions will be remembered longer than the awkwardness of their expression.

It's important not only to feel our own feelings but also to feel the feelings of others. As André Gide wrote, "The important thing is being capable of emotions, but to experience only one's own would be a sorry limitation." The literal meaning of the word "sympathy" is "to feel with." When we enter into the experience of those around us, feeling their feelings with them, wonderful things begin to happen.

There's no use denying that some feelings are "undesirable." Sorrow, for example, is a feeling that we'd rather not feel. But many thoughtful people have discovered that we can't suppress *some* emotions without lessening our ability to feel *any* emotion. We can't blunt some feelings and still stay sensitive to others. Sam Keen was right when he wrote, "The ability to feel is indivisible. Repress awareness of any one feeling, and all feelings are dulled . . . The same nerve endings are required for weeping and dancing, fear and ecstasy." So we need to hold on to the ability to feel, even when it's painful to do so.

Our hearts were meant to do all three: think, choose, and feel. So we impoverish ourselves and we harm our hearts when we fail to do the third of these. And there is more than a little irony here. When we avoid certain feelings, thinking that those feelings would hurt us or somehow diminish us, what we find is that by saving our hearts we have lost them. At last, our hearts are like life itself: it's in the act of yielding to loss that we finally find the thing we were looking for.

In a full heart there is room for everything,
and in an empty heart there is room for nothing.

ANTONIO PORCHIA

SCHOLARSHIP

The office of the scholar is to cheer, to raise,
and to guide man by showing them facts amid appearances.
RALPH WALDO EMERSON

SCHOLARSHIP, FRANKLY, IS NOT SOMETHING MOST PEOPLE
ASPIRE TO. The very word conjures up an image of the ped-
ant, obsessed with heaping together scraps of abstract learning and
totally out of touch with the real world. But what most people object
to is a caricature, if not an outright counterfeit, of real scholarship.
As Emerson suggests, scholarship is something that can be seen in a
positive light, and there is a sense in which all of us need to be interested in some of the same things the scholar is interested in.

Perhaps scholarship has a bad name because so many scholars are
content simply to know what they know. Genuine scholarship, however, is about doing as well as knowing. "A scholar without practice,"
wrote Saadi, "is a tree without fruit." No scholar worth his salt will fail
to do the duties that grow out of knowing the things he has learned.

In a healthy sense, all of us need to take a more scholarly approach to life. That is, we need to have a healthy, eager respect for
what others before us have learned. We need to acquire good study
habits and increase in our ability to gather and arrange information
and knowledge. And we need to be people who do a little research
now and then, adding to the body of human knowledge by figuring
out a thing or two that maybe no one else has been aware of.

Yet scholarship is not just the collection and analysis of information; it's the understanding and application of that information. We're
not just looking for data; we're looking for meaning. The question is
not just *What's the sum total of human knowledge about this subject?* but
What's the significance of what we know? and *How can what we know
make us better people?* Ultimately then, scholarship has to do with
character, both that of the scholar and those with whom he shares his
findings. Learning is about doing, and doing is about doing better as
each day goes by. In the words of Emerson quoted above, the work of
the scholar is "to cheer, to raise, and to guide." Isn't that something
that all of us would do well at least to dabble in from time to time?

True scholarship consists in knowing not what things exist,
but what they mean; it is not memory but judgment.
JAMES RUSSELL LOWELL

August 17

EMPATHY

It is profound philosophy to sound the
depths of feeling and distinguish traits of character.
Men must be studied as deeply as books.

BALTASAR GRACIÁN

OF ALL THE SUBJECTS WE MIGHT STUDY, PEOPLE ARE THE
MOST PROFOUND. By far the most fascinating phenomenon
around us, at least within the terrestrial sphere, people really do have
to be studied in order to be known. It's not easy. It takes both time
and hard work to understand the other human beings with whom we
cross paths. But the effort is well worth making, as anybody knows
who has ever had the pleasure of understanding even one other person.

"Empathy" is a word that describes the knowledge of other
people that we ought to strive for. While often used interchangeably
with "sympathy" (which we'll discuss tomorrow), "empathy" is an important word in its own right. It's a character quality made up of two
separate elements, both of which we need to work on.

Understanding. This is the first, and most obvious, component of
empathy. When we empathize with another person, that means we
listen to them and learn from them in a genuine effort to understand
their situation. And this kind of learning requires more than a pro-
ficiency in theoretical psychology. As Mark Twain said, "One learns
people through the heart, not the eyes or the intellect."

Identification. Understanding another person's situation does not,
by itself, constitute empathy. To have empathy, we must also identify
with the other person. In other words, we must be willing to stand
with them, as if the situation were as much ours as it is theirs.

That we have so little empathy ought to be the cause of great
concern. It ought to disturb us that we don't know those around us
any better than we do. Unfortunately, however, we spend most of
our time worrying whether others understand us or not. This is a
misplaced priority. Almost always, "whether we understand" should
be dealt with before we turn our attention to "whether we're being
understood." In the matter of understanding and empathy, there really
is a sense in which it is more blessed to give than to receive.

That others do not know you is no cause for grief;
grieve that you do not know them.

CONFUCIUS

SYMPATHY

There is no greater loan than a sympathetic ear.

FRANK TYGER

IF "EMPATHY" MEANS UNDERSTANDING SOMEONE ELSE, THEN "SYMPATHY" MEANS FEELING WHAT THEY FEEL. It is "a fellow-feeling" (Robert Burton). Or in the words of Charles H. Parkhurst's familiar definition: "Sympathy is two hearts tugging at one load." To sympathize is to open our hearts to another person's feelings. And mark it well: sympathy is not limited to times of grief or emotional pain. "Anyone can sympathize with another's sorrow, but to sympathize with another's joy is the attribute of an angel" (Arthur Schopenhauer).

Hardly anything is more beautiful or valuable than sympathy. Emerson was right when he said, "Sympathy is a supporting atmosphere, and in it we unfold easily and well." And if we appreciate the freedom that comes from being surrounded by sympathetic people, shouldn't we give that gift more often to those who need our support?

At least two cautions are in order. (1) None of us can ever feel exactly what another person is feeling, and we ought not to pretend that we do. The best that we can do is feel what they're feeling as nearly as possible. (2) We ought not to be condescending when we sympathize. Especially when someone else has suffered a loss that we think we've protected ourselves against, it's hard not to feel (secretly) a little superior to the person that we pity, as if they "had it coming." But we ought to guard against that kind of counterfeit sympathy.

True sympathy costs more than many of us realize. It often requires more time and effort than can be conveniently given. Indeed, it requires more than the giving of anything that we might "have" or "possess." We can't sympathize by skimming off a little of our excess emotion or affluence, giving that which we can easily afford to give — without any sacrifice. No, sympathy means that we invest a significant portion of ourselves in someone else's situation, whether that situation involves grief or gladness. It says, "Whatever you're feeling, I'm willing to feel your feelings with you. And more than that, I'm willing to put my heart at your service. I will do whatever will encourage you."

Pity may represent little more than the impersonal concern
which prompts the mailing of a check, but true sympathy is the
personal concern which demands the giving of one's soul.

MARTIN LUTHER KING JR.

INNOCENCE

It is part of the kindness of God that amid all the change
there are things we can always count on. The unfailing regularity of the
seasons and the reliability of nature; the glory of the stars, the innocence of
the morning; the healing power of time and the sustaining power of hope; the
heart's yearning for love and the soul's hunger for prayer; the endless quest for
truth and the stubborn struggle for justice; the restless urge to create and the
valiant will to overcome — these are some of the things we can count on.
These are the things that hold in a slippery world.

SIDNEY GREENBERG

THAT WHICH IS INNOCENT IS FRESH AND UNTAINTED. It is unspoiled, not having been contaminated by evil or error or unworthiness. We ought to appreciate the things around us that come to us with such freshness, such as "the innocence of the morning." And we ought to hang on to as much of our own innocence as we can.

To be innocent, we don't have to be naive or gullible. As William Blake wrote, "Innocence dwells with wisdom, but never with ignorance." The evidence suggests that Jesus of Nazareth was the most innocent adult who ever lived, but the evidence also suggests that he was nobody's fool. So, contrary to the popular misconception, innocence and simple-mindedness are not the same thing. Consider three of the definitions of innocence in the *American Heritage Dictionary:*

(1) Uncorrupted by evil, malice, or wrongdoing. In this sense, innocence suggests purity. And frankly, in a world that is sadly degraded, one of our main challenges is to remain as unaffected as possible.

(2) Not guilty of a specific crime; legally blameless. When a person is innocent in this sense, it means that he stands before the law as one whose cause is just. In a dispute, to be innocent is to be "in the right."

(3) Betraying or suggesting no deception or guile. Artlessness is the idea here. An innocent smile, for example, is one that is spontaneous. In these days of "technique," this kind of innocence is refreshing.

Aren't all three of these concepts worthy of admiration? Without a doubt, these kinds of innocence are more often found in children than in adults. But wouldn't it improve our adult lives if we retained some of our childhood innocence as long as we live, rather than giving it all up in adolescence? In at least the three senses above, the more innocent we can keep ourselves, the better off we'll be.

The great man is he who does not lose his child's heart.

MENCIUS

August 20
CHIVALRY

> The age of chivalry has gone. That of sophisters,
> economists, and calculators has succeeded, and the
> glory of Europe is extinguished forever.
>
> EDMUND BURKE

HAS THE "AGE OF CHIVALRY" GONE OR NOT? The answer may largely depend upon a person's perspective, or at least that person's definition of chivalry, but it is undeniably true that the emphasis has switched from the knight-like *How can I serve the greater good?* to the consumer-like *What's in it for me?* And even at the level of plain, old mannerliness, something has been lost that we may regret losing.

Chivalry has to do with the medieval institution of knighthood. It refers to the principles and customs associated with that institution. Whether medieval knights did, in fact, idealize such qualities as bravery, courtesy, honor, and service makes little difference, practically speaking. Chivalry simply envisions a realm where these things were important — and says that they ought to be important to us still.

Concepts like chivalry are, of course, touchy topics nowadays. If "chivalrous" means "characterized by consideration and courtesy, especially toward women" (*American Heritage Dictionary*), many modern women would resent the very idea as demeaning. But one does not have to hold a demeaning view of women to believe that at least a few of the old-fashioned courtesies ought to be preserved. The knight may no longer need to lay his cape over the mud so the lady can walk across, but most men could do with a little more "knightliness" in their behavior, not only toward women but toward other men as well. There is, I believe, a larger sense in which all of us ought to be chivalrous, whether we're male or female, young or old. And yes, I confess to hoping there'll always be a few women left who appreciate being treated like ladies by the gentlemen with whom they have dealings.

The gist of chivalry is the spirit that the medieval knight was (at least in our imagination) moved by: *willingness to serve in the cause of right and render help to anyone who needed it.* It doesn't demean anyone to be served. And there's no better service than the service of honor.

> Some say that the age of chivalry is past, that the spirit
> of romance is dead. The age of chivalry is never past, so long as
> there is a wrong left unredressed on earth, or a man or woman left
> to say, I will redress that wrong, or spend my life in the attempt.
>
> CHARLES KINGSLEY

REASON

Reason may be a small force, but it is constant,
and works always in one direction, while the forces
of unreason destroy one another in futile strife.

BERTRAND RUSSELL

THESE DAYS, HUMAN REASON DOESN'T GET THE CREDIT THAT IT PROPERLY DESERVES. Reason may be, as Russell suggested, a "small force," but it is an immensely valuable force. The fact is, we won't get very far in life without it, and we ought to devote more of our energy to the training and exercise of our reason.

It is good that in recent years we've paid more attention to the other parts of our minds, such as our emotions. After all, life is more than just a problem in logic. But as we seek to keep reason in balance, let's not make the mistake of scorning it or despising it altogether. Cut off from our other faculties, reason can be a dangerous thing, no doubt, but the same caution is in order concerning our feelings and intuition. "Reason, ruling alone, is a force confining; and passion, unattended, is a flame that burns to its own destruction" (Kahlil Gibran).

One mistake we make is using our reason to figure things out when we haven't first done our homework. Reason has to have accurate information to work with, and the more information it has, the better it can work. So I agree with Alexis Carrel's comment: "A few observations and much reasoning leads to error; many observations and a little reasoning to truth." Reason can be very helpful when it comes to seeing the relationship between things and drawing helpful conclusions, but it is no substitute for the hard work of fact-finding.

Adlai Stevenson said, "In quiet places, reason abounds." Most of us today lead lives that are both busy and noisy. For reason to be of much use to us, we need to turn down the "volume" of daily life to the point where the voice of reason can be heard and meditated upon.

Especially in times of conflict and controversy, we need, as G. K. Chesterton once said, to strengthen our arguments rather than raise our voices. Shouting and name-calling can't take the place of clear thinking. So today, let's do better by thinking better. Reason is only one of our tools, but we're foolish if we don't use it where it's needed.

Violence in the voice is often only
the death rattle of reason in the throat.

JOHN F. BOYES

August 22
CHARITY

And now abideth faith, hope, charity, these three;
but the greatest of these is charity.

FIRST LETTER OF PAUL TO THE CORINTHIANS

OVER THE PAST FOUR HUNDRED YEARS, THE WORD "CHAR-
ITY" HAS CHANGED ITS MEANING. In the days of Elizabethan
English, when Shakespeare was writing and the King James Version
of the Bible was being made, charity meant love. In fact, it meant
the very highest kind of love, the kind that loves unselfishly, without
regard for return or repayment. But to most people today, charity only
means "giving money to a worthy cause." So let's see if we can't resur-
rect, and learn from, the full meaning of charity in the older sense.

Almsgiving. Giving to the poor and the otherwise needy is
certainly involved in charity, and heaven knows we need more of it.
But while we need more of this kind of charity, we also need more
people who'll engage in it simply for the good that it will do. As Dan
Bennett said, "Real charity doesn't care if it's tax-deductible or not."

Forbearance. There is an English proverb that says, "He that has
no charity deserves no mercy." Charity as mercy or forbearance is a
part of the older meaning of the word, and it would be good for us
to recapture a little of that old spirit. When those around us make
mistakes, we need to learn to treat their failings "charitably."

Love. Here is the heart of charity, even in the two areas above.
It is love that prompts us to engage in acts of charity, whatever their
nature may be. And I suggest that the word "charity" is still a quite
beautiful word to describe the highest, most selfless kind of love.

Charity can be thought of as the glue that holds many other
important things in life together. Qualities like wisdom, strength, and
courage can easily get out of hand, and even do damage, if they're not
enlivened, warmed, and motivated by charity. When we want to do
the charitable thing in a particular situation, it may sometimes tax our
judgment to ascertain what course of action we should take, but the
impulse to act charitably is always honorable. If we were moved by it
more often, the world would surely turn into a better place.

In necessary things, unity;
in doubtful things, liberty;
in all things, charity.

RICHARD BAXTER

DEPTH

Hast thou entered into the springs of the sea?
Or hast thou walked in search of the depth?

THE BOOK OF JOB

THERE ARE DEPTHS OF UNDERSTANDING THAT FEW OF US HAVE FATHOMED — AND EVEN SOME THAT NONE OF US HAVE FATHOMED. It's a much bigger world than any of us have yet comprehended, and even in our own little personal worlds, there are many things that we've not yet explored or been able to explain. We need to be impressed with how much there is to learn out there. How can we fail to be inquisitive? How can we be content with what little understanding we've been able to gain in the past?

We need to strive to be people who have some depth to us. Few of us would feel flattered if someone called us shallow or superficial, and yet that's what many of us are. We don't stand in awe of the mystery of life, and we're content to be uninformed and unacquainted with the amazing intricacy of the world. What little knowledge we have is often no more than the bits and pieces we've stumbled across accidentally. We could do with a bit more depth, couldn't we?

But there is a danger in depth, and that danger is pride. No sooner have we gained a smidgen of depth, than others notice us becoming smug toward the less experienced. Ever so subtly, we adopt the swagger of the sophomore, the "wise fool." We're hardly past the beginner's stage ourselves, but already we feel superior to those who haven't been where we've been and done what we've done. The antidote to pride, of course, is the recognition that compared to the distance between us and God, the distance between any two of us is so small that human pride is simply ludicrous.

Yet if we've learned the lessons of humility, can we not see depth as a gift that we can give? Today, wouldn't others, especially our loved ones, appreciate it if we understood a thing or two that we didn't understand yesterday? But make no mistake: a healthy measure of depth doesn't usually come to the lazy or the negligent. In this world, it takes work to end up being anything more than deeply superficial.

It is easier to perceive error than truth, for error
lies on the surface and is easily seen, but truth lies in
the depth where few are willing to search for it.

JOHANN WOLFGANG VON GOETHE

IMPROVEMENT

Everything can be improved.

C. W. BARRON

WE LIVE IN A WORLD OF POSSIBILITIES. Indeed, there are few things we deal with that can't be taken and improved in some way. Physical things are often raw materials that can be turned into finished products. But other less-tangible things can also be improved: problems can be solved, challenges can be met, potentials can be fulfilled, and goals can be striven for. Nearly every situation we meet presents us with an opportunity to improve something or other.

But what if it were otherwise? Have you considered what your life would be like if nothing could be improved at all? Johann Fichte said it well: "Humanity may endure the loss of everything; all its possessions may be turned away without infringing its true dignity — all but the possibility of improvement." It's true, there can hardly be a worse experience for any of us than the experience of despair. To lose the hope that there is anything we can do that will make anything any better, is to be about as close to death as we can be without dying.

I believe that our desire for improvement, and even our inclination to improvement, is not a coincidence. I agree with Andrew Carnegie, who said, "We know that man was created, not with an instinct for his own degradation, but imbued with the desire and the power for improvement." We are "hard-wired" to want to be better ourselves — and to want to make the things around us better too.

But if our desire for improvement is instinctive, acting on that desire is not automatic. It takes tremendous energy to overcome inertia and act in the direction of improvement, and this energy must be exerted by our will. If we simply live by default, doing no more than what is easy, then dilapidation and chaos are bound to be the results.

So from one standpoint, improvement is optional — a choice must be made. But from another standpoint, improvement is not optional at all. Whatever alternative to improvement there may be, it is not a safe alternative. Our only option is the option between life and death! In our lazier moments, we might wish there were some third way, but really, there is no safe middle ground. Failure to improve is a failure to grow — and a failure to grow is a dire problem indeed.

He who stops being better stops being good.

OLIVER CROMWELL

OVERCOMING

The harder the conflict, the more glorious the triumph.
What we obtain too cheap, we esteem too lightly;
'tis dearness only that gives everything its value.

THOMAS PAINE

CONFLICT AND STRUGGLE AREN'T PLEASANT, BUT IF WE THINK ABOUT THEM IN THE RIGHT WAY, THEY ARE PROFIT-ABLE. Some of the best things in life come to us while we're fighting to overcome difficulties. And yet, as we've suggested, these things don't come our way automatically; they do so only if we think about our struggles in a certain way. It's critical that we adopt a militant attitude toward our obstructions: the attitude of the "overcomer."

There is something we need to be careful about, however. In firing ourselves up to go out and fight "the enemy," we must not make the mistake of thinking that "the enemy" is other people. While it's true that the actions of others can make life more difficult, it would not be the most productive use of our time to fight against them personally, as if they were to blame for our problems. When the time comes to fight, there's much more to be gained by fighting against difficulty in general, rather than attacking people personally. We can be tough on problems and still be gentle with people.

But there are certainly problems to be dealt with, and we need to deal with them actively and forthrightly. We sometimes avoid difficulty as if we thought that ease and pleasure were the main objects in life. But these two things are not the highest human values, and there are times when we need to sacrifice them for more worthy goals. It is, in fact, through difficulty (rather than ease) and pain (rather than pleasure) that we find our character and make our contribution.

So we need to stiffen our attitude and face our challenges, whatever they may be, with the heart of someone determined to overcome. Whether we do this or not is a matter of choice. Yes, we'll lose some skirmishes in the short run, but we can choose to fight with an unconquerable spirit. And if we act with honor, doing with "true grit" the very best that we know to do, then our heads need never be bowed in shame. In this life, difficulty is inevitable, but destruction is not.

He said not, "Thou shalt not be tempested,
thou shalt not be travailed, thou shalt not be afflicted,"
but he said, "Thou shalt not be overcome."

JULIAN OF NORWICH

IMPACT

Let no man imagine that he has no influence.
Whoever he may be, and wherever he may be placed,
the man who thinks becomes a light and a power.
HENRY GEORGE

THE QUESTION IS NOT WHETHER WE'LL HAVE ANY IMPACT BUT ONLY WHAT KIND OF IMPACT IT WILL BE. Impact, or influence, is a fact of life. Those with whom we deal from day to day are impacted by the choices that we make, and most of us would be surprised to find out just how great the impact really is. Much more than we admit, others are hurt by our wrong choices, and to a greater extent than we realize, others are helped by our right choices. In an interconnected and interdependent world, impact is unavoidable.

Today, ponder three things we must do in regard to our impact:

Slow down. Most of us would have a better impact if we simplified our lives and took more time for reflection. "If we really want some things to count, if we genuinely desire some depth to emerge, some impact to be made, some profound and enduring investment to cast a comforting shadow across another's life, it is essential that we slow down . . . at times, stop completely" (Charles R. Swindoll).

Think. As Henry George pointed out above, it is the person who thinks who has a chance to become "a light and a power." So what are our real principles, those that we would die for? What are the things that we value in life? How is it that we really want to impact others? In the end, those who have a lastingly good influence are usually those who've taken the time to think the matter through.

Act. No amount of slowing down and thinking, however, can take the place of acting. If our impact is going to be what we want it to be, we're going to have to summon the self-discipline to do the beneficial things that we know to do. Eventually, we'll be answerable not only for our aspirations and intentions, but for the things we actually did.

But finally, note that worthy impact does not come from what the world calls "greatness" but from what the wise call "goodness." If the full truth could be known, it's not the movers and the shakers who change the world the most, but the down-to-earth folks who do good.

When I think of those who have influenced my life
the most, I think not of the great but of the good.
JOHN KNOX

August 27

VIGILANCE

O polish'd perturbation! golden care!
That keep'st the ports of slumber open wide
To many a watchful night!
WILLIAM SHAKESPEARE

T HE WORD "VIGILANCE" MEANS "WATCHFULNESS." It comes
from the Latin *vigilare* ("to be watchful") and is akin to "vigil."
When we keep a vigil, we stay awake to watch at a time when we
would normally be sleeping. If we said, for example, that a shepherd
kept a vigil over his flock, that would mean he watched over his sheep
by night, keeping a lookout for any danger that might threaten them.
To be "vigilant" in our own lives, then, is to be attentive. It is to be on
guard against problems that might do harm to us or our loved ones.
Vigilant people don't sleepwalk through life — they're wide awake.

Even with respect to literal, physical sleep, there is a time to sleep
and a time to refrain from sleeping. If it's only anxiety that keeps us
awake, that's not good. But Shakespeare spoke of a "golden care" that
might sometimes keep "the ports of slumber open wide." Now and
then, there happen to be some worthy reasons to stay awake. When
a friend is suffering, it may behoove us to sit up and endure the long
night hours with them. Sleeplessness is not always an evil thing.

But even when we're literally awake, we need to be more vigilant.
Our eyes, figuratively speaking, need to be more open and our minds
more awake. Not only will that help us spot potential problems, but
we'll also learn a number of things in the process. In the words of
Yogi Berra's famous quip, "You can observe a lot by watching."

The best synonym for vigilance is "alertness," and here's the reason why: we may be awake, technically speaking, but if we're not alert,
we'll be undone by many situations that could have been mastered.

We probably underestimate the importance of vigilance as a
component of our character. But when we think about it for a moment, it's easy to see how a lack of vigilance can keep our other qualities from being effective. Things like intelligence or courage, or even
skill, can go to waste if we're paying so little attention to what's going
on that we fail to take action when we need to. So today . . . *watch out!*

The battle, sir, is not to the strong
alone; it is to the vigilant.
PATRICK HENRY

SINGING

Song is not Truth, not Wisdom, but the rose
upon Truth's lips, the light in Wisdom's eyes.
SIR WILLIAM WATSON

HAVING A SONG IN OUR HEARTS, IF NOT ON OUR LIPS, MAY NOT BE THE MOST IMPORTANT THING IN LIFE, BUT IT'S MORE IMPORTANT THAN A LOT OF THE STUFF WE SEEM TO VALUE. Music is not an inherent good; it derives its value from the principles of those who compose it and those who enjoy it. But even though it is not, by itself, truth or wisdom, it is, as Watson suggests, "the rose upon Truth's lips" and "the light in Wisdom's eyes."

Some of us are more musically inclined than others, to be sure. And just as surely, not all of us have beautiful voices. But I'm going to go out on a limb and suggest that there is *some value in choosing to sing once in a while, even if it does not seem to come naturally*. It's healthy to sing. It's good for us. When we do it, however unmusical the result may be, the act of singing nudges us in a number of good directions.

Our lives don't have to be problem-free before we can enjoy the singing of a song. An old Chinese proverb reminds us that "a bird does not sing because it has an answer; it sings because it has a song." There isn't a day in any of our lives when there aren't some worthy things to sing about. Whatever may be wrong with the world, it's still true that the good outweighs the bad. And in fact, a determination to sing can be the noble taking of a stand against all that is wrong.

I believe it's important for us to sing while we can. Whether we recognize it right now or not, there is some wonderful "music" in all of us. "Alas for those who never sing, but die with all their music in them" (Oliver Wendell Holmes). There may be some songs we'll need to sing tomorrow, but we dare not let today's songs go unsung.

If there is a conspicuous lack of singing in our lives (either our own or the singing of others that we enjoy humming along with), it would probably pay us to stop and wonder why. Think about hell, for a moment. An environment where there was no music at all would be an evil environment indeed, and to the extent that we never sing, we may be headed in the wrong direction with our lives. If our songs have been silenced, it may be that our characters have been crushed.

The devil doesn't know how to sing.
FRANCIS THOMPSON

DELIBERATION

The necessity of the times, more than ever, calls for our utmost
circumspection, deliberation, fortitude and perseverance.

SAMUEL ADAMS

NO ONE WOULD DENY THAT WE LIVE IN TIMES THAT ARE
DANGEROUS. Monumental problems face us, both individually
and collectively. There has never been a more interesting or exciting
time to be alive, but even so, living today is like walking through a
minefield. And if Samuel Adams could say long ago that "the necessity of the times . . . calls for our utmost circumspection, deliberation,
fortitude and perseverance," the same could be said even more truly
today. Nowadays, to dispense with "deliberation" is to court disaster.

Interestingly, our word "deliberation" comes from *libra,* the Latin
word for a balance or scales. So the Latin verb *deliberare* meant to
"consider" something — that is, to "balance" the arguments for and
against a thing and make a reasoned judgment as to which position
outweighs the other. In English, then, deliberation means thoughtfulness in decision or action. If we do something deliberately, that
means we consider or plan it in advance with a full awareness of
everything that is involved. Deliberate things are done purposefully.

Given the challenges that we face today, it sounds like a good
idea to live our lives more deliberately and purposefully. In the matter
of government, Justice Louis Brandeis said, "Those who won our
independence believed that the final end of the State was to make
men free to develop their faculties; and that in its government the
deliberative forces should prevail over the arbitrary." Think hard about
that statement: *the deliberative forces should prevail over the arbitrary.*
Forethought, discussion, and wise decision-making must take prece-
dence over moods and fads and impulses of the moment.

If the above is true of a nation, is it any less true of an individual? If our society can't get by without weighing all the sides of
our national issues, can we personally survive if we don't know how to
weigh the pros and cons of our own issues? If our culture can't get by
without a healthy measure of intention and purposefulness, can any
of us get by privately without thinking and deliberating? Haphazard,
unintentional living has never taken anyone to a good place.

I went to the woods because I wished to live deliberately.

HENRY DAVID THOREAU

HARMONY

Dust as we are, the immortal spirit grows
Like harmony in music; there is a dark
Inscrutable workmanship that reconciles
Discordant elements, makes them cling together
In one society.

WILLIAM WORDSWORTH

IT IS AMAZING THAT THERE CAN BE ANY SEMBLANCE OF HAR-MONY IN THIS WORLD. Since there are so many "discordant elements" in the world, both outside and inside of us, it is a wonder that there can be any kind of accord or consonance. But there can be. And we ought to pursue the value of harmony more diligently than we do.

Sometimes, we're a bit naive in our concept of harmony. Our vision is out of harmony with what real harmony is like. For example, we often act as if achieving harmony between individuals required removing any differences between them. But unless people are separated by some actual evil, differences shouldn't diminish harmony. In fact, harmony is impossible if everybody is singing the same note.

And when it comes to harmony within ourselves, we can be equally naive. We suppose that perfect inner peace would mean the absence of any difficulty, unpleasantness, or sorrow. But what about God? Assuming that He enjoys perfect peace, does that mean that there are never any difficulties to be dealt with? Never anything but pleasure to experience? Never anything that breaks His heart? How silly. God is not different from us in that He never encounters anything alien — He's different in His attitude toward what He encounters. So Seneca was right: "Let tears flow of their own accord: their flowing is not inconsistent with inward peace and harmony."

But harmony doesn't come without any effort or discipline. And it's a pity that we so rarely pay the price. True, the harmonies that are available to us in this broken world are, at best, only an inkling of true perfection, but even so, we are the losers when we fail to exert ourselves in the direction of harmony. All the discords and disunities in the world notwithstanding, we can still learn to blend our voices better than we have in the past, both on the inside and the outside.

Faith and love are apt to be spasmodic in the best minds.
Men live on the brink of mysteries and harmonies into which they never
enter, and with their hand on the doorlatch they die outside.

RALPH WALDO EMERSON

NECESSITY

The beautiful rests on the foundation of the necessary.
RALPH WALDO EMERSON

VERY MANY OF THE BEST THINGS IN LIFE COME FROM OUR EFFORT TO DEAL RIGHTLY, WISELY, AND HONORABLY WITH NECESSITY. When there is something that has to be done, that need provides an opportunity for the human spirit to soar. If, for example, human beings had never had to get from one place to another, there would be no such thing today as a Ferrari. And if human beings didn't have to have some kind of place to dwell in, the creations of Frank Lloyd Wright would never have come into existence.

Now it's an obvious fact that many people are content to serve necessity with ordinary utility rather than use it to create extraordinary beauty. Homespun usefulness is certainly of great value, and we ought not to despise it. But the fact remains, we owe many of the grandest achievements of our culture to necessity. And it would perhaps take some of the dread and drudgery out of our own days if we'd approach necessity more in the spirit of personal creativity.

A long time ago, Geoffrey Chaucer had one of his characters in *The Canterbury Tales* say, "Hold it wise . . . to make a virtue of necessity." Today, we hear a lot about the importance of "design." In the business world, it's clear that the successful, thriving companies are those that look at the same everyday necessities that everybody else looks at and say, "What can we do to serve those ordinary needs in extraordinary ways?" Wouldn't it make sense to apply that same philosophy to the way we each deal with our own daily necessities?

But on a more serious note, dealing with necessity can often be frightening, and sometimes even terrifying. One of the most paralyzing fears that comes upon us is the fear of suffering horrible, grievous loss as a result of doing something that could not be avoided. It may be, of course, that we're simply deluding ourselves in thinking that a thing is necessary. But if we're frightened by a thing to which there is really no honorable alternative, there is something that can encourage us: the knowledge that doing what is right is its own reward. It's always right to do what is truly necessary — and the softest pillow in the world is the knowledge that we've done what was right.

What is necessary is never a risk.
CARDINAL DE REYTZ

CARING

If I had known what trouble you were bearing;
What griefs were in the silence of your face;
I would have been more gentle and more caring,
And tried to give you gladness for a space.

MARY CAROLYN DAVIES

FEW OF US CAN SAY THAT WE'VE NEVER BEEN ASHAMED WHEN IT CAME TO OUR ATTENTION THAT WE FAILED TO CARE FOR SOMEONE WHOM WE SHOULD HAVE CARED FOR. Whether our unawareness was innocent and inadvertent or the result of negligence, it's painful to find out that we've failed to care. So we'd do well to be more inquisitive when it comes to others' need for our caring.

Caring is a privilege. Caring for others would not be possible if we had not been endowed with some very special gifts. While certain animals "care" for their young in one sense, the kind of caring that human beings are capable of requires a set of remarkable powers. It's a privilege to have been endowed with these powers, and if we ever catch ourselves complaining about having to use them, then we need to adjust our attitudes. Duty is simply the other side of privilege.

Caring is a pleasure. Out of all the happinesses — or perhaps we should say joys — that human beings can experience, none is more exquisite than that of caring. And I don't mean simply the sentiment of caring; I mean the act of caring. The words "It is more blessed to give than to receive" encapsulate one of the most important truths that our minds can grasp. It would behoove us to quit paying lip service to that maxim and start learning that life really does work that way.

Indifference, which is a failure to care, is a horrible sin. I don't believe George Bernard Shaw was overstating the case when he said, "The worst sin towards our fellow creatures is not to hate them, but to be indifferent to them; that's the essence of inhumanity."

Not caring for those around us (especially those to whom we have some special responsibility, such as our families) is a fate worse than death. Yes, it costs us to care. Yes, sacrifices may be required. And yes, it may come to the point where caring for someone even demands that we lay down our lives for them. But listen to me: whatever the price of caring may be, it is nowhere near the cost of not caring.

To try may be to die, but not to care is never to be born.
WILLIAM REDFIELD

OBJECTIVES

Nothing is more terrible than activity without insight.

THOMAS CARLYLE

IT'S AN UNFORTUNATE SITUATION WHEN WE GET SO BUSY THAT WE LOSE SIGHT OF WHAT IT IS THAT WE'RE TRYING TO AC-COMPLISH. But in these busy days, that can easily happen. We can become so deeply involved dealing with the trees that we lose sight of the forest. So it's vitally important for us to take time out regularly to review our objectives and remind ourselves of the purpose for which we are engaging in all of this busyness. In the words of Thoreau, "It is not enough to be busy. The question is: what are we busy about?"

Creating our objectives. If we've never consciously thought about what our objectives are in life, then we need to do that. And in deciding what it is that we want to accomplish, we need to be careful in making those decisions. Using our creativity and imagination boldly, we need to formulate life-objectives that are based on our principles.

Clarifying our objectives. The more deeply we launch ourselves into the business of living life, the more important it is to return to our objectives periodically and clarify them. As we work on our goals, we get a better idea of what it is that we really want to contribute in life, and so we need to sharpen our objectives, continually making them more well-defined. And then, of course, circumstances in life may sometimes indicate that we need to change our principles and our objectives completely. In that case, we need to go back to the drawing board and radically re-envision our purpose for living.

Committing to our objectives. Not even the best objectives can help us if we don't act upon them. So we need to commit ourselves to our purposes in such a way that our commitment shows up in action. Having planned our work, we need to work our plan. And our action needs to be not sporadic but continuous — over the long haul.

Worthy goals and objectives are powerful things. And strangely enough, some of the most powerful objectives are those that are impossible to achieve. It is not the possibility of perfect achievement but the worthiness of the goal itself that provides the power to motivate us. In this broken old world, there are many virtuous things worth beginning, even though we may not be the ones to finish them completely.

The question should be, is it worth trying to do, not can it be done.

ALLARD K. LOWENSTEIN

September 3
RESERVES

Live full today, and let no pleasure pass untasted —
And no transient beauty scorn;
Fill well the storehouse of the soul's delight
With the light of memory —
Who knows? Tomorrow may be —
Night

ANONYMOUS

WITH OUR EMOTIONS, AS WITH OUR MONEY, IT'S WISE TO KEEP SOME RESERVES READY. Admittedly, the point of life is not to see who can build the biggest savings account, and we do need to resist the hoarding instinct. Eventually, everything we acquire will need to be spent, but it's rarely good to spend everything today, all at once. There may be times when that's the very thing we should do, but usually, spending everything by impulse is foolish.

Think about this matter, first, with regard to money and material things. The person who spends everything he makes usually has to impose on other people to bail him out when an unexpected need arises. With no reserves, he has nothing with which to meet the crises that are bound to come up occasionally. And not only that, he has nothing with which to help other people when they're in real need.

But think about this concept also with respect to things like physical strength and energy. It's worth making the effort to eat, exercise, and rest in wise ways, so that the normal demands of daily living don't take everything we've got. Not many weeks will go by that we're not presented with an opportunity to do some worthy work that goes "beyond the call of duty." Folks who have a little strength and energy in reserve are able to seize those opportunities. Others are not.

The meaning of life, then, is to spend and be spent, and the hoarding instinct is evil. So the wisdom of having reserves lies not in the mere act of saving, but in the chance it gives us to *spend them later on things more valuable than the things we probably would have spent them on earlier.* Holding reasonable reserves takes wisdom, to be sure, because it's not always easy to know when to spend and when to save. But we need to avoid both problems: never spending our reserves on the one hand . . . and never having any reserves on the other!

Economy: save money in one store
so you can spend it in another.

ANONYMOUS

September 4
FAITHFULNESS

So faithful in love, and so dauntless in war,
There never was knight like the young Lochinvar.
SIR WALTER SCOTT

FAITHFULNESS IS A VIRTUE THAT'S EASY TO ADMIRE IN OTH-
ERS AND HARD TO ACQUIRE FOR OURSELVES. The tales that tug
at our heartstrings the most powerfully are those that tell of people
who, at great cost, held true to their promises and duties. In the presence of great faithfulness, we're moved to love and admiration.

Maybe it's risky to rate the virtues, but there does seem to be a
sense in which faithfulness is a preeminent quality. "Let us be true:
this is the highest maxim of art and of life, the secret of eloquence
and of virtue, and of all moral authority" (Henri-Frédéric Amiel). The
principle of faithfulness deserves some priority in our thinking. And
if we're looking for a good motto to live by, we could do much worse
than to pick the old Latin slogan: *semper fidelis* ("ever faithful").

The importance of faithfulness is not limited to one or two areas
of our lives; it should govern everything we do, in every relationship. We should be faithful to our spouses, obviously, but that's just
the beginning. Our children also deserve our faithfulness, as do our
parents. Our friends and our neighbors would like to be able to count
on us. At work, our employers (and if we're an employer, then our
employees) need to know that we'll keep our commitments. And yes,
our great institutions and our nation need our loyalty too.

It's the fine print in our contracts that undercuts our faithfulness.
Often, when we think we're being loyal, all we really mean is, "I'll
keep my word, if I don't change my mind" or "if I don't get a better
deal" or "if what I've promised doesn't become inconvenient."

If you have any concept of God as a personal being, think about
the link between that concept and your faithfulness to other human
beings. Isn't it a fact that our trustworthiness in social matters is tied
to our trustworthiness in spiritual matters? If, in a pinch, we would set
aside our commitments to God, wouldn't it be foolish for other people
to expect us to keep our promises to them? If not even God can count
on us, then we're simply not worthy to be trusted, period.

When men cease to be faithful to their God, he who expects
to find them so to each other will be much disappointed.
GEORGE HORNE

ESTEEM

Man's life would be wretched and confined if it were
to miss the candid intimacy developed by mutual trust and esteem.

EDWIN DUMMER

IN THE END, IT'S USUALLY ESTEEM THAT GIVES HUMAN RELA-
TIONSHIPS A CHANCE TO BLOSSOM AND BE JOYFUL. If people
don't regard one another with respect, if they don't look upon one
another favorably, if they don't see the very relationships themselves
as a privilege, then many of life's best qualities are missed. As Edwin
Dummer said, our lives would be "wretched and confined" if we
missed "the candid intimacy developed by mutual trust and esteem."

Unfortunately, very few people today exert any effort to esteem
those around them. If they ever think about the subject of esteem, it's
usually only "self-esteem" that concerns them, or perhaps the question
of whether others esteem them as highly as they would like. Rarely do
we raise the issue of whether we are esteeming other people as highly
as they deserve. Yet that is mainly where the value of esteem lies.

I have a theory concerning the shortage of genuine esteem in the
world, and it has to do with the lifestyle of so many of us nowadays:
we live such busy, self-centered lives that we disconnect from those
around us and make very little real investment in the lives of anyone
other than our own families. And since our relationships cost us so
little in terms of time and effort, we have a good deal less appreciation
for others than we would if we invested ourselves more sacrificially
in them. As Thomas Paine wrote during the American Revolution
concerning the prize of political freedom, "What we obtain too cheap,
we esteem too lightly." No less is true in the realm of human relationships. What we obtain too cheap, we esteem too lightly.

In all of our relationships, esteem ought to be a more highly
valued commodity. We need to work on building mutual esteem with
those around us, and more importantly, having built it, we need to
maintain it. Esteem is fragile and needs our protection. It is far too
precious to be destroyed by "a moment's reckless folly." So when we've
learned to esteem others and we've lived so that they esteem us, let's
be careful not to tear down what we've all worked so hard to build up.

Raised voices lower esteem. Hot tempers cool friendships. Loose tongues
stretch truth. Swelled heads shrink influence. Sharp words dull respect.

WILLIAM ARTHUR WARD

FERVENCY

The effectual fervent prayer
of a righteous man availeth much.

THE EPISTLE OF JAMES

WHATEVER IT'S RIGHT FOR US TO DO, IT'S HELPFUL IF WE DO
IT FERVENTLY. Surely there is already enough halfheartedness
in the world — can't we improve upon the status quo by being wholehearted? And since the word "fervency" comes from the Latin verb "to
boil," can't we boil a little more often and be a little less lukewarm?

Misguided fervency can, of course, be a dangerous evil, and the
uninformed zealot is a well-known source of trouble in any society.
Zeal, or fervor, without knowledge is rarely anything but destructive,
so we need to inform our fervency with things like accurate information and wisdom. In a perfect world, we would never be "all fired up"
about anything except on the basis of *truth*. As William James suggested, "The union of the mathematician with the poet, fervor with
measure, passion with correctness, this is surely the ideal."

But the dangers of ignorant or unbalanced zeal shouldn't scare us
away from the rightful use of fervency. We don't solve the problem of
blind fanaticism by never being fervent about anything, but by opening our eyes, double- and triple-checking our facts, and always being
willing to be corrected. The person who thinks he is just too intelligent and rational to be fervent is being rather foolish. There is no
good reason why a person can't be a mathematician and a poet too.

The fact is, we honor the ideas that we choose to be fervent
about. Julia McFolliard, under whom I studied oil painting as a young
boy, taught me by her passion to respect the discipline of art. And
Robert Winstead, my high school calculus teacher, pulled me into an
admiration for numbers by his eagerness for them. Similarly, we all
confer honor upon the causes that we devote ourselves to fervently.

But what can make us fervent about things in life? Well, many
forces can move a person to be fervent, but none does it better than
love. When we come to love a thing that is worthy of being loved, it
is no trouble at all to be fervent about it. Healthy, balanced fervor is
simply an outgrowth of having come to love a thing in a truthful way.

A lover flies, runs, rejoices . . . Love often knows
no limits but is fervent beyond measure.
THOMAS À KEMPIS

September 7

PERFORMANCE

To lie down in the time of grief, to be quiet under the stroke of adverse fortune, implies a great strength. But I know of something that implies a strength greater still. It is the power to work under stress, to continue under hardship, to have anguish in your spirit and still perform daily tasks.

GEORGE MATHESON

IN ITS MOST BASIC SENSE, TO "PERFORM" AN ACTION SIMPLY MEANS TO "DO" IT. But there are some special meanings of the word that we would benefit from thinking about. For instance, to perform can mean not only beginning something but *carrying it through to completion* (The physician performed surgery). And it can mean *accomplishing something that was expected or promised* (The contractor performed all aspects of the agreement). Thinking of "performance" in these ways, isn't it clear how valuable it would be as a character trait?

You may not have thought about performance as having anything to do with your relationships with other people, but it has a lot to do with them. In fact, healthy human relationships are impossible if the parties don't do, or perform, what is necessary. In the real world, those who can't be counted on (1) to do what is expected, or (2) to carry things through to completion are usually people with a long list of ex-friends. In the words of Owen Feltham, "Promises may get friends, but it is performance that must nurse and keep them."

Paul C. Packer wrote, "It is our individual performances, no matter how humble our place in life may be, that will in the long run determine how well ordered the world may become." If we want to make a difference for good in the world while we live here, the best way to do that is not to aspire to great deeds that will make the evening news but simply to *perform* — that is, do our duties faithfully, however simple or unimportant they may seem to be at the time.

We ought to be, as the old saying goes, "slow to promise and quick to perform." Commitments carelessly entered into often go unfulfilled. But if we are careful in saying what we will do, then the performance of what we said is a powerful thing, much more powerful than the boasts and bluster of those who promise but never perform. There is an ancient adage that warns, "Let not him who puts on his armor boast like him who takes it off." That's well worth pondering.

An acre of performance is worth a whole world of promise.

W. D. HOWELLS

INSPIRATION

I am one who, when Love inspires, attend,
and according as he speaks within me, so I express myself.

DANTE ALIGHIERI

ALMOST EVERY DAY, MOST OF US ARE SURROUNDED BY IN-FLUENCES THAT COULD INSPIRE US TO DO OUR WORK AT A HIGHER LEVEL. When we allow these influences to uplift us and energize us, those around us benefit from that as much as we do. When our work rises above the humdrum to a level of high excellence, the world becomes a better place, even if only in some small way.

While the word "inspiration" often has a religious significance, we are using it here simply to mean "stimulation of the mind or emotions to a high level of feeling or activity" (*American Heritage Dictionary*). All of us know the experience, at least occasionally. A time comes when, because of the season of the year, a piece of music, a conversation with a friend, or any number of other "inspiring" events, we are moved to accomplish something more excellent than we thought we were capable of. Our emotions are stirred, our thinking is provoked, and our abilities surge to an unexpected strength. To act under the influence of "inspiration" is one of life's genuine joys, and we ought to be grateful for the people around us who inspire us.

But the more important question is: to what extent are we having an inspirational influence on them? As much as possible, we need to be people whose influence is such that other human beings find it easier to do good work with us than they would without us. Life's objective is not to be inspired by others but to be inspiring to others.

It would be a mistake to sit down and do nothing until we feel inspired. As Ben Nicholas said, "Most of life is routine — dull and grubby, but routine is the momentum that keeps a man going. If you wait for inspiration you'll be standing on the corner after the parade is a mile down the street." Nevertheless, it's a wonderful experience when, now and then, we feel truly inspired to do our best work. There is no shortage of things that can inspire us, and we should open our hearts up and let ourselves be inspired by them. Better yet, we shouldn't wait for inspiration to find us; we should go out and track it down.

Don't loaf and invite inspiration.
Light out after it with a club.

JACK LONDON

OPTIMISM

There is an optimism which nobly anticipates
the eventual triumph of great moral laws, and there is an
optimism which cheerfully tolerates unworthiness.

AGNES REPPLIER

A N OPTIMISTIC OUTLOOK IS A RESULT OF HAVING CONFI-
DENCE THAT GOOD IS ULTIMATELY GOING TO TRIUMPH
OVER EVIL. It is an attitude that imparts patience in the midst of dif-
ficult circumstances, and also patience with less-than-perfect people.

Optimism doesn't mean that we're naive about the reality of evil
in the world or the extent of the damage that evil has done. While it
believes that one day everything will be fine, optimism is not so foolish as to imagine that everything is fine today. Clearly, everything is
not fine, and genuine optimism looks at the facts with total honesty.

But is there any *reason* to believe that good will ultimately
triumph over evil? I believe there is, even if we limit ourselves to the
empirical evidence of human history and our own personal experience. If we consider the evidence, I believe we can't help but see a
pattern: *truth tends to outlast falsehood, and rightdoing tends to outlast
wrongdoing.* The victories of evil in this world may be shocking and
justice may be long delayed, but facts are stubborn and truth is resil-
ient. Eventually, good has the last say. Why this is so is another question (one that is very interesting, both philosophically and religiously),
but the pattern is undeniably clear. Right is more durable than wrong.

So we can make an intellectual choice to be optimists. In hours
of darkness, we can choose to hold on to what we learned while the
sun was shining. Maintaining our confidence that good will outlast its
enemy, we can stand our ground before the various onslaughts of evil.

Optimism is an important perspective in life not because it
makes us feel better but because it strengthens us and gives us courage. Life happens to be full of battles that have to be fought, and
as Dwight D. Eisenhower said, "Pessimism never won any battle."
Backbone comes from belief — belief that, despite any number of
short-term setbacks, the long-term triumph of good is still sure.

The essence of optimism is that it takes no account of the present,
but it is a source of inspiration, of vitality and hope where others have
resigned; it enables a man to hold his head high, to claim the future
for himself and not to abandon it to his enemy.

DIETRICH BONHOEFFER

September 10
INTELLIGENCE

Intelligence is quickness in seeing things as they are.
GEORGE SANTAYANA

CONTRARY TO WHAT MANY PEOPLE THINK, INTELLIGENCE
IS NOT THE EXCLUSIVE PROPERTY OF PEOPLE WITH A HIGH
"IQ." At best, the so-called "IQ tests" measure only one or two kinds
of intelligence, and it would do us good to see intelligence as a quality
that all of us can enjoy, in one way or another. As Santayana put it,
"Intelligence is quickness in seeing things as they are." To grow in
intelligence means that we learn how to separate fact from fiction and
how to aspire to excellence in our activities, no matter what those activities may be. Each of us has a unique intelligence that can flourish.

It's a good thing that educational experts are coming to realize that there are many more kinds of intelligence than we used to
recognize. Just because a person is not particularly adept at processing
certain kinds of mathematical or verbal data does not mean that they
lack intelligence. It usually only means that their intelligence lies in
other areas. What each of us needs to do is identify our personal intel-
ligences, aptitudes, etc. and develop these to their fullest extent.

But no matter what kind of intelligence we may possess, it's important to recognize that intelligence alone is not enough. The critical
question is what we do with our intelligence once we've developed it.

As far as the practical living of life is concerned, educator John
Holt made a perceptive comment: "The test of intelligence [is] not
how much we know how to do, but how we behave when we don't
know what to do. Similarly, any situation, any activity, that puts before
us real problems, that we have to solve for ourselves, problems for
which there are no answers in any book, sharpens our intelligence."
Intelligence is given to us as a tool with which to solve problems, and
that's exactly what we need to do with it, for the betterment of others.

If we could be known for only one thing, few of us would want to
be known for intellectual ability. But each of us has a mind, and truly,
a mind is a terrible thing to waste. Rather than waste it, we ought to
expand it gratefully. "A good mind possesses a kingdom" (Seneca).

Of work comes knowledge, of knowledge comes
fruitful work; of the union of knowledge and work
comes the development of intelligence.
VINOBA BHAVE

TOOLS

The expectations of life depend upon diligence; the workman
who would perfect his work must first sharpen his tools.

CONFUCIUS

TOOLS ARE DEVICES THAT AID IN THE ACCOMPLISHMENT OF A TASK. Having the right tools for a particular job not only makes the work much easier, but sometimes a job can't be done at all without the right tools. Tools are work multipliers. They take advantage of the laws of physics to increase the work that can be done by a given action. You can, for example, pry something apart with a crowbar that you couldn't pry apart with your hands, simply because the crowbar uses the physical principle of leverage to multiply the force exerted by your hands. Tools helps us do more work and better work.

But if physical tools help us, there are some other, intangible tools that help us even more. Knowledge is a tool. Wisdom is a tool. Talent is a tool, and so are experience, enthusiasm, and a host of other human qualities of character and competence. With these, we can do more work and better work than we could without them. And the more important we believe our work to be, the more important it is to acquire the tools that will aid us in doing that work.

All of us have some tools, of course, but the problem is, we don't have very many. We don't have as many as we need and rather than put more tools in our toolbox, we often try to make our difficulties fit the tools we already have. "If the only tool you have is a hammer, you tend to see every problem as a nail," said Abraham Maslow. We need to wake up to the fact that the world presents us with a variety of tasks and challenges. And every time we get the chance, we need to add new and different tools to those that are currently in our toolbox.

But whatever other tools we may have, whether literal or figurative, here is an encouraging thought: if at least we have our hands, we should be grateful. Let us not undervalue our hands because they are so familiar, for they are really quite extraordinary. With nothing but our own hands, a world of good can be done — if we choose to see their value and make full use of them while the opportunity is ours.

Take a look at those two open hands of yours. They are
tools with which to serve, make friends, and reach out for the best in life.
Open hands open the way to achievement. Put them to work today.

WILFRED A. PETERSON

September 12
BELIEF

> As the essence of courage is to stake one's life on a possibility,
> so the essence of faith is to believe that the possibility exists.
> WILLIAM SALTER

BELIEF IS THE WILLINGNESS TO ACCEPT UNSEEN REALITIES, NOT ONLY IN SPIRITUAL MATTERS BUT ALSO IN THOSE THAT ARE MORE MUNDANE. And not only does it accept them in the safety of the library, belief is willing to stake its life on the truth of its convictions — out there on the front lines where the consequences of being wrong are huge. It doesn't do this blindly or foolishly, but the fact remains, it does do it. To believe is (1) to be sure that a particular possibility exists, and (2) to take a real stand, based on that surety.

First of all, let it be said that we do need to be careful in judging the evidence. Richard Whately, who wrote so powerfully on the idea of belief, offered this caution: "As one may bring himself to believe almost anything he is inclined to believe, it makes all the difference whether we begin or end with the inquiry, 'What is truth?'"

But if some people are too gullible, others are too cynical. In reacting against blind, uncritical belief, let's not overreact and refuse to believe anything at all. Belief is not a vice but a virtue, a character trait that opens the door to many of the best things this world has to offer. So let's be people who are willing to believe when belief is called for.

If you're a person who won't accept anything without empirical evidence, then you've made a choice that will limit you severely before you die. If the only thing real for you is what you can "see," you won't have rich relationships and the legacy you leave won't be worthy. Before you go any further, you'd do well to think about J. F. Clarke's observation: "All the strength and force of man comes from his faith in things unseen . . . Strong convictions precede great actions."

For the time being, the truly great realities almost always fall into the realm of "possibilities." But what shall we do: back away from the evidence, retreat into the cramped cave of what we "know," and simply wait for the end to come? No, we can be much bolder than that. When there is *reason* to believe, we can be *willing* to believe. And acting on the basis of belief, we can move from mere living to real life.

> Be not afraid of life. Believe that life *is* worth living,
> and your belief will help create the fact.
> WILLIAM JAMES

September 13
FUNDAMENTALS

Success is neither magical nor mysterious. Success is the
natural consequence of consistently applying the fundamentals.

JIM ROHN

ALMOST EVERY ACTIVITY IN WHICH WE ENGAGE IS MADE UP
OF SMALLER ACTIVITIES THAT HAVE TO WORK TOGETHER.
Some of these smaller activities are more essential than others. The
ones that are most essential are known as the "fundamentals." These
are the basics, the elements, or the ABCs of the activity. If you were a
beginner, the fundamentals are what a teacher would teach you first.

Right now, for example, I am trying to learn something that I've
always wanted to be able to do: play the banjo in the style that Earl
Scruggs played it. If I work at it, I may eventually be able to play
Earl's *Foggy Mountain Breakdown*, but for now, I am spending most
of my time learning the fundamentals of the instrument: finger rolls
with the right hand, chords with the left hand, etc. If I were so eager
to get to the exciting stuff that I rushed past the basics, that would be
a costly mistake. People often find the fundamentals of a subject boring, but they are very important. In any worthwhile endeavor, there is
no real excellence without mastery of the fundamentals.

The importance of the fundamentals has long been recognized
by athletes, whose paycheck depends on achieving peak performance.
To those who would like to play golf well, Jack Nicklaus said, "Learn
the fundamentals of the game and stick to them. Band-Aid remedies
never last." And Lou Holtz, the football coach, gave this good advice,
"Build your empire on the firm foundation of the fundamentals."

But the comment by Lou Holtz suggests an additional thought.
As can be seen from the word itself, the "fundamentals" are the "foundation" of an activity. Foundations are always important, but their
importance becomes even more obvious with the passage of time.
And in that respect, the foundation of a human life is like the foundation of a building. Shortcuts taken in laying the foundation may not
be noticeable in the early years, but eventually the faulty foundation
begins to crack and the entire structure is in jeopardy. So, my friend, if
your life has become shaky, you need to get back to the fundamentals.

The fundamental things apply,
As time goes by.

HERMAN HUPFELD

CIVILITY

Be civil to all; sociable to many;
familiar with few; friend to one; enemy to none.

BENJAMIN FRANKLIN

IN OUR DEALINGS WITH OTHER PEOPLE, THERE MAY BE MANY
THINGS WE FIND IT IMPOSSIBLE TO DO, BUT WE CAN AT LEAST
BE "CIVIL" TO ONE ANOTHER. To be "civil" is to act like a "civilized"
person. The word comes from the Latin *civis* ("citizen"), and it refers
to the behavior of those who live under a government in an organized
society or "city." Historically, when people have lived in close proxim-
ity, they have found it helpful to treat one another in a "civil" way. So
basically, "civility" is courtesy. It's the way people act who realize that
a group's quality of life is greatly affected by the way its members treat
one another, as opposed to people for whom "might makes right."

Civility does not seem to come naturally to us. Rising above
the behavior of animals involves the use of our freedom of will. It
takes deliberate choice and conscious effort. So we must (1) value the
benefits of civility, and (2) aim to make our communities places where
that is the norm. It won't happen if we don't make it happen.

But in the quotation above, Benjamin Franklin advised being
"civil to all," and therein lies the real challenge. Almost anyone can be
civil to those who are civil in return, but it takes people of uncommon
character to practice civility to all, even to those who are uncivil.

Some would say that being courteous and mannerly to those who
dislike us is timid and cowardly, but John F. Kennedy was right when
he said in his inaugural address, "Civility is not a sign of weakness."
Indeed, it takes far more strength to be civil than to fail to do so.

One of life's great pleasures is to please others. If we had to compromise our principles to be pleasing, that would not be commendable, of course. But within the boundaries of moral integrity, there is
ample room to bring pleasure by being civil and mannerly to those
around us. Graciousness and generosity are habits well worth learning. When we act as civilized people, rather than as brute beasts, we
give a gift that's as agreeable to the giver as it is to the recipient.

The ultimate aim of civility and good manners is to please:
to please one's guest or to please one's host. To this end one uses
the rules laid down by tradition: of welcome, generosity, affability,
cheerfulness, and consideration of others.

CLAUDIA RODEN

RECTITUDE

The only shield to [a person's] memory is the
rectitude and sincerity of his actions. It is imprudent
to walk through life without this shield.

WINSTON CHURCHILL

RECTITUDE MAY NOT BE A COMMONLY USED WORD, BUT ITS
MEANING IS EXTREMELY IMPORTANT, BOTH TO OUR INDIVID-
UAL LIVES AND TO ORGANIZATIONS AND COMMUNITIES. The core
meaning of rectitude is simply "rightness." To rectify something is to
straighten it out or make it right, and so rectitude is the condition or
quality of being right. It means correctness or moral uprightness.

Isn't being right something we ought to aim for? I believe it is,
and by being right I don't just mean being right in an intellectual
argument; I mean being right morally — doing in every situation the
thing that is right. Contrary to what many have been led to believe in
our day, there is such a thing as right, and what is right basically comes
down to doing what is just, as defined by the objective, immutable
standards of justice that all people are subject to. Thomas Aquinas put
it this way: "Justice is a certain rectitude of mind whereby a man does
what he ought to do in the circumstances confronting him."

When we fail to do what is right, we damage the world we live
in, usually more than we realize, but we also hurt ourselves. Without
rectitude, we are severely wounded as human beings, as anyone knows
who has ever lived for any length of time with a bad conscience. As
Churchill observed, rectitude is a "shield" that we need to have. "It is
imprudent to walk through life without this shield," he said.

If we don't have rectitude, we don't have anything worth having.
Without integrity, we are nothing. If we amassed all the wealth in the
world but sacrificed the principles of right conduct in the process, our
wealth would be nothing but cold comfort to us in the long run.

But finally, bear in mind that rectitude is the only way to have
any good influence on those around us. What we are speaks much
more loudly than what we say or do, and so let's resolve to be people
of integrity. People of justice. People who simply do what is right.

The effective impact upon us of men of honor, rectitude,
and goodwill is to arouse kindred impulses within us. We begin
to detect in ourselves undeveloped capacities. The touch of the
heroic awakens in us the slumbering hero.

CHARLES MALCOLM DOUGLAS

DISCERNMENT

The supreme end of education is expert discernment in all things — the
power to tell the good from the bad, the genuine from the counterfeit, and to
prefer the good and the genuine to the bad and the counterfeit.

SAMUEL JOHNSON

WHEN ONE THING IS BETTER THAN ANOTHER, IT IS OFTEN
IMPORTANT TO BE ABLE TO TELL THE DIFFERENCE. Life
is full of choices, and some of them are so far-reaching that our lives
will never be the same after we make them. The character trait of
"discernment" is the "power to tell the good from the bad, the genuine
from the counterfeit." When an important choice has to be made,
discernment is what enables us to judge things accurately. It is skill in
sizing things up — dexterity in distinguishing and deciding. Without
this skill, we make poor decisions, confusing the bad with the good.

There is no way around the fact that we sometimes have to assess
the character of other people and make decisions based on that assessment. When those occasions arise, we ought to be very careful. Some
people have a better character than they appear to have at first glance,
and unfortunately, some people have a worse character than they appear to have. In either case, Lord Chesterfield gave good advice when
he said, "You must look into people as well as at them."

But think about this: "Beware of allowing the discernment of
wrong in another to blind you to the fact that you are what you are
by the grace of God" (Oswald Chambers). When judging things like
conduct and character, not even the keenest discernment would be
helpful if we weren't willing to use it on ourselves. Judging our own
faults rightly is probably the ultimate test of our discernment.

When we are trying, as Samuel Johnson said, "to tell the good
from the bad [and] the genuine from the counterfeit," we often find it
helpful to ask other people for their advice. And when we have access
to someone whose powers of discernment are better trained than our
own, we'd be foolish not to consult their judgment. But in the end,
we're all accountable for our own choices between good and bad. If
we've failed to develop our ability to judge and to decide, we can't
blame the consequences of our poor choices on others. So is improving
your discernment every day a good thing or a bad thing? You decide.

Ask for advice, but do what you think is best.

GREEK PROVERB

SKILL

Force has no place where there is need of skill.
HERODOTUS

WHEN YOU THINK ABOUT IT, MANY OF OUR MOST COMMON MISTAKES IN LIFE ARE SIMPLY VARIATIONS ON ONE THEME: WE RESORT TO FORCE WHEN WE SHOULD BE USING SKILL. We find ourselves in a difficult conversation, for example, and lacking the communication skills to deal effectively with the difficulty, we lose our patience. Arguing, name-calling, threatening, and other brute force tactics become a substitute for skill, and by their use, we admit defeat.

As much as we need skill, most of us go out of our way to avoid the main thing that would teach it to us: difficulty. Very few skills are learned sitting in an easy chair. As the English proverb said, "A smooth sea never made a skillful mariner." So why do we cling to our comfort zone so tenaciously? Why do we decline difficult challenges and opportunities? Are we lazy — or just not interested in the skills that would come from diving into the deep end of the pool?

Some folks have the opposite problem, of course. They try to be skilled at everything, unwilling to be outdone by anybody at anything. But the effort to do that is a losing battle. We need to make some choices in life and focus on the acquirement of a few definite skills. Having done that, we ought to be comfortable with the skills that we have and not envy the abilities that others may have acquired.

Sextus Propertius said, "Let each man pass his days in that wherein his skill is greatest." The concept of "division of labor" is one of the great ideas in the world, and we should learn to be at peace with that concept. I should be eager to do what I am skilled at, and you should do what you're skilled at, each of us doing whatever we do for the common good, rather than for our own personal gratification.

Most of us underestimate the goodness — and also the happiness — that can come from acquiring a few skills and then using them to make a worthy contribution to the world. Even if we recognize that we have some skills, we undervalue them. We think they don't matter. But when we passionately pour ourselves into our skills for the good of others, great things are almost always the result. We've heard it all our lives, but it's still true: it is more blessed to give than to receive.

When love and skill work together, expect a masterpiece.
JOHN RUSKIN

EDUCATION

At present we educate people only up to the point where they can earn a living and marry; then education ceases altogether, as though a complete mental outfit had been acquired . . . Vast numbers of men and women thus spend their entire lives in complete ignorance of the most important things.

CARL JUNG

EDUCATION IS SUCH AN IMPORTANT CONCEPT, IT'S A PITY THAT WE HAVE SUCH A LIMITED VIEW OF IT. We think education is synonymous with schooling, that it is only for the young, and that it is only for the purpose of training someone with a vocational or technical or professional skill. We suppose that education is the concern of the first stage of life only, after which one leaves education behind and enters the second stage of life, that of work, always hoping that one will make it to the third stage, that of retirement. And not only do we limit education in these ways, but we also limit it by seeing it as a slightly negative, or at least suspicious, activity. If a person pursues lifelong education, he won't be considered a "regular" guy.

But real education involves more than what we acquire in school, and it gives us more than what we need to earn a living. Helen Keller said it best, I think, when she said, "The best educated human being is the one who understands most about the life in which he is placed." Education is the never-ending process of learning more and more of what we need to live and thrive in our various situations in life, whatever those may be. It is acquiring not only knowledge but wisdom. And most of all, it is learning how to judge matters accurately, so that we can make fruitful, productive decisions. "Education, properly understood, is that which teaches discernment" (Joseph Roux).

We will never rightly appreciate education until we stop calculating what it can do *for* us and start considering what it can do *to* us. Education is much more than memorization of the facts that need to be known to ply a particular trade; it is the awakening of our imagination to new and better worlds. To be truly educated, then, is to be deeply changed. With the expansion of our character and our competence, we become more forward-striving human beings than we were before. At its best, education not only equips us; it excites us. It says the same thing to us that Dr. Seuss said: "Oh, the places you'll go!"

Education is not the filling of a pail, but the lighting of a fire.
WILLIAM BUTLER YEATS

ACCORD

"Ac-cord" (Latin, *ad corda*) means *heart to heart*. If two
persons like and dislike the same things, they are heart to heart
with each other. Similarly, "con-cord" means *heart with heart*,
and "dis-cord," means *heart divided from heart*.

E. COBHAM BREWER

ACCORD IS NOT ALWAYS POSSIBLE, AND, IN FACT, IT IS NOT
ALWAYS NECESSARY. A world where everybody had the same
tastes and talents would be pretty boring, not to mention unproductive. Even deep differences of principle and value can be good if they
provoke us to grow. Nevertheless, accord is one of life's sweet joys.

The words "accord" and "chord" are obviously related. "Accord"
means agreement, and in music, a "chord" consists of three or more
notes which agree or harmonize when sounded simultaneously.
Thus, accord is a kind of harmony, not of music but of mind. To be
in accord, two minds don't have to think the same thing (that would
be unison, not harmony), but what they think has to be concordant
rather than discordant. People in accord are able to strike a chord!

It's possible, of course, to be in accord with things other than
people. One of the most desirable kinds of accord is consistency between our actions and our principles, and perhaps even more important, between our principles and those that govern the universe. All
of us are interested in happiness, and Aristotle went so far as to say,
"Happiness is activity in accordance with excellence." Discord, in any
form, tends to detract from the joy of life, and there is no unhappier
kind of discord than when our lives are out of sync with our principles
— or worse, our principles are out of sync with truth and justice.

It's not often in life that we find individuals who are "heart to
heart" with us at a deep level. Yes, we may meet many whose convictions and interests overlap ours at some points, but we are fortunate if
we find even one or two people in a lifetime who are in accord with us
on most, or even many, points. What a joy, then, when we find those
few special people with whom we may truly harmonize. Have you
found them? I hope you have. Do you frequently let them know how
happy they make you and how grateful you are? You surely should.

To know of someone here and there whom we accord with,
who is living on with us, even in silence — this makes
our earthly ball a peopled garden.

JOHANN WOLFGANG VON GOETHE

CHANGE

Change starts when someone sees the next step.
WILLIAM DRAYTON

THE SEEING OF POSSIBILITIES IS ONE OF OUR MOST VALUABLE HUMAN ENDOWMENTS. When the status quo is undesirable or unacceptable, we are capable of envisioning other scenarios. We can see other steps that might be taken. And, as William Drayton says, that's when change starts: "when someone sees the next step."

The problem is, we're not always willing to take the next step, and so positive changes often stall before they have any chance to benefit us. "Our dilemma is that we hate change and love it at the same time; what we really want is for things to remain the same but get better" (Sydney J. Harris). We will vote in favor of life's improvement any day — as long as we can continue doing business as usual.

But, as with many of the other good things in life, change requires a degree of balance and wisdom. Dangerous extremes lie on both sides of positive change. On one side, there is the problem of those who are too slow to change, failing to see the benefits of some changes. But on the other side, there is the problem of those who are too quick to change, failing to see the harm that change might do. One of our main challenges in life, then, is to judge specific changes on their own merits, neither minimizing them because we're averse to change or exaggerating them because we have an affinity for change.

The best changes in life are the big ones we're willing to make within ourselves. The world needs changing, no doubt, but the most powerful way to change the world is to change ourselves. If when we look around, the only thing we can see is the need for other people to change, we are to be pitied. We need to change as much as they do. And we miss the point if we think of ourselves as basically high-quality people whose only need for change is to learn better ways of responding to the dysfunctional people around us. High-quality people don't portray their sins as poor responses to other people's failings; they openly acknowledge them as being inexcusable and take full responsibility. They have the humility that makes a person willing to change, and they have the courage that makes a person able to change. High-quality people not only see the next step — they actually take it.

The hearts of the great can be changed.
HOMER

HARVESTS

Who loves a garden still his Eden keeps,
Perennial pleasures plants, and wholesome harvests reaps.

AMOS BRONSON ALCOTT

IN BYGONE DAYS, WHEN MORE OF US LIVED ON FARMS, THE FALL OF THE YEAR WAS ALWAYS ASSOCIATED WITH THE HARVESTING OF CROPS. There is much to be gained from still thinking of autumn that way. Life consists of doing positive, productive work and then bringing in the harvest. We expend ourselves doing worthwhile things, and then we enjoy the satisfaction of having done those things.

Of course, we're not always so fortunate as to see the harvest of crops that we have helped to cultivate. Sometimes our own life ends before the harvest can be brought in. At other times, there must be a division of labor: our work is to plant, and it is someone else's to harvest. At still other times, we simply don't know what the results of our work are. As I write this book, for example, I labor in the hope that someone's life will be touched beneficially. Yet even if that turns out to be true, I may not ever hear about it. It is entirely possible that some readers may reap benefits that will be unknown to me personally. I work, as we all must work, in the simple confidence that there will be a harvest — whether or not I get to take part in it personally.

But sometimes we do get to enjoy harvests, and what a joy that is. To have "planted" in the springtime, "cultivated" in the summer, and then see our work come to fruition and be "harvested" in the fall — well, that's a very satisfying thing indeed. And if we enjoy winter, there's a good reason why. A large part of winter's pleasure is the good feeling that comes from looking back on work that was not only begun and worked on, but also brought to completion and harvested.

So in the unfolding of this year's work, now comes the harvest time. Now comes the season of ingathering, when the bounty of well-worked fields is laid in store. As the ancient writer of Ecclesiastes said, "Nothing is better for a man than that he should eat and drink, and that his soul should enjoy good in his labor." Work itself is not a curse, and honest labor is not to be avoided. It's simply in our nature that we want to do good work while the weather is warm, and then, as the year turns toward fall, we want the happiness of a harvest.

Autumn is the bite of a harvest apple.

CHRISTIAN PETROWSKY

September 22
PATIENCE

The key to everything is patience. You get
the chicken by hatching the egg, not by smashing it.

ARNOLD H. GLASOW

IT IS SAD BUT TRUE: WE MISS OUT ON MANY OF LIFE'S GREAT-
EST BLESSINGS BY GIVING UP TOO SOON. We are not a people
noted for patience or endurance. Accustomed to television programs
where almost every problem can be solved within thirty minutes (the
really tough ones take an hour), we smash any "egg" that doesn't hatch
immediately on our command. For too many of us, the idea of simply
waiting for an answer or a solution is out of the question.

There are some who have the opposite problem, of course. They
wait and wait and wait, failing to take action when action is truly
needed. This kind of patience is only a thin disguise for laziness or
cowardice. But for every person with that problem, I believe more of
us have the other problem: the problem of impatience. We act too
quickly, and our failure of patience costs us very dearly.

Patience is a function of hope. Especially when we're talking
about patience with other people, it is hope that moves us to be patient. When we appreciate the possibilities that lie within others and
when we're willing to affirm their potential, we can patiently endure
their momentary ups and downs. Believing that others have a future
that's worth fighting for, we can work — and wait — with them.

But there is something else that will make us more patient:
recognizing how patient other people have to be with us! And notice
that I put the previous statement in the present. It's not enough to
see how patient others have been with us in the past; we need to see
how patient they still have to be with us. It's bitter medicine, but once
we've swallowed it, we'll forbear the failings of others much longer.

Patience has to rank as one of the preeminent qualities of character. With it we can conquer nearly any adversary; without it we are
vulnerable to nearly any foe. With patience, we enrich the lives of our
families and our friends; without it we diminish their opportunity to
grow. With patience, we find ourselves moving forward and becoming
more alive; without it, we shrivel up and shrink into a pitiful condition. Without patience, we lose most of what life was meant to be.

How poor are they that have not patience!

WILLIAM SHAKESPEARE

INFLUENCE

A man leaves all kinds of footprints when he walks through life.
Some you can see, like his children and his house. Others are invisible,
like the prints he leaves across other people's lives: the help he gives them
and what he has said — his jokes, gossip that has hurt others, encouragement.
A man doesn't think about it, but everywhere he passes,
he leaves some kind of mark.

MARGARET LEE RUNBECK

INFLUENCE IS AN ASSET THAT CAN QUICKLY TURN INTO A LI-ABILITY. If we don't exercise good stewardship of our influence, it can turn in the wrong direction, and when that happens, the very influence that we thought it would be good to have becomes something we wish we could get rid of. But we can't get rid of our influence by wishing it away. If we've influenced others in a negative manner, we can't simply call a halt and decide not to have any more influence. There is something we can do, however, and it's the very thing we ought to do: start working on the improvement of our influence.

But how do we do that?

First, we work on our own character. Whatever we'd like to influence others to be, that's what we ourselves need to be. Talk is pretty cheap, actually. Anybody can say what others ought to do. But if we want to have real impact, we're going to have to walk our talk.

Second, we work on our attitude toward those around us. When we consider those who have influenced us, the point becomes obvious: we are most influenced by those who believe in us. So if we want to improve our influence on others, we need to start believing in them.

Influence is an undeniable and inescapable fact of life. We will be influenced by others, and we will influence them. For better or worse, others will be impacted by our actions — and the impact is probably going to be greater than we estimate. So it makes sense to be careful. *One of the most eye-opening exercises we can do is to imagine what the world would be like if everybody was under our influence and followed our example. Is that a world we'd be comfortable living in?* If not, then we need to make the appropriate adjustments immediately. We ought never to do anything that would worsen the world if our personal practice somehow became the public norm.

So live that your principles might safely
be made the law for the whole world.

IMMANUEL KANT

BIRTH

Baby: Unwritten history! Unfathomed mystery!
JOSIAH GILBERT HOLLAND

WHEN WE'RE BORN, SOMETHING BEGINS THAT WILL BE-
COME MANY DIFFERENT THINGS BEFORE IT REACHES
ITS ULTIMATE GOAL. A human life is an awesomely intricate web
of realities. It involves attitudes and interests, emotions and under-
standings, abilities and achievements. It is a complex intertwining of
character and conduct, with layer upon layer of thoughts, words, and
deeds. Marvelous in its depth and texture, every person's life is a story
with many plots, subplots, themes, and points of view.

What a wonderful thing to be a baby, just beginning to discover
what its history will be and determine how its character will unfold.
Babies do come with inborn traits and tendencies, but from any given
starting point, a thousand different paths could be taken. It's thrilling
to be still in the early stages of that process, a time when no one really
knows what the outcome is going to be. As Yogi Berra quipped, "The
great thing about young people is that they have their whole future
ahead of them." That may be a Yogi-ism, but it's still an exciting truth!

Even if we're old and advanced in years, we can still be people
who're on our way to new things, people who experience the excitement of "birth." We can renew our commitment to the best things in
life and greet each day with the enthusiasm of new life, reborn and re-
juvenated. There are decisions we can make that will revitalize us, and
when we make these choices, we're able to give ourselves to others as
people who're fresh, rather than those who've gone stale.

Back when we were born, lives were initiated that will end up
being something or other, whether we make careful choices about ourselves or not. Even the laziest person, who lives completely by default,
is writing a story. But it's a haphazard story, and it'll be no joy to read.
How much better when the beginning of a life marks the beginning of
a process of improvement! All of us, even the most disadvantaged at
birth, have been endowed with wonderful gifts. The good life means
taking our birth-package of traits and circumstances and turning those
raw materials into a worthwhile product. It can be a difficult process,
without question, but being in the process is a privilege.

'Tis virtue, and not birth that makes us noble.
JOHN FLETCHER

LONGEVITY

If I'd known I was going to live this long,
I would've taken better care of myself.

EUBIE BLAKE

IT IS IRONIC THAT IN A CULTURE SO OBSESSED WITH YOUTH WE ALSO WANT TO INCREASE OUR LONGEVITY. We applaud every advance in medical science that would delay death a few more years, but then we suppose, ironically, that we would continue to be young during those added years. But we can't have it both ways, can we? Consider a few ways our thinking about longevity is confused:

We value longevity, but we don't value old age. Just as everybody wants to go to heaven but nobody wants to die, it's also true that everybody wants to live a long time but nobody wants to be old. Yet if we're serious about increasing our lifespan, we need to start granting more honor to old age. Youth was never meant to be anything but the beginning stage in life, and we shouldn't try to hang on to it so desperately. Old age is a good thing. It's what a long life is all about!

We value longevity, but we want to quit working as soon as possible. I agree with Carl Hubbell, who said, "A fellow doesn't last long on what he has done. He's got to keep on delivering as he goes along." It is inconsistent to want to be both first and last among our peers: the first to retire and the last to die. There's a vital link between productivity and longevity. If we want to boost our longevity, we need to think less about the leisure of retirement and more about the usefulness of work.

We value longevity, but we don't really know why. We have no definite idea what we would do with a long life; we just know that we want one. Consequently, those of us who end up living a long time sometimes have little to show for it in the way of accomplishment. "Often a man who is very old in years has nothing beyond his age by which he can prove that he has lived a long time" (Athenodorus).

The point is, longevity does little good for us if it involves nothing more than additional years of living. What we should want is to spend our years well — whether those years be many or few. A long life is hardly worth aspiring to if it would not be spent making a principled, productive contribution to the world.

It is vanity to desire a long life
and to take no heed to a good life.

THOMAS À KEMPIS

ETHICALNESS

Ethical living is the indispensable condition
of all that is most worthwhile in the world.

ERNEST CALDECOTT

IF WE WISH TO ENJOY THE GOOD LIFE, ETHICALNESS IS NOT AN OPTION; IT'S A REQUIREMENT. If we don't discipline ourselves and subordinate our impulses to ethical principles, then our life is nothing more than a sandcastle that will be destroyed by the next high tide.

Ethicalness benefits us personally. A few years ago, I wrote a book on the importance of taking God seriously. A radio show producer who was considering having me on her program asked what benefit my book would offer her listeners. "Just the benefit," I said, "of going to bed at night knowing that you've done what's right about the biggest issue in life." There are many subsidiary benefits of doing what's right, but in the end, doing what's right is right because it's . . . right!

Ethicalness benefits our families. If you'd like to give your family a remarkable gift but you can't think of anything to give them, may I suggest this: begin living in such a way that every member of your family can count on you to do the honorable thing, no matter what. You will be amazed how much your family will appreciate that gift.

Ethicalness benefits society. If you will live a life of personal integrity, your community will also appreciate it. Indeed, if you're interested in "community service," there is no greater service you can render than ethical citizenship, doing whatever is right toward those around you. When you're gone, you'll be remembered as a person who could be trusted — and there aren't many better ways to be remembered.

We frequently hear it said these days that there is no such thing as objective right and wrong and that such things are purely personal. But no one really believes that. If there were nothing more to ethics than subjective opinion and personal preference, society would soon disintegrate, and the fact that everybody still uses words like "should" and "ought" indicates that we know there are some universally binding rules. For ethical standards to be any good, they have to be binding on everybody. The sooner we admit that fact and start submitting to those standards, the better our quality of life will be.

There is only one ethics, one set of rules of morality, one code:
that of individual behavior in which the same rules apply to everyone alike.

PETER DRUCKER

REJOICING

Gladness of heart is the life of man,
and the rejoicing of a man is length of days.
ECCLESIASTICUS

O NE OF LIFE'S MOST DELIGHTFUL EXPERIENCES IS DEALING
WITH PEOPLE WHO DO A LOT OF REJOICING. There are plenty
of things to grieve about, certainly, and the sorrowful side of life needs
to be given more attention than we sometimes give it. But there is
also much to be glad about. We don't do this world justice if we don't
recognize its joys and appreciate the grace that they represent. People
who do appreciate that grace are refreshing to relate to. Their habit of
rejoicing restores our sense of wholesome balance and proportion.

It's a well documented fact that rejoicing is conducive to better
health. A merry heart really does make for a long life, and that fact
ought to tell us something about our nature. We were built for joy.
Our minds and bodies were designed to run on the fuel of gladness,
and while we have an amazing capacity to endure grief, that capacity
is not unlimited. When we do not rejoice, death hastens toward us.

Rejoicing is one of the best ways in which we can honor other
people. If, despite the sadness in my life, I choose to relate to you
in a joyful, encouraging way, then by that choice I have said, "I care
enough about you to try to maintain a healthy perspective on life. For
your sake, I am willing to see the good as well as the bad."

Rejoicing is, after all, as much a matter of choice as it is a matter of mood. We are not merely helpless victims of our feelings.
Confronted with grievous circumstances, we can consciously choose
to take a broader perspective. We have a will that is free, and we can
determine to live our lives rather than let them "be lived" for us.

Most of us miss a good many opportunities to rejoice. Failing
to count our blessings, we become blind to everything except our
problems. We focus so single-mindedly on certain kinds of emptiness
that we forget how full we are in other ways. Whatever heartaches we
may have, our heartaches are hardly ever the whole story, and if our
priorities are what they ought to be, then it will be no exaggeration to
say that "our cups runs over." Today, let's not miss the joy of rejoicing.

He is a wise man who does not grieve for the things
which he has not, but rejoices for those things which he has.
EPICTETUS

CONTINUITY

Continuous as the stars that shine
And twinkle on the milky way.
WILLIAM WORDSWORTH

IT'S IMPORTANT TO BE A PERSON WHO CREATES CONTINUITY.
For every evil thing in the world that ought to be ended, I believe
there are also good things that need to be continued, and it usually
takes work on somebody's part for that continuity to be achieved.
One generation does not pass down its heritage to the next without
effort and sacrifice. Those who exert the effort and make the sacrifice,
thereby ensuring that the best things in life continue, are to be honored, and each of us would do well to place ourselves in their number.

To be a person who helps create continuity doesn't mean that we
are opposed to change. There is no question that change is sometimes
beneficial. By definition, progress requires change. But the more our
lives are characterized by change, the more essential it is for some
things to continue. We could not long keep our sanity if everything
changed so completely that no day ever had anything in common
with the day that preceded it. There have to be some links between
yesterday, today, and tomorrow. Some things have to hold steady. We
need, then, to have the wisdom to see what those things are — and to
lend a helping hand in the honorable work of preserving them.

At the personal level, there are some things about ourselves that
need to continue, and one of the best kinds of personal continuity is
steadfastness, which means "continuing to try." That kind of continuity
comes from a simple choice or determination. "Strength is the lot of
but a few privileged men; but austere perseverance, harsh and continuous, may be employed by the smallest of us and rarely fails in its
purpose. Its silent power grows irresistibly greater with time" (Goethe).

Without continuity, we can't have any real goodness of character.
The person who is up and down and all around, never carrying any of
his good deeds over from one day to the next, is not a person who can
be counted on. Virtuous character, which is the only kind we ought
to be interested in having, requires that we do some things . . . and do
them again the next day . . . and keep on doing them every day as long
as we live. Continuity is what makes us count-on-able.

Character is simply habit long continued.
PLUTARCH

GALLANTRY

Oh, say, can you see by the dawn's early light,
What so proudly we hailed at the twilight's last gleaming?
Whose broad stripes and bright stars, through the perilous fight,
O'er the ramparts we watched were so gallantly streaming?

FRANCIS SCOTT KEY

GALLANTRY CAN HAVE SEVERAL MEANINGS, EACH OF WHICH IS INTERESTING. The word comes from the Old French *gale,* which meant "rejoicing." So some of the meanings of "gallant" are (1) exuberant or dashing, (2) stately and majestic, or (3) high-spirited and courageous. Also, of course, gallantry can mean consideration and courtesy, especially toward women. Let's look at that meaning first.

Courteous attention to women. Frankly, I wish it were still possible for a man to be gallant or chivalrous in this sense and his actions not be taken as condescending. Shouldn't it be possible for a man to pay "courteous attention to women" because he honors them? But unfortunately, the hands of time can't be turned back, and this kind of gallantry is probably lost forever. It seems to me a grievous loss.

Stateliness and majesty. The "broad stripes and bright stars" that were "so gallantly streaming" in Francis Scott Key's song must have been a majestic sight to his eyes. In today's epidemic of informality and casualness, don't we still need to appreciate a few stately things?

Courage and nobility of spirit. After the previous night's battle, the flag that Francis Scott Key saw "by the dawn's early light" was also gallant in that it inspired courage. Mistakes may surely be made in our choice of things to fight for, but we are in a sad state indeed if there is nothing that stirs our gallantry, nothing for which we would fight.

I suggest, however, that the most important kind of gallantry is not the kind that would face an external foe, but the kind that bravely confronts adversaries that are more inward. For every hundred human beings who would be gallant on the battlefield or in the midst of some other physical crisis, there are far fewer who would show courage and nobility of spirit where it counts the most: in matters of the heart. Whatever other kinds of gallantry we need, we need this kind more.

To fight aloud, is very brave —
But gallanter, I know
Who charge within the bosom
The Cavalry of Woe.

EMILY DICKINSON

PARENTING

As my fathers planted for me, so do I plant for my children.
THE TALMUD

ALL OF US HAVE HAD PARENTS (WHETHER KNOWN TO US OR NOT), AND MOST OF US WILL HAVE BECOME PARENTS BEFORE OUR LIVES ARE OVER. Most of us, therefore, will serve as some sort of bridge between the past generations and those of the future. In our finer moments, what we want is to be a worthy bridge: we want to pass along to our children the best of the parenting that we received.

Doing this is not easy. Parenting is one of the most difficult things any human being ever attempted. And having been told of its difficulty, we may have tried to learn how to do it before we had children, so that when we did have them, we'd know what to do. Yet parenting is a thing mostly learned by doing it. Just as our parents did, we find that we have to learn by trial and error.

Those who end up being good parents are those who are open to feedback, correction, and learning while the process is going on. It takes a commitment to being better parents as time goes by, always being eager to learn anything new that can help us to improve. But not only that, good parents are those who realize that the clock is ticking. The skill must be learned as we do it, yet we don't have an unlimited amount of time to get the hang of it. Our children are growing older every day, and our parenting opportunities are getting fewer.

Many modern parents would do better if we quit trying to use our children as adornments to our own egos and lifestyles and started seeing ourselves as expendable commodities meant to be used up for our kids' benefit. "Parents are," as Peter Ustinov said, "the bones on which children cut their teeth." If we're so full of ourselves that we can't see the sense in that, then we've got a ways to go before graduating from parent school. Parents must be willing to spend and be spent.

The parent-child relationship is one of life's primary learning laboratories. It has important things to teach us about the rights and wrongs of human relationships, and about what the good life is and isn't. It's worth giving every ounce of the very best effort within us.

You don't really understand human nature unless you know why
a child on a merry-go-round will wave at his parents every time around
— and why his parents will always wave back.
WILLIAM D. TAMMEUS

October 1
EXPERIENCE

The value of experience is not in seeing much, but in seeing wisely.

SIR WILLIAM OSLER

IF WE WISH TO MAKE ANY POSITIVE CONTRIBUTION TO THE WORLD IN WHICH WE LIVE, EXPERIENCE IS SOMETHING THAT WE'LL HAVE TO HAVE. For one thing, without any firsthand experience in dealing with the real world, we wouldn't know what kinds of contributions need to be made. It takes a certain amount of hands-on involvement with the world before we begin to discern where the most critical needs really are. As Sir William Osler says, it is experience that teaches us to see wisely. But more than that, experience is where we gain the skills necessary to help meet the needs that we see.

Gaining experience is inconvenient at the very least, and often it goes beyond inconvenience to outright pain. So we tend to shy away from circumstances in which we might gain experience. But we ought not to shy away from them; we ought to welcome them and enter into them. Life has to be lived to be understood. If we don't gain experience, we'll never know anything more than the theory of living.

But to see wisely and to understand life, we have to do more than simply pass through experiences in the world. As Aldous Huxley noted, "Experience is not what happens to you; it is what you do with what happens to you." So we need not only to enter into the experiences that are available to us; we need to think about them, learn from them, and drain from them every drop of wisdom that we can.

The wisest people in the world, however, are not simply those who've learned from their own experiences; they are those who've learned from the experiences of others. In particular, we need to learn from the mistakes of others. We need to be willing to be warned. So Virgil gave good advice when he said, "Believe one who has tried it."

Whatever our work may be, we can't delay doing it until we know how to do it perfectly. Knowledge and skill are essential, but they can't be gained any other way than by experience. So having learned the fundamentals of our work, and having heard the warnings of those who've done it before, let's dive in and get our hands dirty doing the things that need to be done in the world. It's a long and winding road that leads to experience. No shortcut has yet been found.

The work will teach you how to do it.

ESTONIAN PROVERB

October 2
COPING

Success in life is not how well we execute Plan A; it's how smoothly
we cope with Plan B. And for most of us, that's 99 percent of the time.

SARAH BAN BREATHNACH

MOST OF US ARE QUITE FAMILIAR WITH THE CONCEPT OF
COPING. Coping is "the process of managing taxing circumstances, expending effort to solve personal and interpersonal problems, and seeking to master, minimize, reduce or tolerate stress or
conflict" (Wikipedia). In everyday language, that means doing the
best we can to get by in the midst of less than ideal circumstances.

All of us want a more peaceful world, and we tend to define peace
as the absence of stress. But that is unrealistic, at least in the world as
we know it now. Peace is not the absence of stress but the ability to
deal with stress in the right way. That's what we should want.

Coping is one of the most powerful ways that we can contribute
to the quality of our various relationships. Whether it's in the home,
the workplace, or elsewhere, those with whom we interact from day to
day need the hope that comes from seeing others cope effectively with
difficulties. When we offer that example, we do a fine thing indeed.

But stress often takes the form of frightening circumstances, and
consequently, most of us despair of being able to cope because we
don't see ourselves as having enough courage to face life's fears. But I
think that approach puts the emphasis in the wrong place, and I agree
with Barbara Deming, who said, "Think first of the action that is
right to take; think later about coping with one's fears." When doing
what is right is our priority, we'll find that our fears give us less trouble.

The ability to cope involves more than picking up a few handy
"coping skills" from a book or a seminar; it requires the growth and
development of our most inward character — and that takes both
time and hard work. As urgent as it is for us to be able to cope nowadays, there is no easy way to learn to cope. We have to grow up as
human beings. We have to acquire strength and resilience of character. And in particular, we have to attain unity of character — harmony
between our principles and our practice. If we are not at peace within
our own hearts, living consistently with what we say we believe, then
we will find it difficult, if not impossible, to deal with Plan B.

Integrity is essential if we are to cope with life's difficulties.

EURIPIDES

October 3

PATHWAYS

To have his path made clear for him is the aspiration
of every human being in our beclouded and tempestuous existence.

JOSEPH CONRAD

A PATH IS A WONDERFUL DISCOVERY. It indicates that the terrain in which we find ourselves has been explored by someone else. If we follow the path, we will arrive at a place that others have been going to, though we may not know where it is or why others wanted to go there. Consequently, when we find a path in an otherwise trackless wilderness, we feel both safety and mystery. It's comforting to know that the path may lead us out of the woods, but on the other hand, the end of the path may not be a very comfortable place.

Pathways are promising. Our lives may be compared to a journey through territory that is sometimes difficult, and even dangerous; on such a journey, it is a comfort to have a path to follow. As Joseph Conrad said, "To have his path made clear for him is the aspiration of every human being in our beclouded and tempestuous existence." There are few things more frustrating or frightening than wanting to get to a certain destination in life but having no idea how to get there. A pathway may not end up where we thought it would, but at least it gives us some direction. "There's some end at last for the man who follows a path: mere rambling is interminable" (Seneca).

Pathways call for caution. Although pathways can be helpful, sometimes it takes a wise person to know when to follow a path and when to strike out on one's own. There is a certain safety in following the footsteps of others, but safety shouldn't always be our main objective. Many of the major contributions to this world have been made by people who weren't afraid to leave the beaten path and blaze a trail of their own. As André Gide said, "The most beaten paths are certainly the surest, but do not hope to scare up much game on them."

Yet having a path to follow is often important, and we need to appreciate the value of pathways. But if having a path is important, it's even more important to create a path that others can follow. Life in this world is not about being served but about serving, and there are few forms of service more profitable than pathfinding. To get through a difficulty and leave a helpful path is a very thoughtful thing to do.

Pathfinder. A person who goes ahead and discovers or shows others a way.
OXFORD ENGLISH DICTIONARY

WORTH

Nothing worthwhile comes easily. Half effort does not
produce half results; it produces no results. Work, continuous work
and hard work, is the only way to accomplish results that last.
HAMILTON HOLT

GENERALLY SPEAKING, IT IS WORK THAT CREATES WORTH OR
VALUE. A violin is worth more than the pieces of wood from
which it was made because someone worked to take the raw materials
and add value to them. A business, if it had a good year, is worth more
at the end of the year than at the beginning because its employees did
work which added value to the company. Despite the ageless search of
mankind for the proverbial "free lunch," there really is no such thing.
In the whole wide world of human endeavor, there are few exceptions
to the rule: it is work that creates worth. Rarely do we "reap" any more
from a human product than its maker "sowed" in the making of it.

But if human products have worth, so do human beings themselves, and here we need to be careful. There is a sense in which all
human beings have exactly the same worth. Created by the same
Creator, we each possess an equal *inherent* worth. But there is also an
acquired worth which we may have, and this depends on what we do
with what we've been given. Abraham Lincoln and Adolf Hitler both
had the same inherent worth, but most folks would say that Lincoln
used his life to acquire a more worthy character than Hitler. So each
of us needs not only to be grateful for our built-in value as persons; we
need to invest serious labor in building a worthy life while we live.

When we're sizing up the character of others, we need to look
below the surface, since appearances can often be deceiving. But there
is another side to that truth: we ought not to use outward appearances
to deceive others into thinking that we're worth more than we are. As
Aesop said, "Outside show is a poor substitute for inner worth."

As we said at the beginning, it is work that creates worth. If we
want to be people of genuine worth, we're going to have to work at it.
And we might as well admit that work requires sacrifice. To gain the
things of highest value, some lesser things will have to be given up.
Indeed, the very highest things may cost nothing less than life itself.

To gain that which is worth having,
it may be necessary to lose everything else.
BERNADETTE DEVLIN

PROFITABILITY

The successful producer of an article sells it for more than it cost him to
make, and that's his profit. But the customer buys it only because it is worth
more to him than he pays, and that's *his* profit. No one can long make a
profit *producing* anything unless the customer makes a profit *using* it.

SAMUEL B. PETTENGILL

P ROFIT IS ONE OF LIFE'S BASIC CONCEPTS. The root meaning
of the word is "an advantageous gain or return, a benefit." Few of
us do anything for purely abstract reasons. Most of the work in the
world, including the good work, is done by those who stand to receive
some benefit from what they do, if it's only the good feeling that
comes from knowing that one has done something worth doing.

But on the corporate (if not the personal) level, there's no denying that many people today are ambivalent toward the idea of profit.
Somehow, a "non-profit" organization seems more virtuous than any
other kind. But clearly, it's not the pursuit of profit that is objec-
tionable — it's the unprincipled pursuit of profit. There is nothing
dishonorable about the making of a profit, either by an individual or a
business, as long as both the "buyer" and the "seller" receive fair value
in the exchange, as suggested by Samuel B. Pettengill's words above.

Years ago, Justice Louis Brandeis described principled profitability in words that still hold true. Think about this: "While [continued
absence of profit] spells failure, large profits do not connote success.
Success must be sought . . . also in excellence of performance; and
in business, excellence of performance manifests itself, among other
things, in the advancing of methods and processes; in the improvement of products; in more perfect organization, eliminating friction as
well as waste; in bettering the condition of the workingmen, developing their faculties and promoting their happiness; and in the establishment of right relations with customers and with the community."

But here's a final thought, and one more important than all of
the above. To be "profitable" can mean two things: it can mean gaining something advantageous or beneficial, but it can also mean being
advantageous or beneficial. In this second sense, every single one of us
ought to strive to be profitable. That is, we ought always to be asking
the question: *how profitable am I to those who are connected to me?*

He profits most who serves best.

ROTARY INTERNATIONAL

ESTABLISHMENT

Choose to act — rather than delay.
Choose to build — rather than destroy.
Choose to persevere — rather than quit.

ANONYMOUS

A SKYSCRAPER MUST BE ABLE TO BEND OR FLEX SLIGHTLY WITH THE WIND, BUT IT CAN'T DO THAT IF IT'S NOT ESTAB-LISHED ON A SOLID FOUNDATION. In a similar way, we must be established as human beings. To "establish" a thing means to make it "stable." So to enjoy the benefits of establishment, we must be firm and secure. Consider three areas where stability is especially important:

Principles. Our principles are our beliefs about what is real, and about what kind of conduct people ought to engage in. These convictions determine every other thing about us, so it should go without saying that we need to be careful. If we haven't established what our convictions are, then we're at the mercy of every wind that blows.

Character. It takes a while for us to finally figure out what kind of character we really want to have as mature adults, but eventually, we need to have an established character. That doesn't mean we can't grow or change, but it does mean that we know who we are and that the character that we've chosen is stable, rather than wishy-washy.

Conduct. Based on the establishment of our principles and our character, we then need to erect a consistent pattern of behavior. People around us need to be able to count on some predictability in our manner of living. Our lifestyle needs to be one that is solidly built.

All three of the above are important, but of the three, our principles are more basic than our character, and our character is more basic than our conduct. In other words, our character is an outgrowth of our principles, and our conduct is an outgrowth of our character. Too often, we try to reverse these: we try to establish our conduct without having established our character, and we try to establish our character without having established our principles. But that procedure never works, at least in the long run. Life's great challenge, then, is first to find out what the valid, true-north principles are. When we discover these and establish ourselves upon them, both our character and our conduct will stand firm. And out of them, good things will grow.

Character is the evidence that we are built on the right foundation.
OSWALD CHAMBERS

October 7

SOLUTIONS

To spend an hour worrying on our knees is not prayer.
Indeed, there are times when it is our duty, having committed
a problem to God in prayer, to stop praying and to trust
and to do the necessary work to arrive at a solution.

OLIVER BARCLAY

L IFE IS FULL OF PUZZLES AND PROBLEMS THAT NEED SOLU-
TIONS. Indeed, most of our activities on an average day are in one
way or another efforts to find solutions — our work basically consists
of answering questions, filling needs, and so forth. Unfortunately,
we don't always see that this is what our work is, and so rather than
patiently find solutions, we worry. We fret. We pray. We do almost
everything except "do the necessary work to arrive at a solution."

How much better it would be if we threw ourselves gratefully
and productively into the seeking of solutions. There's more than a little truth in the saying that "a problem is only an opportunity in work
clothes." Being faced with tough questions that need sensible answers
doesn't have to be seen as onerous or oppressive; it can be seen as the
special work that only rational creatures have the privilege of doing.

We should be reminded, of course, that solutions are not good
in and of themselves. As Robert B. Reich noted, "Few ideas are more
dangerous than good solutions to the wrong problems." It takes wisdom to see which problems really need solutions and which ones can
safely be passed over, but that is a wisdom we desperately need today.

I believe we need to live and work in the confidence that worthy
solutions can be found, at least to the problems that lie within our
responsibility as human beings. We may not personally find the answers, at least anytime soon. In fact, no one else may find them in our
lifetime. But eventually, there is no valid puzzle to which a solution
can't be found, and it helps us to work with that kind of faith.

It's an admirable aim to want to be a solution seeker. Certainly
we ought to seek solutions rather than create problems. But more
than that, we ought to be those who work at finding solutions and
not those who merely desire them. In the end, there isn't any neutral
ground: if we stand aside and watch while others "do the necessary
work to arrive at a solution," then we've become a part of the problem.

You're either part of the solution or part of the problem.
LEROY ELDRIDGE CLEAVER

October 8
WIT

Wit is a happy and striking way of expressing a thought.
WILLIAM PENN

W E NORMALLY THINK OF WIT AS NOTHING MORE THAN THE
ABILITY TO MAKE A QUICK, CLEVER REMARK. But there's
actually more to it than that, and there's a sense in which we all need
to aspire to a greater quality of wit. The word itself comes from a
family of words with the basic meaning of "seeing" or "knowing."
For example, "unwitting" means unaware or not knowing. So "wit" is
the characteristic of the person who sees the truth of a situation and
expresses his or her observation in "a happy and striking way."

Thinking about life. George Meredith aptly remarked, "The well
of true wit is truth itself." We acquire wit only when we begin to
see how things really are in the world and how they are related. As
Madame de Staël put it, "Wit consists in knowing the resemblance of
things which differ and the difference of things which are alike."

Seeing things from different perspectives. It's a valuable trait to be
able to see commonplace things from different perspectives, and Mark
Twain, a true wit, said, "Wit is the sudden marriage of ideas which
before their union were not perceived to have any relation." A good
example of what Twain was talking about was his own witticism that
"the difference between the right word and the almost right word is
the difference between lightning and the lightning bug" — familiar
things, seemingly unrelated, seen in a new and enjoyable way.

Enjoying the wit of others. Genuine wit allows us to revel in the
perspective of those around us, especially when their observations are
striking. "The wit of conversation consists more in finding it in others
than in showing a great deal yourself" (Jean de La Bruyère).

So wit has to do with some important things, such as thinking
and seeing and thoughtfully relishing conversation about life with
others. If it were only a matter of cleverness or entertainment, wit
would be relatively insignificant. The value of wit, however, lies not
merely in its enjoyableness but in its wisdom. As Dorothy Parker said,
"Wit has truth in it; wisecracking is simply calisthenics with words."
Wisdom and wit are first cousins. We ought to appreciate them both.

What I want to do is to make people laugh
so that they'll see things seriously.
WILLIAM K. ZINSSER

NOBILITY

They that deny a God destroy man's nobility;
for certainly man is of kin to the beasts by his body; and if he be not
kin to God by his spirit, he is a base and ignoble creature.

FRANCIS BACON

NOBILITY, IN AT LEAST ONE SENSE, IS A QUALITY THAT SHOULD BE IMPORTANT TO US NO MATTER WHAT TYPE OF SOCIETY WE LIVE IN. In cultures where there is a royalty or an aristocracy, the nobles are members of the upper classes, the royals or the aristocrats. But nobility can be used in a second sense. It can mean the qualities of high moral character that are normally expected of the nobility, such as courage, generosity, or honor. Isn't it obvious that all of us should be noble in character, whether or not we are noble by birth?

We should always endeavor to think and act nobly *because we are personal beings, free moral agents who bear the stamp of our Creator.* Bacon was exactly right, and his words bear repeating: "They that deny a God destroy man's nobility; for certainly man is of kin to the beasts by his body; and if he be not kin to God by his spirit, he is a base and ignoble creature." Beasts are not capable of nobility. We are.

Genuine nobility does not look down on anyone. In Cicero's words, "The nobler a man, the harder it is for him to suspect inferiority in others." It is nothing but a cheap counterfeit of nobility that fails to recognize the inherent worth of each human being it meets.

Many of the traits we most admire in others are traits that might be called noble. For example, E. H. Chapin said, "Never does the human soul appear so strong and noble as when it forgoes revenge and dares to forgive an injury." Other aspects of noble character are integrity, altruism, benevolence, courtesy, humility, and gratitude.

But finally, we show ourselves to be noble when we rise above discouragement and defeat. It is a part of the grandeur of our nobility as created persons that we can envision, and pursue, a future better than our past. We can feel remorse for our wrongs. We can commit to positive change. In short, we can do what is right — and when we do that simple thing, we act with the greatest nobility in the earth.

Nor deem the irrevocable past
As wholly wasted, wholly vain
If, rising on its wrecks, at last
To something nobler we attain.

HENRY WADSWORTH LONGFELLOW

October 10
FORESIGHT

A prudent man foresees evil and hides himself,
But the simple pass on and are punished.
THE BOOK OF PROVERBS

WE DO OURSELVES, AND ALSO THOSE AROUND US, A HUGE
FAVOR WHEN WE LOOK AHEAD. Not all dangers can be
foreseen, but some can, and it makes good sense to use what foresight
is possible for us. In the wisdom literature of ancient times, one of the
principal differences between the wise person and the fool is that the
wise person uses good judgment in protecting himself from problems
that he can foresee, whereas the fool pays no attention to warnings.
Unwilling to learn from the past, the fool is doomed to repeat it.

To be sure, some folks use foresight as an excuse never to do
anything that involves any risk. "Prudence," said Tehyi Hsieh, "is
sometimes stretched too far, until it blocks the road of progress." If
cowardice or laziness is our problem, we shouldn't camouflage that by
calling it foresight. Prudence is a value and one that is quite important, but frankly, it shouldn't always be the deciding factor.

The opposite extreme, of course, would be equally unhelpful.
Since foresight is not infallible, we must not place too much confidence in it. We may be able to see a little ways down the road ahead,
but usually we can't see very far. Thus our sense of security and optimism can't be based on our foreknowledge of what is going to happen; it must be based on our adherence to valid principles. Travelers
who have an accurate compass can get by without a road map.

What healthy foresight comes down to, therefore, is simply this:
(a) the wise observation of problems that have come up in the lives
of other people, and (b) the taking of commonsense measures to help
protect ourselves from those same problems. In that sense, our foresight is actually based on hindsight: we are willing to learn from past
experience in ways that can make our future much better.

Life often goes along quite comfortably, and we are certainly
thankful when it does. But foresight tells us that it may not always
be so. Happenings on some days may not be as favorable as they are
today. It's a wise person then who takes reasonable precautions — if
not for his own sake, at least for the sake of his friends and loved ones.

Although it rains, cast not away the watering pot.
MALAY PROVERB

FUNCTIONALITY

And let our people also learn to maintain good works,
to meet urgent needs, that they may not be unfruitful.
LETTER OF PAUL TO TITUS

FUNCTIONALITY DOESN'T HAVE A VERY WARM AND WELCOME SOUND TO IT, DOES IT? It sounds like business-speak or techno-speak, rather than the kind of thing a poet or an adventurer would talk about. But before you skip today's reading, think a little further.

If something "functions," it "works." Functional things are helpful. So applying that idea to people rather than things, we might say that functionality is the ability to do things that others find helpful. The more functionality we acquire, the more helpful we can be.

I have long liked the metaphor of the toolbox, in which our knowledge and abilities are our tools. The tools in our toolbox enable us to be useful to others. On the other hand, if it seems that those around us don't find us helpful, it may be that we've never learned how to do anything that anybody needs to have done. If we haven't worked to gain any functionality, we can't contribute to the world.

Functionality has two main meanings, both of which are good.

Operative. If we say that an appliance, for example, is functional, we might mean that it is in good working order. Although we are people and not appliances, we ought to try to keep our personal systems functional — rather than letting them become dysfunctional.

Serviceable. The appliance we mentioned, however, might be functional in that it is practical or handy. And here again, there is a personal application. The happiest people in the world are those who find ways to be of service. They know how to be "handy" to others.

We owe it to those around us to acquire as much functionality as possible as long as we live. The more functions we can perform, the more beneficial we can be, and that gets pretty close to the meaning of life, doesn't it? Although under many circumstances work can become hard and unpleasant, work itself is not the problem and we ought to consider it a blessing. "Work is not primarily a thing one does to live, but the thing one lives to do" (Dorothy L. Sayers). So we ought to want to be as functional as possible for as long as possible. As Richard Cumberland said, "It is better to wear out than to rust out."

To live is to function.
OLIVER WENDELL HOLMES

October 12

PENITENCE

To repent is to alter one's way of looking at life;
it is to take God's point of view instead of one's own.

ANONYMOUS

THE PERSON DOESN'T LIVE WHO DOESN'T NEED TO MAKE
CORRECTIONS. Mistakes are a fact of life. We can't even avoid
wrongdoing by doing nothing, for doing nothing is wrong in itself.
So from time to time, all of us will need to adopt a penitent attitude.
With a genuinely contrite spirit, we will need to alter our way of looking at life and "take God's point of view" instead of our own. And
really, we need to do better than use the word "mistake." Sometimes
the wrongs that we commit are more than just inadvisable; they are
evil. Penitence humbly faces that fact without evasion.

But we need to guard against three misconceptions of penitence:

(1) Penitence is not demeaning. Some people portray penitence as
nothing more than a grovelling, craven spirit, but that is a caricature
of penitence rather than a true picture of it. There is nothing demeaning about humility or contrition. Indeed few things are more noble.

(2) Penitence is more than remorse. While the penitent attitude
involves a broken heart, there is more to it than that. Sorrow is often
merely self-centered, but real penitence goes beyond sorrow to an
acknowledgment of the evil and a commitment to make correction.

(3) Penitence requires action. As Tryon Edwards said, "Right actions for the future are the best apologies for wrong ones in the past."
That doesn't mean that verbal apologies don't need to be made; it just
means that words alone don't suffice. Penitence requires action.

One reason penitence is such a foreign concept to so many of us
is that our lives are so crowded and congested. Rarely are we alone,
and rarely are we quiet. The still, small voice of conscience can't
compete with the loud, incessant drumbeat of our busyness. We are
simply too preoccupied with work and play to notice that some of our
doings are wrong — simply *wrong.* Perhaps we fear the pain of deep
penitence, but truly, it is the door through which we must pass if we
are ever to make any real progress in this fractured world.

In solitude, our heart can slowly take off its many protective devices
and can grow so wide and deep that nothing human is strange to it. Then we
can become contrite, crushed, and broken, not just by our own sins and
failings, but also by the pain of our fellow human beings.

HENRI J. M. NOUWEN

Soundness

You should pray for a sound mind in a sound body.
JUVENAL

IN A HEALTH-CONSCIOUS CULTURE, IT MAY SEEM UNNECES-
SARY TO RECOMMEND THE IMPORTANCE OF "SOUNDNESS," BUT
THERE ARE SOME ASPECTS OF THIS SUBJECT THAT WE TEND TO
OVERLOOK. Essentially, soundness means healthfulness or wholeness,
and that's a widely appreciated idea nowadays. But ironically, modern
culture ends up reducing human soundness to less than it should be.

For one thing, why should we want to maintain soundness?
What's the motivation to seek "a sound mind in a sound body"? Here
we need to rise above the popular monistic or pantheistic concept of
reality which sees "all that is" simply as an amorphous mass of "oneness." Yes, there is a wonderful unity to the "circle of life," but the fact
is, human beings are discrete, distinct personal beings whose actions
impinge on one another. We seek soundness not to merge with impersonal existence or being, but to be of benefit to other personal beings. Soundness is not merely about us; it's about others. Maintaining
ourselves soundly is a gift that we can give to those whom we love.

Authentic soundness is always based on truth and reality. In
the long run, we will not enjoy any significant soundness if we're not
willing to (1) face the facts, (2) take necessary precautions, (3) make
frequent adjustments, and (4) do periodic maintenance and repair.

Not only that, but soundness requires avoiding that which is un-
sound and unwholesome. And that fact applies to the mental side of
life even more than it does to the physical. It's a crazy world in which
we obsess about the physical environment, all the while polluting the
cultural environment with toxic filth, in the name of freedom of speech.

But soundness — real soundness — is not really an extra or an
option for us, at least if we want to contribute positively to the world
while we're here. Soundness, or wholeness, is necessary if we are to do
the important work that the world requires. And so let's pursue it as
an honorable goal. Let's work to maintain sound minds in sound bodies not for our own personal benefit but for the good of our neighbors.

*To meet the great tasks that are before us, we require all
our intelligence, and we must be sound and wholesome in mind.
We must proceed in order. The price of anger is failure.*
ELWOOD HENDRICKS

October 14

FORBEARANCE

Give us grace and strength to forbear and to persevere
. . . Give us courage and gaiety and the quiet mind,
spare us to our friends, soften us to our enemies.

ROBERT LOUIS STEVENSON

TO FORBEAR IS TO RESTRAIN OURSELVES. It is to exercise self-control in the face of provocation. When we are impacted by someone else's failing, there is a tendency for us to strike back. Either we retaliate and "do unto them as they have done unto us," or we pursue "justice," hoping that they'll be punished. To forbear, however, means that we hold back. Because we judge that lashing out would be counterproductive, we pursue a greater good by keeping our temper in check. If necessary, we even forgo the execution of our rights, because we understand the good that can often come from enduring a wrong.

Of course, a point may be reached at which forbearance would cease to be a virtue. It takes wisdom to know when to forbear and when to take action against an unfairness. But in the population at large, there are probably more folks who act too quickly than there are those who act too slowly. If your trouble is that you have an excess of forbearance, then you have a problem that puts you in a minority. Most of us have the opposite problem: an excess of irritability.

Showing mercy. The primary motive for forbearance is usually mercy. There are times when we should refrain from meting out justice to someone because we have compassion on them. In such a case, our heart should move us to tenderness, rather than toughness.

Making allowance. People don't grow and they don't learn to overcome their faults if they're not given a little space for trial and error. So sometimes we forbear the failings of others because we see that making allowance for them is conducive to their growth.

A failure of forbearance often comes down to a failure of gratitude. To be less than forbearing with others is to fail to appreciate the extent to which they have been patient with our faults. And not only that, we set ourselves up for a very strict accounting. If we've not been merciful, mercy will not be shown to us when we need it the most.

Endeavor to be always patient of the faults and imperfections of others,
for you have many faults and imperfections of your own that require
forbearance. If you are not able to make yourself that which you wish,
how can you expect to mold another in conformity to your will?

THOMAS À KEMPIS

RESOLVE

It is a psychological law that whatever we desire to accomplish
we must impress upon the subjective or subconscious mind; that is,
we must register a vow with ourselves, we must make our resolution with
vigor, with faith that we can do the thing we want to do; we must register our
convictions with such intensity that the great creative forces within us will
tend to realize them. Our impressions will become expressions just in
proportion to the vigor with which we register our vows to accomplish
our ambitions, to make our visions realities.

ORISON SWETT MARDEN

NOT MANY OF THE GOOD THINGS IN LIFE GET DONE UNLESS
SOMEBODY DECIDES TO DO THEM. Decisiveness is often the
difference between those who make a positive contribution to the
world and those who don't. But doing good requires more than simple
decisiveness: in addition to making decisions, we have to make them
stick. To finish what we start, we have to have the thing called "resolve."

Deliberation. To deliberate means to "consider" something, and
that which is done deliberately is done "on purpose." Since commitments carelessly entered into are often hastily broken, being more
deliberate is always the first step in learning to be resolute. Before
making decisions to act, we must consider them more carefully.

Earnestness. Having carefully decided to make a decision, we
must make it earnestly, with real determination and firmness of purpose. As Orison Swett Marden put it, we must "register a vow with
ourselves." Our purposes will be realized "just in proportion to the
vigor with which we register our vows to accomplish our ambitions."

Finality. Being resolute means making a commitment, and there
is a difference between making a commitment and "giving it a try."
The person who acts with resolve is the one who knows how to add
finality to his or her intentions. Changes may be made as needed, but
resolute people are not merely at the mercy of every wind that blows.

When we fail to accomplish our objectives, our failure is more
often due to a lack of resolve than a shortage of luck or good fortune.
It isn't circumstances that hold us back, nor is it the difficulty of the
goal itself. Usually, it's our unwillingness to back up our decisions with
intense purpose. We try to do things without *resolving* to do them.

We have more ability than willpower, and it is often an excuse
to ourselves that we imagine that things are impossible.

FRANÇOIS DE LA ROCHEFOUCAULD

October 16
HEART

> The widest thing in the universe is not space; it is the potential
> capacity of the human heart. Being made in the image of God, it is
> capable of almost unlimited extension in all directions. And one of the
> world's greatest tragedies is that we allow our hearts to shrink until
> there is room in them for little besides ourselves.
>
> A. W. TOZER

IT WOULD BE HARD TO THINK OF A WORSE INSULT THAN TO
SAY THAT SOMEONE WAS "HEARTLESS." Few, if any, of the meanings of "heart" have negative connotations; almost always, heart is
something we want to have. But we don't work very hard at having
heart. And although our hearts are capable of quite amazing growth
and expansion, we don't work very hard at having any more heart.

Compassion. One of the definitions of "heart" in the *American
Heritage Dictionary* is "capacity for sympathy or generosity; compassion." In that sense, it seems that we live in an age that is often heartless. Extraordinary calamities and catastrophes may call forth great
sympathy and generosity, but these qualities are often less noticeable
in our daily dealings with one another, where we are often too busy
to help or even to sympathize. "We allow our hearts to shrink," said
A. W. Tozer, "until there is room in them for little besides ourselves."

Courage. Another of the *American Heritage Dictionary's* definitions of "heart" is "inner strength or character; fortitude." We might
say, for example, that a person had the "heart of a lion," and that
would mean the person had an unbreakable spirit, a spirit that would
never concede defeat inwardly, even though setbacks might be suffered outwardly. Having a greater heart in this sense is one of the
most important ways that we can prepare to live in the real world.
Hardships are a fact of life — and it takes a lot of heart to survive.

The word "heart" is one of the great "gift words" in the English
language. Learning to have more heart, in the sense of both compassion and courage, is a wonderfully thoughtful thing to do for those
around us, especially our families. We would make their lives more
enjoyable, to say the least, if we demonstrated frequent growth in our
capacity for sympathy and in the fortitude with which we face life's
hardships. Can we not give this gift? Should we not do so? Yes!

> Give others a piece of your heart, not a piece of your mind.
> ANONYMOUS

POETRY

All men need something to poetize and idealize their life a little
— something which they value for more than its use and which is a symbol
of their emancipation from the mere materialism and drudgery of daily life.

THEODORE E. PARKER

THERE'S A GOOD CHANCE THAT SOME OF THE PEOPLE MOST IMPORTANT TO YOU WOULD APPRECIATE IT IF YOU BECAME A LITTLE MORE POETIC. No, you don't necessarily need to start *writing* poetry, and you don't even need to start *reading* more poetry (although both of those practices have more to recommend them than you might expect). You simply need to start living a *life* that is more poetic. In literature, as we all know, there is prose (think "information") and there is poetry (think "music"). Now, comparing the lives that we lead to literature, aren't there two different parts: the prosaic part of life and the poetic part? Don't our activities fall into two general categories: business and beauty? The answer is yes. And the point is that we all could do with a little more of the poetic.

One of the definitions of a poet is "one who is gifted in the perception and expression of the beautiful or lyrical." Christopher Fry said it well: "Poetry is the language in which man explores his own amazement." Whether we realize it or not, we are being poetic — and we are enjoying poetry — any time we (a) stop to notice that which is beautiful or lyrical, and (b) express our enjoyment in honest ways.

But if there's a dearth of poetry in your life, don't excuse it by saying, "I have too much important work to do, and besides, the people around me aren't very poetic." Rainer Maria Rilke wrote, "If your daily life seems poor, do not blame it on others; blame yourself, tell yourself that you are not poet enough to call forth its riches." The world is full of poetry. There is simply no excuse for not enjoying it.

Whoever we are, we tend to become more poetic when we're under the influence of powerful thoughts and feelings, and what could be more powerful than love? We've all been in love, and in love, we've all felt at least a slight tug in the direction of the poetic. I happen to believe that the tug should be yielded to. There is much to be amazed at, whether it's love or just the wide world itself. When we're amazed by beauty or by virtue, we ought to let ourselves "sing" about it.

At the touch of love, everyone becomes a poet.

PLATO

PERSONALITY

Few men are of one plain, decided color;
most are mixed, shaded, and blended; and vary as much,
from different situations, as changeable silks
do from different lights.

LORD CHESTERFIELD

IF YOU'VE EVER WATCHED PEOPLE IN A PUBLIC PLACE FOR HALF AN HOUR OR SO, YOU'VE PROBABLY BEEN STRUCK BY THE VARIETY THAT THERE IS IN THE HUMAN RACE. Physically, no two people are alike; that much is obvious. But there's an even greater variety in the personalities that people project — and even in the personalities that the same people display in different situations! All these personalities are produced as individuals take the "nature" they were born with and then use that to interact with the external circumstances that come their way. The results are a "mixed bag," to put it mildly.

Hardly anybody is entirely pleased with his or her own personality, but even so, there's a lot of wisdom in learning to accept the personalities that we have. We can adjust them and improve them, but we ought not to despise them. Wishing that we could exchange our personality for that of somebody else is largely a waste of time.

Rather than wishing we had a different personality, what we ought to do is become more proactive in cultivating and enhancing the ones we've got. We do that by getting out there amongst other personalities and getting involved with their uniqueness. Eleanor Roosevelt gave good advice when she said, "If you approach each new person in a spirit of adventure, you will find yourself endlessly fascinated by the new channels of thought and experience and personality that you encounter." And Carl Jung was also right when he said, "The meeting of two personalities is like the contact of two chemical substances: if there is any reaction, both are transformed."

Just as our bodies are instruments through which we do our work, the same is true of our personalities. Two people can do the exact same work and end up making a very different contribution to the world. Personality is what makes that possible. *Viva la difference!*

If you have anything valuable to contribute to the world
it will come through the expression of your own personality
— that single spark of divinity that sets you off and makes
you different from every other living creature.

BRUCE BARTON

October 19
VITALITY

Human vitality is so exuberant that in the
sorriest desert it still finds a pretext for glowing and trembling.
JOSÉ ORTEGA Y GASSET

IT'S EASY TO ADMIRE THOSE INDIVIDUALS WHO HAVE GREAT "VITALITY." It is an attractive quality. Coming from the Latin *vita* ("life"), vitality is the trait of those who, whether young or old, seem to have more life about them. They bubble with a liveliness that is exciting to watch. We appreciate their spirit and their spunk.

But vitality is not only admirable; it is powerful. Those who have vitality are more productive, obviously, but their work also tends to be of a higher quality. Indeed, it is nothing short of astonishing to think about what has been accomplished by vitality. When they have been truly "alive" to their work, human beings have written breathtaking symphonies and invented life-changing innovations and shown death-defying heroism. Vitality is a potent form of leverage.

But it is especially in our relationships that we need to value vitality. We bestow great honor upon others when we present ourselves to them as individuals who are fresh and full of life. "I love you" comes through loud and clear when we live life fully. "It is our uniqueness that gives freshness and vitality to a relationship" (James C. Dobson).

The work that people do in the world is as varied as the people who do it. But whatever it is that we do, most of us could do it more energetically and with more vitality. In the Book of Ecclesiastes, there is this wise statement: "Whatever your hand finds to do, do it with your might." We may fail or fall short (and the bigger our goals, the more often that will happen), but we can at least give our best effort.

Each day tests us with questions like these: How much vitality do we possess? How alive are we? How much energy can we put into our projects? Clearly, we need as much vitality as we can muster if we are to do work that is worth doing. But vitality is not a matter of genetic makeup or environmental circumstances; it's a matter of character. And if it's a matter of character, then it's a matter of choice. So let us choose to work with passion and energy. And when we fail or fall short, let us have enough vitality to get up and get going once again.

Vitality shows not only in the ability
to persist but in the ability to start over.
F. SCOTT FITZGERALD

RELATIONSHIPS

I sincerely believe that the word "relationships" is the key
to the prospect of a decent world. It seems abundantly clear that
every problem you will have — in your family, in your business, in your
nation, or in this world — is essentially a matter of relationships.
CLARENCE FRANCIS

OUR LIVES ARE EITHER BLESSED OR CURSED BY THE QUALITY OF OUR RELATIONSHIPS WITH OTHER HUMAN BEINGS.
As long as we live in the world, our lives are going to be changed, for
better or worse, by the way we interact with those around us. That's
just the way the world is put together, and it doesn't do much good to
wish it were otherwise. To be human is to engage in "relationships."

But really, we shouldn't wish it were otherwise, even when our
relationships are frustrating. The fact is, we need to be connected to
beings like ourselves. "Heaven's eternal wisdom has decreed that man
should ever stand in need of man" (Theocritus). We are communal
beings who would find it very, very difficult to live totally alone.

Sometimes we take a rather superficial approach to improving
our relationships. We read books, listen to recordings, and attend
workshops — all in the hope of finding better relationship "techniques." But our way of relating to others is a function of our character, and so we improve our relationships by improving our character.

None of us does a perfect job of being a partner in any relationship. The most productive step we can take, therefore, is to accept
responsibility for our own actions, and upgrade the quality of our participation in each relationship. We can control only our own behavior.

Ultimately, the manner in which we relate to other people is a
product of our worldview and our understanding of the nature of
reality. If we say, for example, that we believe we've been created by a
personal God, that should make a significant difference in the quality
of our relationships. But if we mistreat those around us, then it is to
be wondered whether we really believe what we say we believe. The
kind of relationships we maintain is an indication of our true, practical convictions — not our theoretical ones. So if we want to improve
our relationships, we should start by asking ourselves what we really
believe about where human beings came from in the first place.

Our sociology reflects our theology.
REBECCA MANLEY PIPPERT

ENERGY

The real difference between men is energy.
A strong will, a settled purpose, an invincible determination,
can accomplish almost anything; and in this lies the distinction
between great men and little men.
ALFRED CARL FULLER

ENERGY IS CERTAINLY ONE OF THE PRIME DETERMINANTS OF ACHIEVEMENT. Those who are energetic achieve greater deeds than those who aren't. Alfred Carl Fuller may have overstated the case in ranking energy as the number one difference "between great men and little men," for one's principles would surely rank higher than one's energy, but it can't be denied that energy is essential to honorable character. Not even the best principles in the world will contribute anything of value if they're not implemented with energy.

It is the combination of valid principles and high energy that we should desire. Principles without energy are ineffective, and energy without principles is destructive. Indeed, Augustine of Hippo gave an interesting definition of sin when he said that "sin is energy in the wrong channel." But think of the power, the uplift, and the benefit that result when principles and energy work together in "synergy."

One of the truly wonderful things about our nature is that we can increase our energy when we choose to do so. We do that, for the most part, by adjusting our motives and our reasons for doing the things that we do. The higher (that is, the more unselfish) our motives, the more energy we have. So if we want to increase our energy, we need to enlarge our desires and elevate our ambitions to a higher plane.

But another thing that influences our energy is the question of for whom we do what we do. For example, try this experiment today and see if it doesn't give you greater energy: *whatever you do, see yourself as doing it not for yourself but as a gift for those whom you love!*

There is hardly a greater energy in the world than benevolence, which comes from the Latin *bene* ("good") and *velle* ("to wish or will"). It is not only one of the most powerful forms of energy, but it's one of the greatest in terms of the good that it accomplishes. Not much can stop us if we're moved by genuine, old-fashioned goodwill.

Goodwill is no easy symbol of good wishes.
It is an immeasurable and tremendous energy,
the atomic energy of the spirit.
ELEANOR B. STOCK

October 22

MISSION

He who wishes to fulfill his mission in the world
must be a man of one idea, that is, of one great overmastering
purpose, overshadowing all his aims, and guiding
and controlling his entire life.

WILLIAM BATE

NOT EVERYONE HAS GONE THROUGH THE EXERCISE OF WRIT-ING OUT A "MISSION STATEMENT," BUT EVERYONE HAS A MISSION NEVERTHELESS. Our mission is our main purpose for living. It is the one thing that we would most like to accomplish or achieve while we're alive. All of us have some such goal or reason for living. We may not have thought about it much. In fact, we may not even be honest enough to admit to ourselves what the real motivation is behind our actions. But whether it is written or unwritten, and whether it is conscious or unconscious, all of us have a motive and we have a mission. There is always some goal or interest that guides our doings.

It pays, then, to be careful about our mission. Rather than drift through life with a mission that is given to us by our surrounding circumstances, we ought to define our mission deliberately and make it as worthy a mission as possible. Out of all the things that we might live our lives for, we ought to decide what we're going to live for. Our mission ought to be one that we've consciously chosen after considering the alternatives before us. Virtually everything else about our lives will be determined by this choice, so we ought to be careful.

One reason to think about our mission is that we hurt those around us, especially our loved ones, when we live aimlessly. Having a well-defined and worthy sense of purpose within ourselves is one of the most positive steps we can take to improve our relationships.

But what about *achieving* our mission? What can we do to help ourselves? Well, most of those who have fulfilled their mission would say that single-mindedness is the key ingredient. We must be in passionate possession "of one idea, that is, of one great overmastering purpose," as William Bate put it. Rather than dabbling, we must learn to focus ourselves and live with concentrated energy. And that is not likely to happen if we don't choose for it to happen. So as to your mission, what choices have you made? Are you pleased with your choices?

Make your life a mission — not an intermission.
ARNOLD H. GLASOW

APOLOGIES

An apology is saying the right thing after doing the wrong thing.
ANONYMOUS

IN A PERFECT WORLD, APOLOGIES WOULD BE UNHEARD OF. But, of course, ours isn't a perfect world. It's a world of inadvertence, error, and, all too often, outright evil. Apologies are the statements that we make to others when we recognize that we've erred, especially when our faults have caused damage or hurt to others. When we apologize, we admit our error and take responsibility for the wrongdoing. To put it in legal terms, we enter a "guilty plea."

While an apology often includes an expression of regret for the trouble or hurt that has been caused, a full apology is always more than that. A dentist, for example, may say he is sorry that what he had to do caused you to hurt, but that is merely an expression of sympathy, not an admission of wrongdoing. When we have actually wronged someone, however, our apology needs to do more than express sympathy. It needs to say, "I was wrong, and if I were presented with the very same circumstances again, I would not do to you what I did."

Some people think that apologies shouldn't be made. They would agree with the line in the old John Wayne movie when he said, "Never apologize and never explain — it's a sign of weakness." It all depends on our value system. If we put a premium on pride, apologies will look weak, no doubt. Yet there are other value systems we might consider.

Like many other good deeds, apologies tend to lose their value when they're overused. Excessive apologies, therefore, are unhelpful and unappreciated. For example, if we committed the very same wrong against a friend repeatedly, each time making a new apology, at some point the friend might be tempted to say, "Look, I appreciate your apologies, as far as they go, but wouldn't it be better if you just quit the behavior? That would be the best apology you could offer." Our friend would have made a point that is well worth pondering.

But wisely considered and honestly offered, apologies are a vital part of any good person's life. If we're fully engaged in the living of real life, we're going to make mistakes on a fairly regular basis. When we make them, it will often be necessary for us to apologize for them. Doing so is not a sign of weakness. It's a sign of true strength.

An apology is a good way to have the last word.
ANONYMOUS

LONGSUFFERING

Hope has a thick skin and will endure many a blow;
it will put on patience as a vestment, it will wade through a sea
of blood, it will endure all things if it be of the right kind, for the joy
that is set before it. Hence patience is called "patience of hope," because
it is hope that makes the soul exercise patience and longsuffering
under the cross, until the time comes to enjoy the crown.

JOHN BUNYAN

IT IS TRUE, AS JOHN BUNYAN SAID, THAT HOPE MAKES US MORE LONGSUFFERING. When our minds and hearts are full of a vision that is exceedingly important to us, and we deeply desire to see that vision realized, we will endure whatever frustrations we may face on the path to our goal. If our hope is sufficiently strong, no interference or injury can break our spirit. Hopeful people know how to hold out.

The word "longsuffering" means the patient endurance of wrongs or difficulties. Literally, it means that a person can bear a burden or suffer a hardship for a long time before giving in to discouragement or vexation. In one sense, it is the opposite of being "short-tempered." The short-tempered person has a short "fuse" — it doesn't take much to set him off. In contrast, the longsuffering person can bear up under even the heaviest load for a very long time. When others have given up or gotten angry, the longsuffering person is still holding out. And he does so because he has not given up *hope*.

It would be to our advantage to spend less time avoiding the hardships of life and more time learning how to endure them. As any sailor knows, it isn't always possible to avoid a storm, and the storms that can't be avoided have to be weathered. Just as a sailor has to ride out a storm now and then, human beings have to be longsuffering. Try as we may to find quick fixes, many of life's most significant problems take a long time to be resolved. In the interim, while they are being resolved, patient endurance is the quality that we need.

Without longsuffering, we won't grow any stronger than we are right now, either in our character, our conduct, or our competencies. Strength comes from dealing with difficulty, and if we don't have the longsuffering to hold out while the difficulty is being dealt with, we won't get the benefit of the hardship. It's *holding out* that helps us.

Strength is born in the deep silence
of longsuffering hearts; not amid joy.

FELICIA HEMANS

WISHES

Hope is wishing for a thing to come true;
faith is believing that it will come true.

NORMAN VINCENT PEALE

FOR ALL OUR WHIMS, WE DON'T HAVE MANY REAL WISHES. A wish is more than a transient urge or a passing fancy. It is a real desire or longing for something. It is a strong inclination based on more than a mood. The things that we wish for are things that bubble to the surface as our inner character interacts with our outward circumstances. They are things that we would really like to see come true. And as Norman Vincent Peale suggests, faith adds the element of expectation. If we have confidence that our wishes are in fact going to come true, then what we have is a combination of hope and faith.

Some people, of course, are nothing more than dreamers. Their wishes never put on any work clothes, and nothing ever comes of their intentions. But as long as we're willing to back up our wishes with hard work, there is a lot to be said for wishing big wishes. The human heart is vast. Its capacity is almost infinite. And it's a pity that we so often content ourselves with wishes that are far below our ability. So let's let ourselves go, at least once in a while. Let's wish for some things that would stretch us to our limits . . . and even beyond.

While we're increasing the size of our wishes, however, we also need to give some consideration to their quality. Too often, our biggest wishes have to do with nothing more than our possessions and our lifestyles. But we've been endowed with the ability to wish for things that are much more important, things that have to do with our character. So add to your wish list some items that would increase your integrity. If a genie ever gave you three wishes, you wouldn't want to waste them on toys or entertainments, would you?

The bottom line is, our wishes need to be consistent with our principles. It's a dangerous game that we play when we wish (however privately) for the fulfillment of desires that are inconsistent with our deepest convictions. So we should keep a close watch on our wishes, lest they come true and we regret it. Or maybe we should simply say it this way: we ought not to wish for things that we wouldn't pray for.

Anything large enough for a wish to light upon
is large enough to hang a prayer upon.

GEORGE MACDONALD

ECONOMY

Economy is half the battle of life;
it is not so hard to earn money as to spend it well.
CHARLES HADDON SPURGEON

THE MORE RESOURCES WE ARE BLESSED WITH, THE MORE
IMPORTANT IT IS TO PRACTICE ECONOMY. There is a sense, of
course, in which the opposite is also true: economy is especially critical
when resources are limited. But the well known principle of accountability says that "to whom much is given, much is expected." The more
we have, the more responsibility we have to use our resources wisely,
and that is hard. As Spurgeon pointed out, earning money is not as
hard as learning to spend it well. Managing our resources (whether
they be many or few) so that the maximum amount of good is done, is
one of our principal challenges as mature human beings.

Sparing. To be economical, we must be sparing — in a good
sense. That is, we must exercise restraint in our expenditures. Economy
means knowing how to subordinate our impulses to our principles.

Frugal. There is a time and a place for luxury, obviously, but if we
are so attracted to luxury that we know nothing of self-denial, then
we're on a slippery slope. Economy means being able to abstain.

Thrifty. An old Latin proverb says, "No gain is so certain as that
which proceeds from the economical use of what you already have."
Economy means increasing our resources by eliminating waste.

Economy is essential if we are to remain free in our thinking and
in our living. One of the worst enslavements is bondage to a particular standard of living, the kind of bondage that occurs when we are
so tied to what we presently own that we "can't do without it." Most
of us these days are fortunate to have much more than we absolutely
need, and the truth is, we can do without much of our present abundance. We may think we couldn't survive having "little," but it would
only take a fire, a hurricane, a tornado, or an earthquake to prove
otherwise. If our abundance was suddenly wiped out, we would find
that we could survive, if we had to, on much less than we thought we
could. So it is a healthy exercise to live economically — spending less
than is within our power — just to stay out of slavery to our stuff.

He will always be a slave who does not
know how to live upon a little.
HORACE

EXEMPLARINESS

He that gives good advice builds with one hand; he that gives good counsel
and example builds with both; but he that gives good admonition and bad
example builds with one hand and pulls down with the other.

FRANCIS BACON

E XEMPLARINESS MEANS SETTING A GOOD EXAMPLE FOR
OTHERS. It doesn't mean setting ourselves up as authorities or
demanding that others pay attention to us; it simply means living in
such a way that others would be helped, rather than hurt, if they did
things the way we do them. Exemplary conduct comes from asking
and honestly answering the question, "What kind of world would it
be if everybody conducted their affairs just as I conduct mine?"

When we are trying to have an influence on someone else, it is
tempting to rely solely on words. Obviously, advice is an easier thing
to give than a good example, and that's why most of us end up saying
so often to our friends and family, "Do as I say, not as I do."

But if exemplariness is difficult and costly, there can be no doubt
that it's worth the cost. As Aristotle observed long ago, *ethos* (our
manner of living) is a more powerful persuader than *logos* (our words)
alone. Influence almost always requires the use of words, but it can
rarely be limited to words. Real impact requires more — it comes from
modeling the principles and practices that we wish others to adopt.

So all things considered, the most powerful and influential
people in the world aren't the eloquent orators or the motivational
masterminds, nor are they the celebrities or the front-page newsmak-
ers. More often than not, they're just the ordinary, everyday folks who
quietly go about the business of living high-quality lives each day.

We have it within our power to give many gifts to those around
us, but no gift is more valuable than the living of an exemplary life. In
fact, nothing else will mean much if our manner of life is not what it
ought to be. If our lives are out of sync with the principles of goodness, no other gifts (least of all those bought with money) can make
up for the damage that we do. So why not improve our exemplariness?
Why not give our fellow human beings the benefit of an example that
can be honorably followed? Whether they ever say so or not, others
will appreciate it. Maybe not now, but eventually they'll appreciate it.

The first great gift we can bestow on others is a good example.

THOMAS MORELL

INSURANCE

Only in growth, reform, and change,
paradoxically enough, is true security to be found.
ANNE MORROW LINDBERGH

MOST OF US CRAVE SECURITY. We fear the prospect of inadequacy or insufficiency — physically, financially, socially, or in almost any other way. And so we try to insure ourselves. Faced with possible losses, deficiencies, and dangers, we try to guarantee that we won't come up short. Yet we tend to look for security in all the wrong places, and our chosen forms of "insurance" turn out to leave us vulnerable still. As Anne Morrow Lindbergh pointed out, true security is a paradox in that it comes from things that seem more threatening than safe: things like growth, reform, and change. There is little real insurance or safety inside our personal comfort zones. To insure our greatest safety, we have to do some fairly risky and "unsafe" things.

The best kind of insurance is a kind that can't be bought with money: it is a matter of *character*. When we pay the price to build a quality character on the inside — based on valid, true-north principles — nothing that happens on the outside can do us any lasting harm.

The bigger question, however, is not how much insurance we have, but how much we provide. In other words, how much security do we add to the lives of those around us? It is a far finer thing to work at making others feel safe than to worry about whether they're making us safe, and in fact we are safest when our focus is on others.

But whether it's insurance for ourselves or for those we come in contact with, true security calls for a long-term perspective. The shortcuts in life that promise easy safety may be tempting, but in the end, the only kind of insurance that will work is doing what is right — and if you haven't noticed, doing what is right is not always easy. Acting justly won't protect us from life's ups and downs right now, but if we're thinking clearly, we won't be concerned about that too much. Our faith will be in ultimate justice, the eventual triumph of what is right when all the facts are known. So anytime we have to choose between what is right and what is easy, let us choose what is right, although it is scary. In this case, the scariest choice is by far the safest.

Justice is the insurance we have on our lives,
and obedience is the premium we pay for it.
WILLIAM PENN

ACTION

It is not the critic who counts, not the man who points out how
the strong man stumbles or where the doers of deeds could have done them
better. The credit belongs to the man who is actually in the arena, whose face
is marred by dust and sweat and blood, who strives valiantly, who errs and
comes short again and again because there is no effort without error and
shortcomings, who knows the great devotion, who spends himself in a worthy
cause, who at best knows in the end the high achievement of triumph and
who at worst, if he fails while daring greatly, knows his place shall never be
with those timid and cold souls who know neither victory nor defeat.

THEODORE ROOSEVELT

THERE IS SOMETHING VERY ADMIRABLE ABOUT PEOPLE WHO
HAVE MADE ACTION A COMPONENT OF THEIR CHARACTER,
PEOPLE WHO HAVE THE WILLPOWER TO DO WHAT THEY KNOW
THEY SHOULD. Those who have trained themselves not just to think
but to act at the impulse of their conscience are to be commended.
They may make some mistakes along the way, but even in failure they
are more to be commended than those who simply do nothing.

Two extremes are possible, of course. On the one hand, there are
those who act too quickly and with too little forethought. But given
the powerful pull of inertia ("the tendency of a body to resist accelera-
tion"), there are probably more of us with the opposite problem: we
spend too much time in forethought and too little in action.

Memories of times when we took no action can be among the
saddest of life's regrets. "The bitterest tears shed over graves are for
words left unsaid and deeds left undone" (Harriet Beecher Stowe).

But is it fair to talk of people who have made action a component
of their character? Yes, it is. There is a vital link between our character and our action. At the deepest level, our action (or the lack of it)
indicates what our character really and truly is. If we say, for example,
that we think democracy is important but we rarely get out and vote,
then the truth is this: we don't really think democracy is important.
So we need to take a hard look at our usual, customary level of action.
Good people may occasionally fail to act as they should, but if self-
examination shows that inaction has become a chronic problem with
us, there's no use telling ourselves that we have a good character.

We know what a person thinks not when
he tells us what he thinks, but by his actions.

ISAAC BASHEVIS SINGER

CONSEQUENCES

> I so love the Spanish proverb "God says, *Choose what you*
> *will and pay for it,*" which stresses that life holds no easy answers,
> that conscious choices are often costly ones. We must live with
> and pay for their consequences. Understanding this,
> we learn what it means to be fully human.
>
> MARSHA SINETAR

WE OFTEN THINK OF CONSEQUENCES IN NEGATIVE TERMS, BUT THE IDEA CAN ALSO BE POSITIVE. For every time that someone says, "Do this or you'll suffer the consequences," there are just as many times when it could be said, "Do this and you'll enjoy the consequences." The word "consequence" simply means "effect" or "result." We live in a world where things happen in "sequence." (One thing leads to another, as the saying goes.) So the "consequence" of an action is its "sequel," the thing that follows it and flows from it. Whether consequences are good or bad depends upon the quality of the actions that produced them. In other words, we reap what we sow.

It's important to see that consequences are inevitable. There is no such thing as an action that doesn't have any result, so it is never entirely true to say, "This won't make any difference." Everything we do makes some difference, for better or worse. We may not see the results, but see them or not, we may be sure that our actions have consequences. With our every action, we make the world a little bit different than it would have been had we not chosen to do that deed.

So we must accept responsibility for the consequences of our actions — especially as they relate to the people around us. "Keep in mind that each of you has your own vineyard. But every one is joined to your neighbor's vineyards without any dividing lines. They are so joined together, in fact, that you cannot do good or evil for yourself without doing the same to your neighbors" (Catherine of Siena).

All in all, we can be glad that our actions have consequences. If that weren't true, we would have no power to effect positive change in the world. So while it is sobering to know that every evil deed does damage, let us be encouraged that good deeds have consequences too.

> Nature imitates herself. A grain thrown into good ground
> brings forth fruit; a principle thrown into a good mind brings forth fruit.
> Everything is created and conducted by the same Master — the root,
> the branch, the fruits — the principles, the consequences.
>
> BLAISE PASCAL

October 31
YOUTHFULNESS

A youth without fire is followed
by an old age without experience.
CHARLES CALEB COLTON

YOUTH SHOULDN'T BE WASTED LIVING PASSIVELY, WITH-
OUT INTEREST AND ENGAGEMENT. "Youth," as Robert Louis
Stevenson wrote, "is the time to go flashing from one end of the
world to the other, both in mind and body." If we let our younger
years pass without putting any "fire" into them, we'll suffer the tedium
of an old age that lacks the color and the texture it could have had.

If we're now old, what's our attitude toward those who're still
young? Does it test our patience to tolerate them, with all their
clowning and their pranks and their mischief? If so, hardening of the
arteries has probably already set in, emotionally if not physically. We'd
do well to maintain gratitude and admiration for the young. Their
natural youthfulness should encourage us to maintain that quality as a
character trait. Youthfulness is too good a virtue to limit to the young!

Theodor Geisel ("Dr. Seuss") probably did more to remind us
of the value of youthfulness than anyone else. "Adults are obsolete
children," he always said. And obsolescence is not only unfortunate;
it's unnecessary. Like Dr. Seuss, we can make the choice to maintain a
youthful outlook long past the point when we lose our physical youth.

Conventional wisdom says that as we get older we have to give
up things. No doubt that's true in some ways, but there's another side
to that story. It can be argued that the reason we get old is that we
give up some things we don't have to give up, like the enthusiasm of
youth. There's no holding back the passage of time, obviously, but it
is possible to stay youthfully interested in the world around us, and
those who've chosen to do so report very gratifying results.

Actually, it all comes down to love. We need to stay in love
with our surroundings, our privileges, and our fellow human beings.
Continued youthfulness amounts to the determined maintenance of
"romanticism" in our lives, the adventurous spirit which wants to taste
life deeply in all of its marvelous, intriguing, and sometimes frustrating variety. It means loving life even after we've come to know it fully!

Age does not protect you from love. But love,
to some extent, protects you from age.
JEANNE MOREAU

November 1

CAUSES

When great causes are on the move in the world, stirring
all men's souls, drawing them from their firesides, casting aside comfort,
wealth and the pursuit of happiness in response to impulses at once awe-
striking and irresistible, we learn that we are spirits, not animals.

WINSTON CHURCHILL

A "CAUSE" IS A GOAL OR PRINCIPLE THAT ONE SERVES WITH DEDICATION. While our "cause-oriented" friends may be somewhat vexing at times, the fact remains: the ability to dedicate oneself to a cause is an ability that only personal beings possess. It is one of our highest endowments, and we ought to appreciate this gift and use it wisely. More of us need to be people who are dedicated to a cause.

In these days when nobody seems to care about much of anything (except whether their bank account is growing), indifference and apathy are plagues upon our society. If those who care deeply about causes can be annoying, they are also refreshing. The zealots remind us of the power of passion, and they prick our conscience.

Do you have a cause that you care about? Are you involved in it at a significant level? Most people have more than one cause, and if they are wise, they prioritize these, giving the lion's share of their attention to the greater causes. Indeed, one mark of maturity is the wisdom with which we prioritize our causes. In our world, there are more things wrong than any one person can be actively concerned about, and we have to pick our battles. We don't want to be guilty of majoring in minors, or giving first-rate devotion to second-rate causes. Most important, we must ensure that our causes are truly just and morally right — and that requires a deep, extraordinary honesty.

But finally, there is one other thing that must be said. It is not enough to be involved, and it is not enough to be involved in a cause that is just. We must also make sure that our involvement is implemented in an honorable way. The end does not justify the means, and we are not free to do "evil that good may come." So once and for all, let us lay aside the foolish notion that things like gossip, innuendo, and mudslinging are excused if our cause happens to be a just one. The more just the cause, the more aboveboard our tactics must be.

If a cause be good, the most violent attack of its enemies will not
injure it so much as an injudicious defense of it by its friends.

CHARLES CALEB COLTON

AFFABILITY

[Sir Thomas] More is a man of angel's wit and singular learning;
I know not his fellow. For where is the man of that gentleness, lowliness,
and affability? And as time requireth, a man of marvelous mirth and
pastimes; and sometimes of as sad a gravity; a man for all seasons.

ROBERT WHITTINTON

WHEN WE MAKE AN HONEST EFFORT TO BE AFFABLE, WE GIVE TO THOSE AROUND US A MUCH-APPRECIATED GIFT. The trait of affability actually combines two traits: to be affable means to be amiable or easy to speak to, but it also means to be mild, gentle, or benign. The combination of these qualities produces a person like Sir Thomas More, who was described by his friend as being a man of "gentleness, lowliness, and affability . . . a man for all seasons." Folks like that are worth their weight in gold. They stir within us a response made up of equal parts admiration and appreciation.

Probably, we respond to affability as we do because we somehow sense that when folks are gentle and pleasant to converse with, they are extending kindness to us, and there aren't many qualities we respond to more gratefully than kindness. When people give us that gift, there's not much we wouldn't do for them in return.

Affability certainly eases the communication process between human beings. Especially when words need to be exchanged that will be difficult to speak and difficult to hear, we listen more openly to those who've learned at least a little "gentleness, lowliness, and affability." Affable people add a touch of grace to their communications.

But I'd go even further: affability eases the process of living life in general. Both those who give this gift and those to whom they give it find that life is not so much a burden as a benefit. It's simply a fact: affable people experience life as being enjoyable in ways that completely escape those who choose to be cold and stand-offish.

So are you blessed to have family members or friends who could be described as affable? If so, don't undervalue them or underestimate the advantage that it is, on your part, to be connected to them. Since it's the "squeaky wheels" (the grouches, the complainers, and the protesters) that get most of the attention, agreeable people sometimes get overlooked and taken for granted. Let's not do that.

An agreeable companion on a journey is as good as a carriage.

PUBLILIUS SYRUS

November 3

FIRE

But true love is a durable fire,
In the mind ever burning,
Never sick, never old, never dead,
From itself never turning.

SIR WALTER RALEIGH

OF ALL THE ENTHUSIASTIC IDEAS IN THE WORLD, "FIRE" IS PERHAPS THE MOST ENTHUSIASTIC. The two words — *fire* and *enthusiasm* — are almost synonymous. When a cause is worthy of our enthusiasm, we appreciate and admire those who are "fired up" about it, and those cold souls who have no fire, well, we pity them.

Most of the great accomplishments in human history have been the result of a passion that burned in someone's heart, and most people understand that. What is not so widely understood is the link between fire (enthusiasm) and learning. Lazy, apathetic people not only fail to accomplish anything, but they also fail to learn very much. Is it not the passionate people who are the real students? I believe so. Indeed, I would go so far as to say that without enthusiasm we never rise to an understanding of the really great truths about human life.

Unfocused and unrestrained enthusiasm can be quite damaging, of course, and so we recognize the need for a person's fire to be governed by valid principles and channeled by self-discipline. Sigmund Freud was exactly right when he wrote, "If the fire rages uncontrolled in a house, we call it a disastrous conflagration; if it burns in a smelting furnace, we call it a useful industrial force." The very last person you want to deal with is the fellow who has a fiery enthusiasm but no acquaintance with the concepts of discipline and governance.

But when a person (a) burns with passion, and (b) knows how to discipline that passion, there isn't much that he can't do. That person will move mountains quicker than ten thousand who know about mountain-moving but don't care whether they get moved or not.

So being passionate is a mighty good thing. Sadly, many people make the mistake of waiting for external circumstances to fire them up. They waste their lives complaining that nothing ever really stirred their interest. But the truth is: you have to strike your own match.

Success isn't a result of spontaneous
combustion. You must set yourself on fire.
ARNOLD H. GLASOW

PRODUCTIVENESS

The happy people are those who are producing something.
WILLIAM RALPH INGE

AT FIRST GLANCE, PRODUCTIVENESS MAY NOT SEEM LIKE ONE OF THE HIGHER VIRTUES, BUT THERE IS AN UNDENIABLE LINK BETWEEN PRODUCTIVENESS AND HAPPINESS. There is no real happiness for us in this world if all we do is consume that which others have produced. We need to be helping and contributing, working and doing things that benefit somebody besides ourselves. When we don't do that, we find that life becomes a tedious, tiresome burden.

Some people make the mistake of defining productiveness only in terms of highly sophisticated or technical work, as if the kinds of things that day laborers do is not worthy of being called productive. But there are many kinds of worthy work in this world, all of which deserve to be appreciated when they are done well. More of us need to think like Thomas Edison, who said: "I have friends in overalls whose friendship I wouldn't swap for the favor of all the kings in the world."

To be productive, of course, we have to know how to do something that somebody needs to have done, so we all need to be expanding our personal skill set. The more tools we have in our toolbox, the more chance we have to do work that is profitable to other people. And the range of skills that we might acquire is almost unbounded. There is hardly anything that you can learn how to do that wouldn't give you a chance to help someone around you, if you did it well.

Skills are not enough, however. The most skilled person in the world won't be productive if he doesn't discipline himself to use his skills responsibly. The lazy, unfocused person may inadvertently do something productive now and then, but he will fall short of the potential that could have been reached if he had been more disciplined.

Productiveness often comes down to enthusiasm; those who are enthusiastic tend to produce more than those who aren't. But if worthy work is to be done, enthusiasm must be matched by expertise. There is simply no shortcut to excellence. We must undergo training, accept discipline, and learn how to do what we do in a skillful way. But when enthusiasm and expertise team up, be prepared: something productive is going to take place, and many lives will be touched.

When love and skill work together, expect a masterpiece.
JOHN RUSKIN

November 5

PROFOUNDNESS

Errors, like straw, upon the surface flow;
He who would search for pearls must dive below.

JOHN DRYDEN

PROFOUNDNESS HAS TO DO WITH "DEPTH." While some thoughts are "shallow," dealing only with what is obvious or superficial (on the "surface"), others have more depth. And whether we like to admit it or not, the more valuable thoughts tend to be the deeper ones: they are not immediately obvious, but require that we "dive below," as Dryden put it. The person who never goes any deeper than first impressions and outward appearances is bound to misjudge many things and miss out on life's richest experiences. So we ought to aspire to "profoundness" — not so others will think we're "deep" but so that we can see things as they are and not merely as they appear.

Profoundness requires extra effort. While it is easy to make snap judgments based on insufficient data, it takes hard work to "dive below" and discover what is really going on. But the extra effort is worth it! The results are truth, right judgment, and fair conduct.

The more profound a truth is, the less likely we are to discover it without serious thinking, and serious thinking usually requires some quietness. "The greatest ideas, the most profound thoughts, and the most beautiful poetry are born from the womb of silence" (William Arthur Ward). In this busy, noisy age, it is hard to find the personal quietness necessary for profound thoughts to reveal themselves to us, but wonderful insights await the person who will take time for silence.

Our friends deserve that we deal with them at a level deeper than outward appearances and surface judgments. What seems "obvious" to us may not really be true, and so we give a great gift to those around us when we do the work to dig a little deeper in our relationships.

But we could be more profound in regard to ourselves as well. One definition of "profoundness" is "coming from the depths of one's being" (*American Heritage Dictionary*). In all that we do, we would do well to act on convictions that lie deep within us. And not only that, we would do well to look deep within ourselves. Strangers to our real selves, few of us have ever plumbed the depths of our own character. But doing that is the first great step on the road to growth.

Who looks outside, dreams; who looks inside, awakes.

CARL GUSTAV JUNG

SOLITUDE

> We have developed a phobia of being alone. We prefer the most trivial and
> even obnoxious company, the most meaningless activities, to being alone with
> ourselves; we seem to be frightened at the prospect of facing ourselves.
>
> ERICH FROMM

SOLITUDE IS SOMETHING THAT MANY PEOPLE AVOID. To these
individuals, solitude is anything but an "enthusiastic idea." They
do not like to be alone, and they endure that condition only when
they are forced to do so by circumstances beyond their control. "What
a commentary on our civilization, when being alone is considered
suspect; when one has to apologize for it, make excuses, hide the fact
that one practices it — like a secret vice!" (Anne Morrow Lindbergh).

But rightly considered, solitude is not a bad thing. It is possible
to have too much of it, no doubt, but the basic idea of being alone is
not one that we should automatically reject or run away from. It is in
solitude that we have the opportunity to ponder the world in which
we live, to meditate on our principles, and to adjust our lives so that
they benefit from a better alignment with our principles. These vital
activities can hardly be done on the run. They require solitude.

Jules Renard said, "Children love to be alone because alone is
where they know themselves, and where they dream." It really is
true that we understood (and enjoyed) the value of solitude more as
children than we do as adults. So the art of creative solitude is perhaps
one of those things about our childhood that we need to recover. We
would do well to remember the daydreams that we dreamed . . . alone.

Many of those who pride themselves on being "people persons"
suffer from a social deficiency that comes from spending too little
time away from society. In the often-quoted words of Albert Guinon,
"People who cannot bear to be alone are the worst company." It is
those who have deepened their character in times of solitude that
have the most to offer when they have the occasion to be with others.

Contrary to popular opinion, there is a huge difference between
loneliness and *aloneness*. Loneliness is painful, but aloneness need not
be so. Indeed, aloneness, wisely practiced, can be one of life's most
rewarding experiences. So gather your courage, be bold, and try it!

> Practice the art of aloneness and you will discover the treasure of tranquility.
> Develop the art of solitude and you will unearth the gift of serenity.
>
> WILLIAM ARTHUR WARD

PROACTIVENESS

I know of no more encouraging fact than the unquestionable
ability of man to elevate his life by conscious endeavor.
HENRY DAVID THOREAU

FREEDOM OF THE WILL IS A TRULY MARVELOUS ENDOWMENT.
We often take it for granted, but the ability to choose our own
character and our own conduct is nothing short of remarkable.

By exercising our will we can, as Thoreau said, elevate our lives
"by conscious endeavor." That doesn't mean that we are capable
of doing anything we want to do, nor does it mean that we have it
within our personal power to solve every problem that confronts us.
What it does mean is that we can make a difference for good by our
choices: we can, by conscious choice, take steps in a better direction.

The pity is, we don't do so more often. Rather than taking positive steps, we worry, we make excuses, we blame and accuse, we rail
against the unfairness of life. In short, we become "reactive" people.

Being "proactive" means acknowledging the freedom of the
human will by taking responsibility for our own character and
conduct — *acting* on our principles rather than just *reacting* to what
happens around us. Proactivity means "more than merely taking initiative. It means that as human beings, we are responsible for our own
lives. Our behavior is a function of our decisions, not our conditions"
(Stephen R. Covey). Truly, there aren't many more worthy challenges
than the challenge of learning to be responsible, proactive people.

In this world, there is much that is beyond our control. Indeed,
most things are beyond our control, and there is no sense in denying
it. But proactive people are glad to exert a good influence wherever
they can, and they recognize that the one thing that always lies in
their control is also the most important: their inward character. We
can choose, by "conscious endeavor," to elevate our character, and
when we fail to do so, blaming our low-quality character on our circumstances, we default on the greatest responsibility of human life.

It's not what happens to us, but our response to what happens to us
that hurts us. Of course, things can hurt us physically or economically and can
cause sorrow. But our character, our basic identity, does not have to be hurt at
all. In fact, our most difficult experiences become the crucibles that forge our
character and develop internal powers, the freedom to handle difficult
circumstances in the future and to inspire others to do so as well.
STEPHEN R. COVEY

EQUALITY

If this is God's world, there are no unimportant people.

GEORGE THOMAS

ONE OF THE BASIC AFFIRMATIONS OF JUDEO-CHRISTIAN RELIGION IS THAT HUMAN BEINGS ARE CREATED IN GOD'S IMAGE. An important corollary of this principle is that all are *equally* created in God's image and therefore have equal value as persons. And what this means is that everybody is important. "If this is God's world," George Thomas says, "there are no unimportant people."

Democratic societies emphasize the equality of all their citizens, and this emphasis is one of the crowning virtues of democracy. In our day, however, it seems that many have misunderstood what this equality means. As Irving Kristol has written, "Democracy does not guarantee equality, only equality of opportunity."

That said, it is nevertheless vital that each of us deal with other human beings as our equals, as far as the image of God is concerned. Remembering that in God's world there are no unimportant people, we need to act accordingly. Neither you nor I will ever meet a human being who is not as important to God as we are. There may be nothing about a person that is attractive or pleasing to us, and that person may, in fact, have so irresponsibly wasted his life that he stands guilty of serious negligence or wrongdoing. Still, he was created by God, and we need to act on the basis of his worth, not his present condition.

We may as well admit that it is hard to do this. We may flatter ourselves as being more "unprejudiced" than others, but in all likelihood, we simply have a different set of prejudices. Honesty compels us to admit that we — all of us — find it difficult to avoid bias and favoritism. And we find it easier to criticize the prejudices of others than to correct our own. Equality is a hard principle to practice.

In the long run, there is only one thing that can give us the power to practice equality in our dealings, and that is love. I speak here not of the weak, sentimental attitude that many mistake for love, but the strong disposition of will that disciplines us to act in the best interests of the other person, whether it is easy at the emotional level or not. This disposition will love others not because they are lovable but because it is right to do so, they having been created by God.

It is only in love that the unequal can be made equal.

SØREN KIERKEGAARD

ASKING

Authentic men aren't afraid to ask for help when they need it.
CHARLES R. SWINDOLL

ASKING IS AN ACTIVITY BOTH SIMPLE AND DIFFICULT. Men, with their pride and their stubborn streak, may have a little more trouble with it than women, but to some extent all of us find it hard to ask questions, especially when the question reveals an ignorance of something that an "in-the-know" person wouldn't have to ask about. Even so, asking is a simple thing to do, and it happens to be one of the most powerful ways that we can experience personal growth.

Not every question is of equal value, of course, and only as we grow in wisdom will we know which are truly the best questions. But a lack of wisdom shouldn't keep us from asking anyway. It's only by asking a lot of questions that we find out which ones are the most significant. We should never outgrow the enthusiasm for questions that we had as children — even the "silly" ones like "Why?" and "What if?" and "Are we there yet?" Such questions keep us moving forward.

Obviously, the willingness to ask requires humility. In the pecking order of worldly importance, those who don't know are always "beneath" those who do, and so we have to swallow our pride to ask a question that says, in effect, "I am a novice, a beginner, a newbie." But in truth, asking is the only way to move beyond being a novice.

Yet even with humility, we won't ask questions if we're not inquisitive and eager to learn. We live in a world of such fascinating complexity, it is hard to imagine a person not being curious about it, but many people are not. They drift through even the most intriguing experiences without seeing or hearing a single thing that elicits a question from them. Consequently, much of life's wonder escapes them. How much better to be engaged with life and eager to . . . ask!

We all hurt ourselves in many ways, but nowhere do we hurt ourselves more than in the questions that we fail to ask. Many good things we don't have and many things we don't know simply because we didn't ask. Whether it's pride or some other thing that holds us back, our failure to ask cuts us off from valuable knowledge that could open doors and introduce us to worlds we've never known.

He who asks a question is a fool for five minutes;
he who does not ask a question remains a fool forever.
CHINESE PROVERB

November 10
POISE

The big things of life are never done by a fussy man.
Poise is one of the earmarks of mental strength.

PRESTON NOLAN

POISE IS NOT A QUALITY THAT MANY PEOPLE PURSUE NOWA-
DAYS, BUT WE WOULD DO WELL TO APPRECIATE ITS VALUE. It
sounds like something from the Victorian Age, and these days, being
Victorian is not very high on anybody's agenda. But let's not be too
quick to poke fun at or write off a character quality like poise.

In its most literal sense, poise has to do with "balance." If, for
example, a basketball is "poised" on someone's index finger, it is in a
state of balance or equilibrium. As a character trait, then, poise means
that a person's thinking is stable and not thrown "off-balance" by awkward or stressful circumstances. We often describe the poised person
as "assured" or "composed." By contrast, the person without poise is
unsure, unstable, and unhelpful; he tends to panic and "lose his cool."

In one of his poems, James Russell Lowell wrote, "Ah, men do
not know how much strength is in poise / That he goes farthest who
goes far enough." There is indeed some strength in poise, and we
would do well to acquire it. Many good things come from the ability
to keep a "level head" when difficult situations arise and hard decisions have to be made. It is poise that tells us how many steps are
enough — and when taking even one more would lead to imbalance.

We live in stressful times, to say the least. As the rate of change
increases exponentially, we can never be sure how long anything
around us is going to stay the same. In this kind of environment,
nearly every day generates some new crisis that threatens to throw us
off-balance. Do we have enough poise to survive life as it now is?

Troubled times call for strong leadership, whether in nations,
communities, or families. And so if you are in any kind of leadership
position — if there is even one person who is under your influence —
then you need to work on increasing your poise. That doesn't mean
being uptight, obsessive, or compulsive, nor does it mean never being
excited or passionate. It means knowing how to keep your balance.

The ability to keep a cool head in an emergency, to maintain poise
in the midst of excitement, and to refuse to be stampeded
are true marks of leadership.

R. SHANNON

BRAVERY

But the bravest are surely those who have the clearest
vision of what is before them, glory and danger alike,
and yet notwithstanding go out to meet it.

THUCYDIDES

WE SHOW OURSELVES TO BE BRAVE WHEN WE MEET DIFFI-
CULTY OR DANGER WITH A DETERMINATION TO DO WHAT
IS RIGHT, REGARDLESS OF OUR FEAR. If we're brave, that doesn't
mean we don't feel any fear; it means that we refuse to let fear deter us
from acting rightly. Bravery means going out to meet the thing feared,
facing it down, and following our conscience.

If we need to be braver than we are (and most of us do), the way
to gain bravery is not merely to think about it. Like many character
traits, this is one that comes to us in larger quantities when we discipline ourselves to use whatever small quantity of it we may have right
now. It's an active thing, rather than a passive one. As Aristotle said,
"We become just by performing just actions, temperate by performing
temperate actions, brave by performing brave actions."

One of the finest gifts we can give to others is the gift of bravery
on our part. The world, including the circle of our personal acquaintances, desperately needs more people who'll set an example of bravery
and thereby encourage others. "Courage is contagious. When a brave
man takes a stand, the spines of others are stiffened" (Billy Graham).
So if we'd like to make a much-needed contribution to the world, it
would be hard to give a better gift than that of our own bravery.

We should understand, however, that bravery is not just needed
by soldiers, law enforcement officers, and rescue workers. Our need
for it is not limited to situations in which our physical lives are in
jeopardy. To the contrary, we need it every day in all those situations
where doing the right thing involves some non-physical danger.
When duty calls, those who honor their conscience and act with
integrity are being brave in the very highest sense. And while our
nation is indebted to those who've fought for its freedom militarily,
the greatness of our country also depends on a host of ordinary heroes
who've had the boldness, day by day, to simply live honorable lives.

It is a brave act of valour to condemn death;
but where life is more terrible than death, it is
then the truest valour to dare to live.

SIR THOMAS BROWNE

November 12

CERTAINTY

It is not certain that everything is uncertain.

BLAISE PASCAL

THESE ARE THE DAYS WHEN SKEPTICISM IS FASHIONABLE. It is trendy to put "truth" in quotation marks and to celebrate ambiguity and paradox. But is it not possible that this movement has gone too far? As Pascal said, "It is not certain that everything is uncertain."

Postmodernism has rightly criticized the unwarranted optimism of modernism, the assumption that we can understand everything, figure out every problem, and fix everything that is wrong with the world. And obviously, the more we know, the more we realize we don't know. But as George Iles said, "Doubt is the beginning, not the end, of wisdom." Humility about what we know, and even what we can know, is the starting point in our quest, but at the end of the quest, there are some great things that can be known with certainty.

Open-mindedness is thought to be an admirable quality, but I've always liked G. K. Chesterton's observation: "Merely having an open mind is nothing. The object of opening the mind, as of opening the mouth, is to shut it again on something solid." Having an open mind serves little purpose if it does not result in some dependable learning.

Life does not always proceed smoothly. There will be times when uncertainty seems to overwhelm us. But at such times we should not make the mistake of believing that the foundations of life no longer exist. Darkness can play tricks on our thinking, and I greatly appreciate the fatherly advice that a favorite teacher gave me at a time when I was very confused and discouraged. "Gary," he said, "when the darkness closes in, don't forget the assurances that were given to you while the sun was still shining." During tough times, we have to hang on to the certainties that our reason has previously found to be trustworthy.

All of us have our uncertainties, and that is only to be expected in a world as perplexing as ours. But our friends and loved ones need more from us than the constant raising of questions; they need us to have some certainty about us and to shine a little light on the path that they must tread. If we can't do that, then perhaps we should just do the courteous thing and remain silent. After all, people don't need our doubts and confusions — they already have enough of their own.

Keep your fears to yourself, but share your courage with others.

ROBERT LOUIS STEVENSON

November 13
UNIQUENESS

Every man is more than just himself; he also represents the unique,
the very special and always significant and remarkable point at which the
world's phenomena intersect, only once in this way and never again.
HERMANN HESSE

IT MAY BE TRITE, BUT IT'S STILL TRUE: EACH OF US IS UNIQUE.
Even "identical" twins are very different from one another. As
Hesse points out, each of us amounts to a unique intersection of many
different phenomena in the world. Our individual configuration of
traits will have happened "only once in this way and never again."

Most of us accept our uniqueness, I suppose. Strictly speaking,
we have no choice but to accept it: it is what it is and there is not
much we can do about it, no matter how we try to conform to others.
But the challenge is to embrace our uniqueness enthusiastically and
appreciate it gratefully. Our individuality means there is good work
that we can do that no one else can do in quite the same way.

But if we appreciate our own uniqueness, we also need to affirm
the uniqueness of others. Other people may be unique in ways that
we find exasperating, but even so, the world would be a poorer place if
the special characteristics of any of its inhabitants were missing.

There is also a uniqueness that should be appreciated about life
itself. As the days of our lives go by, it would help us to enjoy the
uniqueness of each of those days, and indeed, each of the moments
within those days. Many of us (especially the more organized) tend to
plan and prepare our times of happiness. We schedule our delightful
occasions, and we often want them to be just like those we've enjoyed
before. But each day presents us with unique delights, and we should
not resist their one-of-a-kind appeal. "Seize from every moment its
unique novelty, and do not prepare your joys" (André Gide).

If any of us had been given the job of creating the world, we
would have made it more bland. Averse to irregularity and unpredictability, we would have made a "safe" world where sameness was the
rule. But oh, how boring such a world would have been! The uniqueness that pervades the real world may result in an awkward moment
now and then, but the advantage of uniqueness is well worth whatever
downside there may be. I, for one, wouldn't have it any other way.

No two men are alike, and both of them are happy for it.
MORRIS MANDEL

MAINTENANCE

'Tis nothing for a man to hold up his head in a calm; but to maintain
his post when all others have quitted their ground and there to stand
upright when other men are beaten down is divine.

S E N E C A

I N MANY SITUATIONS, WE HOPE TO DO MORE THAN MAINTAIN
THE STATUS QUO, BUT IN TRUTH, "MAINTENANCE" IS A MORE
WORTHY ACHIEVEMENT THAN WE MIGHT THINK. "Maintain"
comes from the Latin phrase *manu tenere*, "to hold in the hand." So
to maintain something means to "hold" it, keep it, or continue it. And
frankly, there are many good things that need to be continued.

Another definition of maintenance is "upkeep" or "the work
of keeping something in proper condition." And most of us have
experienced that there is a lot of that to be done in the world. Left to
themselves, things decay and suffer degradation. Without the worthy work of maintenance, none of the good things in life will keep
working. Think of your marriage, for example. If you don't nourish it
frequently, it will die. If you don't maintain it, it will degenerate.

Maintenance requires, first of all, an appreciation of the thing
that needs to be maintained. If you take your health for granted and
don't recognize its value, you won't do what's necessary to maintain it.
If you're not grateful for your house, you will neglect its upkeep.

But maintenance also requires constant vigilance and hard work.
The kinds of things that have to be done to keep things going often
don't seem very exciting, but they must be done. If we don't do them
faithfully, we are setting ourselves up for serious regret later on.

Of all the treasures that need to be maintained, the most important is love, and therein lies a considerable challenge, for love is,
of all things, the hardest to maintain. No, the maintenance of love
is not hard in the sense of being unpleasant or burdensome, but it is
hard because it is so fragile. Without maintenance, love that has taken
years to create can be ruined by one season of thoughtless negligence.

Love is difficult to sustain, not because it is a positive emotion, but because
it is a complex one. Hate is easy to maintain for a lifetime because it is a
simple one. Love might be compared to the building of a tall and elaborate
sandcastle, taking many hours of painstaking effort, cooperation, balance, and
persistence; and hate might be compared to the foot that comes along and
with one vicious or thoughtless kick destroys in a moment what has been built up.

S Y D N E Y   J .   H A R R I S

November 15

DUTY

There is no right without a parallel duty, no liberty
without the supremacy of law, no high destiny without earnest
perseverance, no greatness without self-denial.

FRANCIS LIEBER

DOING OUR DUTY PROBABLY SOUNDS LIKE A DREARY CHORE, BUT PROPERLY CONCEIVED, OUR DUTIES ARE AMONG OUR HIGHEST PRIVILEGES. And in a culture where freedom often pushes duty aside, we need to be reminded of the need for duty. Without a sense of duty, our freedoms will soon get away from us.

Most of us engage in what T. S. Eliot called the "endless struggle" to think well of ourselves. We want — in fact, we need — to be able to see ourselves in a favorable light. But how can we do that? There is only one way, really, and that is by paying serious attention to our conscience and doing our duty. Goethe was exactly right: "How shall we learn to know ourselves? By reflection? Never, but only through action. Strive to do your duty, and you will know what is in you."

There is no better gift we can give to our loved ones than to discharge our responsibilities faithfully, not only to them but also to others. When people know that we can be trusted to do what we should, no matter what, their relationship with us is surrounded and supported by trust. Not needing to wonder what we might do (or not do), our family and friends can relax in their relationship with us.

Chauncey Wright wrote, "What a fearful object a long-neglected duty gets to be." I agree. There is nothing so tiring as the constant hanging on of some responsibility that we've been putting off. If you have ever finally stepped up to a duty and done something that you had been procrastinating for a long time, you know the wonderful feeling of freedom that results. So there is much to be said not only for doing what we should, but for doing it in a timely fashion — today!

On special occasions, duty can be a "big" thing, but more often it is ordinary. It consists of doing the many "little" things that each day's work places before us. So if you think you can default on your daily duties but still have the character to do what is right when the big occasion arrives and you are in the spotlight, you are sadly mistaken.

Character may be manifested in the great moments,
but it is made in the small ones.

PHILLIPS BROOKS

BOLDNESS

The way of a superior man is threefold: virtuous, he is free from anxieties;
wise, he is free from perplexities; bold, he is free from fear.

CONFUCIUS

THE WILLINGNESS TO BE BOLD, WHEN NEED BE, IS A SIGN OF
STRONG, MATURE CHARACTER. We may wish it were otherwise,
but the world in which we live is full of danger and difficulty, and the
bold are those who will go out and meet these realities head-on. So if
we ourselves aren't bold, we're probably glad to know someone who is.

Boldness, like fire, must be handled with care. Great harm can
be done by "zeal without knowledge," as we all know, but that is not
an argument against wise and disciplined boldness. The person who
never acts boldly because he always plays it safe will never know the
thrill of risk-taking and adventure in the service of a great cause.

Big problems often require bold solutions, and when bold action
is called for, we shouldn't waste time looking for a risk-free way to do
what has to be done. David Lloyd George, the British prime minister
during World War I, said, "Don't be afraid to take a big step if one is
indicated; you can't cross a chasm in two small jumps." Indeed, there
are times when the riskiest thing we can do is play it safe. "In difficult
situations when hope seems feeble, the boldest plans are safest" (Livy)
— and the "hardest" course often turns out to be the "easiest."

Not only do individuals need to be bold, but there are times
when nations and communities do too. Especially today, when the
problems that confront the world are so immense, we can't afford to
be timid or squeamish. Addressing the challenges of the American
people in his day, Theodore Roosevelt said, "If we shrink from the
hard contests . . . then bolder and stronger peoples will pass us by."

Boldness requires a certain amount of character, obviously, but it
also builds character. Just as lifting heavy weights builds stronger muscles, dealing boldly with difficulty makes us stronger spiritually. That
being true, I urge you to choose the more difficult deed whenever you
have the opportunity. Do it with all the boldness you can muster, and
you'll find yourself growing in ways that may surprise you. Don't run
away from choices that would require boldness. Welcome them!

When you cannot make up your mind which of two evenly balanced
courses of action you should take — choose the bolder.

W. J. SLIM

JOYFULNESS

There are joys which long to be ours. God sends ten thousand truths, which
come about us like birds seeking inlet; but we are shut up to them, and so they
bring us nothing, but sit and sing awhile upon the roof, and then fly away.

HENRY WARD BEECHER

IF WE ARE LESS THAN JOYFUL, THE PROBLEM IS NOT THAT JOY
IS UNAVAILABLE TO US; IT IS THAT WE DO NOT CHOOSE TO RE-
CEIVE IT. As Beecher suggests, there are many "joys which long to be
ours." Like birds on our roof, they "sit and sing awhile . . . and then fly
away." Joyfulness courts us, but it can't gain admittance to our hearts if
we keep them closed — or if we're just too busy to be bothered.

Have you ever thought of joyfulness as a virtue or a character
trait to be acquired? Many people think of it otherwise: they look
upon joy simply as a gift granted to the fortunate few, those who are
blessed with lucky lives. But on deeper reflection, what we see is that
joyfulness is a learned attribute. It is the possession of those who,
regardless of circumstances, have learned to think in such a way that
joy has a chance to enter their hearts. If we are not joyful, that makes
more of a comment on us than it does on our circumstances.

As important as it is, however, we defeat ourselves if we try
to track down joyfulness and capture it, as if it were a quarry to
be hunted for its own sake. "Enjoyment is not a goal," wrote Paul
Goodman, "it is a feeling that accompanies important ongoing activity." Like many other desirable things, joyfulness must be experienced
indirectly. It is the by-product of paying attention to other, more
important, things. We find joy while looking for something else!

But ultimately, those who are joyful are those who choose to be
so. Happiness (the experience of pleasant "happenings") may or may
not be ours at a given moment, but joy is a stronger and deeper quality. Happy or not, there is no excuse for failing to make joyfulness one
of our personal attributes. And when we decide to practice the virtue
of joyfulness, we find many other valuable qualities coming our way,
such as courage and strength. Nehemiah made a wise statement to the
people of Israel long ago when he said, "The joy of the Lord is your
strength." Indeed, of all strengths, the strength of joy is the strongest.

I cannot choose to be strong, but I can choose to be joyful.
And when I am willing to do that, strength will follow.

TIM HANSEL

LOVINGKINDNESS

> Lovingkindness is greater than laws, and the
> charities of life are more than all ceremonies.
>
> THE TALMUD

W E DON'T USE THE WORD "LOVINGKINDNESS" MUCH ANY-
MORE, BUT IT'S STILL A VALUABLE WORD. Basically, it means
the type of regard for another person that is characterized by tenderness, mercy, and grace. One dictionary says that it is "tender kindness
motivated by a feeling of affection." Lovingkindness is a compound
word that joins two important qualities: love and kindness. It is love
that shows itself in kindness — and kindness that is enlivened by love.

Most of us acknowledge the importance of love, but in our love,
not many of us are as kind as we ought to be. Indeed, we're often the
most discourteous and ungentle to those who are nearest and dearest to us: our spouses, our children, and our parents. When we find
ourselves "at home," perhaps after a difficult day, it doesn't do any
good to plead that we're tired or that tenderness is not our personality.
Our loved ones deserve that we love them with consistent lovingkindness — and that means exerting the effort to be courteous and gentle.
"Kindness," as someone has said, "is love in work clothes." When love
doesn't do the work necessary to exhibit lovingkindness, it's being lazy.

Strictly speaking, love that does not show up in kindness is not
worthy of being called love. As Amy Carmichael said, "You can give
without loving, but you cannot love without giving." Giving the gift
of lovingkindness doesn't mean that love is weak or that it walks on
eggshells, fearful of doing anything the other person might not like.
There is certainly a time for tough love, but even then, lovingkindness
will make us gentle, unwilling to hurt the loved one any more than is
absolutely necessary. The rule in criticism is the same as in carving:
never cut with a knife what you can cut with a spoon.

In a world full of personal pain, we never give a greater gift than
when we show lovingkindness. "If instead of a gem, or even a flower,
we should cast the gift of a loving thought into the heart of a friend,"
George MacDonald wrote, "that would be giving as the angels give."
Unless you can read other people's hearts, you probably won't know
how much they need your kindness — but love them kindly anyway.

> Be kind; everyone you meet is fighting a hard battle.
> IAN MACLAREN

November 19
ABSOLUTES

Thus absolute truth is indestructible. Being indestructible, it is eternal. Being eternal, it is self-existent. Being self-existent, it is infinite. Being infinite, it is vast and deep. Being vast and deep, it is transcendental and intelligent.

CONFUCIUS

THESE DAYS, THE VERY WORD "ABSOLUTES" IS ENOUGH TO MAKE MANY PEOPLE RECOIL. The idea that there is anything that is fixed and objectively true is unpopular. Many people prefer to say that truth is relative and subjective. Whatever we may say, however, all agree that there are *some* things that are absolute, and when we think about it, what we see is that the current reaction against absolutes is a reaction not against absolutes, but against the foolish way that some people have behaved in regard to their own knowledge.

Some people, for example, seem to think that any opinion they have on any subject is a matter of absolute truth. Others overestimate the evidence and adopt an air of certainty that the facts do not warrant. Still others don't see the extent to which their present knowledge is limited, while others have an attitude that is just plain bullheaded.

But if some people have been overzealous about absolutes, let's not "throw the baby out with the bath water." A commitment to certain absolutes is a vital part of human character. Without such a commitment, we are unstable and undependable. With an "everything-is-relative" philosophy, no one can ever be sure what we might do next, and even our most important relationships are on shaky ground. How much better, then, if we lock our internal guidance systems onto the timeless truths and govern our conduct accordingly.

Facts are stubborn things, as someone has said. If a thing is objectively true, we may deny it, suppress it, misrepresent it, or do any number of other things in an effort to avoid it, but when we're done, the truth will still be there waiting for us to deal with. We will wear ourselves out fighting against the truth long before our efforts have any effect at all in wearing it down. So let's be known as those who are unafraid to stand for the absolutes, those facts that are sure and stable. People who have dealings with us will appreciate the fact that our personal character, grounded in absolutes, is "count-on-able."

Truth is incontrovertible. Panic may resent it;
ignorance may deride it; malice may distort it; but there it is.
WINSTON CHURCHILL

November 20
WARMTH

A warm smile is the universal language of kindness.
WILLIAM ARTHUR WARD

ALMOST EVERYBODY THINKS OF WARMTH AS A POSITIVE PER-
SONAL QUALITY. Given the choice, we'd much rather deal with
people who are "warm" than we would those who are "cold." Why
then do we put forth so little effort to cultivate warmth as one of our
own characteristics? One reason is that we often think we are demonstrating more warmth than we actually are. If we could see ourselves
as others see us, we'd immediately see the need for some adjustments.
So today, let's consider adding additional warmth to our characters.

Notice that I said *characters* and not *personalities*. Warmth is a
quality that all should aspire to, but not everybody has to have what
is often called an "outgoing" personality. Genuine warmth is a deeper
character attribute, one that has more to do with attitude than personality. It means that we add three primary virtues to our character.

(1) *Kindness*. Warmth typically shows itself as courtesy, gentleness, and benevolence — a desire to give kindly help. As the Japanese
proverb says, "One kind word can warm three winter months."

(2) *Openness*. We often use two words to describe those who are
warm: we say that they are "warm and welcoming." In our personal
dealings, we must learn to be hospitable, inviting, and accessible.

(3) *Concern*. To be warm means to be truly concerned about the
other person. It means that we get out of the little box of our own
selfish interests and demonstrate a real desire to serve those around us.

The ultimate test of our warmth is whether we can show it to
those who don't possess it themselves (and do so without being condescending or self-righteous). As Jean Paul Richter wrote, "The last,
best fruit which comes to late perfection, even in the kindliest soul,
is tenderness toward the hard, forbearance toward the unforbearing,
warmth of heart toward the cold." Doing this is not easy, but when
we've learned this skill, we will have learned one of the most potent
sources of influence in the world. It may not be too much to say that
the privilege of influencing others comes mainly from our having
learned warmth of character. *But it must be genuine and not pretended!*

Warmth, friendliness, and a gentle touch
are always stronger than force and fury.
DENIS WAITLEY

PERCEPTIVENESS

A fool sees not the same tree that a wise man sees.

WILLIAM BLAKE

W E OFTEN DO GREAT DAMAGE TO OUR RELATIONSHIPS BY FAILING TO BE PERCEPTIVE. As hard as it is to admit, a friend who is admonishing us may be exactly right when he or she says, "You just don't get it." And by the time we finally do "get it," great harm may have been done by our failure to see certain things.

To "perceive" means to "see" something, not with our physical eyes but with our minds. Two people may "see" the same set of physical circumstances, but one may more fully understand the significance of what has been seen. An experienced crime scene investigator, for example, "sees" more at a murder site than a less perceptive observer. As Charles Kettering said, "There is a great difference between knowing a thing and understanding it." So those who are perceptive not only "look," but they also "see." And they not only "see," but they understand the meaning of what they see. They truly do "get it."

The fact is, we can grow in our perceptiveness. If we lack discernment, we can acquire it. And doing so ought to be one of the highest priorities of our life and work. "Perception of ideas rather than the storing of them should be the aim of education. The mind should be an eye to see with rather than a bin to store facts in" (A. W. Tozer).

But how do we learn to be more perceptive? Here are two ways:

Commitment to reality. There are none so blind as those who will not see, and so to become more perceptive we must honestly want to see things as they really are, and not merely as we wish them to be. We must always want to know the truth — even the painful truth.

Practice, practice, practice. A baseball umpire gets better at calling balls and strikes not by reading books but by getting behind the plate and calling lots of pitches. So we get better at "getting it" by using our perceptive powers over and over, always learning from our mistakes.

The power to perceive is especially important when it comes to the higher and nobler things in life. In trivial matters, no great harm is done if we can't see the difference between good, better, and best. But in matters of love, justice, and beauty, the ability to perceive what is most excellent is an ability that no honorable person can lack.

The perception of beauty is a moral test.

HENRY DAVID THOREAU

GRATITUDE

Gratitude is the memory of the heart.

J. B. MASSIEU

THIS IS THE SEASON FOR THE GIVING OF THANKS. The harvest is complete, provisions have been made for the winter months ahead, and as the snows begin to fall, we take time for one of the year's most delightful customs, the tradition of Thanksgiving.

"Gratitude," as J. B. Massieu defined it, "is the memory of the heart." Just as the intellect can recall truths that are positive and enriching, the heart can remember events that were joyful and blessings that were needed. Gratitude is the appreciative remembrance of these things. It's the recollection of good things that came to us over and beyond our merits. It's the appreciation of grace.

Gratitude happens to be one of the most powerful gifts we're able to give to those around us. Not many of us can resist its power. When someone expresses real appreciation for something we've done, that expression is a gift that calls forth the very best qualities within us. We respond to it with a healthy desire to be even more encouraging to others in the future. So why can't we give that gift more often to those people we deal with daily? They'd respond to our gratitude in the same way we respond to theirs! By giving ourselves to them as grateful individuals, we would have granted them a wonderful grace.

In truth, most of us are grateful to some extent. The problem is, we either don't make that gratitude known or we don't make it known in a timely way. As a Greek proverb puts it, "Swift gratitude is the sweetest." As powerful as the gift of gratitude is, it loses its potency with every day (indeed, every hour) that passes between the reception of the benefit and the expression of our gratitude for it. So that thank-you note needs to be mailed as quickly as we can get it written!

Nowadays, most of us would have to say that our lives have been blessed bountifully. Whatever problems or needs we might have experienced, these are not as great as the good things that we've been privileged to enjoy. It's a fact that we live in an age of affluence. But if we don't properly appreciate the manifold goodnesses that grace our lives, we might as well be poor. Indeed, we *are* poor, in the very worst sense, if our hearts aren't storehouses of gratitude.

It is only with gratitude that life becomes rich.

DIETRICH BONHOEFFER

GENUINENESS

We wander but in the end there is always
a certain peace in being what one is,
in being that completely.

UGO BETTI

AMONG OUR ACQUAINTANCES, THOSE WHOM WE VALUE THE MOST ARE THE FOLKS WHO ARE GENUINE. We recognize that there can be a huge difference between what a person appears to be and what they actually are, and so we appreciate it when we have the opportunity to deal with those who are the "real deal." These are the people (how refreshing they are!) whose words and actions have the ring of truth. They deliver — their deeds live up to their advertising.

Genuineness is largely a matter of sincerity. If a friend is genuinely compassionate, for example, that means that he or she truly does feel compassion. Whatever's on the surface, if a person is sincere you'll find that same quality no matter how deep you drill into their character. Sincerity means that what you see is what you really do get.

Wallace Stevens wrote, "The humble are they that move about the world with the lure of the real in their hearts." When all is said and done, that's what sets genuine people apart: they have the "lure of the real" in their hearts. They prefer that which is actual to that which is only apparent, even when the actual is less than perfect. And in their dealings with others, those who are genuine offer only "the real."

If we had to choose between an article that was authentic and another that was counterfeit, most of us would choose the genuine article. And so it is with people. We prefer those who are true and trustworthy to those who are fake. We want "the real McCoy."

Pretense is a tempting thing, however, and there are few of us who've never engaged in it. We have a definite idea how we'd like others to think of us, and it's tempting to use smoke and mirrors to generate that appearance. But if the conclusion we lead others to is nothing more than an illusion, we haven't accomplished very much.

It's much better to be genuine. That doesn't mean we don't have ideals and dreams. It doesn't mean that it's wrong to put our best foot forward. What it does mean is that we're deeply committed to truth.

Be what you are. This is the first step
toward becoming better than you are.

JULIUS CHARLES HARE

TRAVEL

My heart is warm with the friends I make,
And better friends I'll not be knowing;
Yet there isn't a train I wouldn't take,
No matter where it's going.

EDNA ST. VINCENT MILLAY

DOES IT MAKE ANY DIFFERENCE IN OUR CHARACTER WHETHER WE TRAVEL? I believe it does — or at least it can. Travel doesn't automatically make one a better person, and there are some obvious benefits to the stay-at-home philosophy. But those who travel have an opportunity for personal growth that shouldn't be underestimated. Going outside of the familiar places of our lives opens up new insights and improves our perspective on what's important.

To begin with, let's understand that there's a difference between travel and "tourism." While tourism may be better than no travel at all, it's not the most profitable kind. In the words of an old saying, "A fool wanders, but the wise man travels." Speaking of the older kind of travel, that of the explorer or adventurer, Daniel J. Boorstin wrote, "The traveler was active; he went strenuously in search of people, of adventure, of experience. The tourist is passive; he expects interesting things to happen to him. He goes 'sight-seeing'." The traveler, versus the tourist, goes to unfamiliar, perhaps even difficult, places. Going not to be entertained but educated, he leaves the beaten path, taking the backroads — sometimes even alone. And he comes back with an expanded view of what it is to be a human being in this world.

Travel must never be a running away from home or from ourselves, of course. As Thomas à Kempis observed, "No man safely travels who loves not to rest at home." And Lin Yutang spoke for all travelers when he said, "No one realizes how beautiful it is to travel until he comes home and rests his head on his old, familiar pillow."

But love home as we may, the real value of travel lies in its disorientation. We rarely learn without being disoriented, and so the benefit of travel is that it gets us out of our comfort zone. It breaks up the ruts in our thinking, and it does so by surprising us, catching us off-guard, and thrusting us into exploits we've never dreamed of.

If travel has taught me nothing more, and it certainly has, it's this: you can never know when some trifling incident, utterly without any significance, may pitchfork you into adventure or, by the same token, may not.

S. J. PERELMAN

ETERNITY

We feel and know that we are eternal.

SPINOZA

IN DECIDING ON OUR WORLDVIEW, THE QUESTION OF "ETER-NITY" MUST BE DEALT WITH. Is the space-time continuum in which we presently live, with its beginning and end, all there is, or is there some reality that overarches all of this and extends infinitely backward and infinitely forward? In other words, is there any reality to which the word "forever" can be rightly applied? This is no trivial question. It is one of the most basic questions that we must ask because it has to do with whether there is a God who has always existed, and whether we will continue to exist after our earthly lives are over.

Contrary to popular opinion, science has not disproven eternity. Wernher von Braun, a scientist of no slight stature, spoke for many when he said, "Everything science has taught me — and continues to teach me — strengthens my belief in the continuity of our spiritual existence after death." And the German poet Goethe, who was no country bumpkin, said, "Life is the childhood of our immortality." So affirming eternity doesn't mean that one is intellectually naive.

At the practical level, eternity is a vital question because it bears on our values and principles. As with other elements of our worldview, our belief about eternity helps determine how long-term our perspective is. Very different decisions about our conduct will result if we see those decisions as having eternal consequences, and if our values are shaped by eternal truths, they will have a stability about them that would be hard to maintain if we disbelieved in eternity.

Obviously, many people who say they believe in eternity don't really do so, or they wouldn't conduct their lives so irresponsibly. But if we are truly convinced that an eternal God is our Creator, and that having been created by Him we will spend eternity either with Him or away from Him, the impact of that conviction on our character will make us the kind of people that others are pleased to deal with.

One thing is clear: if eternity waits for us beyond death's door, then we need to factor that into our thinking right now. Whatever advantages we may gain for ourselves in time, if we've neglected to invest in eternity, we will have missed all that really mattered.

No man is rich to whom the grave brings eternal bankruptcy.

HENRY WARD BEECHER

TRANSCENDENCE

*Humanity could only have survived and flourished if it held social
and personal values that transcended the urges of the individual . . . and
these stem from the sense of a transcendent good.*

ARTHUR PEACOCKE

IN YESTERDAY'S READING, WE CONSIDERED "ETERNITY," SO
TODAY LET'S THINK ABOUT "TRANSCENDENCE." To transcend
means to "be greater than" or to "go beyond." If one thing transcends
another, then the first thing exceeds the limits of the second thing.

In the Arthur Peacocke quotation above, the point is made that
our survival has depended on people "transcending" their own selfish
desires, and that is certainly true. Where would we be if no one ever
looked beyond his own interests to the good of the community?

But there is a greater sense in which we use the word "transcendence," and that is when we speak of some reality that is higher
than all of the material universe put together. Such a reality would
be radically "other" than the world in which we live, different from
all material things not only in quantity or magnitude, but in the very
quality of its being. A transcendent God, for example, would be more
than simply "everything that exists" and more than an abstract "force."
He would be distinct from — and superior to — His entire creation.

But is there such a God? Consider the argument of the Apostle
Paul in the Acts of the Apostles, Chapter 17. Speaking to an audience
in Athens, Paul noted that the Greeks' own poets had acknowledged
that we are the offspring of God. So if we know what we are, personal
beings, then whatever power was capable of producing us could not
have been any less a personal being than we are. Only a divine, personal Creator is sufficient to explain what we know about ourselves.
But such a Creator would be transcendent — that is, He would be
"above" and "beyond" us in every significant sense of those terms.

Now the phenomenon that we call "worship" has to do with both
eternity and transcendence. Worship is the recognition (in our hearts
and minds) of eternal, transcendent reality, and the acknowledgment
(in our words and deeds) of that reality. To worship is to stand in awe
before the majesty of what is above us. Amazed and humbled, we
honor the One who brought the world into being and gave us life.

Worship is transcendent wonder.
THOMAS CARLYLE

GRAVITY

The most profound joy has more of gravity than of gaiety in it.

MICHEL DE MONTAIGNE

SOMETIMES WE ERR BY BEING TOO SERIOUS, BUT AT OTHER TIMES WE'RE NOT SERIOUS ENOUGH. Prone to extremes, we struggle to get the balance right from day to day. On other pages, we have dealt with the problem of being too dour or gloomy. Wouldn't it also be in order to consider the opposite problem: a lack of gravity?

"Gravity" is a significant word, more so than is generally recognized in our breezy, casual age. It comes from the Latin *gravis* ("heavy"). In physics, "gravity" is a force that results in what we call "weight." Figuratively, then, we speak of an important matter as being "weighty," and we say that a more trivial matter is on the "lighter" side. If we say a situation is "grave," we mean that it is very serious. And so gravity, when applied to persons, means that one possesses an admirable solemnity or dignity of manner. To possess gravity (or gravitas, as it is sometimes called) means that we recognize when seriousness is needed and dignity is appropriate. And judging from the flippancy with which some live their lives, it would appear that they think seriousness is never needed and dignity is never appropriate!

Perhaps some shy away from gravity because they see it as being inconsistent with joy. But as Montaigne wisely pointed out, "The most profound joy has more of gravity than of gaiety in it." The day you learn the advantage of gravity over flippancy will probably be the day you also learn the difference between happiness and joy. Gravity, or dignity of manner, is not a killjoy; it enhances joy. And if we dispense with all formality and solemnity in our lives, the result is not the carefree enjoyment of constant informality, but the boredom that comes from dumbing everything down to the level of the casual.

There is a sense, of course, in which we ought not to be concerned about our "dignity" at all. If by dignity we mean the pride that makes us want to appear "important," then that kind of pride needs to be gotten rid of. But the interesting thing is this: if we will acquire the virtue of gravity, that virtue will naturally keep us from doing things that would harm us or blemish the good name we have tried to build. A healthy measure of gravity is a wonderfully protective thing to have.

Let not a man guard his dignity, but let his dignity guard him.

RALPH WALDO EMERSON

WISDOM

Keep me from the wisdom which does not cry, the philosophy which does
not laugh, and the greatness which does not bow before children.

KAHLIL GIBRAN

WISDOM, AS WE ALL KNOW, IS DIFFERENT FROM KNOWL-
EDGE. Knowledge has to do with the accumulation of factual
information, while wisdom indicates how that information may be
used to its best advantage. There are two parts to wisdom, both of
which are important. First, wisdom perceives, discerns, and understands. It sees how a situation really is (analysis). But second, having
accurately assessed the situation, wisdom exercises good judgment and
discretion. It tells us what should be done about the situation (action).
In other words, wisdom gives us the best possible answer to these two
questions: "What is going on?" and "What should be done about it?"

Wisdom and prudence are closely related. As Norman Cousins
put it, "Wisdom consists of the anticipation of consequences." It
looks ahead, soberly assessing the likely results of an action, and tells
us the safest way to go or the most advantageous path to follow. And
wisdom is able to do this because it has learned from the experience
of others and seen what usually works and what doesn't. "From the
errors of others a wise man corrects his own" (Publilius Syrus).

The highest use of wisdom is surely in the area of morality.
Cicero observed that the "function of wisdom is to discriminate
between good and evil." Wisdom may give us an advantage in lesser
matters, and for that we should be grateful, but more than anything
else, we should welcome the advice that wisdom gives us in regard to
what is right, just, and honorable. If wisdom doesn't elevate our conduct to a higher, nobler plane, then we've not gotten its best benefit.

The challenge, of course, is to apply wisdom to ourselves. It is
easier to look at someone else's situation and advise them what they
should do than it is to see our own situation objectively and apply
wisdom to our actions. Generally speaking, it is through hardship
and heartache that we learn to be wise in our own lives, and that is
why we ought not to avoid difficulty. If we despise the means through
which wisdom usually comes, we can't truly say we desire wisdom.

People prefer happiness to wisdom, but that is like
wanting to be immortal without getting older.

SYDNEY J. HARRIS

November 29
APPROPRIATENESS

A word fitly spoken is like apples of gold in settings of silver.
THE BOOK OF PROVERBS

IT IS NOT ENOUGH TO DO THE RIGHT THING; THE RIGHT THING MUST BE DONE IN THE RIGHT WAY. Even when we're sure we're doing what is right, we must consider doing it appropriately. If an action is permissible from the strict standpoint of right and wrong, it still may not fit very well or be suitable for a particular person, place, or occasion. If not, a more appropriate action should be sought.

In these days of personal independence and freedom, little thought is given to the question of appropriateness. For many of us, the "legal" question is all that matters: "If you can't show me where it is inherently wrong to do what I want to do, then I'm going to do it." And if someone should say, "Yes, but what you're doing is not fitting or suitable," we would probably reply, "What is 'fitting' is totally subjective, so don't bother me with that." We operate right up to the limit of the law, demanding the right to do anything the law allows.

But the strict rules of right and wrong can never tell us all we need to know about whether we should engage in a specific action or not. Consider, for example, the simple decision about what to wear to a particular event or occasion. Perhaps you are considering wearing something that might be considered unsuitable. Questions like *Is this against the rules?* and *Would I be punished for wearing this?* will only get you so far. At some point, you would need to ask *Is this suitable for a person with values and principles like mine?* and *Will this be beneficial to others?* and *Will this help or hurt the credibility that I want to have with those who are important to me?* The fact is, those who never raise the question of appropriateness are thinking of no one but themselves.

However important appropriateness is in general, it is especially important in our words. "A word fitly spoken is like apples of gold in settings of silver." And let's face it: with our words, timing is crucial.

So if we seek to give good gifts to those around us, we would do well to consider the question of appropriateness, and I'm not just talking about physical gifts. In one sense, everything we do is a gift to those around us. So are we doing things that are suitable and fitting? Are we giving appropriate gifts to those who have contact with us?

The excellence of a gift lies in its appropriateness rather than its value.
CHARLES DUDLEY WARNER

November 30

HELP

*At bottom, and just in the deepest and most important things,
we are unutterably alone, and for one person to be able to advise or even help
another, a lot must happen, a lot must go well, a whole constellation of
things must come right in order once to succeed.*

RAINER MARIA RILKE

HELPING ANOTHER HUMAN BEING IS ONE OF THE HIGHEST PRIVILEGES THAT CAN COME TO US. Although opportunities to try to help are plentiful, it is rare, as Rilke indicates, that everything comes together in such a way that our help ends up being truly helpful. So we should cherish the times when we're able to help someone, exercising good stewardship of every opportunity that comes along.

When the opportunity to help presents itself, figuring out how to help often taxes the wisdom of even the wisest person. It's not always easy to know how to help without making the situation worse. Only wisdom can answer questions like "How?" and "When?" and "How much?" But we only grow in wisdom by getting involved and making an effort, so we should always be ready to help in the best way we can. Over time, we will grow in wisdom and become better helpers.

We should never hesitate to hold out a helping hand — but neither should we hesitate to accept the helping hand of another. In fact, it's not likely that our help will be appreciated (and may not even be accepted), if the other person sees us as being unwilling to be helped by them. Others are willing to be influenced by us only when they believe we are willing to be influenced by them. So it takes humility not only to receive help, but also to give it. The helpfulness of many a gift has been hindered by a lack of humility on the part of the giver.

It helps our humility to realize that all of us have had to be helped at many points along the way. If our present situation is one that we can be thankful for, we need to understand that we didn't get there on our own; we had to have help. And acknowledging the grace that has been shown to us should make us better helpers of others.

Finally, sensitivity is the thing that, along with wisdom, distinguishes great help from the lesser kinds. So if we would help, we must be willing to enter the other person's heart and feel what they feel.

*It is well to give when asked, but it is better
to give unasked, through understanding.*

KAHLIL GIBRAN

ZEAL

Let a man in a garret but burn with enough
intensity and he will set fire to the world.

ANTOINE DE SAINT-EXUPÉRY

IF A PERSON IS MOVED BY ZEAL, THEN THAT PERSON IS A POW-
ERFUL FORCE, EVEN WHEN ACTING ALONE. The human heart is
capable of intense concern. It can be fired with a fervor so hot that it
would sacrifice the gift of life itself in order to gain its goal.

Zeal, of course, is a good thing only if the object of its desire is
good. It's a powerful tool, but in and of itself, its value is neutral. Zeal
takes its value from the use to which it is put, or the causes in which
its services are enlisted. If good can be accomplished by the heart
filled with zeal, so can evil, and so it's critical that we maintain vigilant watch over the moral quality of our desires. The possibility that
we might come to the end of our lives and realize that we've used our
zeal to achieve unworthy ends is a possibility we should want to avoid.
It pays to be careful about what we want in life.

Yet even when the things that we're zealous about are good and
honorable, there is something else to consider: our zeal must not be
blind or unthinking. For example, it's good to be patriotic, generally
speaking. But if patriotic zeal is blind and uncritical ("My country,
right or wrong!"), then we have something less than might be desired.
We need not only to support worthy causes, but we need to know why
we support them. Our enthusiasm needs to be an enlightened one.

And then, of course, our zeal must be disciplined. Like literal
fire, the fire of zeal must not only be stoked; it must be kept inside
the boiler. Our enthusiasm must be trained, channeled, directed, and
governed — or else it'll do more harm than good. Zeal may be one of
the forces by which we do our work in this world, but it's not the only
force. No matter how passionate we are, there'll be times when our
zeal must be held in check while we employ some other, equally valuable, tool or character trait, such as patience or humility or courtesy.

But finally, the main use of zeal should always be the improvement of our own character and conduct. The world needs saving, no
doubt, but truth to tell, most of us could use a little saving ourselves.

Have therefore first zeal to better thyself
and then mayst thou have zeal to thy neighbor.

THOMAS À KEMPIS

RICHNESS

Blood is an inheritance; virtue an acquisition.
MIGUEL DE CERVANTES

THERE ARE ALL KINDS OF WAYS TO BE RICH. Physical, or financial, wealth is what most people would think of first. But today, let's spend a moment thinking about another kind of richness: richness of character. And for purposes of our discussion here, let's do something a little different; let's define richness of character as having a character sumptuously full of choice ingredients. What we should want in life is to have a character that is not flat, one-dimensional, and monotonous, but one that is rich, variegated, and deeply textured.

So what has to happen for our hearts to be "enriched"? Well, first they have to be exposed to things that can enrich them. Whether it's different people, different circumstances, different challenges, or simply different weather, we need to get out of our ruts and let ourselves come into contact with things that can add to the quality of our character. If it's nothing more than taking a different way home from work once in a while, we need to go out of our way to see new things.

But exposure is not enough; we must let ourselves become involved with things that can enrich us. Two individuals may go to a social event and both be exposed to people they've never met before. One, however, may come away enriched while the other leaves completely unchanged. What's the difference? In both cases there was exposure to enrichment, but in only one case was there involvement. So we need to make sure that the experiences that come our way don't simply wash over us; we must open ourselves up to them. Enrichment can't take place if we don't let it work its magic on us.

Ultimately, however, there is no true richness of heart if there has been no exposure to or involvement with the principles of rightness and honor. No matter how richly textured they may be in other ways, if our characters haven't been made more worthy by the acquirement of *virtue,* then we're still paupers. To be rich, in the long run, simply means to do what is right. It means faithfulness to valid principles.

Richness of heart, then, in this last, highest sense, is not the only kind of richness to which we might aspire, but without it, none of the other kinds matter very much. It's what's on the inside that counts.

Without the rich heart, wealth is an ugly beggar.
RALPH WALDO EMERSON

ACCOUNTABILITY

*You can't run a society or cope with its problems
if people are not held accountable for what they do.*

JOHN LEO

WHEN OTHERS REFUSE TO BE ACCOUNTABLE FOR THEIR AC-
TIONS, IT'S EASY TO SEE THE PROBLEM; IT'S A BIT HARDER
TO SEE IT, HOWEVER, WHEN WE'RE THE ONES WHO'RE MAKING
EXCUSES. At times, we can be so subtle in dodging personal responsi-
bility that we deceive our own selves into thinking that it's somebody
else's fault. Most of us jump into the "blame game" far too eagerly.

The word "accountable" means *answerable.* Since it contains the
word "account," let's use the metaphor of bookkeeping to illustrate it.
If I accept accountability, that means I'm willing to let other people
"audit my books." I'm willing for my deeds to be examined against fair
standards of right and wrong, and if the audit shows that I've done
anything amiss, then I'm willing to compensate anyone who's been
hurt and make restitution to the full extent of my ability.

Accepting accountability requires three things, at the very least.

Conscience. We must admit that there are standards that we're
answerable to and have the humility to be guided by those standards.

Commitment. We must discipline ourselves to demonstrate
integrity. That is, we must commit ourselves to doing what's right and
maintain consistency between our principles and our practice.

Courage. We must be willing to accept the consequences of everything we do — and face the firing squad of full justice, if need be.

Accepting full and frank accountability for our own actions is one
of the best things we can do for those around us. It's a gift of great
value, and one that's made all the more valuable by the fact that it's
so rare these days. When others know that we can be counted on to
do our best, and that when we've failed to do what's right, we'll spend
our time making restitution rather than making excuses, they will find
a peace and security in their relationship with us that can't be found
any other way. It's not a complicated matter, really. It's just a bit of
basic morality, a fundamental principle of right and wrong.

*A person may cause evil to others not only
by his actions but by his inaction, and in either case he is
justly accountable to them for the injury.*

JOHN STUART MILL

LEARNING

A man, though wise, should never be ashamed
Of learning more, and must unbend his mind.
SOPHOCLES

THERE ARE FAR TOO MANY WONDERS IN THE WORLD FOR ANY OF US TO QUIT EXPLORING. Even if we're advanced in age and reputed to be wise, there are still many good things left to be learned — and some of these may be facts that will hurt us not to know. If we're truly wise, we'll make a commitment to lifelong learning.

One thing that I've learned so far is that learning things can be scary! New truths force us to reorganize our lives. They may require us to part company with some thoughts and deeds that have previously been a part of our security system. As George Bernard Shaw wrote to someone once, "You have learned something. That always feels at first as if you had lost something." Our "comfort zones," as we call them, are good and we all need to have them, but we can't stay inside them all the time. On the inside of our comfort zones there may be a good deal of coziness, but there's very little learning, and learning is an unavoidable necessity if there's going to be any progress in our lives.

Actually, however, if we can learn to launch out into the realm of new discovery, whatever comfort may be lost is often replaced by a new kind of joy: "I find my joy of living in the fierce and ruthless battles of life, and my pleasure comes from learning something" (August Strindberg). Those who've tried it report that an ounce of new discovery is worth a pound of old, ill-informed comfort.

Learning is particularly important in our personal relationships. It's not too much to say that most of the relationship difficulties we have stem from a failure to be open to new knowledge about other people. We know each other so poorly, and relate to one another so inadequately, because we're content with what we already "know" about others and are afraid to open our hearts to deeper learnings.

So to be learners we must humble ourselves before others, being willing to ask and willing to be contradicted. Adopting these mental postures is not easy, and it doesn't happen by accident. Being a learner calls for a commitment and a bravery that are nothing short of noble.

Learning is not attained by chance. It must be
sought for with ardor and attended to with diligence.
ABIGAIL ADAMS

ENDEARMENT

> But if the while I think on thee, dear friend,
> All losses are restor'd and sorrows end.
>
> WILLIAM SHAKESPEARE

IF ANYONE HAS EVER TOLD YOU THAT YOU WERE "DEAR" TO THEM, YOU'VE BEEN PAID A HIGH COMPLIMENT. Yet regardless of the reaction of others, the responsibility is on our side to acquire characters that tend in the direction of endearment, rather than estrangement. Consider this point from four different angles:

Loved and cherished. To be "dear" to someone means that they feel a fondness and an affection for us. Are we easily loved and cherished? Are our characters and conduct such that they encourage endearment?

Greatly valued. But "dear" can also mean "precious," as in the remark, "In the fire, they lost many things that were dear to them." Are we dear to our friends in this way? If our friendship were lost to them, would they lose anything of significant value in their lives?

Highly esteemed. The salutation "Dear Mr. Jones" is meant to convey respect. When others begin a letter to us in that way, does it take a stretch of their imagination to consider us with high regard or esteem? Has our relationship with them been worthy of their honor?

Earnest and ardent. If somebody said that a certain person "dearly loved golf," that would mean that his or her attraction to that activity was more than casual. What about the passions of your life? Do you love whatever you love in such a way that it's dear to you?

It would be a hardhearted person who would say, "I don't care whether I'm endearing to anybody else or not." And yet, many of us may find that we go to the opposite extreme. Wanting to endear ourselves, we say and do things that are not really very genuine, and things that are not very natural to us, for no other reason than to gain the favor of those whose approval we value. But hypocrisy, flattery, and unctuousness are not endearing, no matter how skillfully they may be employed. What people want is for us to be comfortable in our own skins, to work hard at being the best "us" we can be, and to extend ourselves to them naturally and honestly. When it comes down to it, most folks find snapshots more endearing than glamour shots.

> To me more dear, congenial to my heart,
> One native charm, than all the gloss of art.
>
> OLIVER GOLDSMITH

December 6
INDUSTRIOUSNESS

Industry is a better horse to ride than genius.
WALTER LIPPMANN

WOULD THOSE WHO KNOW YOU WELL SAY THAT YOU'RE A HARD WORKER? If not, then at least two valuable things are being lost: (1) Your friends are losing the value of the contribution you could make to their lives, and (2) you're losing the unique satisfaction that comes from being active and assiduous in your work.

Our English word "industrious" comes from the Latin *industria* which simply meant "diligent." To be industrious is to be dynamic and productive. It is not only to work but to be *hardworking.* And all too often, it's a quality that characterizes the few rather than the many.

In all fairness, it is true that some people go overboard when it comes to work. As Clarence Day wryly remarked, "The ant is knowing and wise; but he doesn't know enough to take a vacation."

But that's not the tendency that's evident in most of our lives. Most of us could add a little more industriousness to our characters and not be hurt by it at all. And that's what we'll want to do when we see our work as it relates to our fellow human beings. When we realize that with our work we honor not only the work itself but also those for whom we do it, we'll naturally want to give it more effort.

That's why it's important for each of us to find two things. First, we need to find work that we can truly see as being our own work: work that taps into our individual endowments and calls forth our greatest passion. And second, we need to identify the people who can most greatly profit from this work. We need to know for whom we're working and dedicate our work to them in all conscientiousness.

Some people, frankly, give work a bad name. They put it off and run from it as if it were a dreaded disease. From their dislike of it, you'd think that hard work is undesirable, that it's something to be done only if there is no other choice, and not a minute longer than it takes to get it over with. But this is a serious, and most unfortunate, misconception. Honorable work and the industriousness that goes with it are two ingredients in any reasonable recipe for the good life. If your friends call you a hard worker, please don't be embarrassed.

Labor disgraces no man; unfortunately, you
occasionally find men who disgrace labor.
ULYSSES S. GRANT

QUESTIONS

He who is afraid to ask is ashamed of learning.
DANISH PROVERB

IN OUR RELATIONSHIPS WITH OTHERS, WE SHOULD BE WILLING TO ASK THE QUESTIONS THAT WE OUGHT TO ASK. That is, we ought, in the matter of questions, to aim for two things: (1) the good sense to see that some things are more valuable to know than others, and (2) the gumption to go ahead and ask the better questions. Both of these are important, more so than you might think.

Knowing what the good questions are. One of the most fascinating aspects of human nature is the amount of interest we bestow upon trivia. To be sure, there are times when we need to relax and be entertained by trivia, but it's not good if our curiosity never goes beyond that. We live in a magnificent world that invites all manner of worthy questions, but all too often those questions go unasked. As Emerson noted, "The sun shines and warms and lights us and we have no curiosity to know why this is so; but we ask the reason of all evil, of pain, and hunger, and mosquitoes and silly people." If the quality of what we know depends on the quality of the questions we ask, then we've got a real, practical need to sharpen our sense of priorities.

Having the humility and courage to ask. Even the best things that we could know will remain forever in the realm of mystery if we can't bring ourselves to do what learners do: ask. It's such a simple thing, but most of us find that it can be difficult. Sometimes we're too proud to let it be known that we don't know certain things, and at other times we just don't have the courage to ask. But in either case, the progress we need to make is impossible if we don't open up and ask.

So it's good to have good questions and it's good to go ahead and ask the questions that we have, rather than remain ignorant. Yet as undesirable as ignorance is, there is something even worse, and that is a lack of integrity. Asking a question should mean not only that we want to know the truth about something; it should also mean that we want to do what's right about that truth. Living a quality life requires more than curiosity — it requires action. If we never get around to using the good answers that have been given to our questions, we forfeit many of the best things in this question-filled world.

He who asks questions cannot avoid the answers.
CAMEROONIAN PROVERB

WILLINGNESS

There is nothing so easy but that it becomes
difficult when you do it with reluctance.

TERENCE

IT'S SAD THAT WE LET SO MANY GOOD DAYS BE RUINED BY
THAT COMMON KILLJOY: RELUCTANCE. Activities that might be
quite satisfying (indeed, activities that at one time were satisfying) are
now seen, for one reason or another, as being required, and so we approach them unwillingly. With our resistance and reluctance, we drain
every drop of joy out of our daily round of duties. It hardly ever occurs
to us that the problem lies with our personal concept of duty.

We tend to draw a pretty hard line between obligation ("have
to") and pleasure ("want to"). We think in terms of work ("have to")
and play ("want to"), and we even divide life itself into two main seg-
ments: employment ("have to") and retirement ("want to"). We hack
away at our "to do" lists as if happiness and delight were things that
could only be enjoyed later. Yet there is no law in the universe that
requires us to see "have to" and "want to" as opposites, and the mere
fact that something is necessary doesn't mean that we can't do it willingly. "The man who does something under orders is not unhappy; he
is unhappy who does something against his will" (Seneca).

Many wonderful doors open to us when we learn the simple
habit of willingness. We can consciously open our hearts and minds
to the things that are ours to do, even those that are obligatory, and
when we do, everything takes on a much better appearance. This
doesn't mean that we try to trick ourselves into thinking that everything we have to do is easy or pleasant. It just means that we give
these things the full assent of our will — and also that we remember
why we're doing them and who the folks are who benefit from them.

When we go to bed at night disagreeably "tired," the thing that
has tired us out is usually not our work or our responsibilities — it's
running away from our work and our responsibilities! A reluctant, unwilling, I-don't-want-to-do-this mindset is one of the most exhaust-
ing things that anybody can endure. So get rid of it. Make a different
choice. Embrace the things that you must do, and you'll find an energy
surging up inside you that you'll have great fun putting to good use.

A willing mind makes a light foot.

THOMAS FULLER

December 9
WORKMANSHIP

He who considers his work beneath him
will be above doing it well.
ALEXANDER CHASE

ISN'T IT IRONIC THAT WE SOMETIMES THINK WE'RE TOO GOOD
TO DO GOOD WORK? We dismiss inferior workmanship with
remarks like these: "My time is too valuable to waste on menial work"
or "That's not my job" or "Let somebody do that who hasn't got anything better to do." When, as Alexander Chase suggests, we view our
work as "beneath us," then we're "above doing it well."

Whatever work we're called upon to do, however, we need to
see our workmanship as an extension of our character. "By the work
one knows the workman" (Jean de La Fontaine). And there is a sense
in which we demonstrate our character most vividly in the doing of
"little" things, those that "don't matter." It's the person who is faithful in that which is least who'll also be faithful in that which is much.
None of us likes to deal with people who only do their best when the
spotlight is shining on them and they believe there's opportunity for
significant praise. We need to be careful not to be that way ourselves.

Not only that, but when we've done less than our best, we ought
not to blame our poor workmanship on external circumstances. When
our work has been less than skillful, it does no good to say, "I could
have done better if I hadn't gotten such bad breaks." That would be
like Abraham Lincoln saying, "I would have been a great president if
there hadn't been a war going on." A good workman never blames his
tools, and "A bad workman never gets a good tool" (Thomas Fuller).

There really are few joys in life more deeply satisfying than the
knowledge that we're constantly improving the quality of what we do.
It feels good to do good work, and it feels even better to know that
we've done better work today than we did yesterday. But high-quality
lives, and the good workmanship that grows out of them, don't just
happen. Continuous improvement requires conscious effort. It requires
paying honest attention to where we are, daily examining the worthiness of our goals, actively learning things that we don't yet know, and
never ceasing to pull our performance up to the level of our ideals.

No fine work can be done without concentration
and self-sacrifice and toil and doubt.
MAX BEERBOHM

December 10

CHALLENGES

The ultimate measure of a man is not where
he stands in moments of comfort and convenience, but where
he stands at times of challenge and controversy.

MARTIN LUTHER KING JR.

WHAT OUR FRIENDS KNOW OF US WHILE THE SUN IS SHINING
IS ONE THING — WHAT THEY FIND OUT ABOUT US WHEN
THE DARKNESS CLOSES IN MAY BE SOMETHING VERY DIFFERENT.
It doesn't take a person of very great character to reflect a bit of glory
when there is beauty and brightness all around, but let a person be
tested by hardship or pain and then, if there's no light coming from
inside that person's heart, the darkness will be dark indeed.

Challenges show us our weaknesses. All of us have some of these,
of course; there is no use denying that we do. But we may not pay
adequate attention to our weaknesses until some crisis makes us aware
of them. And to that end, challenges are good for us. Whatever helps
us see the areas where we're vulnerable is a thing to be thankful for.
Wise people want to know, as soon as possible, where they need to
shore up their defenses, and challenges offer us that opportunity.

But challenges also show us our strengths. Just as we each have our
weaknesses, we each have our strengths also. And just as challenges
force us to look honestly at our weaknesses, the same challenges may
surprise us by bringing to light some strengths that we didn't know we
had. "Within us all there are wells of thought and dynamos of energy
which are not suspected until emergencies arise" (Thomas J. Watson).
When we have to take one of life's hard "exams," we may not make a
perfect score, but often we do better than we ever thought we could.

So, when all is said and done, what's the main thing that we want
from life? Is it simply ease and pleasure? If that's all we want and
we're unhappy when we get anything else, then we probably have our
sights set too low. The fact is, there are several things, such as character growth, that should have a higher priority than ease and pleasure.
And if the goodness of something is judged by what it does for our
character, we'd have to say that challenges and tests, however difficult
or unpleasant, should be placed in the good category.

Our prayers are answered not when we are given what we ask,
but when we are challenged to be what we can be.

MORRIS ADLER

LOVE

Take away love and our earth is a tomb.

ROBERT BROWNING

THE LATIN PHRASE *SINE QUA NON* MEANT "WITHOUT WHICH NOT." When we say that something is the *sine qua non* of something else, we mean that the first thing is absolutely essential to the second. The second thing could not exist without the first.

Is it too much to say that love is the *sine qua non* of human life? Honestly, I don't think that's an overstatement. Many things may be taken away from us, many "essential" things we may have to get along without, but take away love, and what is left is something less than a human life. By this I do not mean that we have to be loved to be human — I mean that we must love. We ourselves must have love for some personal being outside of ourselves. There is nothing any more deeply embedded in our nature than the need to love. Whether or not love is acknowledged, appreciated, or reciprocated, the great happiness of life is to love. It was no one less than Friedrich von Schiller, who wrote the poem *Ode to Joy* and was a leader of German Romanticism, who said, "I have enjoyed the happiness of the world; I have loved."

I came of age on the Mississippi Gulf Coast not far from the Louisiana Creole country. In those lands, there is a beautiful proverb which says, "Tell me whom you love, and I'll tell you who you are." Today, and every day, let's meditate on those whom we love — let's resolve to love them more purely, strongly, tenderly . . . and lovingly!

It should be said, of course, that we do sometimes take love too seriously. It's a force far beyond what any of us mere mortals can handle, and we ought to see the humorous side of our "assaults with the intent to love." We ought to just admit, as some wise person said, that "the game of love can't be played with the cards on the table."

Still it's the most wonderful thing this side of heaven, isn't it? It deserves nothing less than our best effort. We ought to honor it and receive its grace with gratitude. We ought to quit trying to make it be our slave, and instead allow it to be the heart-piercing, two-edged sword that it has always been in the realm from whence it came.

Make your service of love a beautiful thing;
want nothing else, fear nothing else and let
love be free to become what love truly is.

HADEWIJCH OF ANTWERP

DOORS

Hope opens doors where despair closes them.
ANONYMOUS

IT'S ONE OF THE FINEST THINGS IN LIFE TO BE A PERSON WHO OPENS DOORS FOR OTHERS. And no, we don't mean physical doors, although the courtesy involved in doing that old-fashioned deed is a mighty fine gesture in itself. The doors we want to think about in today's reading are doors of opportunity. When we are instrumental in giving hope to someone, and perhaps even assist them in pursuing their hopes, we've engaged in a powerful act of blessing.

One thing, at least, is certain: we can't be door-openers for those around us if we don't keep hope alive within ourselves. If we give in to the crushing forces of despair, we'll get to the point where we don't believe that anything anybody does is going to make any difference for good in the long run. It takes a kind of courage that could almost be described as stubborn and defiant to maintain hope in the face of discouragement. But when we do this and keep the fires of hope burning, we do something that's extremely valuable to those who know us. When they've lost hope, we owe it to them to maintain hope for them and hold the doors open that they'll need to pass through.

Graham Greene once made the comment, "There is always one moment in childhood when the door opens and lets the future in." Can we not take that thought and make use of it in our relationships as adults? Very few of us can say that we turned out to be the people we once hoped we might be. But life continues, does it not? And this may strike you as an unusual thought, but I want you to consider that you have it within yourself to help those around you to reopen the doors of their childhood dreams. You can be a rekindler of hope.

But there is one last thing to think about: not only can we aid others in passing through doors of opportunity, we can also open the doors of our own hearts to them. And in the end, these are the doors whose opening may be the most welcome. To live in this world is to be a traveler. We're all on a journey, and the road grows long. How glad we are to meet those whose hearts are like a wayside inn, with the doors open and a gentle voice saying, "Come in and be refreshed."

> My heart keeps open house,
> My doors are widely flung.
> THEODORE ROETHKE

POSTERITY

*Since it is not granted to us to live long, let us transmit
to posterity some memorial that we have at least lived.*
PLINY THE YOUNGER

SEEN AGAINST THE BACKDROP OF THIS WORLD'S WHOLE HISTORY, A HUMAN LIFETIME IS A VERY BRIEF AFFAIR. Pliny was right: "it is not granted to us to live long." But we can, as he suggested, leave some memorial that we have lived. We can, and we should want to, make some contribution to the world in which we've been privileged to live. As we pass through the world, we can make some improvement, however slight, in the world's condition.

To be sure, not many of us will make any mark that will be remembered after we're gone. A very wise man long ago wrote, "There is no remembrance of former things, nor will there be any remembrance of things that are to come by those who will come after" (Book of Ecclesiastes). There is a sense in which we should forget the future and be content simply to serve our own generation. Serving our own generation, humbly and faithfully, is no small legacy to leave to future generations. In itself, that's a wonderful contribution!

But the fact is, none of us live entirely to ourselves. Each one of us is a link in the chain of generations, and what we do is more than just our own business. We're linked to our ancestors in the past, and we're linked to our descendants in the future. We ought to want to be worthy links and faithful stewards of what's been handed down. "Let us contemplate our forefathers, and posterity," said Samuel Adams, "and resolve to maintain the rights bequeathed to us from the former, for the sake of the latter." There ought to be in our hearts this wholesome two-fold desire: (1) to be a posterity our ancestors would be proud of, and (2) to leave a legacy our descendants will be thankful for.

Not all of us are guilty of this, but I would say that, as a people, we are in danger of losing touch with our ancestors. Nowadays, we live with such a concentration on the ever-insistent "now," we forget the names of even our grandparents, not to mention our more distant ancestors. And if so, this is a tragic loss. We can't disconnect from the past and still have any proper regard for what will come after us.

*People will not look forward to posterity
who never look backward to their ancestors.*
EDMUND BURKE

ROADS

On the old highway maps of America, the main routes were red
and the back roads blue. Now even the colors are changing.
But in those brevities just before dawn and a little after dark — times
neither day nor night — the old roads return to the sky some of its color.
Then, in truth, they cast a mysterious shadow of blue, and it's that time
when the pull of the blue highway is strongest, when the open road is
beckoning, a strangeness, a place where a man can lose himself.

WILLIAM LEWIS TROGDON

IT HAS ALWAYS SEEMED TO ME THAT THERE IS SOMETHING
INEXPRESSIBLY ROMANTIC ABOUT A ROAD. Roads, after all, go
somewhere, and there aren't many roads that don't entice me, intrigue
me, and attract me to their end. As a loner whose work requires a
good deal of travel, I prefer to travel by the roads, preferably the back
roads, rather than by air. I know the time of which Trogdon speaks,
"when the pull of the blue highway is strongest, when the open road
is beckoning, a strangeness, a place where a man can lose himself."

A road is not a bad metaphor for a human life, actually. The
expression "road of life" may be a bit worn-out, but it is nonetheless
true that our lives have many of the characteristics of a road. They
have their destinations, their distances, and even their detours. It pays
to pick our roads carefully — and travel them appreciatively.

One of the nicest gifts we can give to others is to be persons who,
wherever we "go," go gladly and with a spirit of adventure. There are
already too many folks in the world who're treading their path resent-
fully. Can we not be zestfully different: people who motivate (and
amaze) our associates by actually enjoying the journey that we're on?

Perhaps we don't do this because secretly we wish our journey
could be exchanged for someone else's. But there is no good way to
separate our "journeys" from our "selves." The uniqueness of the roads
that we're on is what gives us the opportunity to make a peculiar and
worthwhile contribution to this old world. Individually, we need to
have the courage to follow our own roads with integrity and true
intent. "We can't reach old age by another man's road" (Mark Twain).

> I shall be telling this with a sigh
> Somewhere ages and ages hence:
> Two roads diverged in a wood, and I —
> I took the one less traveled by,
> And that has made all the difference.

ROBERT FROST

DESIRE

Ah Love! Could you and I with Him conspire
To grasp this Sorry Scheme of Things entire,
Would not we shatter it to bits — and then
Remold it nearer to the Heart's Desire!

EDWARD FITZGERALD

NOT MANY PEOPLE WOULD, IN THEIR MORE HONEST MO-MENTS, TELL YOU THAT THEY PRESENTLY HAVE ALL THEIR HEART'S DESIRE. In many ways, this world is an incomplete world, a world of dreams, even a "broken" world, we might say, where we feel our hearts being stirred by longings and aspirations for a perfection beyond the fragmentary happiness that seems to be our lot. We want more than what we've known in the past and the present; for most of us, the future is something we envision with desire, and even hope.

Some would say that we're too naive, that we need to do away with our desires and content ourselves with whatever is real right now. And, of course, when deep desires are unfulfilled, they can feel very much like pain, and so many people think that we should protect ourselves from pain by diminishing our desires. But truly, being people of desire is not a thing to be regretted or avoided. When our desires are governed by wisdom, humility, and respect for the dignity of other human beings, we are at our best when we present ourselves to the world as people of desire. If we're not passionate, we're not fully alive.

Bob Costas, the delightfully thoughtful television sportscaster, made a wonderful statement one year at the beginning of the Winter Olympics. Speaking of the glory of honorable competition and the power of dreams that drive us toward excellence, he said, "We are beaten only when we quit believing in what we wish we could be."

Our dreams matter. Our desires are our dignity. And though we often err by letting our desires be diverted into some pretty unproductive channels, it's not usually our desires that are at fault, only our discipline. We need our desires, and those around us need them too. They need us to want better things. Higher things. Stronger things.

Bad will be the day for every man when he becomes absolutely content with
the life that he is living, with the thoughts that he is thinking, with the deeds
that he is doing, when there is not forever beating at the doors of his soul
some great desire to do something larger, which he knows that he was meant
and made to do because he is still, in spite of all, the child of God.

PHILLIPS BROOKS

OPENNESS

Sincerity is an openness of heart; we find it in very few people.
FRANÇOIS DE LA ROCHEFOUCAULD

E MBARRASSMENT IS ONE OF THE COMMONEST EXPERIENCES IN THE WORLD. There are many things about ourselves that we're too shy to share, and when some of these things work their way to the surface, we feel the flush of embarrassment. It's not really a very pleasant feeling, and so most of us avoid it. We avoid it by locking the doors and closing the curtains of our hearts. And as a result, we get to the point where we're not as sincere as we need to be, if sincerity is defined as "openness of heart." Perhaps we're not blatantly hypocritical or deliberately dishonest; we wouldn't tell a lie or consciously misrepresent ourselves. But there are vast stretches of territory in our hearts that we simply do not reveal to others, sometimes even those who are nearest and dearest to us. For every one of us who is too open, there are ninety-nine of us who aren't open enough.

Openness is probably close to the top of everyone's list of things they look for in both friends and romantic partners. "Anyone who builds a relationship on less than openness and honesty is building on sand" (John Powell). But we need to be careful not to limit our relationships to those who feel comfortable being open with us at the present moment. All of us, to some extent, find it difficult to be as open as we'd like to be, and what we need from one another is safety. We need to extend to one another the security of relationships in which the risk of openness is removed as much as possible, without any pressure to be more open right now than is comfortable for us.

But openness can also be looked at from the opposite direction. If we should open our hearts to let some things "out" (so that others may enjoy them), we should open them to let some other things "in." Like the open mind, the open heart is open to input from outside sources. It's willing to be influenced. And though we should surely be careful about the people and principles to which we open our hearts, it would be a sad mistake never to open them at all. It's a rare day on which we can't be bettered by someone else's thinking. And it's an even rarer day on which we can't be nourished by someone else's love.

The beautiful souls are they that are universal,
open, and ready for all things.
MICHEL DE MONTAIGNE

December 17
VIVIDNESS

Trusty, dusky, vivid, true,
With eyes of gold and bramble dew,
Steel-true and blade-straight
The great artificer
Made my mate.

ROBERT LOUIS STEVENSON

WHO ARE THE PEOPLE WHO HAVE THE MOST NOTICEABLE IMPACT ON US? No two people are exactly the same, of course, and there are many different kinds of influence, but I want to suggest that "vividness" is a quality that often distinguishes those who impact us from those who don't. Their characters may come in a variety of "colors," but they are never murky or muddy gray. They are vivid.

"Vivid" is one of many words that come from the Latin *vivere* ("to live"). In its most literal sense, to be "vivid" is to be "alive." Just for curiosity, let's take three of the basic meanings of "vividness," as outlined in the *American Heritage Dictionary*, and see how these meanings might apply, figuratively, to a person's character:

"Perceived as bright and distinct; brilliant." Vivid people are sharply etched and delightfully distinguished. They've chosen to live their lives with bright excellence, rather than dull, gray mediocrity.

"Full of the vigor and freshness of immediate experience." Vivid people don't just think about life; they interact with it. And they bring to their relationships the "freshness of immediate experience."

"Evoking lifelike images within the mind; heard, seen, or felt as if real." Vivid people, like a vivid painting, inspire images and visions in the minds of others that are vibrant with life as it really and truly is.

So what's our conclusion here? That all of us need to have "lively" or "outgoing" personalities? No, definitely not. The point, rather, is that whatever distinctive characteristics each of us may possess, we need to live our own characteristics vividly. Whatever we are, we need to be what we are, resisting the temptation either to shrink back from life or to try to be what we are and what everybody else is at the same time. The choice should be made carefully, but it should be made decisively: *who are we going to be?* Then, having chosen our colors, we need to engage life with all the heart of a person who is . . . alive!

God does not ask for the dull, weak, sleepy acquiescence
of indolence. He asks for something vivid and strong.
AMY CARMICHAEL

December 18
TOLERANCE

The test of courage comes when we are in the minority.
The test of tolerance comes when we are in the majority.

RALPH W. SOCKMAN

LEARNING WHAT TOLERANCE IS AND HOW TO PUT IT INTO PRACTICE IS ONE OF THE MORE CHALLENGING REQUIRE-MENTS OF WISDOM. It's not easy to distinguish the good kinds of tolerance from the bad kinds, and it's even less easy to implement tolerance wisely in the practical affairs of everyday living. And so it's inevitable that we're going to make mistakes, either in being too tolerant or not tolerant enough. And to top it off, we have to learn how to tolerate those who have a different concept of tolerance than we do.

Sir James Goldsmith made this observation about tolerance: "Tolerance is a tremendous virtue, but the immediate neighbors of tolerance are apathy and weakness." Real tolerance — the genuine article as opposed to its popular counterfeits — is a strong and sturdy quality. Never for a moment does it diminish the seriousness of some of the issues that separate human beings from one another, and it doesn't limit its kindheartedness to people who disagree over matters that it considers insignificant. Yet this is what many do today who hold the "pop" concept of tolerance. If you think an issue is important that they think is just a matter of opinion, then you're being "intolerant," but if you dare to disagree with them on an issue that they see as important, then you'll suddenly see a different side of them, one that looks for all the world like intolerance. So Samuel Taylor Coleridge, who wrote a long time before our modern debate over tolerance, said, "I have seen gross intolerance shown in support of tolerance."

True tolerance (the kind that's tough to learn) wisely balances courage and consideration. It doesn't sweep significant issues under the rug, but neither does it break relationships over disagreements that don't require such a break. It knows how to say to somebody, "I believe you are wrong, and I believe the issue about which we disagree is extremely important — but I respect your dignity and worth as a human being. Let's keep working together wherever we can!"

Tolerance implies a respect for another person,
not because he is wrong or even because he is right,
but because he is human.

JOHN COGLEY

MOTIVATION

It seems to me we can never give up longing and wishing
while we are alive. There are certain things we feel to be
beautiful and good, and we must hunger for them.

GEORGE ELIOT

IS "MOTIVATION" SOMETHING THAT WE OURSELVES HAVE ANY
CONTROL OVER? Some people apparently believe that it is not;
they wait around hoping to "be motivated," as if that condition were
going to drop down out of the sky and sweep them off their feet.

Certainly there are times when we'd like to be more powerfully
motivated, but nothing we do seems to help; the desired enthusiasm
for our goals remains elusive. Even so, we need to be careful not to
avoid responsibility for our own attitudes. The fact that some people
are motivated more consistently than others is not the result of their
having been born that way. It's the result of choices that they make.

For one thing, the quantity of our "motivation" grows out of the
quality of our "motives." Higher, worthier motives produce a motivation that's more forceful and long-lasting. Keith Yamashita, whose
expertise is in motivating large corporations to improve themselves,
has said this: "All meaningful change starts with right aspiration." He's
exactly right, and his point is encouraging because aspiration is something we can do something about. If our motivation seems lacking, we
can reconsider what it is that we're aspiring to. Elevating the quality of
our motives can increase the quantity (or power) of our motivation.

There really are few things more beautiful in life than to behold
someone who is moved energetically by high and worthy goals. Like
all of us, these people need encouragement from time to time. But
basically, they are motivated by a fire that burns from within, and they
don't need constant goading to get busy. They're a joy to work with, to
play with, and to live with. And deciding to be that kind of person is a
gift that every one of us can give to those we care about.

I'd be less than honest, however, if I didn't tell you something else:
greatly motivated people tend to be people who're acquainted with
sorrow. They're not people whose lives are in perfect equilibrium, but
rather they're folks who know a bit about longings and broken hearts.
That's where their passion comes from, and it's not a bad thing.

Never let go of that fiery sadness called desire.

PATTI SMITH

WORDS

*Words were medicine; they were magic and invisible.
They came from nothing into sound and meaning. They were
beyond price; they could neither be bought nor sold.*

NAVARRE SCOTT MOMADAY

L IFE TEACHES TWO THINGS TO THOSE WHO ARE WILLING TO
LEARN: WORDS ARE POWERFUL AND WORDS ARE VALUABLE.
The value of words, in fact, comes from their power to do good. As
symbols which convey thoughts from one mind to another, words are
capable of healing and helping. They have the power to impart hope.
They can instruct and encourage with a potency that's often amazing.

But words can also hurt, as we all know. Out-of-control words
can do more damage in ten minutes than can be repaired in ten years,
and so wisdom counsels us to be careful in our use of language.

Yet in our carefulness, let's not be so careful that we clam up.
As Judith Viorst said, "Brevity may be the soul of wit, but not when
someone's saying 'I love you.'" On the occasion when someone needs
to be uplifted by words that we've got the power to say, that's not the
time to be sparing or stingy. Instead, it's the time to be lavish. We
need not have any qualms about being extravagant when it comes to
encouragement. The more words we can speak to that end, the better.

The main test that our words need to meet is the test of truth.
Not every truth needs to be spoken, obviously, but when we do speak,
our words should never be anything less than truthful. Even when our
intent is to inspire hope in someone else's heart, we dare not twist the
facts to do so. Words that fail the truth test are always wasted words.

Images, including facial expressions and body language, convey
a certain amount of information about us to others, and our actions
are even more revealing. But in the end, it is words by which a human
being reveals himself or herself to another. Since that's true, the words
that we speak, or don't speak, are quite important. By speaking, we
open the doors of our hearts to others; by not speaking, we leave those
doors closed. By speaking, we bestow grace and give ourselves away.
Let us, then, have the courage to do that. May we not hide from the
light of language, but employ words wisely and well. It is, after all, no
small thing to say to another, "I am willing to be known by you."

Speak that I may see thee.

BEN JOHNSON

REST

O rest! thou soft word!
autumnal flower of Eden! moonlight of the spirit!
JEAN PAUL RICHTER

AT THIS TIME OF THE YEAR, AS AUTUMN TURNS TO WINTER, IT IS A TIME FOR THE LAND TO REST. The fields have done their work, the harvest has been gathered in, and now comes the time of rest. The days are short, and the nights are long. The weather has grown cold, and the land, perhaps, lies under a peaceful blanket of quiet snow. It is the time of rest, the "moonlight of the spirit."

Rest and winter, the season of rest, are not valued as they should be. And this is all the more sad because we tend to be a people who are more in need of rest than many. On most days, we are hurried, harried, and harassed. We are driven by the incessant drumbeat of activity. In our culture, extreme busyness is a badge of honor, worn proudly by the important people — the movers and the shakers. And so rather than look forward to the restfulness of winter, we resent being forced to change gears and slow down. We do not properly appreciate what this cycle of the seasons was meant to do for us.

The arrival of winter brings with it the opportunity for more thought and reflection. During the more active seasons, we don't have as much time to evaluate our actions. We're so busy going that we rarely consider whether our destination is any place worth going to. In the winter, however, there is more time to consider our principles and our values, and to make the much-needed adjustments. This is a valuable respite, a season to sit by the fire and . . . ponder.

Quietude has a special beauty about it — and a unique strength. There are few things that epitomize strength any more than a mountain, yet a mountain is a very quiet, peaceful thing. It is majestic in its stillness. Its massive strength is quietly husbanded and not wastefully or frivolously spent. So we should not begrudge that time of the year when our own strength is to be held in reserve. The onset of winter should remind us of the need for rest and replenishment, and for quiet reflection on the meaning of our many activities. If not allowed to rest, our "fields" will fail us, perhaps when we need them most. The busier our summers are, the more we need our winters.

Take rest; a field that has rested gives a bountiful crop.
OVID

December 22
COMMONWEALTH

That which is not good for the beehive
cannot be good for the bees.

MARCUS AURELIUS

T HE CONCEPT OF "COMMONWEALTH" IS ONE OF THE MOST
BENEFICIAL IDEAS THAT WE CAN HOLD IN OUR MINDS. Our
word "wealth" comes from the Old English *wela,* or "weal," which
meant prosperity or happiness. Originally, "weal" (the opposite of
"woe") referred to general well-being, not just to riches, and so the
common "weal" or "wealth" was *the good of the community,* the conditions
in which, together, the members of a society were able to enjoy the
peaceful blessings of life. A government or nation could be described
as a commonwealth if it existed for the common good of its citizens —
and, more importantly, if the citizens themselves were committed to the
common good and not just to their own individual interests.

All of us are connected to other people. We are members of many
groups: families, neighborhoods, organizations, cities, and states, to
name only a few. We are communal creatures by nature, and we thrive
on relationships. Yet while most of us know that our connections are
important, we need to ask ourselves how deeply we're committed to
the principle of commonwealth. When it comes down to it, can we be
counted on to seek the common good? If the people we're connected
to would be damaged by our getting what we want, is it certain that
we'll sacrifice our wants in order to protect the shared benefit?

Words like "community" and "family" engender welcome feelings
in our hearts. But we need a commitment to our connections that
goes beyond feelings. Whatever groups we're privileged to be a part
of, we need to serve those groups with a sense of personal responsibility to the "commonwealth." The good life comes not to those who
take whatever they want, but to those who show their gratitude for
membership in the human race. And good relationships are built by
people who value them enough to nurture them. When the common
good is not served unselfishly, it soon becomes the common evil.

Whoever wishes to assert his will as a member of a community must not only
consent to obey the will of the community but bear his share in serving it.
As he is to profit by the safety and prosperity the community provides,
so he must seek its good and place his personal will at its disposal.

JAMES BRYCE

FELICITY

How small, of all that human hearts endure,
That part which laws or kings can cause or cure!
Still to ourselves in every place consign'd,
Our own felicity we make or find.

SAMUEL JOHNSON

IT HAPPENS, AT LEAST NOW AND THEN, THAT EVERYTHING SEEMS "JUST RIGHT." While the snow falls outdoors, for example, we sit cozily by the fireside with a small group of close friends. There are mugs of hot apple cider. Holiday pastries are within easy reach. Thoughtful conversation is sprinkled with laughter, and there is nothing in this moment except pure, wholesome camaraderie.

"Felicity" is a word that describes the cheerful contentment we feel at such times. It's a word that brings back the welcome memory of our most treasured times. In its basic sense, of course, felicity just means "happiness." (It comes from *felix*, the Latin word for "happy.") But felicity is a special kind of happiness.

When we enjoy felicity we experience a "delightful" sort of happiness, a peace that has in it much gladness, cheer, and gaiety. The dictionary defines felicity as "great happiness, or bliss," but bliss probably sounds a bit over the top to most of us. We'd be more comfortable thinking of a happiness that is bright, sparkling, and festive on the one hand, but also pleasing, calm, and balanced on the other. The feeling is one of cheerful appreciation for our "just right" blessings.

Whether we use the word "felicity" or not, it's obvious that this is the kind of happiness that often comes to us at this season of the year, especially when family and friends gather. And we perhaps wish that our physical circumstances would line up in the same constellation more often, so that felicity could be ours more frequently.

But truly, the sources of felicity are inside us. It is basically the result of character, the by-product of principled living. On special occasions, we're most apt to be surprised by felicity if we've been cultivating a peaceful conscience on days that didn't seem so special.

That discipline which corrects the eagerness of worldly passions,
which fortifies the heart with virtuous principles, which enlightens
the mind with useful knowledge, and furnishes to it matter of enjoyment
from within itself, is of more consequence to real felicity than all the
provisions which we can make of the goods of fortune.

JAMES BLAIR

FESTIVITY

A feast is made for laughter.
THE BOOK OF ECCLESIASTES

ONE OF THE THINGS WE ENJOY MOST ABOUT THIS SEASON IS ITS FESTIVITY. The special gatherings, the tinge of excitement, and, of course, the much-anticipated meals come together in a way that is really quite wonderful. And the food is of more than incidental importance. In its most basic sense, "festivity" means "feasting," and so a festive occasion without food would be a contradiction in terms. But the food is not so much the main ingredient of festivity as it is the catalyst. What we enjoy most of all is what comes from the feasting. Samuel Pepys sensed this when he said, "Strange to see how a good dinner and feasting reconciles everybody." It's the human element, the congeniality, that makes a feast "festive."

We seem to have a built-in need for occasional festivity. Even though too much feasting would not be good for us, it may be that many of us suffer from too little. Our ordinary lives and the routine of our work need to be punctuated by festivities. Now and then we need — we really do need — to enjoy some mirth and merriment. As someone has said, "A life with no festivity is like a long road with no inns."

Some seasons of the year involve holidays that are festive almost by definition. These times come with the turning of the calendar pages whether we make plans for them or not. But other festivities do have to be planned, and there is great wisdom in giving these arrangements some priority. Lives in which no festivities are planned are not "spontaneous." They are dull and tiresome . . . and very often fruitless.

The idea of festivity happens to have an interesting companion, and that is the concept of welcome. To say that others are "welcome" is to say, quite literally, "It is well that you have come!" And is this not the major part of any festivity? It's the welcome presence of other persons who share our delight that turns a humdrum event into a festivity.

So as we feast during this season (however humble our fare may be), let us not be ashamed to enjoy the festive meals that bring us together at the table. But let us also learn the value of having festive hearts. Let us be a people who know the meaning of *welcome!* — a folk whose merry hearts are able to enjoy a feast year-round.

Small cheer and great welcome make a merry feast.
WILLIAM SHAKESPEARE

CELEBRATION

> A holiday gives one a chance to look backward and forward,
> to reset oneself by an inner compass.
>
> MARY SARTON

O NCE IN A WHILE, IT'S GOOD TO CELEBRATE. Many of the traditions with which we celebrate this day of the year are English in their origin, and the English have a special fondness for this sort of thing, as we remember when we read Charles Dickens's *A Christmas Carol.* Blanchard Jerrold quipped, "If an earthquake were to engulf England tomorrow, the English would manage to meet and dine somewhere among the rubbish, just to celebrate the event."

When we look up "celebrate" in the dictionary, we find something like this: "to observe a day or event with ceremonies of respect, festivity, or rejoicing" (*American Heritage Dictionary*). Respect, festivity, rejoicing. All three of these suggest important thoughts.

Respect. At the heart of all good celebration is respect, and to a great extent, it is tradition and history that give respect its power. When we celebrate, we tip our hat to good things that've gone before.

Festivity. Celebration and festivity go together like fireplaces and hot chocolate. Who could imagine celebrating anything important without the presence of good food gratefully enjoyed by friends?

Rejoicing. When the work of the world and its worries have worn us out, we need to be revitalized. The honest-to-goodness joy that bubbles up from worthwhile celebration is one of life's treasures.

For many, today's date has a religious significance. Regardless of the pros and cons of that, however, the traditional "homely" celebrations of this day are really quite wonderful, and we should not miss the opportunity to relish their enjoyment.

When we celebrate, we grow in character by honoring something outside of ourselves. On this particular day, if what we honor is nothing more than our connection to those around us, that's no small thing to celebrate. The act of honoring lifts us above the ordinary and refreshes our outlook. Friendships are strengthened, families are enriched, and our perspective is broadened. Days like today do us a world of good. We ought to "keep" Christmas for all it's worth!

> In celebration the high and the mighty regain their balance,
> and the weak and lowly receive new stature.
>
> RICHARD J. FOSTER

CHEERFULNESS

Wondrous is the strength of cheerfulness
and its power of endurance.
THOMAS CARLYLE

CHEERFULNESS IS SUCH A DELIGHT, WE WISH WE COULD PRE-SERVE IT, LIKE STRAWBERRIES AND PEACHES, TO BE ENJOYED LATER ON. It seems a shame that good cheer is so plentiful during the holidays yet so rare the rest of the year.

In a way, of course, it's good that some seasons are cheerful while others are more workmanlike. Shakespeare was right when he said: "If all the year were playing holidays, to sport would be as tedious as to work." We need rhythms and cycles in life, not constant sameness.

Still, most of us could do with a little more day-in-day-out cheerfulness, and the good news is that we can have it if we try. We can cultivate a more hopeful way of thinking so that cheerfulness becomes what Joseph Addison called "a habit of the mind."

To do this, we need to train ourselves. We must learn to look at life through a lens with a wider angle. True cheerfulness doesn't mean being a Pollyanna, foolishly or naively optimistic, and it doesn't mean denying the ugly realities of life. What it does mean is that we look at more of the truth than that. Whatever uncheerful things there may be, these things are not all there is to reality. There are also joyous things, things that do much more than even the score. The cheer-giving realities happen to be greater and more durable than their cheerless counterparts. Montaigne was not wide of the mark when he said, "The most manifest sign of wisdom is continued cheerfulness."

It is true that some people, by their natural disposition, find it easier than others to be cheerful (just as some find it easier than others to sing on key, hit baseballs, and program computers). But all of us, whether "good-natured" or not, can maintain faith, and we can exercise courage. We can learn the habit of looking at life more comprehensively. And at this season of the year, we can indeed preserve the cheerfulness of the holidays and carry these joys with us into the weeks of work that lie ahead. It's just a matter of being *thankful*.

Since Time is not a person we can overtake
when he is gone, let us honor him with mirth
and cheerfulness of heart while he is passing.
JOHANN WOLFGANG VON GOETHE

SIMPLICITY

Manifest plainness,
Embrace simplicity,
Reduce selfishness,
Have few desires.

LAO TZU

SIMPLICITY IS EASY TO APPRECIATE AND TO HONOR, BUT IT'S QUITE DIFFICULT TO MAINTAIN IN OUR LIVES. For all of us who say we need to slow down and simplify our existence, very few actually do that. There is clearly a "simplicity gap" in our lives.

During the holidays, most people stay fairly busy. In fact, the season is often so hectic that we breathe a sigh of relief when the festivities are over. It's even a "complicated" time of year: there are, it seems, too many people to greet, too many gifts to make or purchase, too many priorities that clamor for attention. The hustle and bustle are fun, of course; there's an air of excitement about it all. But for all its other blessings, this is not a time that is noted for its simplicity.

Perhaps it is especially important at such a time to be reminded of the beauty of simplicity. It has a dignity, a cleanness, and even a power about it that are refreshing. Those persons are fortunate who have disciplined themselves to be simple . . . even while being busy.

Distraction is one of our greatest hindrances in being personally effective. There are so many trees, we lose sight of the forest, don't we? There is great value, therefore, in recommitting ourselves to simplicity. Even if we don't go as far as we should in cleaning out our clutter, it's a big step in the right direction to recognize our distractions for what they are. There can be no real improvement for us if we're not honest.

We'd probably do more to simplify our lives if we ever really experienced the benefit of *focus.* The habit of concentrating on what is most important is a high-leverage habit. When we turn off all the noise, prepare our minds and hearts to do good work, and then get down to the simple things that are our real business in life, wonderful things result. So as this year winds down, let's simplify. Let's take a paring knife to our principles, our values, and our priorities.

'Tis the gift to be simple,
'Tis the gift to be free,
'Tis the gift to come down
Where we ought to be.

SHAKER SONG

QUALITY

If a thing is old, it is a sign that it was fit to live. Old families, old customs,
old styles survive because they are fit to survive. The guarantee of continuity
is quality. Submerge the good in a flood of the new, and the good will
come back to join the good which the new brings with it.

EDWARD V. RICKENBACKER

WHERE DOES "QUALITY" RANK IN YOUR SCALE OF VALUES? If you were an artist, for example, what would you want to be the leading characteristic of your work: critical acclaim? public recognition? commercial profitability? quality of craftsmanship? These are not mutually exclusive, of course; your work might be characterized by more than one of these. But if you had to choose, which would it be?

It's safe to say that "quality" is not held in high esteem by as many people as it used to be. And that's sad. Our lives would be the richer if we regained a sense of quality's importance. Consider the superiority of quality to some things that seem to rank more highly:

Quality is better than newness. New things are exciting, without question, and newness is a value. But as a society, we've become all but obsessed with it, and quality has suffered. Too hastily do we cast aside resources of proven quality in order to pick up on the latest thing.

Quality is better than quickness. In too many areas, our main priority is speed and ease of use. For example, we won't bother learning skills that take a long time to learn. And if the worth of something is not immediately obvious to us, we're in too big a hurry to give it a deeper look. But quality is worth waiting for. It deserves our patience.

Quality is better than popularity. In the age of mass merchandising, we're often content with what is offered to us by the big box stores. Yet many quality "things" — whether products, ideas, or people — never catch on with the public, and we should not neglect these.

To repeat, values are not always mutually exclusive. Something might be of great quality and be new, quick, and popular too. But we need to be careful. As old-fashioned as it sounds, we need to give quality some respect. It's worth the sacrifice of many lesser values.

Quality is never an accident; it is always the result of high intention,
sincere effort, intelligent direction, and skillful execution; it represents
the wise choice of many alternatives, the cumulative experience of many
masters of craftsmanship. Quality also marks the search for an ideal
after necessity has been satisfied and mere usefulness achieved.

WILL A. FOSTER

VALUES

> One of the great arts in living is to learn the art of accurately appraising
> values. Everything that we think, that we earn, that we have given to us,
> that in any way touches our consciousness, has its own value.
>
> GEORGE MATTHEW ADAMS

P ROPERLY EVALUATING THINGS IS A WONDERFUL SKILL. It comes to most people only after they've gotten a little age on them. It usually takes a few years of trial and error before we begin to see which things in life are really more valuable than others.

All of us have some kind of value system, whether we've thought much about it or not. From time to time, it's important for us to clarify what our personal values are. But it's also important to remember that not all values are created equal. The trick in life is to value the things that are valuable and to recognize the inferiority of all else.

To say merely that something is a "value" is not to say very much. It is only to say that a thing is capable of being valued by someone. But the crucial questions are these: How does this value rank in comparison to other values? What is the proper evaluation that should be given to this thing? It takes wisdom to see which values are valuable!

There are, to be sure, some folks who like to say that all values are subjective, that they are nothing but personal tastes. But very few people really believe that. Adolf Hitler had a value system, but most commonsense people understand that his value system was not just subjectively wrong — it was wrong when measured against the objective standards of goodness. It's not meaningless to say that Abraham Lincoln's value system was objectively better than Hitler's.

If we live in a society where everyone is free to value things as they wish, then we enjoy a fortunate freedom. But freedom of thought does not mean that all thoughts are equally valuable. Freedom just means that if I choose to value a thing that has little intrinsic value, I am free to do so . . . and to live with the consequences.

The freedom to value things according to our conscience should encourage us to grow in the quality of our conscience, to learn to evaluate things more truthfully and skillfully. As this year closes, we'll do ourselves (and our relationships) a favor if we upgrade our values.

> Civilization ceases when we no longer respect and no longer
> put into their correct places the fundamental values.
>
> R. P. LEBRET

TREASURE

We should lay up in our minds a store of goodly thoughts which will be a
living treasure of knowledge always with us, and from which, at various times,
and amidst all the shiftings of circumstance, we might be sure
of drawing some comfort, guidance, and sympathy.

ARTHUR HELPS

L IFE IS FULL OF TREASURE. Sometimes its treasures are hidden,
and we don't dig deep enough to find them. At other times, we
fail to appreciate the treasures we've already found. And on other occasions, we can be confused and misunderstand what is treasure and
what is not. But still, life is full of treasure, and we would do well to
ponder that fact and be grateful for it.

The word "treasure" refers to something especially precious or
valuable. We might think of a pirate's treasure, his buried cache of sto-
len money and jewels, or perhaps the gold bullion carefully guarded in
the "treasury" of a national government. But the treasures that most of
us have the opportunity to deal with are of a different kind.

For one thing, we should, as Arthur Helps suggests, "lay up in
our minds a store of goodly thoughts." Our minds and hearts can be
treasuries in the very highest sense if we do the work needed to make
them such. But it does take work. It takes thinking and identifying
the better things that are available to us. It takes meditating on these
things. And it takes choosing, moment by moment, to focus primarily
on these things rather than those that would degrade us. This is what
Enthusiastic Ideas has been all about: suggesting "goodly thoughts"
that we can lay up in our minds and make a part of the treasury of
our thoughts. When we do this regularly, one day at a time, we find
ourselves maturing in wisdom and growing in gratitude.

But finally, here is another thing: our best treasures don't have to
be rare or extraordinary. Unlike gems or precious metals whose value
depends upon their rarity, treasures of the heart can be gathered from
sources that are plentiful. Let us not overlook the wealth of goodness
that surrounds us each moment. It's good to have goals, and the nobler, the better. But goals are best achieved by those who count their
blessings along the way and do not despise their "ordinary" treasures.

Normal day, let me be aware of the treasure you are.
Let me learn from you, love you, savor you, bless you before you depart.
Let me not pass you by in quest of some rare and perfect tomorrow.

MARY JEAN IRION

December 31

ENDINGS

Great is the art of beginning,
but greater is the art of ending.

HENRY WADSWORTH LONGFELLOW

A T THE ENDING OF THIS YEAR, IT WOULD BE WISE FOR US TO REMEMBER THE IMPORTANCE OF ENDING WELL. The year will come to an end whether we end it wisely or not, but we will help ourselves if we think carefully about "endings." To end well, we need a healthy combination of gratitude, humility, and optimism. We must choose to be helped by our memories rather than hindered by them.

When life's endings approach us, especially the bigger ones that involve great change, we're often unwilling for them to occur. We often expend great emotional effort trying to keep change from taking place. But as Hannah Hurnard wrote, "If we try to resist loss and change or to hold on to blessings and joy belonging to a past which must drop away from us, we postpone all the new blessings awaiting us on a higher level and find ourselves left in a barren, bleak winter of sorrow and loneliness." The gifts that the future wishes to place in our hands are greater than those the past has given to us, but many of us will never know. Our hands can't receive what the future has in store if they're still laden with the packages we've picked up in the past. There comes a time when we need to let go of what we've been holding onto so tightly and open ourselves up to new possibilities.

There is a German proverb which says, "Beginning and end shake hands with each other." It is true: everything in life is connected to everything else. Every beginning moves toward some ending, and every ending is connected to some new beginning. The question is not whether there shall be endings and beginnings, but only what we shall do with them as they come to us. Whether our endings are proper and our new beginnings are productive is not a matter of fate or doom. Much depends upon the choices that we make. So let us use well this last day of the year, learning what we should from all that is now behind us. And tomorrow, let us release what has just ended and grasp what will then be just beginning. Let us end today in such a way that tomorrow will be our best beginning yet.

The old order changeth, yielding place to the new,
And God fulfills himself in many ways.

ALFRED, LORD TENNYSON

The word is half his that speaks,
and half his that hears it.

— *Michel de Montaigne*

INDEX

Acknowledgments

THIS WORK STRETCHED OUT OVER MANY YEARS, AND MANY INDIVIDUALS HAVE HELPED OUT AT VARIOUS POINTS. As I indicated in the Preface, this work began in an unusual way, and for quite some time, there was no thought of publishing it. As I began to consider that possibility, and began sending out the readings by email, there were many supporters and encouragers who joined the project.

Thanks, first, to Becky Voyles who in these busy days still works me into her schedule. She has been my right hand for so long I can't remember working without her. Jessica Keet, who did most of the intensive editing of this work, was an absolute joy to work with. She soldiered on even when the work seemed as if it would never end.

Shannon Stinson has been a diligent coworker. An avid reader of many types of literature, she has astutely examined this work. Holly Lankford, a treasured new friend, has been extremely helpful in spotting items that needed fixing. She has been a godsend. Others who have helped are Jessica Sweets, Sherry Morris, and Hannah Roy. Jordan Farquhar again did the tedious work of checking the index.

Ken Craig is a very special friend. Time and again, he has propped me up and refused to let me deviate from the path that I am on. Mike Roy, a colleague in the work at Broadmoor, has frequently and fervently expressed his appreciation for my writing, and his unfailing support has made a difference on days when the writing was hard.

Becky Cawthon deserves a unique thanks for friendship and support. Lee Wildman, who now lives close enough that we can once again enjoy time together, has been everything a man could ask for in a friend. He nourishes my soul and helps me find a way forward. Curtis and Terri Byers have gone beyond the call of duty in helping me to do the work that I do. No one has sacrificed more than they have to establish a safe environment in which I can speak and write.

Phil Henry, my brother, went to New York with me last year, and that journey was refreshing to me in a most memorable way. Thanks, Phil.

And finally, my sons, Brock and Grant, continue to be a source of inspiration and joy. They are stalwart men of integrity . . . and humor!

It is true that I am a solitary man, but never has a solitary man had the support of so many people. When I think about each of you, as I often do, I am deeply humbled. "Thank you" hardly seems adequate.

Resources for Readers

WordPoints.com is a storehouse of information for serious students of the Bible. The WordPoints website grows each month, so check back often. The main entry-page for all of the resources below is at *https://wordpoints.com*.

The WordPoints Blog. News and notes from Gary Henry, plus random observations on the passing scene.

The WordPoints Daybook Series. Information, indexes, etc. for each of the books in the series, including where to buy the books.

Daily Emails. Various daily readings by Gary Henry that can be received by email each morning.

E-books & Downloads. A variety of PDF documents, some available at no charge. These may be reproduced for group study.

Textual & Topical Studies. Study material useful for congregational Bible classes or small group studies.

Sermon Outlines. Biblical study resources in outline form, not just for preachers but for all students of the Bible.

Articles. Collection of lectures and writings by Gary Henry that have appeared in various religious journals.

Seeking God in the Psalms. Monday-Friday topical studies from the Psalms, aimed at spiritual growth — a work in progress.

Daily Family Bible Studies. Monday-Friday themes for families to study and discuss together.

Daily Bible Reading Plan. An organized schedule for reading through the entire Bible each year.

Curmudgeon's Corner. Just for fun, a compendium of cranky quotations on the human race from a lifetime of reading.

Old Southern Recipes: Basic Food Traditions of the South. Also for fun, these are some of Gary's favorite soul food recipes.

About Gary Henry. Personal information about Gary, plus information on Gary's speaking schedule each year.

Frequently Asked Questions (FAQ). Answers to common questions about the WordPoints publishing program.

WordPoints Daybook Series

DAYBOOKS HAVE A RICH LITERARY TRADITION. They are books containing a brief reading for each day of the year, and their value is that they sharply concentrate our thoughts once a day, every day.

The *WordPoints Daybook Series* has redefined the daybook for modern readers. Written by Gary Henry with his well-known blend of candor and courtesy, these volumes have become a familiar part of the daily routine of thousands of readers all around the world.

As a whole, the series takes the reader on a journey. We begin by thinking about elementary character issues and the importance of God, move toward the question of obedience to the gospel of Jesus Christ, and end with a consideration of heaven: the home of the soul.

Book 1 — *Enthusiastic Ideas. A Good Word for Each Day of the Year.* What are the time-tested ideas that should inform our character? (ISBN 978-0-9713710-2-6)

Book 2 — *More Enthusiastic Ideas. Another Good Word for Each Day of the Year.* What are the helpful words that should motivate our conduct? (ISBN 978-0-9713710-3-3)

Book 3 — *Diligently Seeking God. Daily Motivation to Take God More Seriously.* What difference does it make whether we seek God? (ISBN-13: 978-0-9713710-0-2)

Book 4 — *Reaching Forward. Daily Motivation to Move Ahead More Steadily.* Is there anything about tomorrow worth reaching for? (ISBN-13: 978-0-9713710-1-9)

Book 5 — *Obeying the Gospel. Daily Motivation to Act on Our Faith.* How do we make a genuine, scripture-based commitment to Christ? (In preparation)

Book 6 — *Walking with Christ. Daily Motivation to Grow in Our Commitment.* How do we lead lives of authentic discipleship to Christ? (In preparation)

Book 7 — *Going Home. Daily Motivation to Make the Final Journey.* What happens to our hearts as we get closer to the goal of heaven? (In preparation)

"The reader is in for a strong intellectual and spiritual challenge . . . The thought-provoking richness of the 366 essays is reminiscent of the wisdom-dense writings of C. S. Lewis." — Ellen Kennedy

"At once comfortable and elegant . . . a feast for the eye and hand, the soul and mind and heart." — Peggy Rosenthal